English radicalism in the twentieth century

Manchester University Press

English radicalism in the twentieth century

A distinctive politics?

Richard Taylor

Manchester University Press

Copyright © Richard Taylor 2020

The right of Richard Taylor to be identified as the author of this work has been asserted by him in accordance with the Copyright, Designs and Patents Act 1988.

Published by Manchester University Press
Altrincham Street, Manchester M1 7JA

www.manchesteruniversitypress.co.uk

British Library Cataloguing-in-Publication Data
A catalogue record for this book is available from the British Library

ISBN   978 1 7849 9319 1 hardback
ISBN   978 1 5261 5496 5 paperback

First published 2020

The publisher has no responsibility for the persistence or accuracy of URLs for any external or third-party internet websites referred to in this book, and does not guarantee that any content on such websites is, or will remain, accurate or appropriate.

Typeset by
Servis Filmsetting Ltd, Stockport, Cheshire

To Joanna, Lucy and Matthew

Contents

Preface — viii

1. The nature of English radicalism — 1
2. An overview of English radicalism — 14
3. Bertrand Russell — 37
4. Sylvia Pankhurst — 55
5. Ellen Wilkinson — 75
6. George Orwell — 97
7. E.P. Thompson — 118
8. Michael Foot — 142
9. Joan Maynard — 166
10. Stuart Hall — 185
11. Tony Benn — 207
12. Nicolas Walter — 230
13. A distinctive politics? — 247

Select bibliography — 259
Index — 268

Preface

The idea for this book arose when Roger Fieldhouse and I were compiling our study of E.P. Thompson (*E.P. Thompson and English Radicalism*, Manchester University Press, 2013). English radicalism, as Thompson articulated so vividly, has deep roots and has played a pivotal role in progressive politics and culture since (at least) the English Civil War. In this book I have tried to bring together the varied elements that constitute this tradition and its articulation in the twentieth century, through the study of ten 'key figures'.

The approach is one of critical political analysis, within a historical framework. The two introductory chapters discuss the definitional issues, provide a rationale for the continuing relevance and importance of English radicalism in recent and contemporary political culture, and give an outline (in Chapter 2) of the main elements of this tradition from its origins to the close of the twentieth century.

Following the ten case study chapters, there is a brief conclusion, analysing the legacy of the tradition as articulated in the twentieth century, and touching on the developments in the early years of the present century. The chapter concludes with a summary of English radicalism's 'strengths and weaknesses'.

Several friends and colleagues have given valuable advice, constructive criticism and insights in relation to one or more of those radicals discussed. I am also grateful for the loan of numerous private papers, letters and other archival material. In particular I would like to thank my longstanding friends and colleagues Roger Fieldhouse and Mike Newman and my son, Matthew Taylor, who all read and commented in some detail on the whole text. I have incorporated many of the suggestions made, and the resultant book is much the better for their inputs. I would also like to thank the following: Philippa Clark, Andy Croft, David Goodway,

Marion Kozak, Jill Liddington, John McIllroy, Jim McGuigan, Colin Pritchard, Tom Steele and Christine Walter. I have also appreciated Maria Slowey's sceptical Irish perspective on the whole project.

I remain, of course, entirely responsible for the text, for the views expressed and for any infelicities or factual errors.

Finally, this study of twentieth-century English radicalism is dedicated to my children – Joanna, Lucy and Matthew – who in their professional and personal lives embody many of the values and practices which are the subject of this book.

Richard Taylor
Pooley Bridge
April 2019

1

The nature of English radicalism

The central aim of this book is to examine, in historical and political context, the nature and importance of English radicalism in the twentieth century. The analysis is undertaken primarily through the detailed study of ten key individuals, all of whom made significant contributions, in their different ways, to the development of English radicalism across the century.

As with most important social and political concepts 'radicalism' is hard to define precisely. This is in part because it draws on and overlaps with other ideological positions, in part because its context, and thus its impact, has varied over time, and in part because advocates and analysts have had sharply differing views on its proper nature. Here I seek to define 'radicalism', within the *English* radical tradition.

But why *English* rather than British (or even Western European) radicalism? There are illustrious precedents for such a focus (most notably E.P. Thompson),[1] but the case nevertheless needs to be made and the interrelationships with other traditions and other politics need to be delineated.

And how important and relevant is the English radical tradition today? Few would contest the historical importance of this tradition. However, across the whole developed world, the Left, broadly defined, has been in decline since at least the late 1980s. Whilst it may be a matter of regret to those on the Left, it is clearly the case that the internationally pervasive ideology and practice of neo-liberalism appear more firmly embedded than ever, not least in the United Kingdom. So, why might English radicalism remain important politically as well as historically in the early twenty-first century?

Finally, there is the question of the selection of the ten figures chosen to represent English radicalism in the twentieth century: why were they chosen and others excluded; and how far do they embody the key aspects of the tradition?

Definitions

British society in general, and English society in particular, has been predominantly conservative (if not always Conservative), and it has been characterised by a remarkable degree of stability. Since at least the late seventeenth century, constitutional and political structures have evolved through reform, and, despite periods of turbulence, have remained broadly intact. Nevertheless, for centuries there have been movements, political parties and men and women from across the spectrum of radicalism who have opposed economic, political and cultural inequalities and injustices.

'Radicalism' has been a contested concept since the eighteenth century. Raymond Williams has traced its changing definitions through time. In the late eighteenth century, it was largely a term of abuse. By the end of the end of the nineteenth century, it had become 'almost as respectable' as liberalism and the distinction was made in political circles between 'radicals' and 'socialists'. Radicalism was 'often contrasted with "dogmatic" *socialism* or *revolutionary* programmes'. By the mid-twentieth century, 'radicalism' seemed 'to offer a way of avoiding dogmatic and factional associations while reasserting the need for vigorous and fundamental change'.[2]

The often contradictory meanings to which Williams draws attention are reflected in the various studies of English radicalism.[3] Maccoby, for instance, in his multi-volume study of *The English Radical Tradition*, traces the long evolution, as he sees it, from Whigs to radicals to liberals, from the mid-eighteenth to the mid-twentieth century.[4] For Maccoby, by the 1920s the 'old radicalism' had largely dissolved as some of its adherents moved into 'the anti-socialist camp' and others joined the 'new radicalism' of collectivist Labour.

This view of radicals as relative moderates in contrast to 'big state' socialists finds its echoes in other writers[5] and indeed in some left-of-centre political parties in continental Europe (notably the French radical party of the Fourth Republic). Such is not the perspective taken in this study. However, the emphasis upon the free individual, living in an open and free culture (and the corollary of an innate suspicion of the state), constitutes a key characteristic of the English radical tradition, especially in the twentieth century when the power of the state grew so significantly.

The *a priori* centrality of 'the free individual' in the English radical tradition merits further attention. George Watson has observed that 'Liberty is the English ideology';[6] and Edward Vallance rightly emphasises that this was often articulated not as a series of specific policy commitments but rather as a mobilising myth: the radical tradition has recognised 'the importance of recapturing lost freedoms, often located in an Anglo-Saxon Arcadia … and most of all, it saw itself as part of a tradition of people fighting for their liberties'.[7]

The main point of tension between English radicalism and the socialist tradition, both social democracy and, especially, orthodox Marxism, lies in the former's giving absolute priority to *freedom* in all contexts, and the accompanying antipathy to the abrogation of power by the state and its agencies. For socialists, the dangers of an all-powerful state reside primarily in its capitalist nature: capturing and adapting the state for socialist purposes has been the objective. For the radical tradition, however, it is the power of the state *per se* that is the problem. The degree of emphasis given to this argument varies markedly within the English radical tradition, with many on the libertarian Left, notably anarchists such as Nicolas Walter (see Chapter 12), seeing the state as being *the* central problem, whilst others – for example, Russell (see Chapter 3), Wilkinson (see Chapter 5), and Foot (see Chapter 8) – saw civil and social freedoms being deliverable, at least in part, through a democratic, parliamentary socialist state.

There have been others, both on the liberal, social reform Left and on the libertarian Right,[8] who have believed equally passionately in these individual and social freedoms. Whilst *related* to the radical tradition, they differ crucially on a number of levels. For the libertarian Right, the espousal of an unfettered capitalist market system – with all its inherent inequalities and its culture of individual greed and selfishness – is central to its ideology. And, on the liberal social reform Left, there is little if any acknowledgement of the *class* nature of the capitalist system and the consequent need for structural change.

All within the radical tradition have been agreed, however, that a range of freedoms for the great mass of the people had been denied consistently by the ruling orders across all historical periods in the modern era, including those in power in the modern capitalist state. Most, too, would agree with Orwell (Chapter 6) who, had 'a deep feeling that liberty lay with the people, not with the state or some higher intellectual caste'.[9]

Why has this commitment to freedom been so central to the English radical tradition? I would argue that there are two related reasons: first, the ethical basis of English radicalism; and, secondly, the intellectual legacy of the Enlightenment. In his 1952 article 'British Socialism Today',[10] R.H. Tawney articulated the ethical basis of English radicalism (for Tawney this is coterminous with Christian, 'Sermon on the Mount' morality). The movement for radical change in Britain has been 'obstinately and unashamedly ethical'. At its base, he argues that it has been a 'straightforward hatred of a system which stunts personality and corrupts human relations by permitting the use of man by man as an instrument of pecuniary gain'. Conscience is the final arbiter; and it is 'the idolatry of money and success' with which socialists have to grapple 'in our hearts and minds'.[11]

Whilst many in the English radical tradition have been avowed secularists and atheists (or agnostics) – of those discussed in this study, Russell, Foot and Walter, for example – Christianity, especially Nonconformist Protestantism, was of central importance in the formation of English radicalism. For Tony Benn (Chapter 11),

Dissenting, Protestant Christianity was at the very core of his ideology; but several of the others analysed here were also strongly influenced by their Christian, usually Nonconformist, upbringing and culture: including Michael Foot, E.P. Thompson and Joan Maynard.

'Freedom' is such a cardinal value for those espousing English radicalism not least because there is a strong emphasis upon the individual, as opposed to the focus upon the collective, the social class, as the point of reference for orthodox socialists. In this sense, the English radical tradition is philosophically and politically liberal and libertarian. However, this 'radical individualism' contrasts with the possessive individualism, characteristic of liberal capitalist ideology, and its accompanying credo of acquisitive self-interest as the motor of economic growth and social well-being.

The legacy of the Enlightenment was the other major intellectual basis for the radical tradition's adherence to the primacy of 'freedom'. Reason, and the employment of human intelligence to analyse and interpret the world, lay at the heart of the Enlightenment project. Free individuals, thinking and reasoning for themselves, untrammelled by religious or governmental authorities, constituted the essence of a new, optimistic vision of humanity and its potential. William Godwin, a pioneering idealist and one of the intellectual founders of anarchism, argued that 'Man is perfectible, or in other words susceptible of perpetual improvement'.[12] This positive perspective embodied 'the belief in the goodness of man, the bright confidence in human reason, the distrust of governments, the distaste for established churches and authoritarian regimes'.[13] 'The sovereignty of the people' as opposed to the state (personified before the French Revolution by the monarch) became a key tenet of Enlightenment thinking. The cultural and political import of this belief, in the context of post-revolutionary France, was very different from that operating in England. Nevertheless, the belief in the moral and philosophical priority to be given to the 'common people', and their role as the conscious bearers of progressive change, characterised the English radical tradition from the nineteenth century onwards.

All questions were *open* questions. Orthodoxies, particularly religious orthodoxies, were analysed through the lens of human reasoning. This relates to radical Nonconformism, often leading frequently to the sceptical, secular rationalism of men such as Godwin and David Hume. Any organisation or ideology proclaiming unquestioned authority was thus, at the very least, suspect. The overweening state was therefore just as much the enemy as the Roman Catholic Church; later, the collectivist approach of socialists, with their emphasis upon 'the class' rather than the individual, was regarded with similar suspicion, if not antipathy.

Nevertheless, the commitment to *equality* is just as central a value to the English radical tradition: but the emphasis has been upon individual social and political equality, rather than seeing systemic economic change as the key objective. The principal architect of revisionist social democracy in post-1945 Britain, Anthony Crosland, saw the primary objective for social and political progressives (in what he claimed was post-capitalist society) as achieving 'equality of opportunity'.[14] This contention was an important policy preoccupation for successive Labour leaders in the second half of the twentieth century. However, for English radicals this has been an inadequate formulation. Tawney, for example, was vehemently opposed to this revisionist position. 'Nothing could be more remote from Socialist ideals than the competitive scramble of a society which pays lip-service to equality, but too often means by it merely equal opportunities of becoming unequal. Our aim should be the opposite. It should be to effect a complete divorce between differences of pecuniary income and differences in respect of health, security, amenity of environment, culture, social status and esteem.'[15]

The well-springs of this deep belief in equality run consistently through the trajectory of English radicalism. The commitment to equality has had economic and political, as well as social and philosophical, dimensions. Inequities of both wealth and power were central to radicals' demands in the nineteenth and twentieth centuries. Owenism, Chartism and indeed the labour movement *per se* had such concerns as their highest priorities (Chapter 2). However, the demand for a far more egalitarian social structure has always been based upon moral and philosophical arguments. This is in contrast to orthodox Marxist-Leninists, who have argued that, systemically, capitalism entails an unequal, hierarchical structure. For the radicals, it is the manifest injustice of hierarchical societies, whether feudal or capitalist, that lies at the heart of their critique of existing society. Such social structures demean humanity, perpetrators as well as victims (an argument that finds echoes in Marx's early writing on alienation).

The commitment to equality has been linked to a similarly strong commitment in the English radical tradition to the concept of justice, and the rule of law. The relationship between English radicalism and these mainstream beliefs has been complex. Radicals have certainly rejected the Establishment argument that the legal system was part of a neutral state institutional structure. On the contrary, as part of that state institutional structure, the legal system has been essentially a buttress for the existing order. The judiciary is committed to the precepts noted and also to observing scrupulously the rules of evidence, the rights of the accused and all the other pillars of an independent, expert professional legal system. However, it is also the case that judges (and senior lawyers of all types) 'are by no means, and cannot be, independent of the multitude of influences, notably of class origin, education, class situation and professional tendency, which contribute … to the formation of their view of the world … in short [the judiciary] has no more been "above" the conflicts of capitalist society than any other part of the state system'.[16]

The law and its structures have been a site of contestation, often *class* contestation as in the industrial legislation disputes throughout the nineteenth and twentieth centuries. From medieval times right up to the nineteenth century, the law was repeatedly used in explicit, on occasion brutal, ways to impose class rule, originally monarchical rule, and later bourgeois and later capitalist rule. Nevertheless, as

Thompson (Chapter 7) and others have demonstrated, the working-class movement and its allies achieved through struggle the individual and collective legal freedoms referred to. There has been a widely held radical belief that the law should not be subject to political interference; that an independent Parliament should have as one of its key roles the formulation, in open debate, of new legal enactments; that although a professional judiciary and legal structure were essential, the decisions in senior court cases should be in the hands of a lay jury; and that the rights of the individual, through the doctrine of *habeas corpus*, and the *a priori* presumption of innocence until guilt is proven, were sacrosanct.

In summary, then, the legal system has operated consistently in the interests of the ruling order; but its evolution has also revealed an equally persistent belief that the system can act as a bulwark against the authoritarian excesses of the state and the ruling class.

The freedoms under the law have been hard won; but, radicals claim, these tangible freedoms have provided evidence that the system *can* be reformed; that the struggles for popular, democratic rights *could* be won; and that the complex social relationships engendered in the evolution of industrial and post-industrial society *could* become the basis for a truly democratic society.

These then are some of the core values of the English radical tradition. It may be objected that this is not an especially distinctive profile. What is so special about English radicalism?

Its distinctiveness, I would argue, lies in two related characteristics: first, the emphasis upon social movement, extra-parliamentary activity as a means of achieving progressive change; and, secondly, the primacy given to the innate capacity of the 'common people' to believe in, act upon and achieve such progressive change. Although articulated in very different ways, all those considered in more detail in this study believed absolutely in these two precepts.

Social movement, extra-parliamentary activism has always been a minority element in British politics: but it has been through such movements that many of the progressive, radical changes in society have been achieved. Questions of 'agency' – of *how* to attain desired objectives – are central to all modern political formations. But they are of especial importance for those who espouse radicalism, because progressive change is their *raison d'être*.

Since the middle of the nineteenth century, the focus for mainstream progressive radicalism in England has been through the predominantly reformist labour movement and, from 1900, the Parliamentary Labour Party. The failures and frustrations of this formation are of tangential concern here. But three points should be made. First, the labour movement, through the trade unions as essentially defensive organisations, has won many battles (and lost many more) in defence of working-class interests;[17] but this has always been within the series of assumptions that the capitalist *status quo* was a long-term given. (Whatever view is taken of Lenin's overall political writings and practice, he was surely correct in his analysis of the differences between trade union and political consciousness.) Secondly, when the Labour Party has made important advances towards socialist restructuring, it has always been when the Left has had a strong influence: for example, Aneurin Bevan and the creation of the National Health Service. But these occasions have been rare. Throughout its history, the Labour Party has co-operated with, acted as a safety valve for, capitalist hegemony. The Labour Party, far from socialising its supporters and members into socialist activism, has acted more often than not as a *deradicalising* force.[18]

Thus, whilst several of those considered in this book – Foot, Wilkinson, Benn, Maynard – have been MPs and, in some respects, defenders of and advocates for, 'parliamentary socialism', all of them have seen extra-parliamentary social-movement activism as a key corollary to working within the established political system if progressive change were to be achieved. This position is in contrast to many on the Labour Left, who concentrated upon the parliamentary arena. But there are critical dangers here: the political, parliamentary system cannot attain significant change *on its own*; and, just as crucial, there is an almost inevitable cultural incorporation and thus neutralising of radicalism within the confines of the established structures. (As Ralph Miliband observed in the opening sentence of his critique of the Labour Party, *Parliamentary Socialism*: 'Of political parties claiming socialism to be their aim, the Labour Party has always been one of the most dogmatic – not about socialism, but about the parliamentary system'.)[19]

It has thus been the *extra-parliamentary* social movement, rather than the existing parliamentary system, which has been the focus for English radicals. (In the eighteenth and nineteenth centuries it was again *popular movements* outside the mainstream where real progress was made, whether it was the 'Wilkes and Liberty' protests of the late eighteenth century or the Chartists of the mid-nineteenth century.) For many, however, social movement activism and parliamentary struggle have not been incompatible: the Labour Left provided many of the leaders of the nuclear disarmament movement in the late 1950s and early 1960s, for example. The argument here was to fight on two fronts, each supporting the other, as in, for example, the Popular Front politics of the Communist Party at various times. Others, though, like Thompson, had a deep distrust of state bureaucracies and orthodox political parties; Orwell, too, was never really engaged with the Labour Party, 'never one for too much policy', as Colls has it.[20] And anarchists, and many Marxists, were wholly sceptical of the Labour Party and its proclaimed commitments to radicalism.

This focus is intimately related to the second point made at the outset of this part of the argument: the belief that the real engine of progressive change lies with the 'common people'. The kernel of Thompson's argument in *The Making of the English Working Class*, for example, is that it is not some complex of objective historical forces which determines the nature of any given society, but rather the collective, positive actions of human beings who make their own history: '[t]he working class did not rise like the sun at an appointed time. It was present at its own making.'[21]

Thompson had a profound, and romantic, belief in the radical potential and the inherent good sense and egalitarian spirit of the common people. Time and again, both in his historical, academic work and in his peace movement activism, Thompson placed his central reliance for the engine of progressive change upon the 'common people', acting collectively in mass social movements. This central role, he argued, was often undervalued or even ignored by subsequent mainstream politicians and indeed by historians.

Orwell, too, saw the 'common people' as the repository of decency, of ordinary everyday morality and fair dealing. All the commercialism, greed and selfishness of modern industrial society was contested, for Orwell, not so much by formal political parties of the Left (though at certain critical periods he strongly supported one or other of the democratic socialist parties, both in Britain and in Spain) – but in the residual, unchanging good sense of the common people (as opposed to the unreliable, often disreputable and untrustworthy 'intellectuals'). This is a recurring theme through his novels and most famously in his dystopia, *Nineteen Eighty-Four*. With Orwell even more than with Thompson, however, there is a strong element of romantic mythologising: this is especially so in his characterisation of the Proles in *Nineteen Eighty-Four*. (This is discussed in more detail in Chapter 6.)

Although they differed markedly on questions of agency, and on the means of achieving progressive social and political change (and indeed the nature of such change), all those discussed in this book shared a core belief in the key role of the common people, mobilised around issue-based movements: Russell and the Committee of 100 (Chapter 3); Sylvia Pankhurst and the suffragette movement (Chapter 4); Ellen Wilkinson and the Jarrow March of the unemployed (Chapter 5); and Tony Benn and his involvement in several extra-parliamentary movements (Chapter 11).

These then are the central characteristics and ideological tenets of the English radical tradition as it is discussed here. The remaining preliminary questions detailed at the outset can be addressed more briefly. The rationale for the first of these – why is the focus here upon *English* rather than *British* radicalism? – is in part located in straightforward historical context, and in part upon pragmatic issues of scope and focus. The 'island nations' of what is now the United Kingdom of Great Britain and Northern Ireland, and the Republic of Ireland, were very largely separate entities until the seventeenth century. As Robert Tombs has noted, the 'British perspective is most useful for the seventeenth century, when the island nations were entwined politically to a unique degree', though even then, he notes, 'the insular view risks obscuring the fundamental importance to England of the Low Countries, France, Spain and Germany'.[22] Often, he argues, even when part of a (more or less) United Kingdom, the relationships England has had with some other countries (the USA, Germany, for example) and with the British Empire, have been more important than those with the other 'home nations'. In particular, as Stuart Hall amongst others argued (Chapter 10), the interrelationship between English radicalism and the developing anti-colonial, independence movements of the Empire, especially India, have been of central importance, politically and ideologically. Moreover, the whole experience of colonialism has been an integral part of the political culture of twentieth-century England.

Even where Britain has been taken as the focus, it has to be acknowledged, as Edward Vallance does, that 'radicalism in the British Isles did not take on a clearly "British" character until after the Napoleonic Wars'.[23] It is not tenable, in my view, to subsume the 'British' into the 'English', as Vallance appears to do: 'what is offered is an "enriched" English, rather than a genuinely British, history of radicalism', as he puts it.[24] As well as being necessarily misleading, this results in a somewhat unhelpful half-way house.

The focus upon England thus has a solid historical rationale. But it is also important to note that the histories, class formations and ideological perspectives of radical traditions in the other 'home nations' (including Ireland) are very different from those of England. As Thompson put it, the concentration upon England, rather than Britain, is 'not out of chauvinism, but out of respect':[25] Irish, Scottish and Welsh radicalisms deserve proper consideration in their own right.

There are of course close and important interrelationships between radical movements and it is also the case that by the beginning of the twentieth century several factors had enhanced the interpenetration culturally and politically of the radical traditions of the 'home nations'. From the late nineteenth century there was a rapid increase in communication, both physically, as technological progress advanced (railways, roads), and culturally, as greater literacy developed and means of mass communication, notably the BBC, emerged. Similarly, as the nature of capitalism evolved, so collectivist organisations both nationally and internationally came to the fore. Thus, some of the key movements, and indeed individuals, in the development of radicalism were prominent across the whole of Britain, rather than in England alone. Movements such as 'Red Clydeside' and Larkin's Irish trade union movement, for example, were key elements in radical development; and some leading radicals in the United Kingdom were Scottish, Welsh or Irish rather than English: for example, Aneurin Bevan, Jennie Lee and Keir Hardie.

The fact remains, however, that national radicalisms have their own dynamic, their own reference points, in short their own culture and context. There remains an identifiable, meaningful *English* radical tradition: not discrete, of course, but worthy of study and discussion in its own right. (There are problematic issues, for English radicalism, around 'the politics of Englishness', as articulated in the early twenty-first century: these are discussed in the concluding chapter of this book.)

A further question, posed at the outset, is whether the English radical tradition in the twentieth century is worthy of consideration *at all*. There is little doubt that, since at least the seventeenth century, the radical tradition has been important in English history and politics: it has been 'persistent and powerful', as Vallance has it.[26] Further, it is clear that, despite the strictures of Perry Anderson and Tom Nairn,[27] this radical tradition was vibrant from the late eighteenth century to the late twentieth (Chapter 2).[28] Despite the increasing dominance of neo-liberal capitalism in the early twenty-first century, there is no doubt that the radical tradition, in necessarily modified form, is a dynamic political force – and has a central role in progressive political culture.

The final chapter of this study explores this contention in more detail. Here, I would make three brief points. First, as Ralph Miliband said to me some years ago, at one of the many times of political despondency on the Left, whilst capitalism exists, there will be inequalities of wealth and power: it is the nature of the beast. Without concentrations of economic and political control, capitalism cannot function. If objective inequality exists, then objective social class divisions necessarily exist too, and there are conflicts of interest and conflicting perceptions of social reality. Moreover, the contradictions in the capitalist system – both economic and political – will result in continual crises and instability.[29] Precisely when such crises occur, and still more how they are resolved, are open questions, but arise they will; and new radical mass movements will be an important means of articulating these discontents. Secondly, as societies become ever more complex and differentiated, and the interconnections between nation states and individuals increase, so a range of issue movements will be the natural, organic means of expression, in addition to overarching political parties. Finally, the widespread disillusion with mainstream politics and the established mechanisms of parliamentary democracy should not be confused with a lack of interest in or cynicism about politics (and, especially, political radicalism) *per se*. As Tony Benn pointed out on numerous occasions, the radical Left has needed to 'march on two legs': extra-parliamentary activism was as important as a parliamentary presence. Indeed, when he eventually brought to an end his long parliamentary career, he said, only half in jest, that he was leaving Parliament in order to spend more time on politics.

There is abundant evidence, in England as elsewhere, of a continuing interest in and involvement with the long tradition of radical politics, broadly defined: for example, the resurgence of the peace movement, culminating in the huge march against the war in Iraq in 2003; the 'Occupy' movement; the numerous anti-racist and anti-fascist movements of the late twentieth and early twenty-first centuries; and the growth of the environmentalist movement (Chapter 13).

As noted at the outset of this introductory chapter, the central purpose of this book – to analyse and discuss the nature and importance of the English radical tradition in the twentieth century – is undertaken through a series of chapters exploring the ideas and activities of ten exponents of this tradition. Such an approach is not new: Stefan Collini, for example, has adopted a similar structure in his masterly study of British intellectuals in the twentieth century,[30] as has David Goodway in his no less impressive work on anarchism and libertarianism in Britain in the twentieth century.[31] An obvious problem with such an approach, however, is how to make the selection of those individuals to be discussed (and on what grounds others are excluded).

I have chosen the ten people for this study – Bertrand Russell, Sylvia Pankhurst, Ellen Wilkinson, George Orwell, E.P. Thompson, Michael Foot, Joan Maynard, Stuart Hall, Tony Benn and Nicolas Walter – because they represent, in my view, both the diversity of English radicalism in the twentieth century and its cohesion around a series of coherent perspectives. Whilst their differences in background and intellectual, ideological perspectives are often marked, they do share the values and beliefs that constitute the essence of twentieth-century English radicalism. Of course, this selection is not definitive, it could not be: a case could be made for a large number of others. However, I hope that those I have selected at least represent the major strands of the tradition across the century. They range from radical liberals, through a variety of principled, left-wing democratic socialists (many involved with the Labour Party and reformist politics), to those influenced by humanistic Marxism and extra-parliamentary movements, to the full anarchist position. Although the case study chapters follow a broadly chronological order, there are exceptions where the themes considered in relation to two of those selected are very similar (Orwell and Thompson, for example); or where the particular political prominence of the person considered came late in a long political life (Benn, for example).

Such a listing is necessarily schematic and the individuals and their political and theoretical perspectives overlap. The analyses are of the ideas and political perspectives of the people concerned and are not an attempt at a series of 'potted biographies'. Some of those considered were outstanding intellectuals – Bertrand Russell and E.P. Thompson, for example; others were more notable for attempting to put their ideological convictions into practical, political action – Sylvia Pankhurst, Ellen Wilkinson, Stuart Hall, Tony Benn and Joan Maynard, for example. Some are well-known – Bertrand Russell, Michael Foot and George Orwell; others, less so – Joan Maynard and Nicolas Walter. But all have made a distinctive, original and arresting contribution to modern English radicalism.

One further characteristic should be noted: most of those selected wrote eloquently and with style; and some of them wrote quite superbly (in particular, in their very different ways, Russell, Orwell and Thompson). It is a notable, and in my view very attractive, attribute of the best exponents of English radicalism over the last two hundred years that they have written well and with verve and passion. This is fitting, given that of all art forms, the English have excelled in literature, drama and, to use an old-fashioned term, 'letters'.

Notes

The 'place of publication' for the books referenced in all chapters is London, unless otherwise stated.

1. E.P. Thompson, *The Making of the English Working Class* (Gollancz, 1963), Preface, pp. 13–14. References here are to the Pelican edition, Penguin Books, 1968.
2. R. Williams, *Keywords: A Vocabulary of Culture and Society* (Fontana, 1976), Revised edition, pp. 251–2. References here are to the Flamingo edition, 1983.
3. In the early twenty-first century, quite a few other meanings of 'radicalism' have emerged. In the USA, for example, the 'Radical Right' denotes the ultra-conservative, populist, neo-liberal ideology of the supporters of President Trump. Confusingly, 'radical' has also been widely applied to Islamic fundamentalism and the terrorist extremism it has advocated and practised. Clearly, 'radicalism', as defined in this book, is wholly separate from such positions.
4. The numerous books by Simon Maccoby on English radicalism include: *The English Radical Tradition 1763–1914* (Allen and Unwin, 1957); *English Radicalism 1762–1785: The Origins* (Allen and Unwin, 1953); *English Radicalism 1780–1832: From Paine to Cobbett* (Allen and Unwin, 1955); *English Radicalism: The End?* (Allen and Unwin, 1961).
5. For example, W. Thomas, *The Philosophic Radicals: Nine Studies in Theory and Practice, 1817–1841* (Oxford: Clarendon Press, 1979); J.W. Derry, *The Radical Tradition: Tom Paine to Lloyd George* (Macmillan, 1967); G. Watson, *The English Ideology, Studies in the Language of Victorian Politics* (Allen Lane, 1973).
6. Watson, *The English Ideology*, p. 10.
7. E. Vallance, *A Radical History of Britain* (Little, Brown, 2009). References here are to the pb. Abacus edition, 2010, p. 11.
8. There was, in the nineteenth century, a significant strand of radicalism in the Conservative Party, exemplified especially by Disraeli and his 'Young England' movement. By the twentieth century, however, this tradition had largely died out, though there were occasional exceptions: Ian McLeod and Edward Boyle, for example. On the Conservative Party generally, see R. Blake, *The Conservative Party: From Peel to Thatcher* (Fontana Press, 1985); and S.H. Beer, *Modern British Politics* (Faber and Faber, 1965); and, on the Party in the twentieth century, see J. Seldon and S. Ball (eds), *Conservative Century: The Conservative Party Since 1900* (Oxford: Oxford University Press, 1994).
9. R. Colls, *George Orwell: English Rebel* (Oxford: Oxford University Press, 2013), p. 206.
10. R.H. Tawney, 'British Socialism Today', *Socialist Commentary*, June 1952 (reprinted in R. Hinden (ed.), *The Radical Tradition: Twelve Essays on Politics, Education and Literature* (Allen and Unwin, 1964)). References are taken from *The Radical Tradition*.
11. Ibid., pp. 168, 180.
12. W. Godwin, *Enquiry Concerning Political Justice* (1717) Book 1, chapter V.
13. Derry, *The Radical Tradition*, p. 403.
14. A. Crosland, *The Future of Socialism* (Cape, 1956).
15. Tawney, 'British Socialism Today', pp. 178–9.
16. R. Miliband, *The State in Capitalist Society* (Weidenfeld and Nicolson, 1969), pp. 138, 145.
17. R. Miliband, *Parliamentary Socialism: A Study in the Politics of Labour* (second

edition, Merlin Press, 1973); D. Coates, *The Labour Party and the Struggle for Socialism* (Cambridge: Cambridge University Press, 1975).

18 Many on the Left have agreed with Ralph Miliband that the Labour Party has in effect been a deradicalising force. Miliband argued in the 1970s that the Labour Party has always been essentially a party of modest social reform in a capitalist system 'within whose confines it is ever more firmly and by now irrevocably rooted'. *Parliamentary Socialism*, p. 376.

19 Ibid.

20 Colls, *George Orwell*, p. 175.

21 Thompson, *The Making of the English Working Class*, p. 9.

22 R. Tombs, *The English and Their History* (Allen Lane, 2014), pb. Penguin edition, 2015. References here are to the latter, pp. 2–3.

23 Vallance, *A Radical History of Britain*, p. 12.

24 Ibid.

25 Thompson, *The Making of the English Working Class*, p. 13.

26 Vallance, *A Radical History of Britain*, p. 12.

27 P. Anderson, 'Origins of the Present Crisis', *New Left Review* 23; reprinted in P. Anderson and R. Blackburn (eds), *Towards Socialism* (Fontana and New Left Books, 1965), pp. 11–52; T. Nairn, 'The Nature of the Labour Party' in ibid., pp. 159–217.

28 See in particular the polemical response to Anderson and Nairn, E.P. Thompson, 'The Peculiarities of the English', in R. Miliband and J. Saville (eds), *Socialist Register 1965* (Merlin Press, 1965), reprinted in E.P. Thompson, *The Poverty of Theory and Other Essays* (Merlin Press, 1978), pp. 35–91.

29 For a concise account of the inherent contradictions of capitalism, see E. Mandel, *Introduction to Marxism* (Ink Links, second edition, 1979).

30 S. Collini, *Absent Minds: Intellectuals in Britain* (Oxford: Oxford University Press, 2006).

31 D. Goodway, *Anarchist Seeds Beneath the Snow: Left-Libertarian Thought and British Writers from William Morris to Colin Ward* (Liverpool: Liverpool University Press, 2006).

2

An overview of English radicalism

The purpose of this second introductory chapter is twofold: to explore the main themes in the development of the 'English radical tradition' – from its earliest manifestations (in the Peasants' Revolt and later in the Civil War) through to the end of the eighteenth century; and, secondly, to discuss in more detail the main elements of English radicalism in the nineteenth and twentieth centuries. This chapter is intended, therefore, to provide a political and historical framework for the discussion of the selected ten radical figures from the twentieth century.

What follows concentrates upon the main elements, in historical context, that have constituted the English radical tradition. It is not an attempt at a full historical analysis of this tradition.[1]

The origins of English radicalism: from the Peasants' Revolt to the end of the eighteenth century

Kolm has identified two of the mainsprings of early English radicalism. It was 'imbued with the spirit of liberty asserted in a struggle against the ecclesiastical and civil authority' and encompassed 'the demand for and the promise of political and intellectual liberty and equal justice under the law'.[2] Much of the early history of English radicalism was taken up with these linked themes, with Magna Carta, both the reality and the myth, as a central reference point.

The importance of Magna Carta lies not so much in its 'substance as the idea of it ... Myth it may be, but a virtuous national myth that speaks to the belief that the timeless and magisterial law stands above the flawed ruler ... we are free in part because we believe we are free'.[3] There is, though, a danger of reading back into the prospectus of Magna Carta a commitment to modern precepts of radical democracy. Magna Carta, imposed by powerful barons on a weak and unwilling king, was a stage in the struggle between absolute monarchical rule and an ambitious and brutal aristocratic elite.

Edward Vallance has argued that the radical tradition began in earnest with the Peasants' Revolt of 1381. This was not a spontaneous revolutionary uprising: nor was it regicidal. A series of disasters – poor harvests because of climate change, starvation, draconian legal enactments by the state, an untimely declaration of war with France by Edward III and, above all, the onset of the Black Death in 1348 – had had a catastrophic effect upon the mass of the population. 'Not without reason has the fourteenth century been dubbed "the worst century ever".'[4]

The initial disturbances, which triggered the Peasants' Revolt, began in Essex on 30 May 1380 when a number of towns refused to co-operate with the Royal Commission established to enquire into the (widespread) evasion of the new Poll Taxes introduced by the King. The march on London began with only a few thousand but numbers grew rapidly on arrival in the capital; and several uprisings occurred elsewhere in the country. John Ball's radical appeal, in his sermon to the rebel host at Blackheath, has echoed through the ages:

> When Adam delved and Eve span
> Who was then the gentleman?

Briefly, the Peasants' Revolt threatened the viability of the state. The King offered concessions but, once the crisis had passed, draconian penalties were instituted – including the beheading of the Revolt's leader, Wat Tyler – and the promised reforms largely failed to materialise. However, by the end of the fourteenth century, the working conditions and wages of the poor had improved: the ruling class, whilst crushing outright rebellion, recognised the need for some amelioration of the grievances of the mass of the people if revolution were to be avoided. This was a pattern to be repeated across the centuries and provides an important element in the remarkable continuity and stability of the unequal, hierarchical social and political structure in England. It has been against this deep conservatism that English radicals have developed their alternative perspectives and activism.

In some ways, this conservatism applies more to 'the common people' than it does to the governing class. As George Watson has observed, recalling Orwell, the 'English people ... have no tradition of revolution. Their rulers, however, have',[5] as, for example, in the 'Glorious Revolution' of 1688, which brought William and Mary to the throne and finally ended the Roman Catholic, monarchical rule of the Stuarts.

There was one major exception to this largely contained class conflict and clash of ideologies: the English Civil War of the seventeenth century. The complex historical events of the Civil War are not the focus here: the intention is to identify how the ideas and movements generated by these upheavals contribute to the

English radical tradition. Foremost amongst these movements were the Levellers whose ideas were influential in the mid-seventeenth century. Although driven underground after the Restoration in 1660, these ideas never disappeared. They re-emerged in the eighteenth century in radical political movements (the 'Painites', the agitation around 'Wilkes and Liberty' and the pressure for political reform, for example).

Vehement opposition to Roman Catholicism, and a corresponding avowal of Protestant religion, were key elements of the radical focus in the Civil War. The theology was inextricably connected to the politics, however. The belief that people stood in direct relationship to God, and that the intercession of a priestly hierarchy was anathema to the teachings of Jesus in the New Testament, was part and parcel of opposition to monarchical power. Moreover, the Parliamentarians feared that the monarch, in alliance with senior bishops, would by-pass the representative institutions of the state, most notably Parliament.

The Putney Debates of 1647 were the most famous event in the articulation of Leveller ideas. The most memorable statement came from Rainsborowe, who argued that all men who signed the Levellers' 'Agreement of the People' should be eligible to vote: ' "For really I think that the poorest he that is in England has a life to lead as the greatest he ... every man that is to live under a Government ought first by his own consent put himself under that government".'[6] In reality, however, the Levellers were calling not for universal adult suffrage (not even for universal adult *male* suffrage) but for an agreement by plebiscite to a moderately reformed parliamentary system, more akin to the provisions of the 1832 Great Reform Act than to the contemporary universal adult suffrage system. More important, in retrospect, for English radicalism was the identification of 'reserves', those fundamental rights with which elected representatives would not be able to tamper. These were the foundations upon which 'The Liberty Tree', to use Thompson's term,[7] was built: liberty of conscience (including freedom of worship), equality before the law, freedom from conscription, and an independent, fair and inviolable legal structure centred on the jury system.

The Diggers were a more radical, though short-lived and small, movement in the Civil War years, centred on economic demands, principally for the common ownership of land (redolent of later agrarian radicalism: Joan Maynard for example supported land nationalisation, Chapter 9). The Diggers advocated the abolition of private ownership *per se* and the envisioned 'common treasury' of the earth becoming communal again. This was an Arcadian myth *par excellence.*

The importance of such movements for the radical tradition lay neither in their direct influence upon the course of the Civil War nor in their own preoccupations and priorities. The latter, as Robert Tombs has argued, were directed to a 'return to an ancient purity. Their political action was at the service of godly religion struggling to defeat the Antichrist and make ready for a hopefully imminent Second Coming.'[8]

Rather, in retrospect, their importance lies in their advocacy of democratic populism, the inalienable rights of all people in society to be treated fairly and justly, and to have equality before the law.

Fundamental differences of perspective on the 'real nature' of the Civil War and subsequent English history have persisted amongst historians. Within the radical canon, the influential view of R.H. Tawney was that the Civil War was not in essence a struggle for freedom but rather the replacement of feudalism by capitalism. The importance of the resistance 'from below', and the embryonic quasi-socialist ideology it represented, was emphasised by communist historians, notably Christopher Hill.

There are two other particularly notable aspects of the radical tradition up to the end of the eighteenth century: the republican radicalism of Tom Paine; and the beginnings of the struggle for women's emancipation, one of the key themes of English radicalism from the late nineteenth century onwards.

Unlike most other leading radical thinkers and writers in the eighteenth century, Paine had known poverty and hardship and he spoke with an authentic voice to the poor and dispossessed. He had emigrated to America in 1775, and it was here that he published his first influential pamphlet, *Common Sense*, and found his first idealistic cause: the anti-colonial struggle for independence.

Paine's explicitly anti-monarchical, anti-statist language, his generally insurrectionary tone, and his avocation of the common sense and good conscience of the people, alarmed a political Establishment, already jittery in the light of the chaotic revolution in France. In Thompson's view, Paine established a new framework within which radicalism was interpreted for the next hundred years.[9]

Paine rejected the conventional Whig orthodoxy, that the 1688 'Glorious Revolution' (and indeed the notion of a generalised tradition of British liberty) constituted a fundamental, progressive realignment of the polity. On the contrary, he argued, these were at best irrelevancies; the '"ancient constitution" that Burke venerated was no more than a chimera'.[10] Such shibboleths as Magna Carta and the Bill of Rights 'merely set new bounds to the exercise of royal tyranny'.[11] He attacked the 'absurdity' of the hereditary principle, which underlay both the monarchy and the House of Lords.

Moreover, unlike other radicals, who emphasised moral regeneration, via education, to address the negative culture and behaviour of the poor, Paine believed that the solution lay in the ending of poverty itself. This was, in effect, an early advocacy of socialist egalitarianism, not only on moral grounds but also – to put it in modern terminology – because it would lead to a more cohesive, fairer and more dynamic society. Paine proceeded, in the second part of *The Rights of Man*, to advocate in some detail the means by which greater equality should be attained: for example, a sliding scale of inheritance tax, a tax on land ownership and a cut in the general level of taxation.

Paine speaks to the modern radical movement; he made a significant contribution to English radicalism which continues to resonate in our own times.

The modern movement for women's political and social emancipation came to prominence with the women's suffrage movement in the early twentieth century; but, in preceding centuries, perhaps the most striking single observation is how little attention was focused in progressive campaigning upon the unequal relationships between the sexes. Women were excluded from virtually all access to social, political and legal rights. Once the position of women did come to the fore politically, the extension of the suffrage was by no means the only issue. The suffragists highlighted the social, legal and financial discriminatory practice of the state. The extension of the franchise was not a prominent demand in English radicalism prior to the nineteenth century. The first prominent feminist activist was Mary Wollstonecraft. In her book *A Vindication of the Rights of Woman*[12] although she makes her republicanism clear and rails against the unfairness of the restricted suffrage system, the main body of her work 'was directed at the upbringing of women, focusing mainly on the education, or lack of it, given to gentlewomen'.[13]

The solution to the lack of any educational opportunities for women, was, she believed, to create co-educational schools for both the rich and the poor. Some of her attitudes seem distinctly *un*radical to contemporary eyes: for example, she was no egalitarian educationally; she believed that from the age of nine children intended for domestic employment should be educated separately, whilst their middle- and upper-class contemporaries would study the more academic subjects (languages, history, politics and literature). Nevertheless, she had a clear commitment to women's rights. For example: 'I do earnestly wish to see the distinction of sex confounded in society, unless where love animates the behaviour. For this distinction is, I am firmly persuaded, the foundation of the weakness of character ascribed to woman.'[14]

Such passages resonate with the concerns of the women's movement in the twentieth and early twenty-first centuries. But, to repeat the point made at the outset of this section, what is remarkable is not so much the articulation of such views by Wollstonecraft but the rarity of such instances.

English radicalism in the nineteenth and twentieth centuries: the main themes

There have been many strands to English radicalism in the nineteenth and twentieth centuries, including, for example, those movements committed to environmentalist and anti-colonialist/anti-imperialist objectives. The approach taken here is to concentrate upon three of the central elements of English radicalism in this period, all of which are characterised, *inter alia*, by their social movement activism: the *labour movement*, both the industrial trade union element and the Labour Party itself; the *women's movement*, from the suffrage campaigns of the late nineteenth and early twentieth centuries to the 'second wave' feminism of the 1960s and 1970s and beyond; and the *peace movement*, from opposition to the First World War to the anti-nuclear campaigns of the second half of the twentieth century. The aim is to provide a background framework for the more detailed analyses of the ten leading radicals that follow. All were involved in one or more of these movements, and their overall radical values and priorities are illuminated by their activism or writings in these contexts.

The labour movement

Many of the movements of opposition to the new industrial capitalism of the nineteenth century were short-lived, though passionate, protests against the upheavals brought about, economically and socially, in people's lives by the advance of new technologies. The Luddism of the early nineteenth century is only the most prominent of many such movements.

In the labour movement, the more moderate elements believed in parliamentary reform, and exerting pressure through the presentation of petitions demanding universal adult male suffrage, annual parliaments and the institution of a secret ballot. There were others in the growing movement who advocated more radical, even insurrectionary activity, but they were always in the minority. Generally, the British labour movement, and especially the *English* labour movement, was dominated ideologically by a culture of gradualism and political moderation. Martin and Rubinstein have usefully drawn attention to three important characteristics of the British experience: first, 'that, until well after 1945, the majority of working people ... were concerned above all with the struggle for existence ... Self-education ... affected only a minority. Getting and spending have always been the normal human preoccupations'. Secondly, and critically, Britain was different from other European societies in the formative years of the early nineteenth century: the 'roots of trade and industry were deeper; the peasantry had disappeared much earlier; and restrictions on commerce were fewer'. There was relative political stability, a well-established state and constitution; 'it was natural for working-class people to work within the political and social system rather than outside it'. Political reformism and gradualism were the almost inevitable result. Thirdly, 'Britain was deeply divided on grounds of social class. The working class, divided among itself, was cut off from other classes and hostile to ideologies which seemed to reek of middle-class patronage ... The working class was hostile to class war but suspicious of collaborating with middle-class radicals or socialists in either political or industrial struggles. *Without a militant or revolutionary ideology, the working class and its institutions were bound to be defensive. Thus evolved the tenacious institution of labourism*' (my italics).[15]

There were, though, numerous examples of idealistic, even utopian, movements which gained mass backing (usually briefly) from the working class. The most prominent was the Owenite movement for a co-operative system of production and consumption. Robert Owen, a self-made model employer in the cotton textile industries in Lancashire and later New Lanark, was impatient with the purely political reform demands of middle-class radicals. Owen believed that, with a co-operative economic structure and ethos, a new morality and, ultimately, an end to both individual and national and international conflict could be achieved. He saw the Christian religion as inherently individualistic and reactionary. If children were brought up instead to believe in the virtues of co-operation and fellowship, and in fair and generous material conditions, then future generations could be, *would* be, characterised by a more progressive, more moral 'human nature'.

Owen also mobilised tens of thousands of workers in the GNCTU (Grand National Consolidated Trades Union), an attempt to create a single, totalising industrial force dedicated to the overthrow of the capitalist system and its replacement with (an ill-defined) co-operative, socialist alternative.

There were numerous clashes between the governing class and state authorities, and the combined forces of radicalism and working-class militancy, most notably the Peterloo 'massacre' of August 1819. This event, where 15 people were killed and 654 wounded, has entered into Labour mythology.

At the other, more moderate, end of the radical spectrum, pressure was mounting for electoral reform. This was partly because of the influence of the emerging political philosophy of utilitarianism, partly because of the increasingly untenable contrast between the economic power of the new industrial bourgeoisie and their virtual exclusion from the franchise, but also because, amongst the governing class, there 'was a palpable sense that the outright rejection of reform would lead to revolution'.[16] This is not the place to consider the long, slow, painful road to franchise reform. This agitation for parliamentary reform, and the Anti-Corn Law League campaign, led to the greatest mass movement of the nineteenth century, Chartism.[17]

Chartism was essentially a *reformist* movement. Its demands – the six points of the Charter[18] – were for various democratising reforms of, and within, the existing parliamentary system. It was, nevertheless, a movement containing a diversity of perspectives 'ranging from republicans to a few Tory radicals', with some of its leading adherents having revolutionary affinities. In its explicit political aims, Chartism 'failed' – though all but one of its demands (that for annual parliaments) were eventually adopted over succeeding decades. However, its subsequent influence has been profound: it was at the level of the 'lower tier' leadership, as Chase terms it, rather than the better-known leading figures, that 'the movement's enduring legacy was so vital'.[19] It became 'an integral part of the cultural life of local communities, offering ... a powerful morale-boosting memory of working-class political activism and solidarity'.[20]

The most pervasive and most enduring of working-class movements from the nineteenth century was of course the trade union movement.[21] The focus here is upon the ideological and political impact of trade unionism upon English radicalism. It was a long journey from the early, 'secret society', guild origins of trade unions, and the victimisation of the early proponents of union organisation (most famously, the Tolpuddle Martyrs),[22] to the acceptance of the predominantly moderate, defensive and in many ways conservative New Model unions of the middle and later nineteenth century. Their politics began the long tradition of 'Lib-Lab' co-operation, which lasted as a major force in the early Labour Party in the twentieth century.

However, there have been periods where the trade unions and socialist politics have combined to create a movement threatening the established order and arguing for a wholesale transformation of society. The rise of the New Unions in the 1880s and 1890s (union membership between 1888 and 1892 roughly doubled, to 1.5 million) was in part cause and in part effect of the rise of the political socialist movements – the Democratic Federation (later, the Social Democratic Federation, SDF) and the Socialist League.[23] A succession of strikes – the Dockers and London Gas Workers, in 1889, being the most prominent – were inspired by political as well as industrial objectives. There were all kinds of weaknesses – poor organisation, sectarian political disputes and rigid political positions (the SDF in particular), the London-centric nature of most of the activism – but there was enough strength and commitment for working-class socialists to establish, in Bradford in 1893, the Independent Labour Party (ILP). It was only a matter of time now for the disparate elements in the labour movement to coalesce into the (always uneasy) coalition that was to emerge in 1900 as the Labour Representation Committee, soon to be retitled as the Labour Party.[24]

There was also another development in the early years of the twentieth century putting forward a very different and more revolutionary ideology and strategy. Syndicalism in all its various forms briefly dominated the Left between 1910 and 1914, and again was a contributory strand in the turbulent industrial unrest following the end of the First World War and culminating in the General Strike of 1926.

The defining ideas of the syndicalists, though there were sharp differences over both ideology and strategy, were: that a revolutionary transformation was necessary and could come about only through the collective power of working-class people through their trade unions; that the movement should be built through strike action, on an 'industrial union' basis; and that such action should be under workers' control structures, not subservient to an 'external' political authority: such structures would form the initial basis for a new form of co-operative, egalitarian social system.

Such ideas find echoes in the labour movement in succeeding years (in the Institute for Workers' Control in the later decades of the twentieth century, for example): but the years of militancy were relatively brief. The labour movement, in the long term, has been dominated by the (parliamentarist) political Labour Party.

Whether or not the Labour Party is politically capable of achieving radical, progressive change has been one of the central questions preoccupying English radicals in the twentieth century. Amongst those radicals discussed in this book, opinions have differed markedly. Some – Ellen Wilkinson, Michael Foot and Tony Benn – have seen the Labour Party as *the* central reference point, whatever their other differences. Others – notably, Sylvia Pankhurst, George Orwell and E.P. Thompson – have been more ambivalent, or have had a focus much more concentrated upon *extra*-parliamentary, social-movement activism.

What has been the ideological impact of the labour movement upon English radicalism? At the risk of over-generalisation I would summarise the main themes as follows. The labourist argument for radical change in society has been based on predominantly moral grounds (as opposed, for example, to the theoretical analyses of Marxism, where it is argued that capitalism is systemically untenable). From this morally based perspective, radical change is essential because capitalism is inherently unfair and unjust. The moralism of the labour movement drew on the precepts of New Testament Christianity, especially the 'Sermon on the Mount', albeit often in secularised form, and irrespective of the fact that its advocates were often avowed atheists or agnostics. The *culture* of Christian moralism runs deep in the labour movement, the Labour Party and indeed in English radicalism, whether the protagonists are Christian (R.H. Tawney, F.D. Maurice) or agnostics or atheists (Michael Foot, Bertrand Russell).

Also deriving from its Christian, Nonconformist inheritance, labourism has been committed to individualism, not to the *possessive* individualism that has been held to characterise nineteenth century liberalism, but rather to the *free individual* as the key reference point for Labour politics.

Labourism has been committed, much to the frustration of many intellectual leftists, to *pragmatic gradualism*. This, too, forms a significant component in English radicalism. The English are, as Orwell observed, temperamentally hostile to 'continental theorising'. In his view, there is a 'prevailing lack of intellectuality' in the English. They 'are not sufficiently interested in intellectual matters to be intolerant about them'. They 'will never develop into a nation of philosophers. They will always prefer instinct to logic, and character to intelligence.'[25]

Twentieth-century English radicalism has been dominated by these labourist precepts. Neither communism nor any of its dissident variants has ever gained mass popular support in England. This is in contrast to several other comparable Western societies: similarly, anarchism has remained a minority ideology.[26] It is not that such perspectives are unimportant but it is to emphasise that such ideological beliefs and political practices have always been *minority* positions in the English radical tradition.

A further characteristic of English radicalism is its adherence to a rather vaguely defined belief in 'democracy', and a whole series of associated, important values; equality before the law, *habeas corpus*, the right of free expression for minorities and so on. This is all too often conflated with *parliamentary* democracy, a category confusion inherent in labourism, as Ralph Miliband argued persuasively in *Parliamentary Socialism*.

There is also ambivalence in labourism over conceptualisations of the state. On the one hand, there is the innate suspicion by the broadly defined working class of 'Them', as in 'Them' and 'Us'. 'They', as Orwell has it, 'are the higher-ups, the mysterious powers who do things to you against your will'. But, he goes on to note, 'though tyrannical, [they] are not omnipotent. "They" will respond to pressure if you take the trouble to apply it'.[27] On the other, there has been a strong belief in the political *neutrality* of the state. (A position demonstrably mistaken, as Ralph Miliband amongst others has demonstrated.)[28]

Labourism's legacy to English radicalism has thus been a mixed blessing. Nevertheless, however much some may wish it otherwise, its central importance is clear.

The women's movement

Once the extension of the franchise became *the* key area of reform from the time of the agitation leading up to the Great Reform Act of 1832, it was predictable that *women's* voting rights would become a significant issue. However, this did take some time. As Vallance has observed, as late as 1884 there was generally 'an absence of interest in constitutional reform among British socialists. There was a strong sense that, with the enfranchisement of a large section of the male working class under the 1884 Reform Act, British democracy was practically the finished article.'[29] Moreover, there was deep cultural resistance to the idea that women should have political, social or legal independence.

The roles of women were seen, especially by most men, including most working-class men, as 'homemakers' and providers of comfort and support for their male breadwinners. Such attitudes persisted into the twentieth-century labour movement and remained an area of contention, culturally and politically.

Property rights, divorce law reform and the general recognition of women as equal members of society all became significant issues. There was a growing realisation of the importance of equal rights for women (as recognised, for example, by one of emancipation's most eloquent advocates, J.S. Mill). Women were also increasingly prominent in other areas, notably education: for example, Barbara Bodichon and Emily Davies founded Girton College, Cambridge; Frances Mary Buss founded the North London Collegiate School; and Dorothea Beale founded Cheltenham Ladies' College. Women were also engaged in developments in journalism and medicine. There was thus an historical and ideological hinterland to the growth of the women's suffrage movement. As with so many radical social movements in England, the suffrage movement was divided, often with great acrimony, between the 'moderate' original, umbrella organisation, the National Union of Women's Suffrage Societies (NUWSS), and the 'militants' of the Women's Social and Political Union (WSPU).

To draw too sharp a distinction between moderates and militants would be mistaken, however. On the ground, there was much co-operation and, largely, goodwill between the different strands, at least until 1908–9. In Holton's view, it was 'the successful realisation of democratic-suffragist strategy in feminist-labour alliances … which ensured the eventual granting of the vote to women, not militancy as the leaders of the Women's Social and Political Union were afterwards to claim'.[30] It was the coming together of the cause of women's suffrage with more generalised movements for social change, and the realisation that the subordination of women was intimately linked to structural class inequality, that were, Holton argued, the main factors in the eventual success of the campaign.

Most of the attention has been upon the militant suffragettes, their dramatic protest tactics, and the concomitant issues of imprisonment, hunger strikes and 'forced feeding'. However, there is a strong case for arguing, with Holton, that the activities of the WSPU, though dramatic, were not the mainsprings for the eventual attainment of the movement's objectives. Indeed, Robert Tombs maintains that, after Emily Davison's tragic death at the Derby in 1913, the WSPU 'membership collapsed, whereas that of the moderate suffragists shot up'.[31]

In addition to tactical, strategic and personal tensions in the movement, there were fundamental ideological differences which, in one form or another, were to persist in later feminist movements. These centred on humanist and essentialist conceptions, to use Holton's terminology, of women's identity. In the former conceptualisation, common assumptions of differential male and female roles were challenged. Stemming directly from Enlightenment philosophy, it was held that men and women had 'common human attributes' and that their unequal treatment was socially unjust. The essentialist view challenged this. It held that it is 'fixed for all time [that] certain socially determined aspects of what it is to be a woman' are a given: women have inherently 'a higher regard for the sanctity of human life', and tend to be more religious, more altruistic, more moral than men'.[32] They were thus held to be more loving in regard to children and the sick. Some labour movement organisations, notably the SDF, echoed such sentiments and 'revealed a pronounced social conservatism when dealing with any issues relating to women … [they believed women should] remain primarily as wives and mothers'.[33] Such a perspective, which persisted – albeit articulated in different terms – throughout the twentieth century, assumes an unchanging, predetermined, series of female social roles, and by implication these roles are subordinate to those assigned to males, and are distanced from social, economic and political power.

Although the WSPU was led by middle-class radicals (Emmeline and Christabel Pankhurst, the Pethick-Lawrences), and its activists were also largely, but not entirely, middle class, there was considerable working-class radical activism in the wider movement.[34] Nevertheless, this was a movement dominated by middle-class, intellectual, radical women; moreover, there was something of a paradox in a movement founded to extend democracy, becoming, in effect, a 'family dictatorship'.

Whether there would have been significant suffrage legislation in 1914 or thereabouts, remains obviously a matter of conjecture. What is clear is that, with the outbreak of war, the WSPU declined rapidly as its leadership embraced the patriotic call to support Britain and its allies in the ensuing conflict. It had anyway been 'losing ground not just because of its continued advocacy of violent militancy, but also because of its interlinking of the suffrage cause with the ongoing campaign against the evils of prostitution and venereal disease'.[35] Many NUWSS suffragists joined the Union of Democratic Control (UDC), a new anti-war group, which included radical liberals, ILP figures such as Ramsay MacDonald and former WSPU activists such as Pethick-Lawrence.

The fundamental changes brought about by the First World War included a changed perception (and actuality) in the position of women. Women's wartime roles – as workers, nurses and generally patriotic citizens – lessened tensions over suffrage issues. With Lloyd George replacing Asquith as Prime Minister, and with political expediency as well as changing attitudes favouring reform, the enfranchisement of women over 30, 'if they were householders, wives of householders or university graduates, or if they occupied property with a rental value of more than £5 a year',[36] was enacted with remarkably little fuss. Under the 1918 Act, 13 million men and 8.5 million women now had the vote; but most working-class women remained disenfranchised.

As Vera Brittain noted, after all the years of struggle, drama and conflict, this victory '"crept to its quiet, unadvertised triumph in the deepest night of wartime depression"'.[37] Although full equality, in terms of the franchise, was not achieved until 1928, and although this achievement required continual campaigning, women's full enfranchisement had become commonly accepted as inevitable, sensible and fair: a change in public consciousness almost unthinkable a few decades earlier.

Whatever the importance or otherwise of the militants' campaign, it is clear that the *means* – the window-breaking and other similar militant actions – became almost as important as the *ends*. Militant acts were, in one sense, a deep cry of protest against a male-dominated, patriarchal society. The values Emmeline Pankhurst espoused above all others were 'courage, ardour, vitality … The struggle itself was at least as important as the ultimate goal in terms of the opportunity it provided each participant for self-realization, for exerting her will, and for seeing the regeneration of society.' By the end of the campaign 'the vote had become of secondary importance to the engagement in struggle itself'.[38]

The legacy of the movement has been profound. Future generations of feminist activists have drawn inspiration from the example, the commitment and indeed the militancy of the Suffragist, and especially the Suffragette, movement.

From the 1920s to the end of the 1950s, there was a retrenchment and retreat from militant feminism. Significant progress was made in some areas, in addition to full adult suffrage (from 1928). But the 'new' feminists emphasised 'a programme that championed rather than challenged the prevailing ideas about masculinity and feminism … [and] accepted theories of sexual difference that helped to advance notions of separate spheres for men and women'.[39] 'By the 1950s … the movement had suffered an inexorable decline.'[40] These divisions were exacerbated by the Depression and persisting (male) unemployment, which together had consolidated traditional assumptions about the importance of a 'family wage' for the male head of the household. There developed a generally conservative culture which was implicitly hostile to feminism.

'Second wave feminism' of the 1960s and 1970s arose directly from the profound cultural changes in British society, but also drew ideologically upon the history and ethos of earlier feminist campaigns. Both the social reality and the self-perception of women changed radically. The divorce rate tripled over ten years from the early 1960s; church attendances declined sharply; and there was a growth in 'single parent' families. Although it has been argued that the 1960s cultural revolution was particularly beneficial for women, the new, more liberal, society was in many ways hard for women. Parenthood (often as a single parent), a career, persisting inequalities in pay and social esteem, the social pressures created by the new 'permissiveness' and the undiminished sexist culture combined to produce a pressured, unstable life for many women.

In some respects, then, the attainment of women's equality seemed as far away as ever: and equal suffrage, within a two-party system where equality of any sort, and women's equality in particular, was a consistently low priority, had manifestly failed to deliver the hoped-for results. Feminists thus had much to be militant about; and women had a new confidence and sense of independence. There were, broadly speaking, three main ideological strands of the new feminism: liberal, socialist and radical, although on many issues all were united. Key points of agreement included the campaign for equal pay for women, opposition to violence against women (the 'reclaim the night' movement), recognition of household work as 'proper work', and the protection of 'a woman's right to choose', enshrined in the 1967 Abortion Act.

There were, though, distinct ideological differences. Nineteenth-century liberalism argued for equal political and social rights for adult males (and by extension females) on the basis of their citizenship rather than property qualification. Liberal feminists thus gave priority to securing legislative enactments to secure women's equal rights, both social and economic – in the latter case, legislation to make labour markets both fairer and more efficient.

However, socialist feminists argued, such a perspective did little to mitigate *class* inequalities. Given their continuing subjugation in the labour movement – the overwhelming majority were engaged in low-paid, low-status and non-unionised occupations – women should be regarded as a major constituent part of 'the reserve army of labour'. Many socialist feminists also argued, following Engels, that traditional family structures (and the institution of marriage) maintained capitalist economic relations, and patriarchal assumptions about the appropriate roles of men and women in society.

For radical feminists, whereas Marxists see male domination as intrinsic to capitalism, it is 'men, not an economic system, [that] are the primary source of oppression'. Women therefore constitute a class in, approximately, the same way that workers do: 'women [must] take control of their reproduction in order to become free'. Moreover, for many radical feminists, the decision to become lesbian was 'not merely a matter of freedom of choice but ... essential political practice'.[41]

Feminists have always had relationships – usually uneasy if not fraught – with mainstream political parties: for example, Millicent Fawcett and Liberalism; and Emmeline, and especially Sylvia, Pankhurst with the ILP, the Labour Party and the labour movement more generally. In the 1960s and 1970s some socialist feminists were involved with the far Left and anarchistic groups (and notably in the peace movement, as is discussed below). However, the disillusionment of socialist women with the perceived authoritarianism and dogmatism of most of these movements has had a profound effect upon the development of English radicalism in the last decades of the twentieth century. This has been well expressed by Sheila Rowbotham:

> We have stressed ... the closeness and protection of a small group and the feeling of sisterhood ... it has been important that every woman has space and air for her feelings and ideas to grow. The assumption is that there is not a single correctness which can be learned off by heart and passed on by poking people with it ... This is the opposite to most left language which is constantly distinguishing itself as correct and then covering itself with a determined objectivity ... Our politics have tried to allow for the expression of vulnerability and openness to every woman's feelings which consciousness raising at its best implies. We have rejected central organization, hierarchical structures and a leadership.[42]

This perspective illustrates again the importance attached, within English radicalism, to individual freedom, and more generally to the freedom to express ideas and take action as the individual or the group thinks fit, untrammelled by external authority – whether this is the state, the prevailing mores of society or indeed 'the Party'. This is not to deny that such a position creates problems, both of ideological coherence and of organisation; nor is it to minimise or downgrade the commitment to an egalitarian society. But it *is* to emphasise that individual, social and political freedom is a primary and non-negotiable value.

Throughout the twentieth century there was a strong correlation between the culture, priorities and mode of operation between the women's movement and the peace movement, and it is to a consideration of that movement and its relationship to English radicalism more generally that attention is now turned.

The peace movement

The culture and politics of peace movements, from the seventeenth century onwards, have been central to English radicalism. In the earlier years, opposition to war and violence was articulated by Dissenting Christian sects, particularly the

Quakers. This tradition continued to be prominent in the peace movements of the more secular nineteenth and twentieth centuries, usually adopting a fully pacifist stance.

Nineteenth-century Britain was characterised by a belief in progress, in the steady advance of humankind towards a better and more prosperous future, and a conviction that 'history was on the side of peace'. Not only was war seen as an outrage, 'it was also an anachronism'.[43] This optimistic, confident view of the world and Britain's leading place in it was shattered by the First World War.

In 1914–18 the overwhelming majority of the British people *supported* the British government's decision to declare war on Germany. Most Liberals and Labour Party socialists, the leaders of the suffragettes and a large number of prominent intellectuals and writers all supported the war. And, in the first 22 months of the war, nearly 2,700,000 men volunteered to join the army.

There were, though, a variety of groups opposed to the war and this opposition grew as the conflict dragged on and the sheer scale of the slaughter and lack of military success dispelled the initial optimism. Those who were opposed to the war came from disparate perspectives: pacifists, usually but not always Christian (especially Quakers), opposed to war on *moral* grounds; liberal internationalists; libertarians, opposed to what was perceived to be the gross encroachment on civil liberties by an authoritarian state; Labour Party socialist internationalists, especially in the ILP; women's organisations; and Marxist revolutionaries. (As always, 'on the ground' there were many overlaps.)

The focus of the major wartime peace organisation, the UDC, was upon the 'construction of a better international order after the war, rather than attempting to elaborate detailed terms for an immediate negotiated settlement'.[44] The UDC argued that the encroaching state, as the war progressed, was adopting the methods of the autocratic German regime: 'censorship, compulsion, and regimentation'.[45] From modest beginnings, it grew steadily, in part due to the administrative abilities of E.D. Morel; and in part due to its careful bridging of radical liberalism and the more pacifist-inclined section of the Labour Party. By 1917, the UDC had one hundred local branches and approximately ten thousand members; with the membership of affiliated organisations, there were several hundred thousand supporting the broad UDC perspective.

The ILP provided the bedrock of support for the UDC, and it was again the ILP that constituted the leading element in the more radical NCF (No Conscription Fellowship), formed in response to the introduction of compulsory military service through the Military Service Act, January 1916. Led by Clifford Allen, the NCF was aimed at providing organised support for young men of military age who were resisting military conscription. The NCF also had close relations with radical Christian groups, such as the Quakers and the FoR (Fellowship of Reconciliation).

Equally important for the NCF, however, was resistance to what was held to be an increasingly authoritarian state, and protest against the erosion of hard-won civil liberties. As Allen put it, at one of his courts martial, 'I resist war because I love liberty. Conscription is the denial of liberty.'[46] And liberties *were* curtailed, whether rightly or wrongly: for example, *habeas corpus* was suspended; and indefinite imprisonment without trial was legalised. Both the liberal Bertrand Russell and the socialist Keir Hardie saw '*militarism* as a base problem: one that had produced German autocracy and was now undermining English democracy'.[47]

The non-Marxist Left, especially the ILP, was far more effective in its opposition to war than the Marxists of the British Socialist Party (BSP), the successor body to the SDF, and the main constituent organisation in the formation of the Communist Party in 1920. Hardie 'was often the most effective socialist voice against imperialist militarism'.[48]

The mainstream labour movement was divided on whether or not to support the war. Ramsay MacDonald, the Party leader, and many other pacifist-inclined figures in the Party, opposed the war; but the majority of the Party, and the industrial labour movement, gave it wholehearted support. Such divisions over war, disarmament, peace and general foreign-policy orientation, remained a divisive issue in the following decades – and persists as a touchstone of ideological dispute in the Labour Party.

The suffrage movement, too, was deeply divided over the issue of the war. Early in 1915, most of the younger activists in the NUWSS resigned in order to campaign for a women's peace movement; and, in autumn 1915, a Women's International League had been established, with a policy of women's rights and pacifism. This became the Women's International League for Peace and Freedom (WILPF).[49] Catherine Marshall, a feminist activist, expressed sentiments that were to recur, contentiously, throughout the later twentieth century women's peace movements: 'War is pre-eminently an outrage on motherhood and all that motherhood means; the destruction of life and the breaking-up of homes is the undoing of women's work as life-givers and home-makers.'[50]

The majority of the suffragettes followed the lead of Emmeline and Christabel Pankhurst and backed their support for the war: all protest activities were suspended for its duration. A minority, however, took the militant and socialist line advocated by Sylvia Pankhurst (Chapter 4).

In the 1920s pacifist ideas moved towards the centre ground of British politics. The definition and boundaries of the peace movement in this period are hard to delineate. Martin Ceadel's schema is a useful starting point: his term 'pacificism' includes not only 'pure' pacifists but also those who 'give priority to the abolition of war, but do not deny that participation in certain defensive wars is justified in the meanwhile'.

There were three approaches. First was the liberal perspective, which held that 'states could co-operate if they were not blinded by irrational nationalism'; it supported 'confederalism' through the League of Nations and, when that failed, federalism. Second were those who were inspired by socialism, whether Marxist or syndicalist, who 'blamed capitalism for war and sought to overthrow it', through building working-class resistance to war or through working for a '"peace front" of Socialists and progressives to resist Fascism'. Thirdly, there were those radicals who 'blamed elites (aristocrats, diplomats) and vested interests (arms traders, overseas investors) for war scares; their basic remedy was democratic control of foreign policy', though its hostility to the Versailles Treaty led to an early advocacy of appeasement. What they all had in common was 'an assumption that security is not primarily a matter of armaments, that the armed truce is inherently dangerous, and that the international system can be reformed in such a way as eventually to abolish war'.[51]

The core of the former NCF established in 1921 the 'No More War Movement' (NMWM) which had three thousand members by 1927 (and was active until it merged into the Peace Pledge Union (PPU) in 1937). The NMWM trod a difficult line between militant pacifism and (qualified) support for revolutionary resistance to capitalism (for example, in the agitation over the British government's support for the anti-Soviet armies in Russia).

The Wall Street crash led to political turmoil across Europe and the rise of Fascism and Nazism. Not surprisingly, the crisis divided the peace movement as never before or since and its inherent tensions were exposed. A large proportion of the population continued to be, as Ceadel has observed, simultaneously pessimistic – a fear induced by the fear of war and the memories of the horrific trench warfare of 1914–18 – and optimistic: 'an expectation that international relations could be reformed and war prevented'.[52]

The debate through the 1930s, as tensions mounted with successive crises (Manchuria, Spain, Abyssinia, Sudetenland and Munich being the most prominent), ebbed and flowed between 'collective security' through the League of Nations, the implementation of economic and/or military sanctions to prevent illegitimate annexations of territory and the perceived need for rearmament to deter potential aggressors. In addition, there was a persistent minority which advocated absolute pacifist policies. This reached its height in the appeal launched by Dick Sheppard, Canon of St Paul's Cathedral, in July 1935, for support for the statement 'we renounce war and never again, directly or indirectly, will we support or sanction another'. (By September 1939, 130,000 had signed.) In May 1936, this movement became the PPU, 'the largest absolute pacifist organization in history'.[53] In the more mainstream peace movement, the Peace Ballot of 1934–35, although sampling an impressive 11.6 million individuals (38 per cent of the total electorate), and although producing a high level of support for the League of Nations and endorsing overwhelmingly a policy of economic sanctions, was essentially a deliberate political fudge. It appeared to offer the possibility of coercion without bloodshed, of defeating an enemy without recourse to war.

After Hitler's occupation of Czechoslovakia, war was widely seen to be inevitable. When war was eventually declared there were very few 'socialist war resisters' (the

ILP and the Communist Party originally denounced the war as imperialist); but most appeasers were from the Right. By the time of the 'Fall of France', and with the imminent danger of an invasion of Britain, most of the 'political pacifists' recanted, leaving the 'quietists' in a small minority (although the FoR and the Anglican Peace Fellowship expanded; and the circulation of *Peace News* remained at around twenty thousand). By 1940, therefore, the peace movement had been overwhelmed by larger forces; but it continued to exist, and formed the basis for a resurgence of peace movement radicalism in the postwar period.

The ideological roots of what became, in early 1958,[54] the Campaign for Nuclear Disarmament (CND) lay in the traditions of radical protest in the nineteenth and twentieth centuries. After 1945 this tradition found expression in diverse, minority organisations such as Richard Acland's Common Wealth Party, Richard Gregg's and others' adaptation of the theory and practice of Gandhian non-violent resistance, the formation of the National Council for the Abolition of Nuclear Weapons Tests (NCANWT), the campaign led by the British Peace Council – a Communist Front organisation – to protest against the Korean war, and the continuing activities of the individualist, largely Christian pacifist groups.

Political tensions mounted in the 1950s as the Cold War escalated and the immense dangers of nuclear weapons *per se* and of atmospheric testing became apparent. Moreover, the crises of Suez and Hungary, and the reluctance of the Labour Party leadership to take a lead on disarmament, gave rise to increasing frustrations.

From the outset, CND was a coalition. Its self-constituted leadership was socially and politically homogeneous: middle-aged (in the case of Bertrand Russell, the President, considerably more venerable), white, predominantly upper-middle-class, and morally inspired, left of centre Labour Party supporters. There was a belief that Britain, *uniquely*, as the world's third nuclear power, had the opportunity (and indeed the duty) to take a unilateralist initiative to initiate de-escalation and a multilateral disarmament process. The old idea of 'Pax Britannica' persisted.

For the majority of the CND leadership, this was the single, discrete objective of the movement. The complexities of whether or not Britain should remain in NATO, should attempt to formulate (and lead) a 'Third Way', positive neutralist international movement, and of whether nuclear disarmament entailed fundamental social and political change – all these were questions that the CND Executive resolutely refused to consider.

For many in CND, the Labour Party was the main focus; but for others in the growing campaign – which was by the spring of 1958 a mass movement – the Labour Party's machinations, and the mainstream political system, were a part of the problem. It was building a mass movement 'of the people' that was the objective. This was symbolised above all by what became, from 1958, the annual Aldermaston March. It became, in Hinton's words, 'the central unifying experience of the new peace movement', with the 'colour and the noise, the discomfort and exhilaration, the informality and sense of purpose, the intense political discussions and the sentimentalizing songs'.[55]

The Direct Action Committee (DAC), which had initiated the first Aldermaston March, provided the core of the much larger, more ideologically variegated and more influential Committee of 100, which adopted *mass* civil disobedience from its inauguration in October 1960. Although its effective life was short, it captured media headlines and public attention for the unilateralist cause (Chapter 12).

Also during 1960, the campaign for capturing the Labour Party for a unilateralist policy reached its climax when the Party Conference, following the Party's election defeat in 1959, adopted a unilateralist resolution, due partly to the support of several of the larger trade unions, particularly the Transport and General Workers Union (TGWU). It was something of a pyrrhic victory. Hugh Gaitskell, the Party leader, vowed 'to fight, and fight and fight again' to 'save' the Party from what he perceived to be this folly. (He was successful: the policy was duly reversed in 1961.) Following Gaitskell's untimely death, Harold Wilson, a master of political manoeuvring, became leader of the Party, Labour unified in preparation for the 1964 general election, and the nuclear issue was effectively shelved.

From the mid-1960s until the late 1970s, the movement faded from prominence, though it never disappeared. Among the more important legacies of the movement, that of the New Left was especially significant. E.P. Thompson and Stuart Hall (Chapters 7 and 10) played key roles in both CND and the New Left. When the second wave of mass protest was triggered by the escalation of the Cold War in the Reagan/Thatcher era, it was Thompson who played the leading role. In Britain, the movement was 'of unprecedented proportions. In 1984, at the peak of the new movement, CND claimed ninety thousand national members and a quarter of a million in its local groups.'[56]

The initiative for a *European* campaign for nuclear disarmament (which took the organisational form of European Nuclear Disarmament (END) from April 1980) came principally from Thompson, who saw nuclear escalation as a direct threat to human rights. He emphasised popular protest and action rather than working through formal political parties of the Left.

Independently, the other mass mobilisation of the early 1980s was the Women's Camp at Greenham Common, a product of the peace movement and the revivified women's movement. On 12 December 1982, thirty thousand women linked hands to 'Embrace the Base'; this, and the symbolism of their placing flowers, children's toys and clothes and photographs on the perimeter fence received huge publicity and, as Hinton observed, 'was probably as important in bringing cruise missiles to public attention as CND's very much larger, but less imaginative, demonstrations'.[57]

For the majority of the CND leadership, however, the Labour Party remained the key site of political contestation. The conclusive defeat of the Labour Party at the 1983 general election under the leadership of the venerable CNDer Michael

Foot was a humiliating setback.⁵⁸ With the deployment of cruise missiles, and the heavy Labour defeat, the international movement subsided, only to re-emerge in different and dramatic form in the upheavals in the Eastern bloc less than a decade later. In the early twenty-first century, the peace movement organised and led the largest mass movement demonstration ever seen in Britain, in opposition to the war in Iraq.

This chapter has attempted to provide a historical background to twentieth-century English radicalism and an overview of the main strands in its ideology and prospectus for progressive political change. The focus now shifts to the more detailed analysis, within this overall context, of the ten key figures which forms the main part of this study.

Notes

1. References are given in the text to the various historical and political works which provide such detailed analysis. A good overview of English history as a whole, including the place of radicalism, is R. Tombs, *The English and Their History* (Allen Lane, Penguin edition, 2015). On English radicalism specifically see E. Vallance, *A Radical History of Britain* (Little, Brown, 2009), pb. edition Abacus, 2010. References here are taken from the pb. editions.
2. H. Kolm, 'The Genesis and Character of English Nationalism', *Journal of the History of Ideas* 1, pp. 92–4, 1940, cited in A. Aughey, *The Politics of Englishness* (Manchester: Manchester University Press, 2007), p. 25.
3. Editorial, *Guardian*, 13 June 2015.
4. Vallance, *A Radical History of Britain*, p. 47, citing R.A. Griffiths, *The Reign of King Henry VI* (Stroud, 1998, p. 140). 'The worst century ever' was the title given to a Channel 4 series on the fourteenth century.
5. G. Watson, *The English Ideology: Studies in the Language of Victorian Politics* (Allen Lane, 1973), p. 39.
6. Vallance, *A Radical History of Britain*, p. 161.
7. The title of Part One of E.P. Thompson, *The Making of the English Working Class* (Gollancz, 1963), pb. edition Pelican, Penguin Books, 1968. References here are to the pb. edition.
8. Tombs, *The English and Their History*, p. 236.
9. Thompson, *The Making of the English Working Class*, pp. 100–3.
10. Vallance, *A Radical History of Britain*, p. 233.
11. Ibid., p. 234.
12. M. Wollstonecraft, *A Vindication of the Rights of Woman*, originally published in 1792, modern edition, ed. C. Ward (New York, 1996).
13. Vallance, *A Radical History of Britain*, p. 243.
14. Ibid., p. 245, citing a passage from Wollstonecraft, *A Vindication of the Rights of Woman*.
15. D. Martin and D. Rubinstein (eds), *Ideology and the Labour Movement* (Croom Helm, 1979), pp. 9–11.
16. Vallance, *A Radical History of Britain*, p. 356.

17 There is a large literature on the history and politics of Chartism. See, for example: D. Thompson, *The Chartists: Popular Politics in the Industrial Revolution* (Temple Smith, 1984); D. Goodway, *London Chartism 1838–1848* (Cambridge: Cambridge University Press, 1982); M. Chase, *Chartism: A New History* (Manchester: Manchester University Press, 2007).
18 The six points of the Charter demanded universal adult male suffrage, annual parliaments, the secret ballot, the equalisation of electoral constituencies, salaries for MPs and an end to property qualifications for parliamentary candidates.
19 Chase, *Chartism: A New History*, p. 358.
20 Vallance, *A Radical History of Britain*, p. 367.
21 There are several histories of trade unionism in Britain. For example: J. Hinton, *Labour and Socialism: A History of the British Labour Movement 1867–1914* (Brighton: Wheatsheaf Books, 1983); the classic history of trade unionism, following a markedly Fabian, pro-New Model Union perspective, is S. and B. Webb, *The History of Trade Unionism* (1902).
22 The conviction in 1834 of the six Tolpuddle Martyrs for illegally administering oaths to members of their agricultural workers' union, and their subsequent sentencing to seven years' transportation to Australia, became a *cause célèbre* in the labour movement.
23 On the New Unions, see Hinton, *Labour and Socialism*, pp. 40–63; on the SDF, see S. Pierson, *Marxism and the Origins of British Socialism: The Struggle for a New Consciousness* (Ithaca, NY, and London: Cornell University Press, 1973); on the Socialist League, see E.P. Thompson, *William Morris: Romantic to Revolutionary* (second edition, Merlin Press, 1977).
24 See R. Miliband, *Parliamentary Socialism* (Merlin Press, second edition, 1973); S.H. Beer, *Modern British Politics* (Faber and Faber, 1965); D. Coates (ed.), *Paving the Way: The Critique of Parliamentary Socialism. A Socialist Register Anthology* (Merlin Press, 2003).
25 G. Orwell, *The English People* (Collins, 1947), pp. 18, 46.
26 On anarchism in Britain, see D. Goodway, *Anarchist Seeds Beneath the Snow: Left-Libertarian Thought and British Writers from William Morris to Colin Ward* (Liverpool: Liverpool University Press, 2006).
27 Orwell, *The English People*, p. 24.
28 R. Miliband, *The State in Capitalist Society* (Weidenfeld and Nicolson, 1969).
29 Vallance, *A Radical History of Britain*, p. 459
30 S. Holton, *Feminism and Democracy: Women's Suffrage and Reform Politics in Britain 1900–1918* (Cambridge: Cambridge University Press, 1986), p. 6.
31 Tombs, *The English and Their History*, p. 531.
32 Holton, *Feminism and Democracy*, pp. 9, 11.
33 A. McLaren, *Birth Control in Nineteenth Century England* (Croom Helm, 1978), p. 163, cited in ibid., p. 16.
34 See J. Liddington and J. Norris, *One Hand Tied Behind Us: The Rise of the Women's Suffrage Movement* (Virago, 1978); and J. Liddington, *The Life and Times of a Respectable Rebel: Selina Cooper 1864–1946* (Virago, 1988).
35 Vallance, *A Radical History of Britain*, p. 514.
36 Ibid., pp. 523–4.

37 V. Brittain, cited in G. Searle, *A New England? Peace and War 1886–1918* (Oxford: Oxford University Press, 2004), p. 792, cited in Vallance, *A Radical History of Britain*, p. 524.
38 S. Holton, 'In Soulful Wrath: Suffrage and Militancy and the Romantic Feminism of Emmeline Pankhurst', in H. Smith (ed.), *British Feminism in the Twentieth Century* (Aldershot: Edward Elgar, 1990), p. 12.
39 S. Kent, 'Gender Reconstruction after the First World War', in Smith (ed.), *British Feminism in the Twentieth Century*, p. 66.
40 M. Pugh, 'Domesticity and the Decline of Feminism', in Smith (ed.), *British Feminism in the Twentieth Century*, p. 144.
41 E. Meehan, 'British Feminism from the 1960s to the 1980s', in Smith (ed.), *British Feminism in the Twentieth Century*, pp. 191–2.
42 S. Rowbotham, 'The Women's Movement and Organizing for Socialism', in S. Rowbotham, L. Segal and H. Wainwright (eds), *Beyond the Fragments: Feminism and the Making of Socialism* (Merlin Press, 1979), p. 40.
43 J. Hinton, *Protests and Visions: Peace Politics in Twentieth Century Britain* (Hutchinson Radius, 1989), p. 1.
44 Hinton, *Protests and Visions*, p. 45. The 'Four Points' of the UDC's founding statement were in summary: no annexation of territory without the consent of the population involved; parliamentary control over the conduct of foreign policy; a permanent International Council, deliberating in public, to resolve international disputes; national armaments to be limited by mutual agreement, and the pressures of the military-industrial complex to be regulated by the nationalisation of armaments firms and control over the arms trade
45 N. Young, 'War Resistance and the British Peace Movement Since 1914', in R. Taylor and N. Young (eds), *Campaigns for Peace: British Peace Movements in the Twentieth Century* (Manchester: Manchester University Press, 1987), p. 31.
46 Quoted in B. Wilson Cooke, 'Democracy in Wartime: Anti-Militarism in England and the US, 1914–18', in C. Chesterfield (ed.), *Peace Movements in America* (New York, 1973), cited in Young, 'War Resistance', p. 33.
47 Young, 'War Resistance', p. 32.
48 M. Shaw, 'War, Peace and British Marxism 1895–1945', in Taylor and Young (eds), *Campaigns for Peace*, p. 52. As Shaw has argued, Marxists have never satisfactorily theorised war *per se*: it 'was always subordinate to economics and politics, and never really tackled as an intellectual and practical issue in its own right'; ibid., p. 68.
49 For details, see Hinton, *Protests and Visions*, pp. 43–4; and J. Eglin, 'Women and Peace: From the Suffragists to the Greenham Women', in Taylor and Young (eds), *Campaigns for Peace*, pp. 221–59.
50 Hinton, *Protests and Visions*, pp. 43–4, citing M. Kamester and J. Vellacott (eds.), *Militarism versus Feminism: Writings on Women and War*, 1987, p. 40.
51 M. Ceadel, 'The Peace Movement Between the Wars: Problems of Definition', in Taylor and Young (eds), *Campaigns for Peace*, p. 74.
52 Ibid., p. 77.
53 Hinton, *Protests and Visions*, p. 102.
54 On the anti-nuclear peace movement in the 1950s and 1960s, see R. Taylor, *Against the Bomb: The British Peace Movement 1958–1965* (Oxford: Clarendon Press, 1988);

F. Parkin, *Middle Class Radicalism. The Social Bases of the British Campaign for Nuclear Disarmament* (Manchester: Manchester University Press, 1968); Hinton, *Protests and Visions*.
55 Hinton, *Protests and Visions*, p. 162.
56 Ibid., pp. 182–3.
57 Ibid., p. 183.
58 For an account of the general election campaign focusing upon the peace issue, see R. Taylor, 'CND and the 1983 Election', in I. Crewe and M. Harrop (eds), *Political Communications: The General Election Campaign of 1983* (Cambridge: Cambridge University Press, 1986), pp. 207–16.

3

Bertrand Russell

Bertrand Russell provides a unique link between nineteenth- and twentieth-century English radicalism: he was born in 1872 and died in 1970, just short of his ninety-eighth birthday, and he was continuously active intellectually and politically from the 1890s until his death.[1] In ideological terms, he retained an optimistic individualism characteristic of nineteenth-century liberalism at the core of his beliefs, whilst embracing both the empiricist mainstream of the twentieth century and a wide variety of progressive causes from the First World War onwards.

He embodied several of the tensions which characterise English radicalism: he was a democrat *and* an elitist: for example, he wrote in 1935 that the leisured class has 'contributed nearly the whole of what we call civilization. It cultivated the arts and discovered the sciences; it wrote the books, invented the philosophies and refined social relations ... without the leisure class, man would never have emerged from barbarism.'[2] But he was always a radical opposed to the established order. Although he was drawn briefly to support the Bolshevik Revolution in Russia in 1917, he rapidly came to the conclusion that *democratic* socialism was the only viable position. By 1920 he had become, and was to remain, a vehement opponent of Marxism and of the Soviet system. (His ambivalence towards socialism *per se* is discussed below.)

However, although democracy was central to his radicalism, he was no egalitarian. He had, for example, 'conventional views about the distinction between the more and less gifted child; and he thought schools should select rigorously to choose the best'.[3] Whilst he believed strongly in 'equality of opportunity' he was equally convinced that 'all progress is the work of men who are both unintelligible to and unappreciated by the great majority, as his estimate that Darwin was worth thirty million "ordinary men" revealed'.[4] Moreover, his commitment to democracy was qualified; as he wrote to Gilbert Murray in 1949, '"where democracy and civilisation conflict, I am for civilisation"'.[5]

He could be both deeply pessimistic and, at times, deeply optimistic. In his autobiography, for example, he came close to nihilism. 'There is darkness without, and when I die there will be darkness within. There is no splendour, no vastness, anywhere; only triviality for a moment and then nothing. Why live in such a world? Why ever die?'[6] And there is evidence, in his early years, of persisting thoughts of suicide.[7] However, he repeatedly emphasises his optimism about the potentially utopian future for humanity. In his last volume of autobiography, he wrote that, whilst he acknowledged that the world was in many ways a horrible place and the universe an impenetrable mystery, he envisioned the day 'when hate and greed and envy die because there is nothing to nourish them. These things I believe, and the world, for all its horrors, has left me unshaken.'[8]

Some of these ambivalences and tensions lie at the core of English radicalism. How to reconcile a commitment to democracy with the need to protect and extend the values and culture of the Enlightenment? How to combine the open, tolerant, free-thinking society with the need to confront and transcend the powerful, negative forces of capitalism? And how best to ensure the widest possible liberty of the individual within an increasingly powerful nation state system? Russell grappled with these and similar questions throughout his life, at both the abstract and the practical levels.

Unusually, in his case it is legitimate to separate to a large extent his professional, academic work in philosophy from his voluminous writings and activities on social, moral and political issues. Nevertheless, there are connections. The original spur for his interest in philosophy was his quest for *certainty*. For some years, he believed that this would be found through mathematics and logic. Eventually, however, although he had '"set out with a more or less religious belief in a Platonic eternal world, in which mathematics shone with a beauty ... [he came] to the conclusion that the eternal world is trivial, and that mathematics is only the art of saying the same thing in different words"'.[9]

This quest, combined with his lifelong conviction that loneliness and isolation were in large part the cause of human misery (over and above misguided practical, political practices), impelled his social and political writings and activities. His consistent belief was, as Ryan puts it, that 'the universe was a large, cold place, wholly indifferent to the affairs of suffering humanity, and from this glacial indifference only passionate love offered a consolation and an escape'.[10]

Russell's writings and activities were numerous and took place over such a long period, that it is hard to summarise the key elements in his social and political thought and activism. However, I have attempted to identify the main elements that constitute his contribution to twentieth-century English radicalism under the headings of: politics; social and ethical issues; and the struggle for peace.

Politics

Russell was liberal and libertarian to the core: 'he shared his parents' conviction that anything less than perfect equality of opportunity was simply wicked'.[11] He supported unequivocally a series of progressive social campaigns: including women's suffrage (he stood for Parliament in 1907 as a women's suffrage candidate), contraception and a secular, free-thinking approach to education. He took it for granted that liberals should support such causes. However, there was clearly a tension here between his patrician, intellectual belief in the importance of fostering the innately powerful intelligence of men (and women) of genius, and his commitment to the principles of egalitarian democracy.

The goal of politics must be to create a society where individual men and women had as full a range of freedoms as possible: he acknowledged that *collective* action, and government itself, were necessary, but for Russell they were necessary *evils* and eternal vigilance was imperative. 'I know', he wrote in a letter, cited in his autobiography, 'that for collective action the individual man must be turned into a machine ... yet it is the individual soul that I love ... its loneliness, its hopes and fears, its quick impulses and sudden advances'.[12] Again, in his early work on the 1917 Bolshevik Revolution, he expresses a similarly unequivocal view: 'Government and the rule of law, in their very essence, consist of restrictions on freedom and freedom is the greatest of political goals.'[13]

Russell was thus, in Ryan's phrase, 'an ambivalent socialist'.[14] His early rejection of Marxism as a political philosophy and analysis persisted throughout his life. He thought the labour theory of value was 'simply wrong', and that 'most of Marx's predictions [were] false': for example, immiseration had not occurred; far from escalating class conflict, the middle class had grown; and the importance of nationalism had been ignored. The 'combination of the dialectical method and a materialistic analysis [was] a logical confusion but a rhetorical triumph'.[15] Marx, he argued, was wrong on two main counts: he was muddle-headed; and his thinking was almost entirely inspired by hatred. Moreover, his theory of class conflict was erroneous: he made an unwarranted generalisation from the specific situation of England and France a hundred years ago. All this, dismissive as it was, 'was neither here nor there'. Marxism, he argued, was not a political party or an economic theory: it was 'a complete self-contained philosophy of the world and of human development; it is, in a word, a religion and an ethic'.[16]

Much of this critique is contained in his first book, *German Social Democracy* (1896); but his real detestation of Marxian socialism was reserved for the reality of Marxism-Leninism in action. He was the first prominent left-wing intellectual in Britain to argue that the Soviet system was not the model for the new society but a cruel, despotic and illiberal regime. He recognised that the horrors of the Soviet Union were the result not primarily of Marxism *per se* but of centuries of brutality, imperialism and superstition in Russia. The practical message of these early works, and of his attitude to the Soviet Union throughout his life, was that this Marxist version of socialism was wholly inapplicable to advanced Western societies.

Not that Russell was supportive of Western capitalism, far from it: he was opposed to capitalism and imperialism because they fostered war and aggression abroad, and greed, cruelty and inequality at home. But he fitted awkwardly into the socialist tradition: he was a liberal, individualistic radical. Whilst recognising the evils in capitalist society and the need for these to be at least ameliorated through socialist policies, he was also insistent that individual freedoms, tolerance and untrammelled scientific and cultural enquiry were all of paramount importance.

He was uninterested in institutions and processes (save that he was inherently suspicious of state bureaucracy and interference with individual freedoms): what he sought was 'two kinds of freedom above all. The first was the freedom from war and imperialism ... The other was the large emotional and intellectual freedom which is most easily described by contrasting it with the anxious narrow-mindedness to which ... existing industrial societies mostly consigned their victims.'[17]

He took a similarly libertarian view of the 'common ownership' of industry. It was not so much who owned the means of production, he argued, that was important but how industry should be *governed*: it was therefore an issue of power rather than property. And it was the lust for power, allied to dogmatic beliefs which, for Russell, lay at the heart of humankind's political problems. ('Dogma', he said in a 1965 interview, 'is a very great mistake and does an immense amount of harm – with no exceptions. One should hold one's beliefs tentatively.')[18]

He thus opposed strongly the Fabian model of nationalisation. With G.D.H. Cole and others on the more libertarian Left, he supported a Guild Socialist system which was, he argued, in *Proposed Roads to Freedom*,[19] a sensible British compromise between romantic, impractical anarchism and the rigid, hierarchical bureaucratic system of state control, advocated by the Fabians.

His politics were a somewhat eccentric blend of utopianism and *realpolitik*: this became particularly apparent in his persistent campaigning for peace, in extreme old age, from the late 1950s until his death. His ambivalence towards socialism was based partly upon his inherent dislike and distrust of party organisations, and centralised, bureaucratised power; and partly on the belief that, whilst democratic socialism was the only solution to war, greed and inequality, the liberal values of freedom of thought and action and of the cultivation of all that was best in Western civilisation might fare badly under a fully socialist system.

Following J.S. Mill (appropriately, as Mill was his godfather), Russell was a heavily qualified utilitarian. He believed in the 'greatest happiness' principle; but only some (superior) types of happiness were worth preserving. Utilitarian criteria which 'ran counter to deeply felt intuitions about freedom or other deeply held values' had to be abandoned.[20]

Underlying his belief in the freedom of the individual was his commitment to scientific endeavour. He became increasingly convinced that the disinterested pursuit of truth through scientific enquiry, using analytical and empirical methods, was at the centre of the intellectual project of the modern age. 'Like Spinoza whom he admired and Kant whom he detested, Russell thought the impersonal knowledge produced by science one of the glories of mankind. That knowledge was the nearest thing to the Godlike element in man.'[21] In this, as in other ways, he was an Enlightenment man through and through.

Aside from his lifelong concern with peace issues (discussed below), a consistent element in his politics was his belief in world government. From the time of the First World War until the 1960s, he advocated 'world government' in various guises of collective security, usually through the leadership of the USA, as clearly the dominant power of the twentieth century. There were two obvious problems with this advocacy. First, even if the *desire* may have been legitimate, its practicality was highly questionable; and Russell remained extremely vague about the details, both of the process of achieving such a goal and of what resulting structures could emerge. There was more than an element of the philosopher-king about such pronouncements. Secondly, this advocacy sits ill with his equally persistent distrust of centralised power in the nation state. Still more, his increasing hostility to American capitalism and its aggressive overseas wars, make his advocacy of international American hegemony unconvincing.[22]

Russell's politics were thus conflicted but always principled. He was a liberal in a collectivist age; a democratic socialist, who believed fully neither in democracy nor socialism; and he had a passionate, emotional conviction that the human spirit could secure the triumph of all that was best in western civilisation, whilst at the same time holding that objective, scientific enquiry was the highest form of intellectual endeavour.

By the 1920s, Russell was convinced that only through education could a better world be achieved; and, he argued in *The Prospects of Industrial Civilization*, co-authored with his second wife, Dora Black, in 1924, that the root of education is an adequate psychology. It is to a consideration of Russell's views on education, and their practical application that attention is now turned. This will also necessitate a broader consideration of those aspects of his moral and ethical writings that relate to English radicalism.

Social and ethical issues

For Russell, the key task for a good teacher is to instil a 'reverence' for the world and all its mysteries and beauty. He believed that both the state and the Christian churches were fundamentally opposed to such an enlightened approach to education. For the state, education had two primary policy objectives: to instil a competitive, acquisitive ethic to equip children with the skills to engage with the world of wealth and power; and to indoctrinate children with the belief that their country (and, in Britain's case, Empire) was always justified in its military adventures, always had the moral high ground (and, usually, God on their side). For the churches, the aim was to indoctrinate children with religious belief, with its accompanying fear and superstition.

Education, for Russell, should be aimed rather at teaching children '*how* to think, not instilling orthodoxy, or even heterodoxy'.[23] Moreover, it should also be imbued with liberal values to enable children in their everyday lives to be friendly, freed from anxiety, tolerant, and above all *interested* in the world. Thus he emphasised the importance of empirical, scientific enquiry and saw such curricular emphasis as being at the centre of a modern educational system.

This approach would counter 'the priests and the politicians' who would try to keep children 'brutal, ignorant and unhappy'.[24] Children educated in a liberal ethos would be predisposed to prefer 'peace to prestige, contentment to profit, cooperation to power'.[25] To achieve an educational system based upon these moral and social principles was thus central to Russell's radicalism, and is indicative of the importance attached to education in English radicalism.

For Russell, education 'demands ... love plus science. Ignorant love will make mistakes; science deals in means not ends, and, guided by hatred, greed or the love of power, it will achieve untold horrors'.[26] In *The Principles of Reconstruction*, Russell wrote that the existing educational system encouraged conformity, an unquestioning belief in orthodoxies, and the holding of 'positive opinions on doubtful matters rather than [letting children] see the doubtfulness and be encouraged to independence of mind'. Thus, instead of discipline, education ought to aim at 'preserving independence and impulse ... instead of credulity, the objective should be to stimulate constructive doubt, the love of moral adventure, the sense of worlds to conquer by enterprise and boldness in thought'.[27]

However, there were tensions in his position. In the political as well as the educational context, Russell was no egalitarian, as has been noted: understandably so, perhaps, given his ultra-aristocratic background, incomparable intellectual ability and elite academic environment. He believed, without qualification, in the innately differential ability of children. As Alan Wood has observed, Russell believed that 'a good deal of needless pain and friction would be saved to clever children if they were not compelled to associate intimately with stupid contemporaries'.[28]

But he was also, as noted, in favour of 'equality of opportunity': 'what was wicked was handing out education on the basis of privilege rather than ability'.[29] The inevitable differences of ability should not, he believed, lead to gross inequalities of wealth and power. It was crucial that, through education, humankind's tendencies towards cruelty and superstition should be countered by liberal, humane education 'inspired by love and guided by knowledge'.[30] Such rather vague homilies cannot mask the ambivalences in Russell's educational philosophy.

In the final analysis, he argued, education is fundamental, both to human happiness and to the securing of a peaceful, civilised world. Russell argued that, for all their wonders and mysteries, the laws of nature, the natural world, the universe itself, are neither good nor bad, and are 'not concerned to make us happy or unhappy. All such philosophies spring from self-importance, and are best corrected by a little astronomy.'[31] But in the realm of *value*, the reverse is the case. Human beings are 'the ultimate and irrefutable arbiters of value ... It is for us to determine the good life, not for Nature – not even for Nature personified as God.'[32]

The centrality for Russell of formulating and implementing a liberal educational system stems in part from his rejection of organised religion and particularly of the Christian conception of an omnipotent, omniscient and loving God. As befits a thoroughgoing liberal and empiricist, Russell was agnostic rather than atheist: 'he did not deny that God *might* exist; he simply thought it overwhelmingly unlikely'.[33] Few have written such witty, destructive and pithy rejections of Christianity.[34] Russell dismissed all the traditional theistic arguments: 'first cause', 'design', Kant's moral argument for God and so on. Similarly, he argued that the doctrines of the Church – resurrection, transubstantiation and so on – were simply absurd. And in particular he could not reconcile the existence of evil with the notion of an omnipotent, loving God. Unlike many free-thinkers, as Ryan has observed, he 'was not impressed by the personality of Christ himself'.[35] He especially deplored the fear of hellfire and damnation with which Christ repeatedly threatened unbelievers.

As with his opposition to Marxism, it was the actual lived experience and practical application of Christianity through the organised Churches, rather than the manifest philosophical shortcomings of religion, that lay at the heart of his antagonism. (In an interview a few years before his death, Russell said that he was 'much happier when I ceased to believe in God than I had been before. Religion is not only false but cruel'.)[36] Guilt, sexual repression, fear of death – and ultimately fear of ourselves and our own natures – all led to human misery and existential unhappiness. 'Fear', Russell wrote in *What I Believe*, 'is the basis of religious dogma, as of so much else in human life'.[37]

Russell's opposition to religion thus connects to his insistence upon individual freedom and the enlightened pursuit of happiness, and knowledge, as being the fundamentals of the good life. However, it is important to recognise that Russell had in many ways a religious – and often puritanical – approach to morality. Despite his protestations to the contrary, he was tormented by the vast pointlessness of the universe. He had the 'preacher's conviction of the sinfulness of mankind'[38] and he repeatedly contrasted the misery of the world as it is – because of human folly, superstitious religion, capitalist greed, nationalism and war – a 'fallen world' indeed, with the utopian future that lay within our reach.

The struggle for peace

This leads into the most persistent and passionate political crusade of Russell's long life – his campaign, or rather his various campaigns – for peace. The lyricism and passionate conviction of his belief in peace, captured in his inimitable style, is articulated in his memorable radio broadcast, *Man's Peril*, in 1954. There is more than a whiff here of the pulpit, and of the moral exhortation of the revivalist preacher.

Measured by geological time, Russell argued, human beings have existed for a brief period, a million years at most. Yet, in the last six thousand years especially, we have achieved

> something utterly new in the history of the universe, so far at least as we are acquainted with it ... In the great world of astronomy and in the little world of the atom, man has unveiled secrets which might have been thought undiscoverable. In art and literature and religion, some men have shown a sublimity of feeling which makes the species worth preserving. Is this all to end in trivial horror because so few are able to think of man rather than this or that group of men? Is our race so destitute of wisdom, so incapable of impartial love, so blind even to the simplest dictates of self-preservation, that the last proof of its silly cleverness is to be the extermination of all life on our planet? ... I cannot believe that this is to be the end ... There lies before us, if we choose, continual progress in happiness, knowledge and wisdom. Shall we, instead, choose death, because we cannot forget our quarrels? I appeal as a human being to human beings: remember your humanity, and forget the rest. If you can do so, the way lies open to a new Paradise; if you cannot, nothing lies before you but universal death.[39]

I cite this at some length to illustrate Russell's lifelong concern with issues of war and peace, based upon a quasi-Manichean view of the continual struggle between good and evil. Although this comes from late in his life, at the beginning of his campaign against nuclear weapons, its moral insistence and its intensity typify his approach to issues of war and peace from the First World War onwards. (His critics would argue that it also typifies his over-simplification and over-dramatisation of morally and politically complex issues.)

Russell's engagement with issues of war and peace began with the Boer War. His reaction to this conflict is instructive. First of all, he was not then, and never became, a pacifist; nor was he a straightforward anti-imperialist. He was a qualified utilitarian, and a thoroughgoing consequentialist.[40] It seemed to many on the Left that there was a simple injustice in the crushing, by a rich and powerful nation, Britain, of a poor minority, the Boers. Russell's response was that 'political justice was whatever was demanded by the larger interests of the human race'; and in this instance he believed that the longer-term interests of civilisation would be best served by a British victory.[41] He was, though, outraged by British treatment of Boer women and children, and by the establishment of concentration camps. His stance was to characterise his subsequent approach to issues of peace and war; and it lay at the centre too of his perspective upon English radicalism.

Russell's involvement in opposition to the 1914–18 war through the Union of Democratic Control (UDC) and, later, the No Conscription Fellowship (NCF), changed his life. He lost his Cambridge University post because of his controversial stance; and he became well known as a public speaker and indeed something of a celebrity. His initial opposition to the war was based on similar arguments to those of other liberal critics: he thought it foolish and avoidable; and he disapproved of Britain supporting the reactionary Tsarist regime in Russia.

It was at this time that he developed political friendships in the NCF – in particular with Clifford Allen, a pacifist, and Fenner Brockway, a lifelong socialist and anti-imperialist – that were to bring him permanently into liberal, and libertarian Left, circles. He left the NCF in 1917, feeling that he had little more to contribute.

He was, however, promptly imprisoned for six months as a result of an article he wrote for the *Tribunal* journal on the implications of the German peace offer to the Bolsheviks. He argued that, if peace were delayed until the European powers were worn to a standstill, the likely result would be an American occupation of France and Britain. 'The point of this', he argued, 'would be to prevent insurrection from the working classes, and intimidate them back to work. The American army had done it for many years at home. Russell readily – if charitably – admitted that it may not have been in the government's mind to use American troops to put down the English working class, but that was only because there was nothing whatever in the government's mind'.[42]

This mischievous piece exasperated the government; rather unwisely, he was prosecuted for 'insulting an ally'. On appeal, he was granted 'first division' status as a prisoner, which carried significant privileges, including a plentiful supply of books: he read two hundred and wrote two! Russell always seemed to have had the best of it with the authorities, leaving them looking flat-footed and pompous. This resulted in part from his intellectual ability and agility, in part from the confidence instilled by his aristocratic background and in part from his mischievous irreverence and his pleasure in undermining arrogant authority.

Russell's initial response to the rise of Fascism, and later Nazism, in the 1930s was consistent with his stance on the First World War. In *Which Way to Peace?*, 1936, he advocated, in the context of an appeasement policy, a form of pragmatic pacifism. This was, typically, support not for the moral pacifism of Dick Sheppard's Peace Pledge Union (PPU), though he was a signatory to the pledge;[43] nor for the particular brand of activist pacifism advocated by Gandhi;[44] but rather to a '"political pacifism", which opposed neither the rule of force in principle, nor of war as such, but objected specifically to any war likely to break out in the immediate future in Europe'.[45] As in the 1914–18 war, he believed that war in Europe would have more disastrous consequences than any other course of action. As the European situation worsened, Russell concluded that he had been wrong in his appeasement approach, and 'came to be ashamed of *Which Way to Peace?*'.[46] By 1939, he had become convinced that Hitler *had* to be defeated if civilisation were to survive. The scales of his pragmatic consequentialism had tipped irrevocably: war was the only viable course of action.

Russell was by no means alone in his *volte face* in the 1930s: by the time of the outbreak of war, only a small number of absolute pacifists remained opposed to countering the menace of Nazism with force. These were, by any criteria, exceptional times: and at least Russell was consistent in applying his pragmatic consequentialism as the arbiter of his judgement.

Russell had no such doubts over the supreme threat posed by the development of the atomic bomb – though there were to be dramatic changes in his political position of how best to counter this threat. As Clark has noted, there 'is no doubt that the salvation of the human race from a nuclear holocaust was the last great attachment of Russell's life'.[47]

In the years immediately after the bombing of Hiroshima and Nagasaki, Russell argued that it was crucial for the attainment of peace that the USA should use its (temporary) monopoly of atom (and later hydrogen) bombs to exert pressure on the USSR to engage in disarmament and a less aggressive foreign policy in Europe. If the Russians should decide not to co-operate, as he thought likely, his view was that a war with the USSR would be the lesser of two evils. In numerous articles, speeches and private letters, he stated this argument unequivocally in the later 1940s.[48] His twin objectives in this first phase of the nuclear age were thus to secure peace through coercion, if necessary involving preventive war; and, secondly, thereby advance towards his old goal of world government.

Such views attracted a very hostile response, and not only from socialists, pacifists and communists. *Reynolds News*, for example, argued in an editorial, 'The distilled essence of all the wisdom he has accumulated in a long life is this message of death and despair... Lord Russell, the famous philosopher, advances the oldest and most blood-drenched fallacy in History: "the war to end wars"'.[49]

Although he held these views only relatively briefly in 1948,[50] his distrust of the USSR persisted: he believed that Stalin had fundamental ambitions for territorial expansion. It was Russia's success in developing its own atomic bomb in 1949 which changed Russell's view on nuclear policy: an aggressive foreign policy towards (or indeed by) the USSR was now likely to result in mutual destruction. But Russell did not at this stage favour a neutralist stance, which he later advocated with some force: for all his criticisms of the USA, he saw it as 'a broadly liberal, democratic, individualist society of the same cultural stamp' as Western Europe. And he believed that the USA was right to develop the hydrogen bomb:[51] primarily because he believed that the USSR would go on to develop its own H-bomb anyway, and the thought of Stalin's Russia having a monopoly of nuclear weaponry was, to him, an anathema. Within this context, Russell, in the earlier 1950s, advocated a cessation of nuclear weapons testing, supported the renunciation by Britain (the only other nuclear power at that time) of nuclear weapons and argued for a nuclear-free Europe.

With the escalation of the Cold War, and the various political disasters of the 1950s and early 1960s, the tensions between the super-powers increased. Russell advocated from 1956, and with increasing urgency of both rhetoric and action, the unilateral renunciation by Britain of nuclear weapons and the creation of a neutralist European bloc. This was, as Ryan has noted, a 'real change of heart'.[52] However, the reasoning underlying his position was consistent: he was always an advocate of objectively necessary action to attain the political goals which lay at the heart of his radicalism. He saw the threat of nuclear war as the greatest danger facing humankind and he therefore believed that radical protest was essential, the only limits on that action being that it should not conflict with the sacrosanct principles of his liberal, individualistic radicalism. His belief in the necessity of dramatic action was expressed with passion and inimitable style. The underlying logic was the *pragmatic radicalism* that permeated his politics and has been so central a component of the English radical tradition.

Alongside his increasing political involvement in nuclear issues, Russell became the moving force in the establishment of the 'Pugwash movement' of leading scientists from both the West and the communist world, arguing for scientists from *all* nations to play their part in the struggle against nuclear weapons and the dangers of nuclear war.[53] Russell was also one of the small group that gave birth to the Campaign for Nuclear Disarmament (CND) and he became its President in February 1958. Canon Collins became Chairman.[54] Although Russell had not been active in the precursor movements, he had been well aware of these and was a sponsor of the National Council for the Abolition of Nuclear Weapons Tests (NCANWT), probably the most important of the early movements.

There are two issues of particular importance about the early years of Russell's involvement with CND. Firstly, he always took a highly pragmatic view of the movement and its objectives. He did not share the Gandhian ideological position of the Direct Action Committee (DAC),[55] still less the anarchistic and insurrectionary politics of the Committee of 100. But he *did* believe that the nuclear threat was so extreme that dramatic action, above 'merely meetings and marches', was essential. He thus supported the *tactics* of the Committee of 100 but not the various ideological stances which characterised its leading activists. Russell saw the nuclear issue as a discrete, single issue. For Russell, as for Collins and most of the CND leadership, unilateral nuclear disarmament by Britain was a single, focused, political objective, which could facilitate and lead an international movement for multilateral nuclear disarmament.

Russell had, however, been clear for many years that, on occasion, civil disobedience was justified, indeed essential. (Here, he differed markedly from the rest of the CND leadership.)[56] As early as 1936, he had written that, although civil disobedience was 'a dangerous doctrine', at the same time 'almost all great advances have involved illegality. The early Christians broke the law; Galileo broke the law; the French revolutionaries broke the law; early trade unionists broke the law. The instances are so numerous and so important that no-one can maintain as an absolute principle obedience to constituted authority.'[57]

He was, therefore, as ever, a pragmatic consequentialist; his ideological position remained as it always had been, that of the radical liberal individualist.

Secondly, whereas those establishing the campaign saw Russell as a 'figurehead giving academic respectability and white-headed publicity',[58] he saw himself as taking a far more active role. As Peggy Duff has observed, Russell 'was not exactly dictatorial but he liked laying down the law. And I think the Canon [Collins] made a mistake... in the first year or so. He saw Russell as a sort of figurehead to be trotted out on occasions whereas Russell really wanted to be in charge.'[59]

By the summer of 1960, Russell had become impatient with Collins's over-cautious leadership,[60] and responded with enthusiasm to the radical proposal from Ralph Schoenman, a young, radical American postgraduate student at the London School of Economics, to establish a new civil disobedience movement for the nuclear disarmament cause, the Committee of 100. This is not the place to discuss the extraordinary story of Schoenman's relationship with Russell, and the strong influence he had upon Russell until shortly before the latter's death. (Russell eventually broke with Schoenman in September 1969.) The combination of Russell's international reputation and fame, and Schoenman's vigorous, articulate and persuasive radicalism, inspired the new movement.[61]

The Committee of 100's first 'sit-down' demonstrations – in February, April and September 1961 – attracted huge publicity, not least because the spectacle of Russell, at 89, being sentenced to two months' imprisonment, led to headlines around the world. Russell took full advantage of his court appearance to make a passionate, articulate speech on the nuclear threat.

From prison, Russell issued a typically dramatic statement: 'You, your families, your friends and your countries are to be exterminated by the common decision of a few brutal but powerful men ... Our ruined, lifeless planet will continue for countless ages to circle aimlessly around the sun, unredeemed by the joys and loves, the occasional wisdom and the power to create beauty which have given value to human life. It is for seeking to prevent this that we are in prison.'[62] Once again, Russell had made the authorities appear callous, vindictive and, most importantly, oblivious to the disaster to which the world was inexorably heading.

September 1961 was, however, to be the high point of the Committee of 100's activism. The decision to escalate the civil disobedience action simultaneously to a variety of sites, mainly nuclear bases outside London, was a serious tactical error. The relative failure of these demonstrations, plus the harsh prison sentences given to the young activists who really did the organisational and political work in the Committee, 'burst the bubble' and the Committee thereafter declined (though continuing in existence until 1968). There were, however, more fundamental reasons for this decline: whereas Russell supported civil disobedience 'purely to get attention',[63] others had widely differing, and more complex, ideological motivations, ranging from Gandhian pacifism to anarchism. The Committee of 100 thus suffered the same fate as CND: as with many single-issue movements, differences of orientation, ideology and style could be masked in times of success. Once the movement began to decline, its problems and divisions became all too evident.[64]

Russell, long experienced in the ebb and flow of relatively short-lived protest movements, turned his attention (after the Cuban Missile crisis in October 1962)[65] towards more international concerns. In September 1963 he established the Bertrand Russell Peace Foundation (BRPF). The BRPF focused upon American involvement in Vietnam: but almost any perceived American misbehaviour came under attack: for example, the BRPF was instrumental in the establishment of the 'British Who Killed Kennedy Committee', and later the International War Crimes Tribunal.

There was increasing evidence of Schoenman's influence upon Russell's pronouncements. Whereas in the past Russell had always castigated *individuals* for their supposed misdeeds, consistent with his liberal individualism, he now 'seemed to have acquired the habit prevalent among the 1960s radicals of blaming everything on "the system"' and of seeing 'the sole cause of evil in the world [as] American imperialism'.[66]

His almost obsessive anti-Americanism in this last phase of his life was partly attributable to the influence of Schoenman. But it was also because Russell believed that the US war in Vietnam 'was proof that western, civilized, rational, liberal, scientific man had reverted to something lower than the beasts'.[67] This led him into some dubious judgements: for example, his unequivocal support for the National Liberation Front in Vietnam; and similarly for the Palestine Liberation Organisation.

These were, however, surely understandable frustrations from a man in his midto late nineties who had campaigned all his life – and continued campaigning right to the end – for a better, more humane and more civilised world, and for the liberal, individualist values which characterised the good society.

Conclusion

Most of those radicals considered in this book, although they have many differences in ideology, outlook and background, have much in common. Russell stands alone. He made a major contribution to English radicalism in the twentieth century, by any criterion, and was unique in several ways. Most obviously, he had an exceptionally long life, *and* he was intellectually and politically active continuously from early adulthood right up to his death: as noted, he thus spanned the nineteenth and twentieth centuries, not only chronologically but intellectually.

He was always politically radical, and by instinct, upbringing and emotional commitment a liberal (though not a Liberal). But he was uninterested in party politics. Moreover, he was never a committee man, 'broad brush' rather than concerned with the detail of structures and administration. This is most graphically evident in his long-held demand for world government, about which he was consistently enthusiastic, but he tackled neither the contradictions between his advocacy and his insistence upon national and international freedom, nor the complexities of achieving and implementing such an ambitious goal.

He was cool and detached in his analysis of the 'best' political course of action to adopt: his consequentialist frame of reference remained consistent throughout his life. (But he seems never to have considered the obvious dangers of such a position: the unpredictability and unreliability of calculating with any precision the likely effects of any particular course of action.) On the other hand, he was passionate, utopian, romantic and visionary in his conceptualisations of human potential.

He opposed nationalism consistently; but he was a passionate patriot. Indeed, on many occasions he observed that love of England was almost the strongest feeling he possessed. In an interview a few years before his death, he said, albeit with a twinkle in his eye, that 'At the time when it looked as though Hitler would conquer England, I minded enormously, *enormously*; much more than I minded him conquering France!'[68]

His attacks on religion in general, and the Christian Churches in particular, were trenchant, witty and telling: and his polemicising against religion remained uncompromising to the end of his life. And yet he was the most spiritual of men; he had much of the Nonconformist preacher in him, railing against the wickedness of humanity in a fallen world; and he proclaimed the utopian possibilities of humankind, freed from the iniquities of capitalism and the curse of imperialism and war.

Russell was a socialist – of sorts: but he could never resolve the tensions between the primary goals of individual freedom and the paramount need to protect and extend Western civilisation and its values, and the demonstrable necessity of collective, governmental action to achieve socialist objectives. American free-market capitalism and its accompanying imperial war machine were anathema to him, especially in the last two decades of his life; and the Marxism-Leninism of the USSR, in both theory and practice, even more so. He was sceptical, at best, about the Labour Party: and the industrial labour movement and its culture were, not surprisingly for an aristocrat steeped in nineteenth-century liberalism, alien territory. Although it should be noted that he was, for a time, supportive of Guild Socialism and its vision of genuine industrial democracy through workers' control.

Thus, as with English radicalism in general, his politics were located in the interstices between the orthodox Left formations. It was in social movements that he found his most fruitful vehicles for radical dissent, from the NCF to the Committee of 100 and the BRPF. It was in such contexts, and in his enthusiasm for humanistic educational provision, that Russell found the outlets for combining his commitments to fostering individual freedoms and enlightenment, and his radical, individualist political ideals.

Russell belonged, as Ryan claims, to two aristocracies. 'Besides being a member of the aristocracy of birth, he was a member of the aristocracy of exceptional talent.'[69] His achievements and his life were remarkable: in this one context alone – his contribution to English radicalism – his influence and his legacy were profound. Despite his aristocratic background, elite environment and exceptional erudition,

Russell was disarmingly human. He was charming, vulnerable, witty, extremely articulate and a 'mischievous sage'.⁷⁰ The unresolved dilemmas he wrestled with, the mistakes he made and his numerous *volte faces*, testify to his continuing concerns with the nature of radicalism and how best to resolve its problems.

There is one final attribute of Russell's which is of key importance: his ability to write clear, sparkling prose. There is a freshness to his writing, some many decades later, whether in his more accessible philosophical work (for example, *The Problems of Philosophy* or his *History of Western Philosophy*) or in his political, campaigning articles, papers and speeches.

He was, in all these ways, an exceptional man. With hindsight, it is clear that, over an exceptionally long life, he was often wrong both substantively and tactically about many political issues; but he was passionate and principled, and he held tenaciously and consistently to a series of radical beliefs, which lie at the core of English radicalism.

Notes

1 Literally so: on 31 January 1970 he dictated to his Secretary, Christopher Farley, a memorandum which was sent to the International Conference of Parliamentarians in Cairo, 'condemning the latest Israeli air-raids on Egypt, and lambasting the Israelis for their treatment of Palestine refugees'. He died on 2 February 1970. R. Clark, *The Life of Bertrand Russell* (Weidenfeld and Nicolson, 1975), p. 638.
2 B. Russell, *In Praise of Idleness* (Allen and Unwin, 1935, reprinted 1960), p. 19.
3 A. Ryan, *Bertrand Russell: A Political Life* (New York: Hill and Wang, 1988; also published by Penguin Books, 1988. References here are taken from the Hill and Wang edition), p. 107.
4 Ibid., p. 81.
5 Russell, letter to Murray, 27 April 1949, cited in Clark, *Life of Russell*, p. 631.
6 B. Russell, *The Autobiography of Bertrand Russell* (Allen and Unwin, 3 vols, 1967, 1968, 1969), vol. 2, pp. 158–9.
7 See Clark, *Life of Russell*, pp. 31–3.
8 Russell, Autobiography, vol. 3, p. 223.
9 B. Russell, 'Reflections on My Eightieth Birthday', in *Portraits from Memory* (Allen and Unwin, 1956), cited in Clark, *Life of Russell*, pp. 630–1.
10 Ryan, *Russell: A Political Life*, p. 123.
11 Ibid., p. 3.
12 Russell, *Autobiography*, vol. 2, p. 105.
13 B. Russell, *The Practice and Theory of Bolshevism*, 1920 (reprinted, Allen and Unwin, 1962), p. 82.
14 Ryan, *Russell: A Political Life*, title of chapter 4.
15 Ibid., p. 29.
16 Ibid., p. 28.
17 Ibid., p. 91.
18 Bertrand Russell, interviewed by Ralph Miliband, in 1965 (archival film, Connecticut

State University, USA, lent to the author by Marion Kozak, the wife of the late Ralph Miliband).
19 B. Russell, *Proposed Roads to Freedom*, 1918; new edition Echo Press, 2007.
20 Ryan, *Russell: A Political Life*, p. 13.
21 Ibid., p. 106.
22 For a contrary view, see ibid., pp. 173ff.
23 A. Huxley, 'The Relevance of Style', in R. Schoenman (ed.), *Bertrand Russell: Philosopher of the Century* (Allen and Unwin, 1967), p. 91.
24 B. Russell, *Education and the Social Order* (Allen and Unwin, 1931), p. 115.
25 Ibid., p. 116.
26 Ryan, *Russell: A Political Life*, p. 114
27 B. Russell, *The Principles of Social Reconstruction*, 1916, cited in R. Egner and L. Dennon (eds), *The Basic Writings of Bertrand Russell 1903-1959* (Allen and Unwin, 1961), pp. 406–7.
28 A. Wood, *Bertrand Russell: The Passionate Sceptic* (Allen and Unwin, 1961), p. 165.
29 Ryan, *Russell: A Political Life*, p. 107.
30 B. Russell, *What I Believe*, 1925, included in Egner and Dennon (eds), *Basic Writings of Bertrand Russell*, p. 372.
31 Ibid., p. 371.
32 Ibid.
33 Ryan, *Russell: A Political Life*, p. 50.
34 Russell's best-known publication on this theme is 'Why I Am Not a Christian'; but his outspoken views on religion appear in numerous works from the early twentieth century (for example, *Mysticism and Logic*, 1918).
35 Ryan, *Russell: A Political Life*, p. 51
36 Miliband, interview with Russell, 1965.
37 Russell, *What I Believe*, 1925, in Egner and Dennon (eds), *Basic Writings of Bertrand Russell*, p. 370.
38 Ryan, *Russell: A Political Life*, p. 54.
39 'Man's Peril', BBC Radio broadcast, published in *The Listener*, December 1954, in Egner and Dennon (eds), *Basic Writings of Bertrand Russell*, pp. 729–32.
40 'Consequentialism' is the belief that the morality of an action is to be judged solely by its consequences. This is based upon two principles: whether an action is right or wrong depends only upon the *results* of that action; and secondly, that the more beneficial consequences an action produces, the better that action is.
41 Ryan, *Russell: A Political Life*, p. 34.
42 Ibid., pp. 62–3.
43 In October 1934 Sheppard invited people to sign a pledge stating that 'we renounce war and never again, directly or indirectly, will we support or sanction another'.
44 For detailed discussion of Gandhian Direct Action pacifism, in the context of the British anti-nuclear peace movement of the late 1950s, see R. Taylor, *Against the Bomb: The British Peace Movement 1958–1965* (Oxford: Clarendon Press, 1988), chapter 4, pp. 115–89.
45 C. Moorehead, *Bertrand Russell: A Life* (Sinclair and Stevenson, 1992), p. 428.
46 Ibid., p. 428.
47 Clark, *Life of Russell*, p. 517.

48 For example, in a letter to Dr Marseille, a US professor, in May 1948, Russell stated that 'I think war would be worth while. Communism must be wiped out, and world government must be established ... I do not think that the Russians will yield without war.' Cited in ibid., p. 524. There is a detailed, evidence-based, discussion of Russell's views in this period in Clark, *Life of Russell*, pp. 517–30.
49 Editorial, *Reynolds News*, 21 November 1948, cited in ibid., p. 525.
50 Russell confirmed on several occasions that this had been his view at the time. For example, in an interview on BBC television, in 1959, with John Freeman, in *Face to Face*, Russell stated that: 'What I thought all along was that a nuclear war in which both sides had nuclear weapons would be an utter and absolute disaster ... not that I advocated a nuclear war, but I did think that great pressure should be put upon Russia to accept the Baruch proposal, and I did think if they continued to refuse it might be necessary actually to go to war.' Cited in Clark, *Life of Russell*, p. 528.
51 Ryan, *Russell: A Political Life*, pp. 183–4.
52 Ibid., p. 190.
53 Among those involved were Joliot-Curie and Albert Einstein, who had signed the appeal letter just before his death. The meetings were hosted and funded by the wealthy Canadian industrialist Cyrus Eaton, who had made his home at Pugwash, a village on the St Lawrence. The first meeting was held in July 1957: several of those attending were Nobel Prize winners. For details of Pugwash, see Clark, *Life of Russell*, pp. 538ff. Most of the organising work of the Pugwash group was undertaken by Professor Joseph Rotblat, Professor of Physics at St Bartholomew's Medical College in London; he had previously been in the British nuclear weapons team at Los Alamos and had had a distinguished career in nuclear physics research.
54 For details of the birth of CND, and its prehistory, see Taylor, *Against the Bomb*, pp. 5–71. See also Clark, *Life of Russell*, chapter 21, pp. 553–69.
55 See Taylor, *Against the Bomb*, pp. 115–89.
56 For example, Jacquetta Hawkes recalled, in 1978, that there was, from the moment of the creation of the Committee of 100, 'the division between those who wished to break the law and felt that things must be done very quickly ... the basic thing was that most of us didn't want illegal action, that was quite definite'. Hawkes, in conversation with Richard Taylor, January 1978 (*Against the Bomb*).
57 B. Russell, *Which Way to Peace?* (Allen and Unwin, 1936), p. 207, cited in Clark, *Life of Russell*, pp. 573–4.
58 Clark, *Life of Russell*, p. 553.
59 Peggy Duff, in conversation with Richard Taylor, January 1978 (*Against the Bomb*).
60 The relationship between Russell and Collins had been difficult from the outset; they deteriorated markedly in 1960–61. Collins's assessment of Russell, a few years later, is probably accurate: Russell was, Collins said in his autobiography, 'an aristocrat to his fingertips, and he has all an aristocrat's impatience with democratic ways. He is a man for whom I have great respect and high regard. A little vain perhaps; but he has much to be vain about.' Collins, *Faith Under Fire* (Leslie Frewin, 1966), p. 325. In private conversation, however, Collins was a lot more critical: 'Russell was a very vain old man, a great man, a very great man, but a very, *very* vain man.' Collins, in conversation with Richard Taylor, January 1978 (*Against the Bomb*).

61 On Schoenman, see Clark, *Life of Russell*, pp. 570–628; and Taylor, *Against the Bomb*, pp. 210–16.
62 *Guardian*, 14 September 1961, cited in Taylor, *Against the Bomb*, p. 223.
63 Russell, interview with *Playboy* magazine, March 1963, cited in Clark, *Life of Russell*, p. 574.
64 For a detailed discussion of the Committee of 100, see Taylor, *Against the Bomb*, pp. 190–274.
65 Russell took a firmly anti-American line in the crisis. He sent telegrams arguing for conciliation, moderation and a pledge of non-intervention by the USA in return for the removal of the missiles from Cuba, to U Thant, Macmillan, Kennedy and Khrushchev. 'Astonishingly, both Khrushchev and Kennedy replied, and the world was treated to the spectacle of the two most powerful men in the world arguing with each other through the sitting room of a ninety-year-old philosopher.' Ryan, *Russell: A Political Life*, pp. 201–2.
66 Ibid., p. 197.
67 Ibid., p. 206.
68 Miliband, in conversation with Russell, 1965 (archival film, see note 18 above).
69 Ryan, *Russell: A Political Life*, p. 2.
70 Ibid., p. xi.

4

Sylvia Pankhurst

The women's movement has been a central element in the development of English radicalism in the twentieth century, as was discussed in Chapter 2. The suffragist and suffragette movements of the early years of the twentieth century had a profound influence on the subsequent women's movement and this has extended far beyond the issue of 'the vote' itself. Women's consciousness of gender inequality, not only politically but economically, socially and culturally, was one of the dominant characteristics of radical culture in late twentieth-century Britain. Moreover, this has been the primary cause of the fundamental questioning of gender roles more generally in relation to 'life/work' practices, family structures, sexual mores and much else besides.

In terms of ideology, and of social movements' strategy and tactics, the fractious history of the suffrage movements has been especially important. Should the campaign for women to have the legal right to vote be a *single*-issue movement, 'classless' and linked to no other political party or set of demands? Or should it rather be allied to more general campaigns for a fully democratic society? Specifically, what should the relationship be, if any, between the women's movement and the struggle for socialism? Leading on from this – and of particular contention in the suffrage movement – should the movement concentrate on legal, open, constitutional pressure through the existing institutional system or should it, in contrast, be militant, involve illegal, on occasion violent, action against property, and be clandestine and at least potentially insurrectionary? Finally, should the movement be democratic, in terms of its internal decision-making processes, or led by a self-selecting dedicated group of those totally committed to the cause?

These dilemmas have been of central concern to English radicalism, in all its forms, in the twentieth century and later. These questions were never resolved satisfactorily, nor could they have been: they are inherently a continuing 'political problematic'. Different contexts have required a different balance of approaches, ideological, strategic and tactical, and continue to do so. However, in the turbulent years of the suffrage campaign such dilemmas were especially prominent.

Consideration of a 'representative' figure from the suffrage movement is thus essential for a study of this sort. However, singling out any one individual to represent such a diverse movement is impossible. Recent historians of the suffrage movement, notably Jill Liddington and Sandra Holton,[1] have argued that insufficient attention has been paid to 'the strong local traditions of radicalism among women'.[2] There were 'tens of thousands of women in suffrage societies up and down the country who backed the demand for the vote'. Moreover, they argue, 'we know little about the working-class women – other than Annie Kenney and her sisters'.[3] (Liddington's biography of Selena Cooper, a working-class suffrage campaigner, is an exemplary study illustrating this point.[4])

There is force in the argument that it was the less dramatic constitutional campaigning of the mass of 'ordinary women' which in the end was more important in attaining the vote for women than the militant, high-profile activities of the suffragettes. Also contextually important in achieving the specific objective of 'Votes for Women' were the inexorable economic and social changes associated with the First World War, the rise of a mass, industrial, collectivist society, and the consequent changes in the position of women.

Why then select Sylvia Pankhurst for consideration in this chapter, rather than a working-class suffragist, such as Selena Cooper, or one of the leading influential figures from the suffragist movement, such as Millicent Fawcett or Catherine Marshall? Surely the Pankhursts, as a family and individually, have been given undue prominence in suffrage movement histories (and consequently in the conceptualisation of the 'window-smashing' militants of the movement in the popular consciousness)? And this has reinforced the historical romanticism which attributes political and social change to the 'sacrifice from those ... individuals heroic enough to resist tyranny and in this way render themselves forces of history'.[5]

Sylvia Pankhurst was undeniably a central member of the Pankhurst clan; and she had many of the personality traits common to her family. However, she also had distinctive, interesting and important radical attributes. She was a passionate campaigner for women's suffrage; but she was very much more than this. She was a lifelong socialist and always insisted that the causes of women's suffrage and socialist advance were inherently connected; she was one of the few campaigners to realise the importance of the anti-colonial struggle (in contrast to both her mother Emmeline and her elder sister, Christabel); she was an active anti-racist (and was the first editor of a British newspaper to employ a black journalist); she was a leading figure in the communist Left in the turbulent years leading to the foundation of the Communist Party of Great Britain (CPGB) in 1920–21; she was one of the first radicals to recognise the threat posed by fascism from the late 1920s; and she devoted the later decades of her life to a series of committed campaigns to free Ethiopia from colonial control, first by Italy, then by Britain. In all these contexts she was intensely active. As her son, Richard Pankhurst, has observed, 'her life was her struggle'.[6]

This range of activism was remarkable and encompassed a spectrum of political concerns central to the English radical tradition. Her political life thus links the single issue of suffrage to wider, cognate radical causes. As Sheila Rowbotham has observed, there have been 'two Sylvia Pankhursts', as conceptualised by historians. Feminists have 'focused on the suffrage movement'; and labour historians on 'her role in the formation of the Communist Party ... the whole Sylvia has proved elusive'.[7] It might also be added that most historians have ignored, or seriously downplayed, her dedicated involvement with anti-colonial campaigns in general, and Ethiopia in particular, from the late 1920s onwards.

This chapter thus considers Sylvia Pankhurst 'in the round' and her contributions to a spectrum of English radicalism's concerns in historical context. With all her faults, and they were many, she was consistent in 'her fierce and uncompromising independence, her ruthless adherence to principles that she believed to be right regardless of the cost in terms of support'.[8] The structure of the remainder of this chapter is as much thematic as it is 'a history', although a broadly chronological approach is adopted. The purpose here is to analyse Sylvia Pankhurst's politics and her shifting allegiances, always within the context of her unchanging core principles.

The Pankhurst family and Sylvia Pankhurst's early years[9]

Pankhurst was born into a thoroughly radical, upper-middle-class family: from her earliest years she absorbed and internalised the intense moral radicalism of her adored father, Richard: ' "wonderful father; the lode star of our lives" '.[10] He was her 'hero and her guiding light'. In one sense, she dedicated her life to achieving his ideals. Like her father – and like Keir Hardie, her friend, mentor and later lover – her moral and political perspective owed much to both John Ruskin and William Morris.

When she died, in 1960, the words of her father's 1884 election address were framed above her bed: ' "This is the hour of the people and the poor ... This is a time of hope for the life of labour. Old society was based on war, new society rests on work ... Over the production of wealth preside the laws of nature, but over the distribution of wealth presides the heart of man." '[11]

When the Independent Labour Party (ILP) was formed in 1893, the Pankhursts were among the first to become members. They saw the ILP as providing the ideal, radical vehicle for achieving an equal and just society through parliamentary reform, supplemented as necessary by (legal) public protest. In later years, Emmeline became distanced, to say the least, from such perspectives. (At the time of her death in 1928, she had been adopted as the Conservative candidate for a parliamentary seat.) Richard Pankhurst, however, was a staunch supporter of the ILP and its moral socialism for the few remaining years of his life. And Sylvia too became a member as soon as she was old enough, when she was 16.

Sylvia Pankhurst, born in 1882, was the second daughter in the family: Christabel was born in 1880; subsequently, her siblings were Frank, 1884 (who died aged four); Adela, 1885; and Henry Francis (Harry), 1889. From the outset, there were tensions between the sisters: Adela, for example, recalled that, in her view, Sylvia ' "dominated the family because she had a supreme self-love and a tenacity of purpose greater than belongs to most people" '. Moreover, Adela did not share Sylvia's adoration of their father: ' "To what a treadmill he condemned us helpless, hopeless children" '. Adela was in fact ' "terrified" ' of her father.[12]

Whatever the truth or otherwise of such recollections, there is no doubt that Sylvia, like her father, believed that 'principles came first no matter what the financial or personal cost'.[13] Once she had established a principled stand, she held to it assiduously. ' "I never consulted anyone" is a recurrent theme in her writings about her life.'[14] As one of her biographers has commented, a little acidly, 'she was, after all, in temperament a Pankhurst and accustomed to leading a group of devoted followers'.[15] It is perhaps not surprising that she continued to inspire both admiration and exasperation, if not dislike, during her lifetime and for some years subsequently. Bernard Shaw, for example, thought 'that there were only two opinions about her. One was that that she was miraculous. The other was that she was unbearable.'[16] Barbara Castle, on the other hand, wrote that she had been 'one of the great influences of my life. Sylvia … never allowed the issue of "Votes for Women" to dominate her. She believed, passionately, in the context of the current politics, that all citizens, including women, should be included in the international fight for justice – and that you should not isolate one little section of that fight. She had enormous physical and political courage.'[17]

In addition to her father (and to Ruskin and Morris), she was influenced by Dickens and his moral passion for justice and for the plight of the poor and oppressed.[18] It soon became clear that, in addition to her strong political commitments and enthusiasms, Sylvia had real artistic talent.[19] After a succession of local scholarships, she won a scholarship in 1904 to London's Royal College of Art. By this time she had lost her father, who died of a perforated ulcer in July 1898, when Sylvia was only 16.

Lonely, already somewhat estranged from her mother and sister Christabel, it is hardly surprising that, living alone in London, she was drawn increasingly to Hardie, who, though 25 years older and married with children, had a semi-detached relationship with his family, and shared her political idealism and moral passion. Their love affair lasted from 1904 to 1913 or 1914. Hardie died in 1915, but her deep affection for him lasted for the rest of her life. Her only son, born when she was 45, was named Richard Keir Pankhurst, after the two men she had loved the most.

This is to anticipate, however. Her promising artistic career in London was soon overwhelmed by the demands of the rapidly growing suffragette movement and the related pressures of her family commitments. The Women's Social and Political Union (WSPU) was formed by Emmeline Pankhurst in 1903. Its formation came about as a direct result of Sylvia's invitation to decorate the lecture hall of the ILP in Salford. She was delighted at the invitation, especially as the hall was to be dedicated to the memory of her father: the foundation stone of the hall had been laid in November 1898, shortly after Richard Pankhurst's death. However, the delight was short-lived. To her dismay, Pankhurst discovered that women were not allowed to join that branch of the ILP: and that even some members of the ILP Executive were actively opposed to votes for women. It was as a result of this that Emmeline Pankhurst called a meeting at the Pankhurst home attended by six women. The result was the formation of the WSPU. (Sylvia was not present at this meeting.)

Sylvia Pankhurst's artistic talents were well to the fore in early WSPU poster design and propaganda. Indeed, she gave the WSPU 'its visual identity: she foregrounded working-class women', indicative of her strong belief that the movement should focus its political work upon engaging with the mass of ordinary, disadvantaged women.[20] 'The extent to which Sylvia envisaged the campaign being led by working-class women is evident in the WSPU membership cards she designed ... The sole image is a procession of women whose rolled up sleeves, clogs and aprons make them instantly recognisable as women workers.'[21]

Pankhurst and the WSPU in the early years

Tensions between Sylvia and her mother and sister, Christabel, were present from the start. These tensions were an inextricable mix of longstanding difficulties over familial relationships and mounting disagreements over ideological and strategic perspectives. Initially, Sylvia tried to combine her WSPU role, as National Secretary, with her artistic studies: but Annie Kenney, who had been sent to London to help, recalled that the 23-year-old Sylvia ' "looked over-burdened and distraught" '.[22]

From the outset, Pankhurst concentrated on work with working-class women from the East End. 'She presented the vote as an integral part of obtaining the social changes these women were already engaged in fighting for.'[23] Her leadership role in the WSPU was short-lived, however. Her mother insisted that, once Christabel had completed her studies, she should assume control of the WSPU. However, Sylvia pre-empted this by resigning as Secretary: she recognised that, even at that early stage, she was not ' "fully in accord with the spirit of [Christabel's] policy" '.[24] From late 1906, Christabel took charge and 'rapidly began to break all links with the labour movement';[25] she insisted upon strict neutrality towards other political parties and movements.

Moreover, the Pankhursts (Emmeline and Christabel) effectively abolished any semblance of internal democracy in the WSPU, and assumed control. (Many dissenting suffragettes resigned and established the Women's Freedom League.) By 1907, the WSPU was urging supporters to abandon any 'class feeling'. As Katherine Connelly comments in her biography of Sylvia Pankhurst, in practice 'the claim to be classless in a rigidly class-divided society meant uncritically accepting the status quo. Being part of a "classless" organisation was clearly far more appealing to women whose socially privileged position was not going to be challenged.'[26] Thus, in effect, the WSPU insisted on middle-class women being in control and fighting the cause *on behalf of* working-class women.

Although remaining in the WSPU – for the time being – Sylvia ignored her sister's diktats and, after the first few of many spells of imprisonment for militant action, she campaigned against the shockingly poor treatment of prisoners and also undertook fieldwork research into a variety of working-class occupations and cultures, concluding that 'men and women benefited by working together'.[27] This underlined her disagreement with Christabel's increasingly Manichean views: Sylvia rejected the perspective that saw 'a world of masculine evil and female victimization. The working-class men who supported the suffrage movement were oppressed too.'[28] She believed that the suffrage cause, though of central importance, had to be seen as a part of the wider struggle for social and political emancipation, and for the attainment of a socialist society. Sylvia was the only member of that remarkable family (apart from her father, Richard), who maintained this position.

Pankhurst nevertheless continued to give public support to the militant tactics of the WSPU. She was also unstinting in her support for those suffragettes undergoing the horrors of forced feeding in prison; indeed, she herself endured repeated imprisonment and life-threatening hunger strikes on numerous occasions. But because for her the issue of women's suffrage and emancipation had to be seen in *class* terms, she disagreed with her mother and sister over the question of *who* should be enfranchised.

It became increasingly clear that, for Emmeline and Christabel Pankhurst (and for some of the leadership of the National Union of Women's Suffrage Societies (NUWSS)), it was enfranchisement of more privileged and educated women that was the priority, and maybe even the only ultimate objective. In part, this can be seen as an endorsement of the gradualist, inch-by-inch strategy: one step would lead to another. But it was also the case that, in 1913, Christabel Pankhurst had argued against a working-class suffrage movement. Both Christabel and Emmeline Pankhurst 'wanted a WSPU of women who were handpicked or aristocratic'.[29]

The government's decision in 1918 to widen the franchise to include women over the age of 30, who were either householders or married to householders, was supported by many in the suffrage movement, including Emmeline and Christabel Pankhurst. In contrast, Sylvia identified the cause of women's suffrage and the struggle for socialism as coterminous. Moreover, her socialism was not of the top-down state or municipal socialism advocated by the Fabians and progressives. She believed in socialism from the bottom up, with workers controlling both industry and government.

Increasingly out of sympathy with the WSPU, Sylvia made two trips to the USA, in 1911 and 1912. In accord with her developing political position, she campaigned on a range of issues: women's suffrage, certainly; but also better treatment for prisoners; support of a New York laundry workers' strike; and explicit condemnation of racism. Outspokenly critical of their attitude towards the black community, in a speech to the Women's Community Club in Missouri she said that in her view their state was the most backward in the Union. She also highlighted the plight of Native Americans. For Pankhurst, it was the struggle for equality, fairness and justice, irrespective of class or race, that was the objective. Such views may seem a commonplace of the Left one hundred years later, but at the time few were prepared to endorse or support such a stance: many of those active in the American suffrage movement condemned her, or at the very least were 'uncomfortable' with such campaigning. Moreover, her tour was no 'hole in the corner' event. She was only the second woman to address the Senate and House in joint convention; and she spoke at several famous venues, including Carnegie Hall and Boston State Hall. She accomplished all this, effectively on her own, at the age of 29–30.

Sylvia Pankhurst, the East London Federation and the struggle for Irish independence

By 1912, it was clear that the WSPU was 'in decline and becoming isolated not just politically but from the rest of the movement'.[30] Martin Pugh argues that the real impetus lay with the NUWSS and its pressure upon, and subsequently negotiations with, Lloyd George and other senior ministers; but he also acknowledges the relevance and importance of Pankhurst's move to the East End and her establishment, in 1912, of the East London Federation (ELF). She was successful in gathering together significant numbers of working-class women, despite an initial suspicion of middle-class radicals 'parachuting in' to working-class areas, and considerable hostility and violence. Pankhurst showed courage and determination in such adverse circumstances in her persistent advocacy of 'building liberation from below'. The ELF organised several meetings each night and encouraged working-class women to report on their grievances, and to develop these concerns to build a self-confident movement, which included, but was not dominated by, the demand for female enfranchisement.

Pankhurst *engaged* with local working-class women. She did not talk *at* them but *with* them; she listened to their grievances and their political and social priorities. Although she could often be domineering, self-opinionated and even stubborn, she demonstrated in her East End years that she had a deep moral empathy with and understanding of the plight of working-class women and the community in which they lived.

After bitter exchanges with Christabel (and to a lesser extent with her mother, Emmeline), and having undergone yet another spell of imprisonment, Sylvia was pursuing an increasingly separate political path to the WSPU. Through 1913 there were mounting tensions. The final straw, for Christabel, had been Sylvia's decision to speak at a mass rally on 1 November 1913, organised by George Lansbury, in support of the victims of police brutality in the Dublin strike of the Irish Transport and General Workers' Union. Her speech was received rapturously and she was cheered loudly. 'A furious Christabel, who now considered her sister to be breaking every rule in the WSPU book', was determined that Sylvia and the ELF should be expelled from the WSPU. This decision was confirmed when Sylvia, accompanied by Norah Smyth, met with Christabel and Emmeline Pankhurst in January 1914.[31]

Pankhurst's response was to amend the name of the ELF to ELFS – the 'S' signifying Suffragettes – much to the irritation of her mother and her sister. Sylvia also launched her newspaper, *The Woman's Dreadnought*. In an early article she reiterated her belief in the necessary connection between the struggle for the vote and the struggle for socialism, and she confronted directly the elitist, class-based attitude of the WSPU. As one of her biographers has observed, Christabel, and some other suffragettes, shared 'contemporary preoccupations with the future of "the race"'.[32] Advocates of such a view, Sylvia argued,

> forget that comparatively, the leisured comfortably situated women are but a little group, and the working-women a multitude … The essential principle of the vote is that each one of us shall have a share of power to help himself or herself and us all. It is in direct opposition to the idea that some few, who are more favoured, shall help and teach and patronize the others.[33]

Sylvia's 'emphasis on emancipation from below informed the paper's aim to amplify the voices of working-class women',[34] and again signified her commitment to the principles of English radicalism.

Eventually, in the light of the persistent pressure from Pankhurst and the ELFS, the previously intransigent Prime Minister, Asquith, agreed to receive a deputation of six working-class women on 18 June 1914. Asquith's response was certainly positive. 'His claimed support for an "unrestricted" franchise suggests he was contemplating women voting on the same terms as men.'[35] However, before any further developments were possible, the world was plunged into the cataclysm of the First World War.

Before considering Pankhurst's opposition to the war, in contrast to most of her fellow campaigners, brief note should be taken of her consistent support for the Irish campaign for Home Rule. In addition to her supporting Lansbury's meeting at the Albert Hall, she and Norah Smyth had organised a 'People's Army' in 1913, to support the suffragettes but also 'to defend the organised working class'. She also supported the Dublin Easter Rising in 1916, and was especially shocked by the execution of James Connolly, whom she had spoken alongside in 1913 and whose '"rebellion struck deeper than mere nationalism"'.[36]

Her support for the cause of Irish nationalism was a part of her commitment to anti-colonial struggles in a variety of contexts. Such issues were to assume much wider significance as fascist aggression, and more general imperial rivalries between the European powers in Africa and Asia, intensified. Such far-sighted, anti-colonialist analysis and activism were rare in the early decades of the twentieth century. Pankhurst was one of very few to engage not only with Irish issues in this period but also a little later with the pressure for Indian independence. And the last decades of her life were devoted, as noted earlier, to the cause of Ethiopia.

Attention should now be turned, however, to Sylvia's anti-war activism, from 1914 onwards; and subsequently to her central involvement in communist politics from 1917 to the early 1920s.

Sylvia Pankhurst and anti-war activism

The international socialist movement and the women's movement had, in theory, a set of similar beliefs, prior to the declaration of war. In 1913, for example, the International Woman Suffrage Alliance (IWSA) stressed anti-militarism as a principle of the suffrage movement; and the Second International, the body to which almost all socialist and social democratic bodies were affiliated, 'vowed to organise general strikes to bring Europe to a halt in the event of war being declared'.[37] Such views were given forceful expression at a demonstration in Trafalgar Square on 2 August 1914. However, opposition to the war soon crumbled, and the Second International collapsed as a result. The ILP and many of its members, including Keir Hardie and George Lansbury, opposed the war, but most labour movement leaders backed the government position.[38]

The leadership of both the NUWSS (including Millicent Fawcett and Helena Swanwick) and the WSPU, plus the large bulk of the members and supporters of both organisations, supported the government's war policy; and they gave up their campaigning for the vote for the duration of the war. Indeed, many, including Emmeline and Christabel Pankhurst, became prominent and strident supporters of the 'war effort'.[39] The WSPU's newspaper, *The Suffragette*, was retitled in 1915, *Britannia*.

In sharp contrast, Sylvia opposed the war vigorously from the outset from an internationalist, socialist perspective: on 1 August 1914, she wrote, in *The Woman's Dreadnought*, '"it is practically certain that every war of modern times has been fought with the purely materialistic object of forwarding the schemes and protecting the interests of powerful and wealthy financiers"'.[40] On the day Britain declared war, Pankhurst was in Dublin reporting for her newspaper on the killing by British soldiers of three people at a demonstration. 'Her presence in Ireland underlined her opposition to workers being divided by nation, race or gender, believing that workers had a common interest in uniting against the powerful.' She saw that the First World War would encourage workers 'to fight each other for the material gain of their rulers'.[41]

Pankhurst's opposition to the war never wavered, but she did recognise that her position was very much a minority point of view, not least in the working-class community of the East End. Unlike the WSPU, the ELFS, in accord with Sylvia's principles, was democratic (though she assumed, not without justification, that she should occupy a leading role). Thus, the ELFS demands were broadened, not to downplay the insistence on women's suffrage, but to include a range of further objectives to protect the living standards and welfare of the working class. The ELFS did not demand the denunciation of the war but it *did* demand that the war should not result in increased suffering and exploitation of working-class men and women. It was not until 1915, when anti-war sentiment was rising, that the organisation was able to adopt an explicit anti-war stance. The opposition to the war lost the organisation many members: only a few hundred remained. Nevertheless, Pankhurst used these to good effect, and many more working-class women (and some men) were assisted and supported in numerous ways during the war years.

She supported conscientious objectors and war resisters, but most of her energies went into developing welfare systems for the hard-pressed community. The ELFS established a Distress Bureau to help those who were grappling with poverty, illness and the complexities of the state's (minimal) welfare bureaucracy. The Women's Hall distributed free milk for malnourished babies, engaged doctors and nurses (on a very part-time basis) and set up a 'Cost Price Restaurant' in Bow, soon to be followed by other such initiatives. Later, a nursery and another shop were added to the ELFS's provisions. Pankhurst was, however, always intent on avoiding the organisation becoming a 'quietist charity' and was keen to develop personal initiative and craft and other skills. A toy-making business was established and, by January 1915, the ELFS was employing, in addition to secretarial staff, ' "59 regular indoor workers on relief work" ', mostly on a full-time basis.[42] Moreover, she insisted that women were paid no less than the minimum wage that men received in the district.

In line with her developing emphases upon socialism and anti-war activism, the ELFS changed its name in March 1916 to the Workers' Suffrage Federation (WSF): it changed again in 1918 in recognition of the growing importance it attached to socialism (discussed below) to the Workers' Socialist Federation (WSF).By this time, the WSF 'was no longer an East End-based organization but a national federation with branches in England and Scotland'.[43] The WSF campaigned against conscription, introduced in 1916; against the Defence of the Realm Act, which enabled the state to take over the factories whose work was considered vital for the war effort and to regulate and requisition their output; and against the Munitions Act, which outlawed strikes (and any profiteering) in munitions industries.

The WSF was centrally involved in the Trafalgar Square demonstration of 8 April 1916, where twenty thousand gathered to oppose these repressive measures and, more generally, to call for an end to the war. Numerous other demonstrations followed, including one in December 1916, addressed by, amongst others, a young Clement Attlee.

Increasingly, Pankhurst and the WSF worked with the ILP and the British Socialist Party (BSP) in opposing the war. She became more and more disillusioned with the Labour Party itself. Not only were anti-war motions defeated by the Party Conference, she was rudely treated and abused by delegates. 'It was these wartime experiences with the Labour Party that convinced her of its bankruptcy and of the futility of working with it.'[44] By 1918, as a result of the war, the 1916 Easter Rising in Dublin and not least the Russian Revolution of 1917, Sylvia Pankhurst 'was no longer a socialist suffragette but a revolutionary dedicated to the struggle for socialism'.[45]

Sylvia Pankhurst and communism, 1917/18–1921

With undiminished, indeed heightened, enthusiasm, Pankhurst embarked on the revolutionary path. She 'developed a hard anti-Labour Party, anti-electoral, anti-trade union leadership stance and discarded her former position that suffrage was the vehicle for social transformation'.[46] In truth, Pankhurst, as noted above, had never been enamoured of the Labour Party or of the parliamentary system in general: as her son Richard Pankhurst recalled, many years later, 'she was never over-enthusiastic about Parliament'; similarly, the historian Mary Davis has observed that Sylvia was 'never very happy about Parliament, frankly'.[47] Pankhurst thus belongs to that strand of English radicalism which prioritises social movement and grassroots activism and is deeply suspicious of, if not downright hostile to, gradualist, parliamentarist reform perspectives.

For Pankhurst, the critically important aspect of the Bolsheviks' October 1917 Revolution was their creation of soviets (or workers' councils) as the fundamental structure of the new socialist democracy. Ideologically, this fitted exactly with Sylvia's core belief that power must reside in the hands of the ordinary people, with direct democracy, and not in bureaucratic, so-called representative structures, which bedevilled both bourgeois society and reformist parliamentary parties, such as the Labour Party. Her move to a revolutionary position was no doubt enhanced by her falling in love, in late 1917, with the Italian revolutionary anarchist Silvio Corio, subsequently the father of Sylvia's son, Richard.[48]

Pankhurst and the WSF worked with other far-left organisations, including the BSP, the Socialist Labour Party, and some members of the ILP and the National Union of Railwaymen, to counter government propaganda against the Bolshevik Revolution. The WSF took a clear internationalist and anti-colonialist stand and affiliated in 1919 to the new Third International. Pankhurst became more than ever convinced that revolutionaries should not seek affiliation to parliamentarist parties such as the Labour Party. Concerned that the WSF would be outflanked on this issue at the Communist Unity Convention called for 1 August 1920, the WSF arranged its own Convention for June 1920 and voted to take the title of the Communist Party (British Section of the Third International) (CP) (BSTI).

Lenin disagreed with the WSF stance and urged her to attend the Second Congress of the Third International, held in the summer of 1920 in Russia, so that matters could be resolved. She attended with Willie Gallacher (later, a Communist MP) and J.T. Murphy. Lenin argued that the communists needed to make contact with the mass of the workers and that, as the Labour Party was the mass party of the working class in Britain, affiliation was necessary. Only then could the Labour Party be exposed as '"an organization of the bourgeoisie, which exists to systematically dupe the workers"'.[49] Lenin, not surprisingly, carried the day, by 58 votes to 24 with two abstentions.

Pankhurst was impressed by Lenin's determination to bring the communist argument to the mass of the workers, and eventually she agreed to work with the broader CPGB, which had been founded at the Unity Convention in August 1920. The new CPGB was firmly committed to seeking affiliation to the Labour Party: this was, of course, never achieved; despite repeated attempts, the Labour Party rejected all such overtures.

Back in the East End, Pankhurst and the WSF became focused on the anti-racist struggle, the East End being a notably ethnically mixed area, where there had been racist riots and several black men had been killed. It was at this time that she employed Claude McKay, the Jamaican journalist, as noted earlier, on the *Dreadnought*. McKay, writing under a pseudonym, produced some of the most trenchant journalism of the day, especially in his coverage of the relations between the white working class and black workers. Working with a young seafarer, McKay wrote articles encouraging working-class men in the armed forces to refuse to strike-break. McKay also encouraged white, black and Chinese workers to turn their anger not on each other but on '"the huge stores of wealth along the water front. The country's riches are not in the West End ... they are stored in the East End, and the jobless should lead the attack on the bastilles, the bonded warehouses."' This was regarded by the authorities as incitement to looting. Pankhurst, as editor, was sentenced to six months' imprisonment. In court, she affirmed her revolutionary stance: '"it was useless trying to palliate an impossible system. This is a wrong system, and has got to be smashed. I would give my life to smash it."'[50]

The merger between the CPGB and the CP (BSTI) was duly approved on 29/30 July 1921. Pankhurst, at that date, was in prison: on her release in May 1921 she was welcomed by her East End friends, but there was no CP presence. The rift was healed only at the formal level and there remained mutual resentment and hostility, personally as well as ideologically.

Never really comfortable in the CP, despite her admiration for Lenin, Sylvia became increasingly unhappy with what she (and many others) saw as the rightward policy drift in the Soviet Union: she backed the 'Workers' Opposition', and was particularly close to Alexandra Kollontai. In the domestic context, she advocated a similarly uncompromising line. In the Poplar Rent strike of 1921, for example, when Labour Councillors, including three of the Lansbury family, were sent to prison for refusing to collect rates for anything other than local services, Pankhurst, whilst respecting the Councillors' action, urged the workers not to settle for gradualist reforms but 'to fight for nothing less than full communism'.[51]

Given her stance in general, and the increasingly centralised control of the CP, tensions were inevitable. The specific cause of her expulsion focused on the future of her retitled newspaper, *The Workers' Dreadnought*. She argued that she should be free to argue the abstentionist line, and, generally, the policy of the Left opposition, within the CP as the editor of an independent publication. The CP insisted on central, Party control of all publications by CP members. The impasse was resolved only by her expulsion from the Party in September 1921. Not that Pankhurst was giving up: she concluded a lengthy article in *The Workers' Dreadnought* on 17 September 1921, ' "And so I leave the Party but not the movement." '[52]

Pankhurst and *The Workers' Dreadnought* (still calling itself the 'Organ of the Communist Party') continued publication, publicly criticising Lenin for the 'New Economic Policy' and generally abandoning Marxist-Leninist communism. In October 1921, she called, in the *Dreadnought*, on communists to support the new Fourth International, founded by dissident communists. Pankhurst established her own group, the Communist Workers' Party (CWP). This was a propagandist, sectarian group with no real roots, and was, as almost everyone on the Left realised, hopelessly grandiose and unrealistic. It was not her finest hour. She had one last burst of activity in her East End years, backing the Unemployed Workers' Organization (UWO), a radical, direct actionist group, established in opposition to Wal Hannington's much larger National Unemployed Workers' Movement (NUWM), within which the CP had a major influence. Formed in March 1923, the UWO's life was brief and inglorious: by early 1924, it had ceased to be viable and merged into the NUWM.

Finally, in July 1924, the *Dreadnought* ceased publication. 'Sylvia was tired, a rebel apparently without a cause. But not for long.'[53]

Sylvia Pankhurst and the anti-fascist struggle

Pankhurst had been one of the first to realise the danger of the rise of Mussolini and the fascists in Italy. Many both on the Left and, particularly, on the Right initially welcomed this development: Bonar Law, Winston Churchill, the *Daily Mail* and *The Times*, for example, were enthusiastic proponents. Similarly, she was the 'first editor in Britain to foresee the new dangers emerging in Germany and the young Adolf Hitler's rise to power'.[54]

In July 1924, she, Corio and Norah Smyth, 'her devoted, loyal friend and comrade',[55] moved to Woodford in Essex. A new phase of her life, and her activism, was about to begin.

Initially, Pankhurst concentrated her energies on two projects: turning the cottage to which she, Corio and Norah had moved into 'Red Cottage', serving tea and refreshments to lorry drivers and other travellers; and devoting herself to a series of writing projects.[56] But it was the rising threat of fascism that soon captured her attention. As early as 1922, she had warned that ' "Fascism [was] the White Terror of modern Capitalism" '.[57] Tensions rose in Italy and by October 1922 Mussolini was in power. Pankhurst and Corio worked with anti-fascists in the Italian community in London; and in the early 1920s they were instrumental in founding the organisation 'Friends of Italian Freedom League'. Their fears were confirmed when the socialist deputy, Giacomo Matteotti, was kidnapped and murdered by Mussolini's fascists.

In 1927, Sylvia and Corio's son, Richard Keir Pankhurst, was born. Three years later she published a campaigning book:[58] 'a pioneering political analysis of maternity',[59] which argued for reform of the abortion laws; and, '[s]ixteen years before the establishment of the National Health Service, Sylvia called for "an entirely free and efficient maternity service open to all" '.[60]

From the outset, Pankhurst saw the threat to women posed by fascism: as 'a totally reactionary force ... it would violently deprive women of their rights'.[61] She launched a petition in 1932 protesting at Mussolini excluding women professors in Italian universities. Once Hitler had taken power, she wrote a chapter on 'Women under the Nazis' in her series *Fascism As It Is*. She exposed the torture of women opponents of the Nazis, the expulsion of women from the professions and the enforced sterilisation of women.[62]

Pankhurst was involved in a series of other anti-fascist initiatives: in 1932 she established the Women's International Matteotti Committee (WIMC) to campaign against the persecution of Matteotti's widow, Velia, by the fascist government. She spoke at anti-fascist rallies, and in 1937 she 'returned to the East End, the scene of so many battles with the police, this time to do battle with the British Union of Fascists'.[63]

As one of her biographers has claimed, 'Sylvia's mobilisation of women in opposition to fascism helped reclaim the radical, democratic suffragette tradition'.[64]

Sylvia Pankhurst and Ethiopia

Pankhurst began the 1930s campaigning for peace, like so many on the Left. In 1930, she joined the Women's International League for Peace and Freedom (WILPF) and she was also Treasurer of the Women's World International Committee Against War and Fascism. But, again like many others on the Left, by the end of the decade 'she concluded that a war was needed to defeat fascism'.[65]

Pankhurt's main concern was the fascist conquest of Ethiopia by Mussolini: indeed, her involvement with this cause became her passion, her *raison d'être*; and

Ethiopia became eventually her home and final resting place. But she also saw from the outset that the cause of saving Spain from the quasi-fascist revolt led by Franco in 1936 was intimately linked to Ethiopia. She attributed 'both to the prejudices of rightwingers who felt more threatened by black people and republicanism than by fascism'.[66] She deplored the refusal of the Western powers to support the anti-fascist cause.

More left-wing activists prioritised the cause of Spain. Why was this and why did Pankhurst concentrate her energies on Ethiopia?[67] She had for some years linked the causes of anti-racism and anti-imperialism: the struggle against fascism emphasised the importance of this perspective. '"People stood by while Ethiopia was vanquished: this is only Africa: this is not a White Man's country. They listened to Italian propaganda: these are primitives, their customs are barbarous."'[68]

Her focus on Ethiopia was in part the result of her respect for the Emperor, Haile Selassie, the ousted monarch. This, though a somewhat strange cause for a left-wing socialist and republican, typified her obsessive political personality. It also, more rationally, reflected her anti-imperialist, anti-racist and of course anti-fascist sympathies. Moreover, as Barbara Winslow has observed, 'Pankhurst loved to defend the underdog and she saw in Selassie much more a defeated victim of fascism than a reactionary monarch'.[69] However, it should be noted in fairness that Haile Selassie had been a 'modernising' monarch: there were in the early 1930s, 'huge strides made in education for boys and girls, a printing press was established, a written constitution was introduced and legislation passed to phase out slavery'.[70] Indeed, 'Haile Selassie was revered throughout Africa and the black world ... There was still a great deal to be achieved but Haile Selassie was supervising a remarkable renaissance.'[71]

Once the effective complicity of Britain and France had been secured, Mussolini saw no obstacle to his invasion and conquest of Ethiopia in 1935. Pankhurst understood, before many others on the Left, that appeasing fascism 'would lead to war not peace, and resisting fascism would lead to peace not war';[72] and she campaigned through the press, letters to politicians and public statements, to this effect.

In response to Mussolini's invasion, she launched a new newspaper in May 1936, *New Times and Ethiopian News* (NTEN), a title inspired partly by Chaplin's film *Modern Times*. She published many articles by anti-racists, Ethiopian writers, Italian anti-fascists and leading members of the Pan-African movement. Despite censorship, the paper carried 'reports of the three-day massacre in Addis Ababa in which thousands of Ethiopians were killed'.[73] The war crimes committed by fascists, including the bombing of Red Cross units and the use of poison gas by the Italian Air Force, were also reported. Such persistent, radical journalism was necessary: even the *Manchester Guardian*, as it then was, described the Italian dictator as having '"shrewdness and Italian fineness of perception"'.[74]

Not that Pankhurst was oblivious to the mounting conflict in Europe: she commissioned the sculptor Eric Benfield to create a unique monument to mark the moral outrage at mass aerial bombing. The 'stone bomb' was unveiled the year before Guernica. Pankhurst saw aerial bombardments as '"cruelly unfair methods of gassing and bombing the innocent"'.[75]

Her main focus, however, remained Ethiopia, which became 'a symbol for black anti-imperialists because it emerged as the only independent African country from nineteenth-century imperialism'.[76] Selassie was exiled in Britain, spending most of his time living in Bath, a town for which he retained a great affection. Eventually, in 1940, Britain declared war on Italy. Pankhurst spent much of her time in a somewhat arcane, but eventually successful campaign to persuade the BBC to play the Ethiopian national anthem when other Allied anthems were played. However, she did not lose sight of larger world issues. She undertook, in the NTEN, a Left critique of Stalinism, and exposed the horrors of the Show Trials, the assassination of Trotsky and other atrocities committed by Stalin's regime in the name of communism. Her break with Stalinist communism was now complete.[77]

Selassie flew from Britain to Khartoum at the end of June 1940. Addis Ababa was captured by British forces on 6 April 1941 and, although he was eventually permitted to return to his capital, Ethiopia was now classed as 'occupied enemy territory'; an Anglo-Ethiopian agreement was signed on 4 February 1942, but 'it was a far cry from full independence'.[78] Sylvia continued campaigning for full independence and for the union of Ethiopia and Eritrea. Her continued activism irritated the British government. In a letter from a Foreign Office official in 1947 to the British Minister in Addis Ababa, Sylvia was described as a '"horrid old harridan [who] should be choked to death with her own pamphlets"'.[79] As Katherine Connelly comments, more than thirty years after the end of the suffragette movement, Pankhurst was 'still driving the British government to distraction'.[80] Her persistent campaign after the war to have *Italian* war criminals included in the Nuremberg war crimes trials was unsuccessful, despite there being considerable evidence of atrocities having been committed.

Pankhurst continued in her various campaigns on behalf of Ethiopia, notably raising funds for the Princess Tsehai Memorial Hospital, named in honour of Selassie's daughter, who had trained as a nurse in Britain, had been a friend of Sylvia's and had died tragically young. (Funds were raised and the hospital successfully created, thanks largely to Pankhurst's prodigious efforts and networking skills.)

After Corio's death in 1954, at the age of 77, and that of her old friend Emmeline Pethick-Lawrence in 1956, Pankhurst decided to move permanently to Ethiopia with her son, Richard. She closed her newspaper but, once in Ethiopia, she (typically) began another, *The Ethiopian Observer*. She became something of a folk hero in Ethiopia and was certainly held in high esteem by Selassie and his family. As he wrote, in 1941, '"Your unceasing efforts and support in the just cause of Ethiopia will never be forgotten by myself or my people."'[81]

Sylvia Pankhurst died on 27 September 1960, aged 78, and was buried 'in land allotted for Ethiopian Patriots in the grounds of Ethiopia's Holy Trinity Cathedral'.[82]

Conclusion

Throughout her life, Sylvia Pankhurst was both a feminist and a socialist. For her, these inextricably linked pillars of progressive politics were supplemented by her prescient anti-racism and anti-imperialism. She was a ' "voluntarist" – believing that political will was all that was needed to overcome all material circumstances'.[83] Her moral imperatives were the driving force in her politics, which were 'rooted more in the nineteenth century than in the twentieth; she always clung to the ideas of her father and of Keir Hardie'.[84] Her politics owed more to Morris than to Marx. She was not a great strategist: as her frustrations with the various political formations she had been involved with grew (the Labour Party, the ILP, the WSPU, the CPGB), so her politics became more extreme, and in many ways more unrealistic. Committed as she was to the women, and men, of the working-class communities of the East End and elsewhere, she failed to carry people with her on her 'revolutionary road'. Her 'fierce and uncompromising independence' and her 'ruthless adherence to principles that she believed to be right' (as noted at the outset of this chapter) may have been admirable qualities, but in the end they lessened her influence on the socialist movement.[85] Arguably, however, the same cannot be said in relation to her lasting influence on feminism. Her success, supported by Keir Hardie, in convincing the Prime Minister, Asquith, of the plight – *and* the determined militancy – of working-class women played an important part in achieving universal suffrage. In this sense, she has a significant place in the development of socialist feminism in the later twentieth century.[86]

Moreover, her persistent opposition to racism, colonialism and imperialism, and Fascism – all in the context of a feminist frame of reference – make her one of the few internationalist socialist feminists of the period. She had a profound and consistent belief in a socialism 'from below', achieved by struggle within and by working-class communities. She 'helped ordinary people to speak for themselves' and tried to instil her values and political beliefs into the movements she founded and worked in so assiduously. She was consistent in her support for the 'underdog', and in her belief that equality, fairness for all, irrespective of class and race, were the central objectives of progressive politics. Throughout her life, she was a true radical in both her political beliefs and her political activism.

Notes

1 See for example, S. Holton, *Feminism and Democracy: Women's Suffrage and Reform Politics in Britain, 1900–1918* (Cambridge: Cambridge University Press, 1986); J. Purvis and S. Holton (eds), *Votes for Women* (London and New York: Routledge, 2000); J. Liddington and J. Norris, *One Hand Tied Behind Us: The Rise of the Women's Suffrage Movement* (Virago, 1978); J. Liddington, *Rebel Girls: Their Fight for the Vote* (Virago, 2006); J. Liddington, *Respectable Rebel: The Life and Times of Selina Cooper 1864–1946* (Virago, 1984).

2   Liddington and Norris, *One Hand Tied Behind Us*, p. 11.
3   Ibid., p. 14.
4   See Liddington, *Respectable Rebel*.
5   S. Holton, 'The Making of Suffrage History', in Purvis and Holton (eds), *Votes for Women*, p. 21.
6   Richard Pankhurst, in the film *Sylvia Pankhurst: Everything Is Possible*, WORLDwrite, January 2011.
7   S. Rowbotham, 'Foreword', in B. Winslow, *Sylvia Pankhurst: Sexual Politics and Political Activism* (UCL Press, 1996), p. ix.
8   Winslow, *Sylvia Pankhurst*, p. 192.
9   Sylvia Pankhurst is referred to in this chapter as 'Pankhurst', unless the context necessitates differentiating her from other members of the Pankhurst family. On these occasions, 'Sylvia' or 'Sylvia Pankhurst' is used. For a detailed history of her varied activism, especially her 'suffrage years', see the texts cited in the references to this chapter and in the Bibliography.
10 Pankhurst, *The Suffragette Movement* (Longmans, 1931), cited in S. Harrison, *Sylvia Pankhurst: A Maverick Life 1882–1960* (Arun Press, 2003, pb. edition, 2004), p. 14. In contrast to her evident affection for her father, Sylvia's relationship with her mother, recalled many years later in 1931, was from the beginning much more distant. But it 'was not anger [she felt] but regret'. Harrison, p. 14.
11 Harrison, *Sylvia Pankhurst*, p. 24.
12 Ibid., pp. 15–16. Adela always felt alienated from her family; at her mother's and Christabel's instigation, she emigrated to Australia and never returned to live in Britain.
13 K. Connelly, *Sylvia Pankhurst: Suffragist, Socialist and Scourge of Empire* (Pluto Press, Revolutionary Lives Series, 2013), p. 6.
14 Winslow, *Sylvia Pankhurst*, p. 144.
15 Ibid.
16 G.B. Shaw, cited in Harrison, *Sylvia Pankhurst*, p. 3 (no source given).
17 Harrison, *Sylvia Pankhurst*, citing a letter from Castle to the author (n.d.), pp. 2–3. See also B. Castle, *Sylvia and Christabel Pankhurst* (Penguin Books, 1987).
18 And, according to Harrison, other visitors to the Pankhurst family home also exerted a strong influence on Sylvia: Malatesta, the Italian anarchist refugee; Dadabhai Naoroji, the first Indian MP in the Commons; Tom Mann, the trades unionist; Annie Besant; and 'perhaps most memorable of all ... Louise Michel, a heroine of the Paris Commune', ibid., p. 21.
19 On Sylvia's artistic attributes and achievements, see J. Bullock and R. Pankhurst (eds), *Sylvia Pankhurst: From Artist to Anti-Fascist* (Basingstoke: Macmillan Academic, 1992).
20 R. Pankhurst, Sylvia's son, in the film *Sylvia Pankhurst*, 2011.
21 Connelly, *Sylvia Pankhurst*, p. 22.
22 E. Pethick-Lawrence, *My Part in a Changing World* (Victor Gollancz, 1938), cited in ibid., p. 21.
23 Ibid., p. 24.
24 Pankhurst, *The Suffrage Movement*, cited in Connelly, *Sylvia Pankhurst*, p. 25.
25 Connelly, *Sylvia Pankhurst*, p. 26.
26 Ibid., p. 29.

27 Ibid., p. 33.
28 S. Rowbotham, 'Foreword' to Winslow, *Sylvia Pankhurst*, p. x.
29 Winslow, *Sylvia Pankhurst*, p. 8.
30 Ibid., p. 24.
31 M. Pugh, *The March of the Women: A Revisionist Analysis of the Campaign for Women's Suffrage, 1866–1914* (Oxford: Oxford University Press, 2000), p. 253.
32 Harrison, *Sylvia Pankhurst*, p. 151.
33 *Woman's Dreadnought*, 8 March 1914, p. 3, cited in Connelly, *Sylvia Pankhurst*, p.61.
34 Ibid.
35 Ibid, p. 66.
36 S. Pankhurst, *The Home Front* (Hutchinson, Longman, 1931, reprinted Virago, 1977), p. 322, cited in ibid., p. 85.
37 Connelly, *Sylvia Pankhurst*, p. 67
38 Arthur Henderson, who replaced MacDonald as leader of the Labour Party, joined the wartime coalition government. Most trade union leaders, including veteran left-wingers such as Ben Tillett and Will Thorne, also supported the war.
39 Although it should be noted that some, like Millicent Fawcett, whilst accepting that the government could not take up the issue of women's suffrage during the war, exercised a 'patriotism [that] was firm if relatively restrained'. Pugh, *The March of the Women*, p. 284.
40 Connelly, *Sylvia Pankhurst*, p. 67.
41 Ibid.
42 ELFS, First Annual Report, 1915, p. 18, cited in ibid., p. 75.
43 Winslow, *Sylvia Pankhurst*, p. 76.
44 Ibid., p. 87.
45 Ibid., p. 104.
46 Ibid., p. 105.
47 *Sylvia Pankhurst*, film, 2011.
48 Sylvia and Corio remained together, although they never married, until his death in 1954.
49 Documents of the second Congress 1920, vol. 11, New York: Pathfinder Press, 1991, p. 739, cited in Connelly, *Sylvia Pankhurst*, p. 108.
50 *Workers' Dreadnought*, 16 October 1920, p. 3, and 6 November 1920, p. 1, cited in Connelly, *Sylvia Pankhurst*, pp. 112–13. The changed title of the paper reflected the increasing priority given by Pankhurst to the socialist element of the radical movement.
51 Ibid., p. 115.
52 Winslow, *Sylvia Pankhurst*, p. 173.
53 Harrison, *Sylvia Pankhurst*, p. 215.
54 Ibid., p. 214.
55 Winslow, *Sylvia Pankhurst*, p. 185.
56 In both of these, she achieved success. Her main publication at this period was the 638-page book *India and the Earthly Paradise* (Bombay, 1926). According to the historian Mary Davis, the book 'deserves attention as one of the very few British anti-racist and anti-imperialist attempts to analyze Indian culture, traditions and history'. Harrison, *Sylvia Pankhurst*, p. 218.
57 *Workers' Dreadnought*, 11 November 1922, p. 1, cited in Connelly, *Sylvia Pankhurst*, p. 118.

58 The book was entitled *Save the Mothers: A Plea for Measures to Prevent the Annual Loss of about 3000 Child-bearing Mothers and 20,000 Infant Lives in England and Wales and a Similar Grievous Wastage in Other Countries* (New York: Alfred A. Knopf, 1930).
59 Connelly, *Sylvia Pankhurst*, p. 125.
60 Ibid., p. 126.
61 Ibid., p. 127.
62 See 'Fascism As It Is', in K. Dodd (ed.), *A Sylvia Pankhurst Reader* (Manchester: Manchester University Press, 1993).
63 Winslow, *Sylvia Pankhurst*, p. 188.
64 Connelly, *Sylvia Pankhurst*, p. 129.
65 Ibid., p. 130.
66 Ibid., p. 134.
67 It was not that she ignored Spain. She 'participated in a women's delegation organised by the All London Aid Spain Council to the Foreign Office [which was] told that the government's priority was to prevent an international war. Sylvia responded "It is an international war!"' Ibid., p. 135, citing R. Pankhurst, 'Sylvia Pankhurst and the Spanish Civil War', text of paper given to the Sylvia Pankhurst Memorial Lecture 2004, at Wortley Hall, Sheffield, 17 September 2004, p. 6.
68 *New Times and Ethiopia News*, 1 August 1936, p. 4, cited in Connelly, *Sylvia Pankhurst*, p. 134.
69 Winslow, *Sylvia Pankhurst*, p. 189.
70 Connelly, *Sylvia Pankhurst*, pp. 130–1.
71 Harrison, *Sylvia Pankhurst*, p. 243.
72 Connelly, *Sylvia Pankhurst*, p. 132.
73 Ibid., p. 133.
74 Editorial, in *New Times and Ethiopia News*, 2 September 1939, cited in Harrison, *Sylvia Pankhurst*, p. 248.
75 *New Times and Ethiopia News*, 4 July 1936, p. 6, cited in Connelly, *Sylvia Pankhurst*, p. 134.
76 Connelly, *Sylvia Pankhurst*, p. 139.
77 See Harrison, *Sylvia Pankhurst*, p. 251; and Connelly, *Sylvia Pankhurst*, pp. 137–8.
78 Ibid., Harrison, p. 253.
79 R. Pankhurst, *Sylvia Pankhurst: Counsel for Ethiopia* (Hollywood: Tsehai Publications, 2003), p. 17, cited in Connelly, *Sylvia Pankhurst*, p. 146.
80 Ibid., Connelly.
81 Haile Selassie, 17 May 1941, cited in Harrison, *Sylvia Pankhurst*, p. 249.
82 Connelly, *Sylvia Pankhurst*, p. 147.
83 Ibid., p. 148, citing Mary Davis, *Sylvia Pankhurst: A Life in Radical Politics* (Pluto Press, 1999), p. 82.
84 Winslow, *Sylvia Pankhurst*, p. 190.
85 Ibid., p.192.
86 I am indebted to Philippa Clark for drawing my attention to this point.

5

Ellen Wilkinson

Ellen Wilkinson represents an important strand in twentieth-century English radicalism. She was quintessentially a labour movement figure, whose politics derived from her working-class, Northern background, her family's Methodism, her immersion in trade unionism and its proletarian culture, and her sustained commitment to what might be termed 'labourist feminism'.

Although she died prematurely, aged 55 in February 1947, her political life was intense, wide-ranging and passionate. Moreover, she was closely involved in almost all the great left-wing movements of the first half of the twentieth century, a period of unusually dramatic and tragic events, both national and international. At various times, Wilkinson was active and prominent in Guild Socialism, the Communist Party, the women's suffrage movement, the anti-war movement, the Independent Labour Party (ILP) and the agitation over the Spanish Civil War and over Indian independence, Popular Front movements against fascism, and numerous left-wing organisations within the political labour movement. She was 'an inveterate leaguer – from the Plebs League to the Women's International League for Peace and Freedom [WILPF] to the League Against Imperialism to the India League'.[1] In addition, she was an MP for 19 years and, from 1940 to her death, a member, first, of the wartime coalition government and latterly of Attlee's Labour Cabinet. Throughout this whole period, she was notably active in international socialist politics and was, despite her persistent ill-health, a tireless 'political traveller'.

She had a natural talent for the public stage and was a charismatic orator: she was known variously as 'five foot of dynamite',[2] the 'elfin fury', 'Our Ellen', ' Little Miss Perky',[3] 'Five Feet of Pugnacity'[4] and, more maliciously, 'virago intacta'.[5] Through all the twists and turns of her political affiliations and beliefs,[6] what motivated her was a burning sense of social injustice and the unfairness of the capitalist system. Her 'politics tended to be value-driven rather than party driven'.[7] She was an emotional pragmatist rather than a theoretician: her eloquence was matched by her anger and indignation at the sufferings of the poor and oppressed. She drove herself unrelentingly and, as one of her biographers notes, she had an 'inability to refuse help to worthwhile causes'; and this led to 'overworking and over-committing herself ... Rush, hurry, unpunctuality, muddled papers, were as endemic as her difficulties in meeting journalistic deadlines.'[8]

She was, too, a lifelong feminist (and one of her earliest serious involvements was with the women's suffrage campaign, discussed below); but, for her, feminism was a part of, and inseparable from, the struggle for socialism. In addition, especially in her earlier years, she was impatient with the suffragettes of the Women's Social and Political Union (WSPU) for abandoning '"Manchester" for "Mayfair"',[9] and its domination by middle-class women who had little interest in or understanding of the plight of *working-class* women.

Unlike many working-class socialists of the period, Wilkinson was always an internationalist and she devoted her energies to a variety of campaigns and movements for social justice across the world. She never lost her enthusiasm and idealism for the international 'socialist project'.

Her unremitting commitment to the cause and her continuing high profile give support to Morgan's judgement that she was ' "arguably Britain's most important woman politician" '.[10] Yet Wilkinson was unable to resolve the fundamental dilemmas confronting democratic socialists working within the confines of the reformist Labour Party in the twentieth century; and these constitute too some of the central problems for English radicalism in the period. Can radical change come through mass social movements? or through trade-union mobilisation and activism? or through a left-wing Parliamentary Labour Party? or through 'Popular Front' politics? or through some sort of revolutionary struggle?

At various times, Wilkinson gave priority to each of these perspectives; and it is significant that her trajectory, as with many socialist activists who enter Parliament, concluded with her full involvement in 'Establishment' government politics, although it can be argued, even from a radical perspective, that the 'crisis years' of the Second World War justified such a position.

To understand Wilkinson's important contribution to twentieth-century English radicalism this chapter looks first at her background and attitudes, then at her changing ideological perspectives, her feminism, her trade union activism, her internationalism and her parliamentary and ministerial career.

Background and attitudes

Wilkinson was born, one of four children, in October 1891 in Manchester, into a 'secure, upper working class, respectable' family.[11] Her father, originally a worker in the cotton mills, had left school aged eight, had learned to read and write at Sunday school, and by the time of her birth had worked his way up to his post as an insurance agent. Her mother suffered repeated bouts of cancer and died in 1916; and it was her father, Richard Wilkinson, who instilled a spirit of ambition in his children: despite his lack of any formal education, of his four children three went to college, and two of them obtained degrees.

Her father's Methodism was an important element in her ideological development. Although the 'patience and resignation it taught were not for her', [12] the Nonconformist moral radicalism of Methodism and its quasi-puritanical culture left its imprint on Wilkinson. (She was a lifelong teetotaller, for example.) Despite her membership of the Communist Party in the early 1920s and her adoption, at least for a time, of Leninist materialist orthodoxy, she could still claim in 1939 that '"I am still a Methodist ... you can never get ... its special glow out of your blood"'.[13]

Her Methodism was soon complemented by a fervent belief in socialism. At school, encouraged by a liberal-minded teacher, she read the ethical socialist Robert Blatchford. She became, in her own words, '"an ardent, in fact a flaming, socialist"'.[14] She joined the ILP aged 16; and, although something of a rebel at school, won a national scholarship to read history at the University of Manchester, a remarkable achievement for a young woman at this time, and still more so given her working-class background.

At university, Wilkinson, although revelling in the intellectual excitement of studying history and in the range of books and ideas that the university offered, devoted much of her time and energy to radical socialist politics. (And later, in 1924, she observed that she had been '"astonished to discover when I came into contact with the National Council of Labour Colleges [NCLC] how little real history I had been taught"'.)[15] She became involved, *inter alia*, in the University Socialist Federation and the Fabian Society, as well as in numerous outside political activities (for example, a strike in Manchester). It was at this time that she came to know leading figures in the socialist movement, including Sidney and Beatrice Webb, G.D.H. Cole, Palme Dutt, Clifford Allen and Katherine Bruce Glasier. (She was also engaged briefly to Walter Newbold, who became in 1922 the first Communist Party MP in the House of Commons.)[16]

On leaving the University of Manchester in 1913, Wilkinson took a post as full-time organiser for the National Union of Women's Suffrage Societies (NUWSS). This experience, and two years later her full-time work in the trade union movement, completed her 'political formation'. The course was set for a life of committed socialist activism, inspired by a fierce working-class moralism.

The far Left

In the years immediately before and after the Russian Revolution of 1917, syndicalist, Guild Socialist and communist perspectives were part of a fluid, developmental and, in some respects, exciting and optimistic period in the unfolding of 'the socialist project'. Wilkinson became secretary of the Manchester National Guilds League (NGL) in 1917–18. She was on the revolutionary left of the NGL agitation, 'arguing for workers' control of production through national guilds, eviction of the employers and an end to the profit system'.[17] Wilkinson was a member of a small group, delegated to consider with other pro-Soviet organisations the way forward and formulate a programme of action. Their proposals, accepted by the NGL at a special conference in December 1920, argued for a revolutionary approach to Guild Socialism and envisaged the necessity for the violent overthrow of capitalism. It was thus an explicit rejection of Fabian gradualism, although it was also argued that the Soviet model was inappropriate for Britain, and the belief in a Guild Socialist system was reaffirmed. (This shift to the Left by the NGL prompted the resignation of several Executive members, including R.H. Tawney.)

Wilkinson remained a member of the NGL after she joined the Communist Party (CP), which was established in July 1920; indeed, she never resiled from her belief in workers' control – an emotional, gut belief more than a continuing intellectual conviction. It was her CP involvement that, for the next few years, defined and dominated Wilkinson's politics. At the CP Convention, the ultra-Left's proposal to reject parliamentary activity was defeated (in line with Lenin's strictures on 'ultra-leftism' in *Left-wing Communism: An Infantile Disorder*). Wilkinson supported the view that 'parliament and elections were a platform for revolutionary propaganda rather than a means to bring socialism';[18] and she enthusiastically adopted the 'Communist principles of proletarian dictatorship, democratic centralism and revolution'.[19]

Wilkinson visited the Soviet Union in 1921 and, though shocked by the hardship and poverty, she strongly supported Lenin's purported 'back to the masses' strategy and she wholeheartedly agreed with the Soviet leaders' initial internationalism. As Wilkinson remarked, it was '"no more possible to have a Communist Russia in a capitalist world than to have a Communist Manchester in a Capitalist Britain"'.[20] Although, like many other socialists, Wilkinson was uneasy about the continuing lack of democracy in the Soviet Union, she argued that the Revolution *had* to be defended as it was in the front line of the struggle for international socialism.

By late 1922, the tide of revolutionary fervour in Western Europe had ebbed: *international* socialism was no longer an imminent possibility. This, combined with the consolidation of centralised power in the Soviet Union and the adoption of the New Economic Policy, and domestically the persistently masculine culture of the CP, led to her disillusionment with the Party. Moreover, it became clear that the CP was not to be allowed to affiliate to the mainstream Labour Party and, equally important, that it had only marginal influence on the trade union movement. For Wilkinson, the honeymoon period with communism was over. As the Stalinist grip tightened on the Soviet Union through the 1920s and beyond, Wilkinson became more and more critical. Moreover, though she retained elements of her

Marxist-Leninist analysis (for example, on the nature of imperialism, as exemplified in her two substantial pamphlets, both co-authored with Dr Edward Conze, *Why Fascism?* (1934) and *Why War?* (1934)), her long-term *emotional* political priorities reasserted themselves. The moral crusade for an egalitarian socialism lay at the centre of her politics. For Wilkinson, this struggle was articulated through a combination of trade unionism, parliamentary socialism, and feminist campaigning. This relatively rapid transition testifies to the primacy of such concerns throughout Wilkinson's life and to her pragmatism, her belief in adopting whatever means seemed most likely to achieve her long-term *un*changing, political objectives. Thus Wilkinson's ideological and short-term political priorities varied widely and often in seemingly contradictory ways, but her commitment to her fundamental socialist *values* remained consistent.

In 1924 she resigned from the CP and from then on was fully committed to the Labour Party. In part this decision was politically self-interested: she realised that the CP was, for the foreseeable future, a political cul-de-sac. Her future as a left-wing socialist lay within the Labour Party and the mainstream trade union movement. However, until her ministerial career began in 1940, she remained something of a maverick left-winger, and she maintained close contact with former CP comrades, notably Palme Dutt: 'until the last six years of her life it would be wrong to view her as being a figure of mainstream Labourism'.[21] But it was also a principled decision. She abhorred the increasingly bureaucratic centralism and authoritarian culture of the CP; and she had come to accept that democratic argument and debate were the only legitimate ways to achieve worthwhile change. Nevertheless, as one of her biographers has emphasised, she was 'never a "red baiter"' and she 'never wholly rejected the basic theory of the class war and long believed that the interests of workers and employers within a capitalist society were in perpetual conflict'.[22]

The trade union movement

In July 1915, Wilkinson was appointed women's organiser for the AUCE (Amalgamated Union of Co-operative Employees). Her involvement with this union and with NUDAW (National Union of Distributive and Allied Workers) continued for the rest of her life. For Wilkinson, given her background in Guild Socialism and the women's suffrage movement, both industrial unionism and the defence and development of *women* workers' conditions and rights were of primary concern. Female trade union membership rose rapidly during the First World War: a 160 per cent increase to a total of 1,224,000 in 1918. Her strong support for equal pay for women undertaking effectively 'men's jobs' during the war led her into dispute with the union hierarchy in the AUCE and resulted eventually in her dismissal from her post, though she was rapidly reinstated. She was involved throughout the war and in the years immediately after, with a series of industrial disputes on behalf of women's industrial struggles for justice and equality.[23]

Wilkinson was very active in the 1926 General Strike. She toured, with her close friend J.F. Horrabin, to speak at more than forty strike meetings across the country. She was inspired by the militancy, commitment and warm humanity of the strikers and their supporters; and she, in turn, was in her element as a passionate speaker. In contrast, back at TUC headquarters in London, she found the chaos and pressure of the office, and the '"constitution-mongering antics"' of the TUC, exhausting and dispiriting.[24] Not surprisingly, she was highly critical of the TUC General Council's decision to call off the General Strike. She argued that the TUC was at fault in several respects: its reluctance to engage in the strike and its consequent lack of preparation, in contrast to the government and employers; its attempt to put pressure on the miners to call off the strike; its lack of nerve when it came to confrontation with the government and the Establishment at large; and, tellingly, the acceptance by the TUC of the government's shrewd depiction of the strike as being a threat to the Constitution. Such '"useful bogies [are] used by the government class when it suits them"', as Wilkinson put it.[25]

Wilkinson threw herself into the continuing struggle to support the miners. She visited the USA, at the request of the miners' leader, A.J. Cook, and raised considerable sums of money in support of the strike, and gained favourable publicity. She spoke at the Durham Miners' Gala in 1927, 1929, 1934 and 1937; and she continued her close association with the miners as MP for Jarrow (her constituency included two pits).

Her trade union activism was intertwined with her political life, both ideologically and practically. Ideologically, she retained her loyalty both to the union movement and to the working-class culture for which it stood; her Guild Socialist and industrial unionist outlook co-existed, albeit somewhat uneasily, with her more orthodox role as a trade union official. Practically, she owed much to NUDAW sponsorship of her parliamentary career and her various roles in the political labour movement: for example, NUDAW nominated her for Labour's National Executive Committee (NEC) as early as 1924 and she served two spells on that body, from 1927 to 1929 and 1937 to her death.

Finally, Wilkinson's commitment to improving women's position in society was articulated primarily through her trade union activity. Whether this took the form of prosaic but important reforms such as the provision of better toilet and bathroom facilities, or the more generalised campaign for equal pay, women's issues were always prominent in Wilkinson's politics.

Suffrage, feminism and 'women's issues'

High on her agenda as women's issues were and remained, Wilkinson, as already noted, always saw these in the context of the wider struggle for socialism and within an overall socialist perspective. As her most recent biographer, Laura Beers, has argued, her 'feminism was imbricated by class analysis ... [She] entered politics to advance the class struggle, and her championship of women's rights was most often framed within the context of the advancement of the working class.'[26]

Her support for the constitutional suffrage movement, rather than the WSPU, may have been due partly to 'political careerism', but, in the view of Beers, it was principally because of her 'background in debate and public speaking. She believed that thinking men and women could be persuaded of the logic of women's suffrage without resort to violence and intimidation.'[27]

During her time in the CP, Wilkinson believed, with Trotsky, that 'class exploitation and women's oppression were connected and the franchise would not emancipate working women; only through revolution could women achieve real freedom'.[28] Also, at this period and later, Wilkinson was at pains to emphasise that women's social and political role should not be restricted to 'home and motherhood'. She praised the Soviet ambition to provide communal care for children so that women could be liberated to play a variety of other roles. And in 1917 she wrote in the AUCE journal, with enthusiasm, of the modern, independent young woman who was keenly involved with a range of social activities, work, sport and fashion.[29]

Once elected as an MP, in 1924, Wilkinson became closely involved with the small number of other women MPs, of *all* parties. Indeed, Nancy Astor played 'mother hen' to her and other young female MPs. Wilkinson regarded her as one of the '"decent members"' of the other side.[30] However, Wilkinson never lost her focus on the plight of working-class women, and the importance of the demands for equal pay and equal rights for women.

On some issues, however, Wilkinson was more ambivalent. She became somewhat estranged from most Labour women over her unwillingness to support birth control, let alone abortion. (Almost certainly this was due to the sizeable Roman Catholic vote in her constituency: she was a politician, after all!) Her policy on family allowances was perhaps more instructive; there was a clear feminist case for support, but most trade unions were opposed because such benefits were seen to threaten both male wages and, generally, male autonomy. Writing in *Tribune* in 1938, Wilkinson wrote that as '"a feminist, I have a certain sympathy. But my trade unionist reaction is precisely the same as Jack Lawson's"': that is, opposition on the grounds indicated.[31] Nevertheless, generally, Wilkinson was persistent in her defence of women's interests.

As she distanced herself from the CP and Marxist analysis in the 1920s, she moved from a revolutionary perspective on women's liberation and empowerment to a reformist view. In some respects, therefore, she moved closer to 'Bloomsbury feminism'; indeed, she became a regular visitor to Cliveden and her circle of friends included Vera Brittain, Winifred Holtby and Lady Rhonnda (and she regularly met with such intellectual luminaries as Bertrand Russell, C.E.M. Joad, Harold Laski and Kingsley Martin).

With the rise of Fascism and Nazism in the 1930s, and the resulting international crisis, 'women's issues' and feminism necessarily became less of a priority for Wilkinson. Although she never ceased to campaign on women's issues, it was increasingly international affairs, and especially confronting the growing menace of fascism and war, which dominated her politics in the 1930s.

Socialist internationalism

From the time of her involvement in the CP, Wilkinson always regarded as axiomatic that the struggle for socialism was international. Through the 1920s and 1930s Wilkinson 'linked war and imperialism'.[32] She was, for example, an early and consistent supporter of Nehru's campaign for Indian independence, preferring Nehru to Gandhi as she believed that the former understood better the nature of global capitalism and imperialism. Her support for Indian nationalism, and for Nehru in particular, remained strong for the rest of her life, and was 'inflected with class and gender politics and sought to overcome the cultural distance between British and Indian workers'.[33] Similarly, she supported actively the cause of Irish independence, '"being half-Irish myself"',[34] and regarded James Connolly as one of her political heroes.

Despite her belief that pacifism without socialism was merely sentimental, she nevertheless collaborated actively with pacifists. Such obvious political contradictions typified Wilkinson's emotional approach to politics. Charitably, this can be explained by her commitment to socialist ideals and their attainment through a variety of means in different circumstances. From a more jaundiced perspective, however, they can be seen as indicative of her political inconsistency, resulting in part from her 'political pragmatism' and her lack of any rigorous underpinning theoretical analysis; and in part from her predisposition to be swayed by emotion. Such ambivalences inhere more generally too in the political perspectives of English radicalism in the twentieth century. It has been the moral imperative to achieve change, in Wilkinson's case *socialist* change, that has dominated many radicals' perspectives, rather than logical, structural analysis and consistent adherence to a political programme or political party.

Wilkinson's international activism intensified through the 1930s, largely in response to the growing threat of fascism. It was the Spanish Civil War that finally led Wilkinson to decide that 'she was a socialist first' rather than a pacifist, and that '"in Spain [she] would be with the workers on the barricades"'.[35] By 1937, she had come to back the Labour Party's position of support for 'collective security' and for the League of Nations.

She made numerous international visits to garner support for the anti-fascist cause: to the USA (twice), France, Germany and Spain. She was as heavily involved as anyone in the labour movement in campaigning for support for the Republicans in the Civil War; however, unlike Orwell and many others on the Left, she was hostile to the anarchists and such groups as the POUM. For the anarchists, the fight against fascism was secondary: their prime objective was to foment libertarian revolution. For her, the overriding objective was to win the war against the fascists. She saw the anarchists' position as at best diversionary. Whatever the rights and wrongs of this perspective, it does illustrate Wilkinson's continuing identification, in many policy areas, with the CP.

Not only did Wilkinson engage with the Spanish cause with great energy and persistence: she was emotionally and personally committed. As she wrote to Otto Katz in 1938: ' "Spain is draining me dry" '.[36] Franco's victory in 1939 was a devastating blow for everyone on the socialist Left; but Wilkinson was especially affected. Her health, never strong, deteriorated and she suffered from nervous exhaustion.

Wilkinson was a consistent campaigner for Popular Front politics: this *was* a consistent, coherent perspective. It was moral values and the attainment of a more egalitarian, more just, socialist society that was the objective. Wilkinson thus co-operated closely at various times with Conservative, upper-class women over 'women's issues' (as noted, with Nancy Astor and Lady Rhondda amongst others); at other times with radical churchmen (for example, Dick Sheppard and the Peace Pledge Union); and with Communists.

As the international crisis of the 1930s developed, Wilkinson became increasingly critical of appeasement and of Chamberlain's leadership. When Winston Churchill became Prime Minister in 1940 Wilkinson became an enthusiastic supporter, not only of the wartime coalition government, but of Churchill personally, as is discussed below. The defeat of Nazi Germany became for Wilkinson, as for many on the Left, *the* priority. And, from 1940 until her death in February 1947, Wilkinson became fully committed to 'the parliamentary road', to her role as a junior minister in the coalition government, and subsequently to the postwar Labour government as a Cabinet minister. She even became a (qualified) supporter of the British Empire. But she never lost her commitment to radical socialism, and consistently campaigned for a more egalitarian and more just society. It is to a consideration of her parliamentary career and what it tells us about her radicalism and how it changed and was articulated from the 1920s until her death that attention is now turned.

Parliamentary career: from radical backbencher to government minister

Wilkinson's parliamentary career began as an extension of her trade union activism. Her union, NUDAW, supported her nomination for Ashton-under-Lyne in 1922; although she lost the seat, she performed creditably, and was subsequently adopted for Middlesbrough East in 1924, for which she was subsequently elected. From then on, except for the years of Labour's disintegration, 1931 to 1935, following the 1931 crisis and the formation of the national government, Wilkinson remained an MP until her death.

She immediately proved to be a natural parliamentarian: a feisty, witty House of Commons performer, revelling in irreverence, and enjoying the limelight. For two years, 1924 to 1926, she was the only female Labour MP. (Susan Lawrence was elected in 1926.) However, in her early years, she was uneasy in her new role, for two primary reasons: first, she was indignant at all the arcane procedures of the Commons and wanted the Labour Party 'to stand for the "ending of all that show and theatrical glitter and tinsel"';[37] and secondly, and more importantly, she retained her belief that only through a combination of parliamentary and extra-parliamentary social-movement activism could fundamental socialist restructuring be attained. In a sense, she never resiled from this belief: but, slowly but surely as her seniority in the Labour Party increased, the balance shifted towards a concentration upon the *parliamentary* context. This was certainly the case after 1940, when her ministerial career began.

This has been one of the central tensions in the 'labourist mainstream' of English radicalism in the twentieth century. Tony Benn, for example, as discussed in Chapter 11, was the most prominent advocate of this 'marching on two legs' approach; at the same time, he was a passionate parliamentarian for most of his adult life.

Wilkinson was an excellent constituency MP. This role was not undertaken as a 'chore' or even a duty: she had a natural, emotional empathy with her own disadvantaged, poor and needy constituents. She always felt, with justification, that she came from their social milieu, that she understood, and had lived, their oppression. Many MPs regarded their constituency work, dealing with the largely prosaic concerns of local people, as a necessary evil: Wilkinson never did.

In 1929, with an enlarged electorate, Wilkinson increased her majority to a comfortable 3199. The Labour government depended upon Liberal support but Wilkinson argued that Labour should adopt socialist measures and 'appeal beyond parliament and ... mobilise opinion in favour of broad socialist policies'.[38] She distanced herself from the ILP and moved towards the Society for Socialist Inquiry and Propaganda (SSIP), the Labour Left pressure group involving, *inter alia*, the Coles, Lansbury and Cripps. She supported the Labour government during the early years of the Depression, but, as the economic and financial crisis deepened in 1931, opposed absolutely any suggested reduction in unemployment benefit.

Inevitably, Wilkinson lost her seat in the 1931 election, following the split at the top of the Labour government. Wilkinson, opposed only by a National Liberal, Ernest Young, a Tory '"decoy duck"' in her view,[39] lost by 6329 votes: even so, she received only 135 fewer votes than at the previous election.

In January 1932, Wilkinson was nominated by NUDAW as the Labour candidate for Jarrow, and was duly adopted. She was forever afterwards identified with Jarrow, and in particular the 'Jarrow March'. Three years before the March, in January 1933, she organised a well-supported 15-mile march to challenge the Prime Minister in his own constituency to protest at the closure of Palmer's shipyard. As the Depression deepened and unemployment grew, the Northern industrial areas suffered acute economic and industrial decline. The campaign in Jarrow centred on the blocking, by the bankers and the steel employers, of a proposed steelworks in the town.

Although the Jarrow March (or 'Crusade' as it is sometimes known) is associated largely with Wilkinson, the idea in reality came from local Labour councillors. Nevertheless, the March was masterminded by Wilkinson and it was she who handled adroitly what would now be termed the 'public relations' aspects: for example, all the men were smartly turned out, soberly dressed and serious in demeanour; they were led by David Riley, the Chairman of the Council, in a suit and bowler hat; and the organisers were careful to avoid any involvement with the CP or with the communist-backed National Unemployed Workers' Movement (NUWM). However, according to Vernon, it was the Council, rather than Wilkinson, which was responsible for the distancing from the NUWM. [40]

It was largely due to Wilkinson that the March came to represent 'Depression Britain' in the 1930s: and her considerable reputation with the general public as 'Red Ellen' owed much to the Jarrow March. The March from Jarrow to London began on 5 October 1936, receiving support and friendship from a wide variety of individuals and organisations *en route*, including the Co-operative Society, Territorial Army organisations and the Rotary Club. The government resolutely ignored the March; and Wilkinson, in tears, presented the eleven-thousand-signature petition to the 'Bar of the House', but with no success. Despite its initial failure, the March, like many other more sustained and prominent social-movement campaigns, had a lasting, long-term impact on Labour and radical culture. This has been a consistent aspect of radical activism in twentieth-century England (and elsewhere, of course). The absence of immediate, tangible successes for social-movement activism has often led to disillusionment, or 'movement fatigue'. On the other hand, such movements tend to erupt again, in response to external political events: each 'wave' of activism accretes a significant number of politicised, long-term radicals, and these movements build and consolidate.

Whatever else may or may not have been achieved by the Jarrow March, the Reverend Donald Soper was surely correct in observing that the March, and Wilkinson in particular, '"gave to the Labour Movement and to the political world the concept that unemployment is intolerable"'.[41] It is also the case that Wilkinson immersed herself, emotionally as well as politically, in Jarrow and its history, culture and political problems.

Wilkinson wrote several books, and much journalism, but her book on Jarrow is undoubtedly her most substantial and lasting work. *The Town that Was Murdered* was published by the Left Book Club in 1939.[42] Although she had assistance from a talented young researcher, George Bishop, later knighted as a successful industrialist, the book was very largely her own work.

Wilkinson situated her analysis within the international crisis of capitalist modernity. Her approach, though drawing on substantial historical research, was political and polemical. The tone is set in the opening lines of her Introduction. 'The poverty of the poor is not an accident, a temporary difficulty, a personal fault. It is the permanent state in which the vast majority of the citizens of any capitalist country have to live. That is the basic fact of the class struggle.'[43] Thus, she argued, a community and its worthwhile industries could be, and were, swept aside by the irrational vagaries of global capitalism. She employed her intellect, and historian's training, to contextualise the moral atrocities of unemployment, poverty and degradation which affected Jarrow. Not that her approach was confined to the present: she traced Jarrow's long history, its Roman origins, the pirate raids and the Norman Conquest, the monks of Jarrow and the influence of Bede. With the advent of the industrial revolution and the rapid development of the capitalist economy and its accompanying social structures, Jarrow, like many other towns in industrial areas, changed markedly.

In the nineteenth century, coal owners, and the local ruling elite as a whole, resisted any regulation and any attempts at trade union organisation; and they imposed archaic employment practices and low wages. Wilkinson emphasised the inherent dignity and moral steadfastness of the ordinary working people and their community; and she contrasted this with the oppression, hypocrisy and immorality of the capitalist ruling class.

From the mid-nineteenth century onwards, Palmer's shipyard brought employment and a measure of prosperity to the town, as the population grew. 'Challenging the image of Palmer cultivated over the decades as a great benefactor, Wilkinson observed that he saw no obligation to provide his company town with decent housing or social amenities. There was no water supply until 1864.' The result was 'squalor, epidemics and slums'.[44] In Wilkinson's view, there was little improvement until the outbreak of the First World War, when the shipbuilding industry expanded and Palmer's prospered.

The story of Palmer's after 1918 'provided a telling indictment' of the capitalist system.[45] After the boom came the slump: most small investors, including many of the workforce, lost all or most of their savings. Whilst Palmer's remained a high-quality, skilled shipbuilding firm, the vagaries of capitalism continually undermined its financial basis.

Wilkinson argued that Britain, as an island, maritime nation with an extensive empire, and a high level of both imports and exports, depended upon shipbuilding to counter the threat that Fascism posed. It could be argued, one of her biographers has observed, that Wilkinson had drifted ideologically 'from internationalism to national and imperial defence'.[46] The closure of Palmer's during the slump indicated to Wilkinson that the problems faced by the ravaged town – and by wider British society – could be solved only if the ' "workers took control of this country of ours. It is time that they planned it, organised it and developed it so that all might enjoy the wealth." '[47]

The book was thus both a detailed history of Jarrow and a passionate polemic: it was thus not a *scholarly* book, but it does indicate that 'Ellen's was a potent pen'.[48]

Wilkinson was returned as MP for Jarrow in 1935, with a majority of 2350 over her Conservative opponent, and remained as MP there until her death.[49] In 1935 she was the only female Labour MP; as noted, she had long had close relationships with those campaigning on women's equality issues in other parties. And, throughout the 1930s, she wrote regularly for publications such as *Time and Tide*: her network of socialist thinkers and writers, and feminist campaigners, became extensive, and was by no means confined to working-class or labour-movement activists.

She was, by common consent, an extremely accomplished House of Commons speaker. As one of her fellow MPs, Jack Lawson, recalled: '"In her voice was power and music with a tone like that of a well cast bell"; and her Commons performances were electrifying, "even though the despatch box was too high for her, and she had to stand aside from it."'[50] She was passionate, emotional and frequently moved to tears, often in public.

Most of Wilkinson's attention in the 1930s was directed to international affairs and the crises caused by the rise of fascism, as discussed in the previous section. She did, however, also devote time and energy to a number of domestic issues, especially in relation to the struggle for women's equality: for example, she led, effectively, the Joint Committee on Women in the Civil Service (JCW) campaign in Parliament from late 1935 through to the spring of 1936. She forced a debate and, surprisingly, her proposed amendment to secure equal pay for women civil servants, was carried. This victory was, however, short-lived: five days later the Prime Minister brought it back to the Commons and, effectively, made it a motion of confidence in the government: the decision was overturned, and women civil servants had to wait until 1956 to achieve this objective.

Wilkinson was bitterly critical of the appeasement policy of Chamberlain's government, and also of his reactionary domestic policies in face of the continuing economic and social hardships resulting from the long Depression. The situation changed markedly in the crisis of 1940 and the formation of the wartime national government led by Churchill. Wilkinson was appointed a junior minister, first and briefly as Parliamentary Secretary to the Ministry of Pensions and then as Parliamentary Secretary to Herbert Morrison, Home Secretary and Minister of Home Security.

Churchill was keen to have a broad coalition and for it to be seen and acknowledged as such. More to the point in the context of this study, Wilkinson's attitude to Churchill, and to a lesser extent her politics as a whole, underwent a transformation, as noted earlier. In the past she had regarded him as the quintessential class enemy: a heartless oppressor of the poor and needy. Her view changed radically in the 1930s: Wilkinson revelled in Churchill's oratorical, parliamentary skills, and enthused over his debates in the Commons with Philip Snowden: the '"large smiling, expansive Winston" could impulsively shape a brilliant speech from "half a fact and a couple of rumours"'.[51] 'She was loyal to Winston Churchill in a way she never was to Clement Attlee.'[52] She enthusiastically advocated the broadest Popular Front coalition, from 'Pollitt to Churchill'. And not long before her death, when she received a plaque commemorating the coalition, she recalled the time when '"we served our Captain to save Britain" and how those "great days" had eclipsed other memories'.[53]

Although she never lost her socialist zeal and her passionate advocacy of social justice and equality, it is the case that her socialist internationalism changed during the war years into a qualified support for the British Empire and for the defence of Britain as the primary objective. Some critics, both at the time (Kingsley Martin, for example) and currently (one of her recent biographers, Matt Perry, for example), have seen this as a clear shift to the Right. However, circumstances, especially in the critical years 1940 and 1941, were extreme, maybe unique. Britain *did* stand virtually alone for a time against Nazism; Churchill *was* a great war leader. And in an essay of 1941, Wilkinson argued that Nazism had come to the fore as big business's response to the threat of socialism in the era of mass production.[54] This was hardly a right-wing perspective. In the view of another of her biographers, Laura Beers, Wilkinson's Marxist analysis continued to be central and 'acted as a spur to her politics'.[55]

Whatever the rights and wrongs of Wilkinson's change of perspective in her final years, there is no doubt that she was an extremely effective and courageous Home Office minister. She had a real rapport with the working class in the great cities whose communities were subjected to persistent bombing from the Luftwaffe. She was responsible for the shelters policy and personally oversaw the opening up of the London tube stations (and made sure that they were equipped with sanitation and were safe and reasonably comfortable, especially for women). As always, she worked tirelessly and visited frequently not only the East End in London but also the suffering communities in Coventry, Glasgow and other cities, and was often personally exposed to considerable danger. Wilkinson was responsible for the Firewatchers and, controversially, introduced conscription for women to join the service.

Although she was under pressure to visit the USA to boost support for US entry into the war, Churchill 'refused to let Wilkinson go as her work in Britain, primarily maintaining morale in the face of the Luftwaffe, was vital'.[56] Wilkinson wore herself out during the war. There was a streak of restlessness, even obsessiveness, in her character; and she began to suffer a series of accidents – car crashes, nearly drowning. But she ignored her frequent illnesses and consequently had to go to hospital. Winifred Horrabin noted that '"she looks so ill and small and weary"'.[57]

Following the victory in Europe in May 1945, Labour decided (against Attlee's advice) to opt for an immediate general election. Wilkinson was chair of the Party's NEC and thus presided at the May 1945 Conference and delivered a stirring and passionate opening address. It was, in Philip Noel Baker's view, '"Ellen's finest hour. No one will ever forget the nerve, the verve, the wit, the confidence and the joyful challenge with which she led the Conference."'[58]

Wilkinson was centrally involved in the ensuing campaign. She wrote an influential Labour Party election pamphlet, *Plan for Peace: How People Can Win the Peace*, and she co-authored the election manifesto, *Let Us Face the Future*, with Michael Young, Herbert Morrison and Patrick Gordon Walker. She was the only woman of the nine Labour politicians selected to deliver party political broadcasts, and Mass Observation 'found that [her] speech had the broadest sociological appeal'.[59]

Labour won a historic victory in 1945; and Attlee proceeded to lead what was by common consent one of the greatest and most important administrations in modern British history.[60] Nevertheless, Wilkinson continued to intrigue to replace Attlee as leader with Herbert Morrison, a campaign she had been waging – more or less openly – for some years. (This is partly explained, perhaps, by the strong likelihood that she and Morrison had had a long-running affair.)[61]

Nevertheless, Attlee appointed Wilkinson to his Cabinet as Secretary of State for Education. (He had originally intended that she should become Minister of Health, in the event a post held by Aneurin Bevan, the architect of the National Health Service.) Attlee, always astute, saw the necessity for having an able woman in his Cabinet; he saw Wilkinson as an ' "enthusiast for education" '; and 'it seems that her allies were powerful enough, her reputation strong enough and Attlee magnanimous enough to include her'.[62]

Despite her heavy new ministerial responsibilities, and her worsening health, Wilkinson continued with her relentless political travelling to support her lifelong internationalism, including exhausting tours to Germany's devastated communities. In common with many other former communists and/or Marxist intellectuals, she focused much more upon an 'idealist logic of the inculcation of a new generation in a culture of peace-making'[63] than upon quasi-Leninist theories of war and imperialism. Indeed, by this stage, again like many other former communists, she had distanced herself completely from Stalinist Russia.

One of her most significant final international commitments was to UNESCO, at whose inaugural meeting she took the chair and spoke, with passion and commitment; and she was instrumental in the appointment of Julian Huxley as the organisation's first Director General.[64]

Her main responsibility, however, lay with the education brief. Her main task, and a formidable one with far-reaching consequences lasting well into the twenty-first century, was to implement the 1944 (Butler) Education Act, or a slightly modified version of it. The two key proposals were: the reorganisation of the state secondary system into grammar, technical and (secondary) modern schools, with the destination of children being decided via the 11 plus examination; and the raising of the school leaving age (ROSLA).

The '11 plus' selection process channelled children at an early age into 'academic', 'vocational' or 'general' schools. Subsequent history would suggest, at least to those of a socialist or generally egalitarian bent, that the proposals were fundamentally flawed. Be this as it may, the task was undoubtedly administratively complex. Wilkinson's 1946 Education Act conscientiously attempted to begin the process of implementation, but she was never an enthusiast.

Even allowing for her understandably somewhat lukewarm attitude to the reorganisation, Wilkinson's 1946 Act failed to address some key aspects of educational inequality. It entrenched the provision of state funding for religious (Christian) schools; and it did nothing to reduce the privileged position of the public (independent) schools, still less lay the foundations for their abolition. (But then neither has any subsequent Labour government broached this sensitive area.)

For Wilkinson, the focus was rather upon ROSLA: she had been inspired by R.H. Tawney's address to one hundred Labour MPs as early as February 1930, emphasising the importance of this measure. Not only would it reduce unemployment: more importantly, it was, for Wilkinson, a 'basic matter of social justice'.[65]

Wilkinson's educational ideas derived from her own overall political ideology, and personal educational experience. She was suspicious of any emphasis upon vocational, instrumental education, believing that this was often used to buttress the class-confirming, inegalitarian culture of British society. As she put it graphically in a 1927 article, such an approach had the implicit aim 'of making good little bricklayers for local industry rather than good citizens'.[66] Wilkinson was thus emotionally and fundamentally a believer in critical, liberal education whose primary policy objectives should be to enhance social, political and cultural knowledge and understanding, and to build a vibrant, critical and informed democracy.

She had a long association with the NCLC and its General Secretary, J.P.M. Millar; and was suspicious of the larger, more influential and institutionalised Workers' Educational Association (WEA). This conception of adult education as a social movement, intimately linked not only to the labour movement but to broader movements for cultural, social and political emancipation, was an important aspect of English radicalism in the twentieth century.[67] Education in this context, and particularly socially committed adult education, has been seen as a key cultural formation in the struggle to radicalise, in democratic forms, the existing culture; and many of the leading proponents of twentieth-century English radicalism were involved with adult education.

Given the number of adverse contextual factors noted, and of course the extremely restricted resources available in the aftermath of the war, Wilkinson's record of achievement as Secretary of State was creditable and significant. This was not the verdict of some observers at the time, or of some later analysts. The Chief Education Officer for the North Riding of Yorkshire, Frank Barraclough, for example, claimed that she '"was no longer the Red Ellen I had admired in the 1930s ... from being an important Crusader, Ellen became mainly a sick and ailing administrative Minister"'.[68] And it is probably the case that Wilkinson did not have a comprehensive, theorised position on socialist education policy: compare her, in this respect, with Anthony Crosland or Shirley Williams. However, as has been noted throughout this chapter, Wilkinson was neither a theorist nor did she have a consistent, intellectually coherent approach to politics. Her (considerable) strengths and virtues lay elsewhere.

Nevertheless, given the difficult context, I would reiterate that her record is creditable, especially in the light of the serious deterioration in her health. Wilkinson introduced the provision of daily free milk for all school children in 1946 – a real health benefit, especially for children from poorer families – which continued until, notoriously, Margaret Thatcher reversed this policy in her term as Secretary of State for Education in the 1970 Heath government ('Margaret Thatcher, Milk Snatcher', as the Opposition slogan had it at the time). Also, Wilkinson secured the extension of maintenance grants and state scholarships, via Local Education Authorities, for a greater number of able students from modest backgrounds to go to university.

Her own experience of a grammar school education, and the opportunities thus opened up for her, influenced her views profoundly. Her emotional commitment to egalitarianism conflicted with her equally profound belief in a meritocratic educational system. Without her grammar school, she would probably not have had a political career at all. At an emotional level, she was thus resistant to the proposals to have a fully comprehensive schools structure. Although she reduced the number of grammar schools, and she insisted on their taking more non-fee-paying pupils, she defended strongly the viability and legitimacy of such schools. Moreover, there was, at this period, no groundswell of support for a fully comprehensive secondary system, in the Labour Party or elsewhere. Such ideas were largely confined to the more radical educational experts. The '"grammar school was still regarded as the 'way-in' for the bright boys [sic]"'.[69]

Her educational credo, and her romanticism about education, are perhaps best summed up in her Foreword to *The New Secondary Education* (published posthumously as a government paper in 1947): '"Everything to do with children must have room to grow ... Schools must have freedom to experiment ... Laughter in the classroom, self confidence growing every day, eager interest instead of bored uniformity, this is the way to produce the Britons who will have no need to fear the new scientific age, but will stride into it, heads high, determined to master science and to serve mankind."'[70] Moreover, she believed that *all* children should have access to the arts: literature, foreign languages and, especially, history. The ruling orders were apprehensive, she believed, that, if history were taught properly, critically, intelligent children would ask awkward questions: as she put it in a personal note on an early draft of *The New Secondary Education*, '"Don't worry how we got India, let's go and do some nice work at the forge!"'[71]

In hard, practical terms, her greatest achievement was the raising of the school leaving age to 15. This was no mean feat. Although the policy had been agreed in principle by the Labour government, significant extra resources were required for actual implementation: thirteen thousand more teachers and abut two hundred thousand more secondary school places. Given the extreme pressure on the economy, the pressing demands for other public expenditure and the severe austerity of postwar Britain, there was considerable pressure to defer any extension. Wilkinson fought with great tenacity, and although she had influential support from outside the government, most notably from R.H. Tawney who welcomed this '"bold and decisive announcement"',[72] she had to contend with 'heavyweight' opposition in Cabinet, including both Cripps and Morrison. She eventually won, though only after she and several other Cabinet Ministers had threatened resignation over the issue; and implementation was agreed for 1 April 1947.

Her very last ministerial engagement was, fittingly, to preside at the opening of the Old Vic Theatre School on 15 January 1947. The weather was icy cold, the venue was open to the sky. Wilkinson contracted pneumonia and she died on 6 February 1947. There were persistent rumours, both at the time and since, that, disheartened politically, overwhelmed with work and weakened by prolonged illness, she took her own life. There can be no definitive view on this, though the official inquest recorded a verdict of accidental death: but the overwhelming probability is that she died as a result of her illness and an accidental overdose of the pills that gave her at least some relief from her persistent asthma. In the end, she simply drove herself too hard: a tragic, heroic figure, dedicated to the socialist cause in which she had so fervently believed all her life.

Wilkinson's national and international reputation, and the widespread affection for her, are indicated by the large number of condolences received from all over the world; and by the attendance at her national memorial service of King George VI, the Prime Minister (Attlee) and most of the Cabinet, the Archbishop of Canterbury and Winston Churchill.

Conclusion

It remains to attempt an assessment of Wilkinson's contribution to English radicalism, and her impact upon the labour movement and socialist development.

At the core of Wilkinson's lifelong and total commitment to the socialist cause lay a simple but profound morality: for her, politics was about justice and equality, and the creation of a society where free individuals would be encouraged to develop to their full potential through involvement in education and, in the widest sense, cultural life. Complementary to this moral core, Wilkinson always believed in and practised a humanitarian internationalism.

As one of her biographers has noted, Wilkinson is not easily classifiable.[73] In part, this is because she was never a theorist, nor was she a deep or reflective thinker. Indeed, she could at times be 'muddled and confused'; and, worse, gullible.[74] She was always a socialist, a (particular type of) feminist, and an internationalist; and, as noted, at different periods an active trade unionist, a syndicalist, a revolutionary; and she was too an able parliamentarian and latterly, a minister from 1940 until her death. Despite becoming a leading political figure both nationally and in Westminster, 'her radicalism remained a crucial part of her political identity'.[75]

Generally, English radicalism, in the twentieth century and before, was characterised by a strong moral imperative; and has been correspondingly weak on theoretical analysis. The moral bases of her socialism, her humanitarianism and her internationalism derived from her initial Methodist grounding. Her socialism thus had much in common with the ILP, as was the case with many working-class socialists.[76] It was the moral and political objectives, and the consequent campaigning, that were seen as primary: the *means* used to attain these objectives were secondary and 'fluid'. Hence there is a logic, in its own terms, for Wilkinson's involvement over time in a variety of organisations and theoretical structures, even though some of them were clearly incompatible.

However appealing and likeable a character Wilkinson may have been – and there is no doubt that she *did* inspire almost all of those who knew her, across the political spectrum – such an approach also exemplifies one of the key weaknesses of English radicalism in the twentieth century. Without clear, cogent analysis, and without dealing with the key question of 'agency', radicalism is liable to become, like Wilkinson, 'muddled and confused'.

In the end, like several others considered in this book, Wilkinson 'chose to work within the structures of political power, believing that parliamentary democracy was a more effective route for radical activists than criticising and organising from outside'. For Wilkinson, the Labour Party, in Parliament, could offer a way forward if it 'would only decide to be more courageous'.[77] It must also be acknowledged that the powerful culture of Parliament itself not only became congenial to Wilkinson, it became an essential aspect of her self-identity. Especially after 1940, Parliament became her natural political home.

Despite these unresolved dilemmas, and despite huge setbacks for the working class and for the cause of socialism in her lifetime, Wilkinson's achievements were remarkable: not least, given her working-class origins and her struggles as a woman in a male-dominated culture, her resilience and political adroitness in rising through the ranks of the labour movement and the Parliamentary Labour Party, to high office. Personally, she was not without her faults: but, like Barbara Castle, her occasional hot temper and impetuosity were more than compensated for by a generosity of spirit; ' "the kindest and most generous friend that anyone had the good fortune to possess" ',[78] as one of her close friends observed. She was a ' "heroic and lovable figure, with integrity and first rate moral and physical courage" ',[79] a socialist and a democrat to her fingertips. She had a warmth and a natural rapport with working-class people, unmatched by any other Labour figure of her time; and she had an unquenchable belief in the essential goodness of humanity, given the right sort of social and economic conditions.

Notes

1 L. Beers, *Red Ellen: The Life of Ellen Wilkinson, Socialist, Feminist, Internationalist* (Cambridge, MA: Harvard University Press, 2016), p. 3.
2 B. Vernon, *Ellen Wilkinson 1891–1947* (Croom Helm, 1982), p. 6. She was in fact 4 ft 10 in.

3 Ibid., Preface; p. 1; p. 75; p. 237.
4 Beers, *Red Ellen*, p. 231.
5 M. Perry, *'Red Ellen' Wilkinson: Her Ideas, Movements and World* (Manchester: Manchester University Press, 2014), p. 3 (the description was recalled by Lady Juliette Huxley).
6 For example, in the trade union movement; see ibid., pp. 119ff.
7 P. Bartley, 'Ellen Wilkinson (Red Ellen) Wilkinson: From Suffragist to Government Minister', *Theory and Struggle*, Journal of the Marx Memorial Library 117, 2016, p. 76.
8 Vernon, *Wilkinson*, p. 117.
9 Perry, *Wilkinson*, p. 104.
10 K.O. Morgan, *Labour People: Leaders and Lieutenants, Hardie to Kinnock* (Oxford: Oxford University Press, 1987), p. 101, cited in ibid., p. 2; similarly, one of her recent biographers judges that 'In her day "Red Ellen" as she became known, was arguably the most famous, certainly the most outspoken British woman politician'. P. Bartley *Ellen Wilkinson: From Red Suffragist to Government Minister* (Pluto Press, 2014), p. xi.
11 Vernon, *Wilkinson*, p. 1.
12 Ibid., p. 17.
13 E. Wilkinson, *Methodist Recorder*, 16 March 1939, cited in ibid., p. 19.
14 E. Wilkinson, *Myself When Young*, cited in Vernon, *Wilkinson*, p. 9.
15 Vernon, *Wilkinson*, p. 28, citing Wilkinson's address to the Annual Meeting of the NCLC, 1924. Wilkinson retained her close involvement with the NCLC for the rest of her life. Her close personal, probably sexual, relationship with J.F. Horrabin, editor of *Plebs*, the journal of the NCLC, was no doubt one element, but only one, in this persisting support for the organisation.
16 For a highly critical account of Newbold, and his strange subsequent career, see Vernon, *Wilkinson*, pp. 35–8.
17 Perry, *Wilkinson*, p. 21.
18 Ibid., p. 24.
19 Ibid.
20 Wilkinson, *The Communist*, 27 August 1921, cited in ibid., p. 27.
21 Perry, *Wilkinson*, p. 56.
22 Vernon, *Wilkinson*, p. 64.
23 See ibid., pp. 119–32.
24 Wilkinson, 'Introduction', in S. Nearing, *The British General Strike* (New York, 1926), p. xviii, cited in Perry, *Wilkinson*, p. 138.
25 Plebs journal, June 1926, cited in Perry, *Wilkinson*, p. 140.
26 Beers, *Red Ellen*, pp. 4, 455.
27 Ibid., p. 40.
28 Perry, *Wilkinson*, p. 76.
29 AUCE journal, 1917.
30 Wilkinson, *People*, 21 June 1926, cited in Perry, *Wilkinson*, p. 79.
31 Wilkinson, *Tribune*, 8 July 1938, cited in Perry, *Wilkinson*, p. 95.
32 Perry, *Wilkinson*, p. 155.
33 Ibid., p. 170.
34 Ibid., p. 157, citing Wilkinson, *Time and Tide*, 28 December 1935.

35 Ibid., p. 186.
36 Letter to Katz (n.d. October/November 1938), cited in ibid. p. 337.
37 Perry, *Wilkinson*, p. 205.
38 Ibid., p. 222.
39 *North Eastern Daily Gazette*, 12 October 1931, cited in ibid., p. 226.
40 Vernon, *Wilkinson*, p. 142.
41 Soper, cited in Vernon, *Wilkinson*, p. 137.
42 E. Wilkinson, *The Town that Was Murdered: The Life Story of Jarrow* (Left Book Club, Gollancz, 1939).
43 Ibid., p. 7.
44 Perry, *Wilkinson*, p. 287.
45 Ibid., p. 288.
46 Ibid.
47 Wilkinson, *The Town that Was Murdered*, p. 284, cited in ibid., p. 289.
48 Vernon, *Wilkinson*, p. 137.
49 There was only one general election in this period, in 1945. Wilkinson was elected with an increased majority of 11,007.
50 Jack Lawson MP, in *Methodist Magazine*, April 1947, cited in Vernon, *Wilkinson*, p. 85.
51 Wilkinson, *Time and Tide*, 16 April 1932, cited in Perry, *Wilkinson*, p. 351.
52 Bartley, *Wilkinson: Red Suffragist to Government Minister*, p. 120.
53 Churchill Archive CHUR2 495 Wilkinson to Churchill, 22 June 1946, cited in Perry, *Wilkinson*, p. 351.
54 E. Wilkinson, 'Social Justice', in Fabian Society, *Programme for Victory: A Collection of Essays Prepared for the Fabian Society*, London, 1941.
55 Beers, *Red Ellen*, p. 447.
56 Perry, *Wilkinson*, p. 361.
57 W. Horrabin, Notebook, Personal Notes, Psychology, 1945, cited in ibid., p. 363.
58 P. Noel Baker, Labour Party Conference Annual Report 1953, cited in Vernon, *Wilkinson*, p. 196.
59 Perry, *Wilkinson*, p. 366.
60 See, for varying accounts, R. Miliband, *Parliamentary Socialism: A Study in the Politics of Labour* (second edition, Merlin Press, 1973), especially chapter IX, 'The Climax of Labourism'; K.O. Morgan, *Labour in Power 1945–1951* (Oxford: Oxford University Press, 1984); A. Sked and C. Cook, *Post-War Britain: A Political History* (Penguin, 1979).
61 For varying accounts of the relationship between Wilkinson and Morrison, see Vernon, *Wilkinson*, pp. 126–9, 236–8; Bartley, *Wilkinson*, pp. 98–9; Beers, *Red Ellen*, pp. 386–7.
62 Perry, *Wilkinson*, p. 368.
63 Ibid., p. 371.
64 Wilkinson also chaired the first meeting of UNESCO's preparatory convention on 18 January 1946. For Wilkinson, UNESCO's significance was 'that it could disseminate an approach to culture and education so that the child could conceive of a world without war and learn the economic, political, social and cultural interdependence of the world'. Ibid.
65 Ibid., p. 374.
66 Wilkinson, *New Leader*, 29 July 1927, cited in ibid., p. 373.

67 See for example, R. Fieldhouse, *A History of Modern British Adult Education* (Leicester: NIACE, 1996); R. Taylor and T. Steele, *British Labour and Higher Education 1945–2000: Ideologies, Policies and Practice* (Continuum Studies in Educational Research, 2011); K. Ward and R. Taylor (eds), *Adult Education and the Working Class: Education for the Missing Millions* (Croom Helm, 1986; and Routledge, second edition, 2012); and L. Goldman, *Dons and Workers. Oxford and Adult Education Since 1850* (Oxford: Oxford University Press, 1995).
68 Letter from Barraclough to D. Reid, 25 September 1974, cited in Perry, *Wilkinson*, p. 374.
69 Lord Goronwy Roberts, interview with B. Vernon, cited in Vernon, *Wilkinson*, p. 218.
70 Wilkinson, 'Foreword' to *The New Secondary Education*, HMSO, Pamphlet No. 9, 1947, cited in *ibid.*, p. 221.
71 Wilkinson, cited in ibid., p. 223.
72 Letter from Wilkinson to Attlee, citing Tawney's support in a letter to her, Bodleian Library, University of Oxford, ms. 23.171, 5 October 1945, cited in Perry, *Wilkinson*, p. 381
73 Bartley, *Wilkinson*, pp. 134ff.
74 Vernon, *Wilkinson*, p. 236.
75 Beers, *Red Ellen*, pp. 454–5.
76 See, for example, S.H. Beer, *Modern British Politics* (Faber and Faber, 1965); and Tom Nairn, 'The Nature of the Labour Party', in P. Anderson and R. Blackburn (eds), *Towards Socialism* (Fontana and New Left Books, 1965), pp. 159–220.
77 Bartley, *Wilkinson*, p. 139.
78 Susan Lawrence, interview with Margaret Cole, *Fabian Quarterly*, February 1947, cited in Vernon, *Wilkinson*, p. 237.
79 Lord Redcliff-Maud, cited in Vernon, *Wilkinson*, p. 237.

6

George Orwell

Orwell was fundamentally *English* in his persona and ideology; and wholly *radical*, within the context of the English radical tradition. Although he died in early 1950, what he wrote and, still more, what he stood for – or what has been interpreted as standing for – have a contemporary relevance. His major works have never been out of print and continue to reach new generations, and address vividly some of the central political and ideological issues of the modern world. If any single person can be said to embody twentieth-century English radicalism, it is George Orwell.

For most of his short life, he was a fairly obscure figure. It was only after the publication of his two most famous books, *Animal Farm* and *Nineteen Eighty-Four*, that he became well-known, and financially solvent.[1] (His posthumous fame exceeded by far anything he had experienced in his lifetime.) There has been 'an avalanche of critical and biographical studies ... Orwell [has] joined that shelf of authors who had far more written about them than they wrote themselves'.[2]

What was it that caught the imagination, that touched the political and moral concerns, of such large numbers of people, not only in Britain but across the Western world (and Communist Eastern Europe)? And what precisely was the nature of his English radicalism?

Orwell was essentially a 'political writer': as Crick emphasises, both words are of equal weight.[3] Writing in 1946, Orwell reflected that: 'What I have most wanted to do throughout the past ten years is to make political writing into an art'.[4] Although he claimed, regretfully, that in 'a peaceful age I might have written ornate or merely descriptive books, and might have remained almost unaware of my political loyalties', he became increasingly convinced that he had no alternative, in the troubled times in which he lived, but to concentrate upon politically committed writing.

'Every line of serious work that I have written since 1936 has been written, directly or indirectly, *against* totalitarianism and *for* democratic Socialism.'[5]

These two commitments lay at the centre of Orwell's political identity. One of the common mistakes of interpretation in relation to Orwell is the claim that he was primarily if not exclusively a polemical critic of communism and, in effect, an apologist for Western capitalism in the Cold War context of the later 1940s. Even Thompson, in his perceptive polemic 'Outside the Whale', comes close to this caricature of Orwell's position:

> Orwell is like a man who is raw all down one side and numb on the other. He is sensitive – sometimes obsessionally so – to the least insincerity upon his left, but the inhumanity of the right rarely provoked him to a paragraph of polemic. To the right ('decent people', 'average thinking person'), every allowance; to the left ('bearded fruit-juice drinkers who come flocking towards the smell of "progress" like bluebottles to a dead cat'), no quarter.[6]

Orwell was certainly opposed to Stalinist communism, and bitterly scornful of those intellectuals on the Left who had given support to this totalitarian ideology and its many atrocities through the 1930s and 1940s: but it is resoundingly evident that he opposed with equal vehemence the evil of fascism and Nazism, and had fundamental criticisms too of the Americanised capitalism of the West. The 'message' of *Nineteen Eighty-Four* is not a fatalistic pessimism about a future Stalinist state. It is rather, in his own words, a *warning*. 'The moral to be drawn from this dangerous nightmare situation is a simple one: *Don't let it happen. It depends on you.*'[7]

Orwell's commitment to democratic socialism was equally profound but it was hedged around with qualifications; moreover, it was a position he took some time to reach. Significantly, the only mainstream British politician 'whom Orwell thoroughly respected, partially identified with and whose ear he would like to have had'[8] was Aneurin Bevan, perhaps the most eloquent proponent of democratic socialism that Britain has produced.[9]

The focus of this chapter is upon the nature of Orwell's political commitments and his considerable contributions to English radicalism. However, there is an intrinsic connection between his politics, his life experience and activism, and his writing. The political discussion is thus preceded by a brief biographical outline.

Life and the formation of values

Orwell, originally Eric Blair, was born in Bengal in 1903 into what he termed '"the lower-upper-middle class", the shabby genteel "poor whites" of the English social system'.[10] His father was 'a servant of the Empire', working in the Opium Department in India, in Burma as a policeman and later serving in the First World War; and his mother was a half-French member of a commercial family in India. In

1904, she returned to England with her three children, her husband remaining in the subcontinent until his retirement in 1911.

After an unhappy time at a boarding preparatory school, recalled in exaggerated but evocative and grim detail in his subsequent essay, 'Such, Such Were the Joys',[11] Orwell gained a scholarship to Eton, which he attended from 1917 to 1921. On leaving, the only way he would have been able to pursue the 'traditional' route to Oxford or Cambridge was by gaining a scholarship. His father was, at best, lukewarm about university and Orwell (Eric) himself was certainly 'not set ... enough to want to swot'.[12] Instead, he followed his father, and joined the Imperial Police in Burma. Although he was there only from 1922 to 1927, the experience was formative. He went to Burma as something of a loner, anti-authority and with vaguely radical inclinations. His experience in Burma made him a passionate, lifelong opponent of imperialism (and provided the framework for his novel *Burmese Days*).[13]

At Eton, as he recalled in *The Road to Wigan Pier*, 'I seem to have spent half the time in denouncing the capitalist system and the other half in raging against the insolence of bus conductors'.[14] After Burma, his rejection of established society and its mores was based on firmer ground. His opposition to class inequality and racial discrimination, so blatantly apparent in Burma, and to cruelty and philistinism, remained central to Orwell's politics. In Burma, he acquired '"an immense weight of guilt that I had got to expiate". It would be fair to say that he spent the second half of his life trying to do just that.'[15]

Yet he was in no coherent sense at this stage a socialist. His politics rested on his advocacy of justice, fairness and human dignity, values that were at least partly inheritances of his solidly bourgeois background and educational environment.

He worked hard to become a writer, but also was determined to experience at first hand a different, harsher life which would contrast with the stultifying conformity of his parents' milieu. He lived rough in Paris and London, suffering with some masochism the extremes of poverty and degradation. The result, in literary terms, was the still remarkable book *Down and Out in Paris and London*.[16] Working briefly as a private school teacher (which he hated) and as a bookshop assistant from 1934 to 1936, he began publishing articles and became a moderately successful journalist, producing 'efficient reviews and impressive essays'.[17] In addition to *Burmese Days*, he published three further novels: *A Clergyman's Daughter*, *Keep the Aspidistra Flying* and, the most successful in literary as well as ideological terms, *Coming Up for Air*.[18]

However, it was through his political and socially committed writing, and subsequently his essays, that Orwell became well-known. More importantly, it was this aspect of his writing that both articulated and defined his politics. As one of his biographers, Gordon Bowker, has claimed: as 'a novelist Orwell had his shortcomings... [but as] an essayist he was supreme'.[19] It is because he 'reflected a peculiar English version of commonsense and decency',[20] and because he wrote with such appealing clarity and honesty that his essays and polemical pieces have survived and are still read today. (These aspects of Orwell's achievement are returned to below.)

His first substantial work of this type was *The Road to Wigan Pier*, the first part of which was a study of working-class life in the industrial North of England in early 1936, and the contrasting degradation and steadfast decency of the people he encountered. The second part was an idiosyncratic, passionate, confused and much-quoted credo of Orwell's beliefs. But it was his experiences in the Spanish Civil War, where he volunteered to fight with the Republican forces against the fascist insurrection, that formed the basis of his subsequent libertarian socialism. As Crick observed:

> Orwell did believe in socialism before, as *The Road to Wigan Pier* and reviews written at that time prove. But he did not '*really* believe': it had been an intellectual matter and a moral compassion for other people's sufferings. In Catalonia he experienced it for himself. He was no longer condescending, he was engulfed in comradeship.[21]

Seriously injured in Spain, and already suffering from the lung disease which was to kill him (exacerbated by his lifelong smoking habit), he was deemed unfit for service in the Second World War. He joined the Home Guard from 1940 to 1943, and worked for the BBC as a Talks Assistant and Talks Producer for the India section of the Eastern Service from 1941 to 1943, and then as Literary Editor of *Tribune* from 1943 to 1944.

He had a chequered sexual life.[22] Even one of his staunchest advocates, Christopher Hitchens, has a chapter entitled 'Orwell and the Feminists: Difficulties with Girls'.[23] Hitchens's opening sentence sets the tone for the ensuing discussion: 'George Orwell's relationship with the female sex was in general a distraught one, and he had a tendency to let it show.'[24] He had difficulties, too, with women characters in his novels. There are few strong female characters and none, with the arguable exception of Julia in *Nineteen Eighty-Four*, shows 'the least trace of intellectual or reflective capacity'.[25] On the other hand, it has to be acknowledged that he married, happily, a spirited and intellectually capable woman, Eileen O'Shaughnessy, in 1936. Orwell believed himself to be sterile. Whether or not this was the case, they did not have children and, in 1944, they adopted a son, Richard. Eileen died, unexpectedly, undergoing a relatively minor operation in 1945.

There are other questionable aspects of Orwell's writing and personal character. In his early years especially, he was, on occasion, anti-Semitic; however, by the late 1930s he was a consistent and vocal opponent of anti-Semitism in general and of the extreme Right's anti-Semitism in particular. He gave voice to this in his 1945 article 'Anti-Semitism in Britain'.[26] However, temperamentally, there remained a strain of anti-Semitism in his outlook. In the view of his longstanding friend Malcolm Muggeridge, ' "he was at heart strongly anti-Semitic" '.[27] In another context altogether, some of the criticisms of his historical inaccuracies and perceived condescension to working-class, Communist Party (CP) volunteers in the International Brigade in the Spanish Civil War would seem to carry weight.[28]

Overwhelmingly, though, his was an eloquent, persistent voice on behalf of decency, fairness, equality and justice in a hostile context. Moreover, unlike many on the Left, he acted courageously in trying repeatedly to put his values and beliefs into practice.

Orwell at last achieved real fame with the publication in 1945 of the superlative, bitter and deeply moving allegory *Animal Farm*. This was followed by his most famous book, *Nineteen Eighty-Four*, completed, largely in 'retreat' on the Isle of Jura, with great difficulty because of his rapidly deteriorating health. He went into hospital in 1949 in London, where he married Sonia Brownell, shortly before his death on 21 January 1950, aged 46.

An English socialist

Orwell's socialism emerged and developed from his life experience. He was a principled, pragmatic moralist, not a theoretician. At no stage in his life did he formulate his position into a coherent and all-embracing analysis. Similarly, although latterly generally supportive of the Labour Party, he had no interest in 'party politics' or 'politicking', and still less in the world of Westminster intrigues and party positioning.

His politics was, rather, grounded on two of the basic perspectives of English radicalism: liberal, humanistic moral principles; and 'common sense', empirical, arguments from contingent political factors. The first of these led him to focus, as noted, upon the core values of justice, fairness, decency and equality. The 'contingent political factors' of this fraught period led him, secondly, to devote himself through his writing to oppose Fascism and Nazism in the 1930s and 1940s; and subsequently, with equal vehemence, to oppose the rise of totalitarianism in Stalin's Soviet Union. Moreover, it was the *intellectual culture* underlying this ideology that was, in Orwell's view, as dangerous as the directly political aspects of communism: and it was the horrors of such totalitarian culture that was so vividly realised in dramatic form in *Animal Farm* and *Nineteen Eighty-Four*.

From the time of *The Road to Wigan Pier*, and still more after his experiences in Spain, Orwell defined himself as the 'plain, blunt, honest man – a friend not of "the people", certainly not of "the proletariat", but of the "common man"'.[29] He 'set himself up to be "the conscience of the Left" … subverting the pomposity of both statesmen and intellectuals'.[30]

This self-image was closely related to Orwell's near obsession with class. He was all too aware of his relatively privileged class position and was conscious too that 'England is the most class-ridden country under the sun' ('The Lion and the Unicorn'). England, more so than other parts of Britain, was 'a land of snobbery and privilege, ruled largely by the old and silly'. He was consistently dismissive of the English ruling class, characterised by what he termed the 'Blimp' mentality. In the same essay, for example, he argued that, since the mid-nineteenth century, 'somehow the ruling class decayed, lost its ability, its daring, finally even its ruthlessness …'. By the 1920s and 1930s, the incompetence of the ruling class had become risible: Baldwin could not even be dignified with the epithet of a 'stuffed shirt. He was simply a hole in the air.' How was it, Orwell asked rhetorically, that between 1931 and 1939, 'at every decisive moment ... every British statesman [did] the wrong thing with so unerring an instinct?' His answer was that, because they no longer had any objectively viable role, they had become 'an entirely functionless class ... simply parasites ... Clearly there was only one escape for them-into stupidity. They could keep society in its existing shape only by being *unable* to grasp that any improvement was possible.'[31]

This dismissive attitude was surely at least partially incorrect: the ruling class has shown itself to be remarkably adept at changing its culture, priorities and political 'principles' to attune to rapidly changing circumstances. However appealing Orwell's caricature may have been, the harsh realities of capitalist power are rather more complex. But the ruling class and its inadequacies were not in fact the main target for his critique. His real venom was reserved for the communist-inclined middle-class intelligentsia; and this mirrored his veneration for the idealised working class. Two still vivid caricatures from *The Road to Wigan Pier* serve to illustrate his perspective on the former, the middle-class intelligentsia. He characterised the typical socialist not as a working-class 'rabble-rouser' but as:

> either a youthful snob-Bolshevik who in five years' time will quite probably have ... been converted to Roman Catholicism; or, still more typically, a prim little man with a white-collar job, usually a strict teetotaller and often with vegetarian leanings, with a history of Non-conformity behind him, and, above all, with a social position which he has no intention of forfeiting.

He goes on to describe the eccentricities of socialist activists:

> the mere words 'Socialism' and 'Communism' draw towards them ... every fruit juice drinker, nudist, sandal-wearer, sex-maniac, Quaker, 'Nature Cure' quack, pacifist, and feminist in England [to ordinary men] a crank meant a Socialist and a Socialist meant a crank.

and:

> Look at Comrade X, member of the CPGB and author of 'Marxism for Infants'. Comrade X ... is an old Etonian. He would be ready to die on the barricades, in theory anyway, but you notice that he still leaves his bottom waistcoat button undone. He idealizes the proletariat, but it is remarkable how little his habits resemble theirs.[32]

It is clear that such invective is, at least in part, an exercise in self-flagellation, attempting to expiate his guilt at being inescapably the old Etonian, upper-middle-class leftist he was affecting to ridicule and despise.

The other side of this political and psychological coin was his sentimental identification with the 'common people'. Examples of this permeate his work, from the drunken young stevedore in *The Road to Wigan Pier*, whose initially threatening appearance resulted not in violence but in the offer of a cup of tea; to the deeper socialist comradeship of Catalonia; to the idealised working-class family, again in

The Road to Wigan Pier;[33] and finally to the 'proles' of *Nineteen Eighty-Four*, who embodied the fundamental human values: 'they were not loyal to a party or country or an idea, they were loyal to each other ... [they] had stayed human'.[34]

As he observed, wistfully, of the working-class home referred to in *The Road to Wigan Pier*, it 'is a good place to be in, provided that you can be not only in it but sufficiently *of* it to be taken for granted'.[35] But that was precisely the point: he never was, nor could he ever be, '*of* it'; and this *déclassé* distancing frustrated and depressed him.

Orwell's perspectives on class, so central to his politics, thus resulted in an ideological cul-de-sac. To oversimplify: Orwell saw the ruling class as anachronistic and incompetent; the middle class as either stultifyingly conformist and philistine or, worse, as articulating the sham radicalism described in *The Road to Wigan Pier*; and the working class – the 'proles' of *Nineteen Eighty-Four* – as sentimentalised and, in an undefined way, bearers of human values for the future.

There are three observations to be made in the context of Orwell's socialism. First, his notional commitment to the working class was 'wholly embedded in the existing proletarian community; it therefore could not move beyond the perspectives of a class-divided society'. By describing the working class as it is and not as it might be, it could be argued, as Peter Sedgwick has it, that Orwell 'is supporting the status quo'.[36] There is thus little if any discussion of the alienation and deformation of working-class culture and politics under capitalism and how, through socialist or other radical social movements and political parties, such conditions might be ameliorated. Orwell's conception of the working class was thus not only sentimentalised, it was implicitly static. Secondly, Orwell's socialism was strongly individualistic. He was, as Stuart Hall has argued, 'instinctively an *individualist* ... He belonged to the *libertarian* socialist, rather than the collectivist socialist, tradition.'[37] Thus, his joining the Independent Labour Party (ILP) in 1938 was no accident: the ILP was, in Crick's words, 'Left-wing, egalitarian, a strange English mixture of secularised evangelism and non-Communist Marxism'.[38] Thirdly, because of his aversion to 'theory', and because he thus had no analysis of class structures,[39] Orwell's view of the English class system, whilst acutely observed, was superficial. As Raymond Williams has put it: 'class is a powerful and continuing economic relationship-as between the owners of capital and the owners only of labour and skill ... [with Orwell this relationship] is effectively masked'.[40]

There were thus, in my view, serious inadequacies and confusions in Orwell's conceptualisation of social class and its place in the theory and practice of socialist radicalism. However, all this can be argued to miss the central point. Orwell's politics was about articulating and putting into practice 'socialism as a moral code'.[41] And, for Orwell, insistently, this moral code centred on individuals' commitments to justice, fairness, decency and equality. These values were held tenaciously by Orwell, as noted, especially from his time in Spain onwards. Other more intellectually sophisticated left-wing socialists in the 1930s, 1940s and beyond were often in effect apologists for Stalinist communism (and earlier, leading socialists, such as the Webbs and George Bernard Shaw, had been stout defenders of the Soviet Union).[42] 'It is often said in mitigation... that they could not really have known what Stalinism was like' and that, when they *did*, 'they also managed to repress their misgivings for the good of the cause'.[43] But Orwell never went through a Stalinist phase. Writing in 1940, he said that '"such horrors as the Russian purges never surprised me, because I had always thought that – not *exactly* that, but something *like* that – was implicit in Bolshevik rule"'.[44]

Orwell's commonsense, moral conception of socialism was, in this crucial case, more reliable than the 'theorised' socialism of the intellectual Left. It is significant, as Hitchens has argued, that the radical intellectual leaders of the eventual revolt against Soviet repression in Eastern Europe all paid 'some tribute to George Orwell. So the alliance – between communities of workers and alienated sceptics – did come to something after all.'[45]

Radical patriotism

There is a close relationship between Orwell's socialism and his patriotism. In his two essays 'My Country Right or Left' and 'The Lion and the Unicorn' Orwell articulates vividly his patriotic sentiments.[46] It has to be borne in mind that the emotional tenor of the writing is explained at least in part by the fact that these pieces were written in 1940–41 when a Nazi invasion of Britain seemed imminent, and when Britain was facing the darkest days of the Second World War. A love of England, albeit with a host of qualifications, is a fundamental value shared by almost all of those who have espoused English radicalism. Orwell shared this view, and recognised the strength and depth of such patriotism: 'Christianity and international Socialism are as weak as straw in comparison with it'. It is 'usually stronger than class-hatred, and always stronger than any kind of internationalism'.[47]

Orwell was clear that the crisis of 1940 had shown him that 'I was patriotic at heart, would not sabotage or act against my own side, would support the war, would fight in it if possible'. It was not rational, socialist reasoning that underlay Orwell's support for the war. On the contrary, 'the long drilling in patriotism which the middle classes go through had done its work, and... once England was in a serious jam it would be impossible for me to sabotage. But let no one mistake the meaning of this. Patriotism has nothing to do with conservatism. It is devotion to something that is changing but is felt to be mystically the same.'[48]

What are the essential elements of Orwell's conception of England and Englishness? Orwell exhibits both a deep affection for England and Englishness, and a deep frustration about the attitudes and culture produced. The distinctiveness of England is bound up, Orwell claims, 'with solid breakfasts and gloomy Sundays, smoky towns and winding roads, green fields and red pillar boxes. It has a flavour of its own'; and, in a celebrated passage, he describes the 'clatter of clogs in the

Lancashire mill towns, the to-and-fro of the lorries on the Great North Road, the queues outside the Labour Exchanges, the rattle of pintables in the Soho pubs, the old maids biking to Holy Communion through the mists of the autumn morning'.[49]

Orwell clearly approved of what he considered to be the most marked characteristic of English culture: 'the gentleness of English civilization'. And yet this gentleness is 'mixed up with barbarities and anachronisms ... [despite the English] respect for constitutionalism and legality'. There was a 'belief in "the law" as something above the State and above the individual, something which is cruel and stupid, of course, but at any rate *incorruptible*'.[50]

At the very end of *Homage to Catalonia*, Orwell reflected upon his emotions on returning to England from the stark horrors of the Spanish War:

> southern England [is] probably the sleekest landscape in the world. It is difficult when you pass that way ... to believe that anything is really happening anywhere. Earthquakes in Japan, famines in China, revolutions in Mexico? Don't worry, the milk will be on the doorstep tomorrow morning, the *New Statesman* will come out on Friday. The industrial towns were far away ... Down here it was still the England I had known in my childhood: the railway-cuttings smothered in wild flowers, the deep meadows where the great shining horses browse and meditate ... and then the huge peaceful wilderness of outer London, the barges on the miry river, the familiar streets, the posters telling of cricket matches and Royal weddings, the men in bowler hats, the pigeons in Trafalgar Square, the red buses, the blue policemen – all sleeping the deep, deep sleep of England.[51]

This encapsulates perfectly Orwell's divided feelings of personal, emotional identity with, and love for, England, and his political exasperation at its deep, impenetrable conservatism, quietism and insularity.

In the end, Orwell, in what has become a well-known metaphor, likened England to

> a family, a rather stuffy Victorian family, with not many black sheep in it but with all its cupboards bursting with skeletons. It has rich relations who have to be kow-towed to and poor relations who are horribly sat upon, and there is a deep conspiracy of silence about the source of the family income. It is a family in which the young are generally thwarted and most of the power is in the hands of irresponsible uncles and bedridden aunts. Still, it is a family. It has its private language and its common memories, and at the approach of an enemy it closes its ranks. *A family with the wrong members in control* – that, perhaps, is as near as one can come to describing England in a phrase (my italics).[52]

Relationship to anarchism, the Labour Party and Trotskyism

Orwell's politics were defined largely by his moralism, his pragmatism, his deep opposition to totalitarianism and his patriotism. But there are other, more secondary, aspects of his perspectives that should be noted.

In the late 1920s Orwell described himself as a 'Tory anarchist'.[53] He certainly had strong conservative (though never Conservative) leanings as the discussion of his patriotism has shown, and as is further illustrated by his essays (see below). In terms of anarchism, although George Woodcock claims that anarchism 'remained a restless presence in his mind right to the end' of his life,[54] as Woodcock himself wrote earlier (1946), Orwell was not an anarchist but ' "an independent socialist with libertarian tendencies" '.[55] Moreover, after 1939, Orwell 'never again defended it [anarchism] and often attacked it'.[56] In Crick's view, Orwell 'did not accept anarchism in principle, but had, as a socialist who distrusted any kind of state power, a speculative and personal sympathy with anarchists'.[57] Anarchist writers have generally agreed. David Goodway has written that although Orwell 'displayed an empathy with Spanish anarchism ... he was never in his maturity any kind of anarchist ... yet at the same time he exhibited pronounced anarchist tendencies and sympathies, for he was a libertarian socialist'.[58] Anarchists have thus viewed Orwell as a kindred spirit. Vernon Richards, Colin Ward, David Goodway and George Woodcock have all written about Orwell with affection and respect.[59] Nicolas Walter summarised anarchist attitudes to Orwell: 'Unhappy the country that needs such a person, perhaps, but happy the country that gets it.'[60]

In contrast, even though he supported the Labour Party in general terms for the last fifteen years or so of his life, his attitude was at best lukewarm. Although he acknowledged that, in England, the Labour Party was the only socialist party 'that has ever seriously mattered', it had, in his view, never achieved anything of significance. It was largely a party of the trade unions, whose primary aim was to secure wage rises and job security for working-class people. But this depended upon the 'prosperity of British capitalism', and thus upon the British Empire: the 'standard of living of the trade-union workers ... depended indirectly on the sweating of Indian coolies'.[61] The dilemma for the Labour Party was that, once in power, it would have to carry out its rhetorical socialist promises, and thus risk economic collapse and political and social rejection – or 'stop talking about Socialism. The Labour leaders never found a solution ... They had degenerated into a Permanent Opposition.'[62]

Orwell wrote little about the Labour Party and even less about socialist policy. In 'The Lion and the Unicorn', he discussed briefly the definition of socialism in the British context. It entailed common ownership of the means of production, 'approximate equality of incomes ... political democracy, and abolition of all hereditary privilege, especially in education'.[63] This led on to an extended description of a broadly radical socialist prospectus, reiterating and extending some of the points above and adding an anti-imperialist dimension. Orwell predicted in this essay, incorrectly, that in the short term 'we shall see the rise of something that has never existed before, a specifically *English* Socialist movement. Hitherto there has been only the Labour Party ... There was nothing that really touched the heart of the English people.'[64]

This encapsulated Orwell's view of the Labour Party. It was worthy, and, because there was no viable alternative at present, it had to be supported: but it was essentially uninteresting as it was incapable of achieving the sort of radical changes that Orwell desired; and still less was it a vehicle for his vision of socialism as a 'moral code'.

Orwell's relationship with Trotskyism was more tangential. It is the case that Orwell served in Spain with the POUM, a small quasi-Trotskyist political party; and, when he subsequently formally joined the ILP, he espoused the latter's 'virtually ... Trotskyist, theory of international relations'.[65] However, although Trotsky was 'a rich source of ideas and imagery' for Orwell, he was never convinced by, or even interested in, Trotsky's explanation of Stalinism or his defence of Leninism.[66] He was in no sense a thoroughgoing Trotskyist. At just this time, 1939, he made it clear that he believed that the horrors of Stalinism were inherent in the whole Bolshevik project. 'It is probably a good thing for Lenin's reputation that he died so early. Trotsky, in exile, denounces the Russian dictatorship, but he is probably as much responsible for it as any man now living, and there is no certainty that as a dictator he would be preferable to Stalin, though undoubtedly he has a much more interesting mind. The essential act is the rejection of democracy.'[67]

Although he had a quasi-Trotskyist belief in the potential for a British revolution – 'red militias billeted in the Ritz' – up to 1944, by the later 1940s he had come to see the prospects for fundamental, radical change as 'bleak'.[68] The best that could be hoped for, in the longer term, was 'the creation of a "socialist United States of Europe"'.[69] However, he, like Russell before him, acknowledged the danger that the United States would obstruct any such move.

Orwell's commitment to revolutionary socialism, let alone to a theoretical Trotskyist perspective, was not only brief but was anyway always secondary to his general patriotism and to his belief in the moral code of his individualistic socialism. His ideological commitments had undergone a tremendous battering in the 1930s:

> He had exposed himself to so much hardship and then fought so hard; had got a bullet in the throat in Spain; had been severely ill ...: had given so much of his energy to what seemed a desert of political illusions, lies and bad faith. Between the myth of 'England' and this profound European disillusion he had to make what settlements he could find.[70]

From all this trauma, psychological and emotional as much as political, Orwell salvaged his original values and reinterpreted them in the changed context. From now on, his primary commitment and concern was to defend his version of democracy, and the values that underpinned it, against totalitarianism.

The writer

At the outset of this chapter, attention was drawn to Bernard Crick's assertion that equal weight should be given to Orwell's proclaimed purposes – to 'make *political writing* into an art' (my italics).

His success as a writer is certainly one of the main reasons for his lasting appeal. His idiosyncratic, distinctively English style of writing has a lasting freshness. He set down rigorous rules for good writing in 1946, in 'Politics and the English Language',[71] emphasising the importance of simple, clear expression, free of jargon, stale metaphors and Latinate – or still worse Americanised – language.

He also gave strong emphasis to the importance of *honesty*. 'Political language – and with variations this is true of all political parties, from Conservatives to Anarchists – is designed to make lies sound truthful and murder respectable, and to give an appearance of solidity to pure wind'.[72] This was linked to the need to protect intellectual liberty from '[o]n the one side ... its theoretical enemies, the apologists of totalitarianism, and on the other its immediate, practical enemies, monopoly and bureaucracy'.[73] In the already encroaching totalitarian climate of the 1940s, Orwell argued that there was growing pressure to turn the writer into an unquestioning, uncritical purveyor of the state's current ideological orthodoxy. In the recent past, Orwell wrote, freedom of the intellect had to be defended against Conservatives, Roman Catholics and fascists. 'Today one has to defend it against Communists and "fellow-travellers."'[74]

Thus we reach one of the central points of Orwell's critique of totalitarianism, so brilliantly captured in the nightmare world of 'doublethink', 'Newspeak', and the 'Ministry of Truth' in *Nineteen Eighty-Four*: from 'the totalitarian point of view history is something to be created rather than learned. A totalitarian state is in effect a theocracy, and its ruling caste, in order to keep its position, has to be thought of as infallible ... [It] demands, in fact, the continuous alteration of the past, and in the long run probably demands a disbelief in the very existence of objective truth.'[75] (There are shades here of the later, dangerous illusions of postmodernism.)[76] It took Orwell's genius as a political writer to give dramatic life to these dangers in his two most famous books.

However, his writing was by no means confined to these directly political arenas. His talent, and his lasting appeal, lies as much in his wide-ranging essays, his journalism and review articles as in his political books.[77] As an essayist, he is in the great tradition of English radicals, Hazlitt, Swift *et al.*; and he was also 'a brilliant journalist'. Such essays as 'Shooting an Elephant' and 'A Hanging' are lasting examples of the art of the essayist: vivid, intense, evocative and, though not *directly* political, stimulating 'political reflection for the first time in many new readers', however politically innocent they may be.[78]

His range was wide. Some slight pieces, such as 'A Nice Cup of Tea', 'In Defence of English Cooking', 'The Moon under Water' and 'Hop-picking', are still a joy to read: and they illustrate, in a tangential way, the *Englishness* of his radicalism.[79] But there are more substantial pieces of acute cultural observation and comment too. There is much to be said for Hitchens's view that Orwell 'pioneered "cultural studies" without giving the subject a name'.[80] 'In his Essays on "Boys' Weeklies"', on violence ("Raffles and Miss Blandish") and on pornography ("The Secret Life of Salvador

Dali"), he was a moralist who made pioneering studies of unsophisticated, as well as of intellectual, literature to expose anti-humanitarian values.'[81] Those essays gave eloquent expression to the *decency* that inhered within the culture of the common people. They also indicate that, although his politics were clearly left-wing, his cultural inclinations were conservative. There is some truth in the generally hostile view of Alaric Jacob that Orwell 'not a widely travelled man ... was at heart an Edwardian Little Englander'.[82] Embedded in the nostalgia for a lost Edwardian childhood, there is a more modern 'green' strand to his writing. He was a conservationist before his time: one of the central themes of *Coming Up for Air* is the destruction of the natural habitat by the encroaching philistine forces of modern capitalism.

Orwell observed that the English lack artistic ability, *except* in the field of literature, which, as he said, is the one art form that does not travel well. He maintained that, apart from Shakespeare, 'the best English poets are barely known in Europe'. The only poets who are widely read 'are Byron, who is admired for the wrong reasons, and Oscar Wilde, who is pitied as a victim of English hypocrisy'. Linked to this, he maintained, has been 'the lack of philosophical faculty, the absence in nearly all Englishmen of any need for an ordered system of thought or even for the use of logic'.[83]

Although he was unashamedly English in his writing style and concerns, as he was in his personal life and habits, he was never insular. He was widely read in French and Russian literature (the latter in translation) and contemporary American writing too. But it was English literature that held his attention most frequently. His essays on Dickens and Swift, and his 'Lear, Tolstoy and the Fool', are thoughtful, insightful and intellectually subtle pieces of literary criticism. Moreover, he was uncompromisingly *modern* in his understanding and appreciation of controversial modernist work. 'Orwell championed and understood James Joyce's *Ulysses* at a time when some traditional intellectuals denounced it as meaningless filth' and the popular press applauded its censorship in Britain. He defended with vigour Henry Miller, 'whose cynicism and deliberate apoliticism he cordially detested'. He found artistic excellence in figures such as Eliot and Kipling, whose 'world views' were alien to him. And, most difficult of all, he defended the awarding of a prize to Ezra Pound, 'while condemning him utterly as a person'. (Pound was a fascist, a war-criminal and an explicit anti-Semite and racist.)

Orwell was also a talented though eccentric journalist, excelling not in political or other reporting but rather in the 'characterful and speculative essay'. His 76 'As I Please' columns in *Tribune* became a model for young journalists: a mixture of 'protesting, denouncing, needling, nagging, mocking, teasing and celebrating', all written with either profundity or humour or both.[84]

Religion

As with many other English radicals in the twentieth century, Orwell was greatly influenced by the 'Dissenting culture'. Whilst his focus of attention was upon the political, social and economic causes of contemporary problems, and the political changes that were needed to counter them, the notion of 'socialism as a moral code' was based upon Christian ethics. It was 'this duality' which, according to one of his biographers, 'defined his philosophical outlook'.[85] Such secularised moralism lies at the heart of English radicalism: it has inspired many of the leading figures considered in this book.

However, again in common with many other English radicals, Orwell lost his Christian faith at an early stage. By the age of 14 or 15 he had concluded that he was an 'unbeliever'. Nevertheless, at Eton, he permitted his Confirmation to go forward, being 'admitted to the Communion of the Church of England by the Bishop of Oxford. Thereafter his relationship with the Anglican Church would always be one of fond irreverence.'[86] He had 'an ironic attachment to the liturgy, the humane political compromises and the traditions of the Church of England'.[87] In the nostalgic, romantic affection for the culture, rather than the theology, of Anglicanism, Orwell had much in common with that very different man of English letters, Philip Larkin.[88]

The cultural and moral heritage of the Anglican version of Christianity was thus central to Orwell's perspectives. But it should be emphasised that this was a *secularised* attachment. He was a 'Humanist, even a Rationalist'.[89] It was the moral code that was important to him, not the theology; also, the Dissenting Churches' opposition to authority, their individual witness against war and injustice, and their emphasis upon the essential equality of all humanity before God all appealed to his libertarian inclinations.

Such empathy most definitely did *not* apply to Roman Catholicism, which he loathed. For Orwell, '"the poor, unoffending old Church of England"' compared well to the '"dogmatic intolerance"' of the Roman Catholics.[90] It was the spread of Catholicism and the '"deceptive bluff"' of Roman Catholic apologists which most provoked his angry criticism.[91] He also emphasised the frequent collusion of the Roman Catholic Church and Catholic intellectuals with Fascism. Orwell saw close parallels between the Inquisition and the secular totalitarianism of the mid-twentieth century.

Orwell wrote little directly about religion but he was always fully aware of its importance culturally, psychologically and politically. In his essay on Arthur Koestler, he observed that, faced with the horrors of the twentieth century and the virtual collapse in the hopes of attaining an 'Earthly Paradise' through political movements of the Right or Left, the 'only easy way out is that of the religious believer, who regards this life merely as a preparation for the next'. However, 'few thinking people now believe in life after death ... The real problem is how to restore the religious attitude while accepting that death is final'. (And, he added, 'men can only be happy when they do not assume that the object of life is happiness'.)[92]

In the end, Orwell always came back to the humanist, moral basis of socialism, which 'could co-exist with Christianity, but not with the belief that man is inherently a fallen creature'. Those who believed in the possibility of human progress in the modern world were, Orwell argued (according to Crick), Machiavellians, bureaucrats or utopians. Orwell 'came down on the side of the utopians'.[93]

> If one studied the genealogy of the ideas for which writers like Koestler and Silone stand, one would find it leading back through Utopian dreamers like William Morris and the mystical democrats like Walt Whitman, through Rousseau, through the English diggers and levellers, through the peasant revolts of the Middle Ages, and back to the early Christians and the slave revolts of antiquity.
>
> The pamphlets of Gerrard Winstanley, the digger from Wigan, whose experiment in primitive Communism was crushed by Cromwell, are in some ways strangely close to modern Left Wing literature ... Underneath [the belief in an 'earthly paradise'] lies the belief that human nature is fairly decent to start with, and is capable of indefinite development.[94]

In the extremis of his final months of illness, with the possibility of imminent death, the pull of the Church of England was strong. On 18 January 1950, Orwell made out a new Will. He directed 'that my body shall be buried (not cremated) according to the rites of the Church of England in the nearest convenient cemetery'. An ironic request, in a way, for such a proclaimed humanist and agnostic; but, as Crick has observed, it was perhaps 'not so surprising. He loved the land and he loved England and he loved the language of the liturgies of the English Church.'[95]

'The List'

It remains, as a postscript, to discuss the issue of the notorious 'List', which Orwell, at the prompting of his old friend Celia Kirwan (now working for the Information Research Department section of the Foreign Office), submitted in 1949 to the government 'in confidence'. In addition to the names of 35 suspected 'Fellow-Travellers', there were brief comments by Orwell on each of those listed. As he observed, some of the comments were possibly libellous, hence the need for confidentiality. Orwell's reputation as an anti-authoritarian champion of the libertarian Left, and a defender of freedom of speech, appeared to be seriously undermined by his 'collaboration' with the government in the escalating Cold War.

With hindsight, Orwell's decision to submit such a list appears ill-advised, to put it charitably. It seemed to confirm the view of those on the Left who argued that he had 'sold out' and had become a tool of 'capitalist propaganda': he had compromised his intellectual integrity. There were, however, mitigating circumstances. As Hitchens has observed, 'in the late 1940s Orwell ... considered the survival of democratic and socialist values to be at stake in the struggle against Stalin'.[96] It is also of note that he produced in the early 1940s a list of 'Nazi sympathisers he thought should be removed from positions of influence'.[97] He was in no doubt of the equivalent threat to the values he cherished posed by Stalinist totalitarianism.

In 1948, he wrote that we were faced '"with a world-wide political movement which threatens the existence of Western civilization, and which has lost none of its vigour because it has become in a sense corrupt"'.[98]

Moreover, there was only one person on that list whom Orwell accused of being a Soviet agent – 'and even there the qualifying words "almost certainly" are applied'.[99] This was Peter Smolka (also known as Smollett), the civil servant who had put pressure on Jonathan Cape to refuse to publish *Animal Farm*. Smolka was subsequently found to be an agent of Soviet security.

There were other mitigating contextual factors. Orwell was, by the time he gave the list to Celia Kirwan, an extremely sick man; and Kirwan, with whom Orwell had once tried, unsuccessfully, to have an affair, was no doubt persuasive. And almost 'one-third of the entries end in the verdict "Probably not", or "Sympathiser only", in the space reserved for Party allegiance'.[100]

Finally, he was always strongly against banning the Communist Party. '"To suppress the Communist Party *now*, or at any time when it did not unmistakably endanger national survival, would be calamitous', he wrote in 1947.[101]

However, when all is said and done, there is little excuse for Orwell acting in this way. He had always held that suspicion of the state and its inherent totalitarian tendencies lay at the heart of libertarian socialism. Moreover, and complementary to this, individual freedom of thought and expression was a key, 'non-negotiable' value. Orwell was naive in his seeming inability 'to grasp that a list sent in to a secret government agency ... might be used against such people on a wider front and severely damage their careers'.[102] This whole sorry episode must be judged, at the least, a serious lapse of judgement.

Conclusion

Orwell thus had his faults. Nevertheless, with all the caveats, Orwell's integrity and political and literary importance shine through. His style, his 'crystalline prose' and the moral socialism for which he stood are the 'most durable achievement of a good and angry man'.[103] He was consistent, from his time in Spain onwards, and often in the most difficult of circumstances, in his commitment to the core values of justice, fairness, decency and equality. Bernard Crick, at the conclusion of his fine biography, summarises Orwell's lasting legacy:

> In striving to keep a deliberate balance between public and private values, between creative work and necessary labour, between politics and culture, Orwell's life and his writings should both guide and cheer us. He hated the power-hungry, exercised intelligence and independence, and taught us again to use our language with beauty and clarity, sought for and practised fraternity and had faith in the decency, tolerance and humanity of the common man. And what is even more heartening, he was all that and yet as odd in himself and as varied in his friends as man can be.[104]

Notes

1 George Orwell, *Animal Farm* (Secker and Warburg, 1945); George Orwell, *Nineteen Eighty-Four* (Secker and Warburg, 1949).
2 C. Ward, 'Orwell and Anarchism', in Freedom Press, *George Orwell at Home (and among the Anarchists)* (Freedom Press, 1998), p. 15. Among the major biographies and other studies on Orwell are: B. Crick, *George Orwell: A Life* (Secker and Warburg, 1980; Penguin edition, 1982); C. Hitchens, *Why Orwell Matters* (New York: Basic Books (Perseus), 2002); G. Woodcock, *The Crystal Spirit* (Cape, 1969); P. Stansky and W. Abrahams, *The Unknown Orwell* (Constable, 1972); M. Shelden, *Orwell: The Authorised Biography* (Heinemann, 1991); C. Norris (ed.) *Inside the Myth: Orwell: Views from the Left* (Lawrence and Wishart, 1984); J. Meyers, *A Reader's Guide to George Orwell* (Thames and Hudson, 1975); D.J. Taylor, *Orwell: The Life* (Chatto and Windus, 2003; paperback edition, Vintage, 2004). This is by no means an exhaustive bibliography: there has developed a sizeable 'Orwell industry'. The original, magisterial biography by Bernard Crick, although Sonia (Brownell) Orwell disliked it, remains 'by far the best single book yet on Orwell's whole career' (N. Walter, 'Orwell and Anarchism', in *Orwell at Home*, p. 50).
3 Crick, *Orwell*, p. xiii.
4 Orwell, 'Why I Write', originally in *Gangrel*, No. 4, Summer 1946, reprinted in B. Crick (ed.), *Orwell: Essays* (Penguin, 1994), p. 5.
5 Ibid., pp. 4–5. Orwell cited a poem he had written in 1935: 'A happy vicar I might have been / Two hundred years ago, / To preach upon eternal doom / And watch my walnuts grow / But born, alas, in an evil time, / I missed that pleasant haven....'
6 E.P. Thompson, 'Outside the Whale', in *The Poverty of Theory and Other Essays* (Merlin Press, 1978), p. 15. This was originally published in Thompson (ed.), *Out of Apathy* (Stevens and Sons, 1960). See Chapter 7 below for a discussion of Thompson's contribution to English radicalism.
7 Press Release, dictated to his publisher, Frederic Warburg, and cited in Crick, *Orwell*, p. 395.
8 Crick, *Orwell*, p. 333.
9 See Chapter 8 below for a discussion of Bevan in relation to Michael Foot. See also Bevan, *In Place of Fear* (Heinemann, 1952).
10 Walter, 'Orwell and Anarchism', p. 47.
11 Orwell, 'Such, Such Were the Joys', *Partisan Review*, September–October, 1952, reprinted in S. Orwell and I. Angus (eds), *The Collected Essays, Journalism and Letters of George Orwell (CEJL)* (Penguin, 1968), Vol. IV, *In Front of Your Nose 1945–1950*, pp. 379–422.
12 Crick, *Orwell*, p. 72. As Crick observed, only a minority of boys from Eton went on to Oxford or Cambridge, so such a route was not really 'traditional'.
13 Orwell, *Burmese Days* (Gollancz, 1934).
14 Orwell, *The Road to Wigan Pier* (Gollancz, 1937), p. 123 (paperback edition Penguin 2001).
15 Walter, 'Orwell and Anarchism', p. 48.
16 Orwell, *Down and Out in Paris and London* (Gollancz, 1933).

17 Walter, 'Orwell and Anarchism', p. 48.
18 Orwell, *A Clergyman's Daughter* (Gollancz, 1935); Orwell, *Keep the Aspidistra Flying* (Gollancz, 1936); Orwell, *Coming Up for Air* (Gollancz, 1939).
19 G. Bowker, *George Orwell* (Little, Brown, 2003), p. 432
20 Ibid.
21 Crick, *Orwell*, p. 214.
22 Bowker, *Orwell*, devotes considerable space and much conjecture to this aspect of Orwell's life and personal psychology.
23 Hitchens, *Why Orwell Matters*, chapter 6, pp. 141–54.
24 Ibid., p. 141.
25 Ibid., p. 148.
26 Orwell, 'Anti-Semitism in Britain', *Contemporary Jewish Record*, April 1945. However, as *Hareetz*, the Jewish News Journal has pointed out in a 2012 article, it is at least possible that there remained a residual, emotional anti-Semitism in Orwell's outlook. Anshel Pfeffer, *Hareetz*, 3 December 2012.
27 M. Muggeridge, *Like It Was: The Diaries of Malcolm Muggeridge*, ed. J. Bright-Holmes (Collins, 1981), p. 364, cited in T. Ricks, *Churchill and Orwell: The Fight for Freedom* (Richmond: Duckworth, 2018), p. 36.
28 See. B. Alexander, 'George Orwell and Spain', and R. Stradling, 'Orwell and the Spanish Civil War', in Norris (ed.), *Inside the Myth*, pp. 85–125.
29 Bernard Crick, 'Introduction: An Essay', in *Orwell: Essays*, pp. viii–ix.
30 Ibid., pp. xi–xii.
31 Orwell, 'The Lion and the Unicorn: Socialism and the English Genius' (Secker and Warburg, 1941), reprinted in *CEJL*, vol. 2, pp. 74–134, and in Crick (ed.), *Orwell: Essays*, pp. 138–88. Quotations in this chapter are taken from this latter edition, pp. 149–51.
32 Orwell, *Road to Wigan Pier*, pp. 150–1, and 40.
33 'The next moment the stevedore collapsed on my chest and flung his arms around my neck. "'ave a cup of tea, chum!" … I had a cup of tea. It was a kind of baptism. After that my fears vanished', ibid., p. 133; 'a working-class interior at its best. Especially on winter evenings after tea, when the fire glows in the open range and dances mirrored in the steel fender, when father, in shirt-sleeves, sits in the rocking-chair at one side of the fire reading the racing finals, and mother sits on the other with her sewing …', ibid., p. 104.
34 Orwell, *Nineteen Eighty-Four*, pp. 134–5 (pb. Penguin edition).
35 Orwell, *Road to Wigan Pier*, p. 104.
36 P. Sedgwick, 'George Orwell: International Socialist: The Development of Orwell's Socialism', *International Socialism Journal*, 1969, p. 30.
37 S. Hall, 'Conjuring Leviathan: Orwell on the State', in Norris (ed.), *Inside the Myth*, p. 218.
38 Crick, *Orwell*, p. 162.
39 Crick observed that, to 'judge by the second half of *The Road to Wigan Pier*, Orwell had not studied the classic texts of Marxism closely; and there is no evidence elsewhere in his writings, letters or among the books he possessed that his knowledge of Marxism was anything but secondary'. Crick, *Orwell*, p. 201.
40 R. Williams, *Orwell* (Fontana Modern Masters, 1971), p. 24.
41 S. Ingle, 'A Note on Orwellism', *Political Studies*, xxviii, No. 4, December 1980, p. 592.

42 'Sidney Webb, co-author with his wife Beatrice of the notorious volume *Soviet Russia: A New Civilisation?*, which in its second edition dropped the question mark just in time to coincide with the Great Purges ... Shaw managed to be stupidly lenient about both Stalin and Mussolini'. Hitchens, *Why Orwell Matters*, pp. 5–6.
43 Ibid., p. 56.
44 Orwell, Private Diary 1940, cited in ibid., p. 59.
45 Hitchens, *Why Orwell Matters*, p. 57. Hitchens cites Czeslaw Milosz, Vaclav Havel, Rudolf Bahro, Miklos Haraszti, Lesek Kolakowski, Milan Simecka and Adam Michnik.
46 Orwell, 'My Country Right or Left', 1940, *Folio of New Writing*; and 'The Lion and the Unicorn'.
47 'The Lion and the Unicorn', pp. 138, 146.
48 'My Country Right or Left', pp. 136–7.
49 'The Lion and the Unicorn', p. 139.
50 Ibid., p. 144.
51 Orwell, *Homage to Catalonia* (Secker and Warburg, 1937; pb. edition, Penguin Modern Classics, 1989). Citation taken from this latter edition, p. 196.
52 Orwell, 'The Lion and the Unicorn', pp. 149–50.
53 Walter, 'Orwell and Anarchism', p. 55, citing Orwell's close friend Richard Rees, 1961, *George Orwell: Fugitive from the Camp of Victory*.
54 Woodcock, *The Crystal Spirit*, p. 245.
55 Woodcock, *Politics*, December 1946, cited in Walter, 'Orwell and Anarchism', p. 52.
56 Walter, 'Orwell and Anarchism', p. 66.
57 Crick, *Orwell*, p. 308.
58 D. Goodway, chapter 6, 'The Spanish Revolution and Civil War – the Case of George Orwell', pp. 123–48, in Goodway, *Anarchist Seeds Beneath the Snow: Left-Libertarian Thought and British Writers from William Morris to Colin Ward* (Liverpool: Liverpool University Press, 2006), pp. 144–5.
59 V. Richards, 'Orwell the Humanist', in *Orwell at Home*, pp. 9–14; Colin Ward, 'Orwell and Anarchism', in ibid., pp. 15–46; Goodway, 'The Spanish Revolution and Civil War', in *Anarchist Seeds Beneath the Snow*; Woodcock, *The Crystal Spirit*.
60 Walter, 'Orwell and Anarchism', p. 75.
61 Orwell, 'The Lion and the Unicorn', p. 171.
62 Ibid., pp. 172.
63 Ibid., p. 160.
64 Ibid., p. 181.
65 Crick, *Orwell*, p. 246. Trotsky himself, however, was very critical of the POUM.
66 J. Callaghan, 'Engaging with Trotsky: The Influence of Trotskyism in Britain', in E. Smith and M. Worley (eds), *Against the Grain: The British Far Left from 1956* (Manchester: Manchester University Press, 2014), p. 29.
67 Orwell, Review of N. de Basily, *Russia under Soviet Rule*, in *New English Weekly*, 12 January 1939, in *CEJL*, vol. 1, p. 381.
68 Callaghan, 'Engaging with Trotsky', p. 33.
69 Ibid.
70 Williams, *Orwell*, p. 65.

71 Orwell, 'Politics and the English Language', 1946, *Horizon* (included in Orwell, *Essays*, 2000). Citations are taken from the latter, p. 359.
72 Ibid.
73 Orwell, 'The Prevention of Literature', *Polemic*, No. 2, January 1946, included in Orwell, *Essays*, pp. 328–40, p. 329.
74 Ibid., p. 331.
75 Ibid., pp. 332–3.
76 See T. Eagleton, *The Illusions of Postmodernism* (Oxford: Blackwell, 1996); and for a discussion of postmodernism in the context of higher education, see R. Taylor, J. Barr and T. Steele, *For a Radical Higher Education: After Postmodernism* (Buckingham: SRHE and Open University Press, 2002).
77 Orwell's *CEJL* in 4 volumes, 1968 (Penguin edition 1970) have never been out of print. Since then, an exhaustive 20-volume collection has been published: P. Davison (ed.), *The Complete Works of George Orwell* (Secker and Warburg, 1988).
78 Crick, *Orwell*, p. xvi.
79 Respectively, *Evening Standard*, 12 January 1946; *Evening Standard*, 15 December 1945; *Evening Standard*, 9 February 1946; and *Diary*, August 1931.
80 Hitchens, *Why Orwell Matters*, p. 58. There is perhaps less to be said for Hitchens's view that 'Post-colonial studies owes something to Orwell'. p. 58.
81 Crick, *Orwell*, p. xvi.
82 A. Jacob, 'Sharing Orwell's "Joys" – But Not His Fears', in Norris (ed.), *Inside the Myth*, p. 63.
83 Orwell, 'The Lion and the Unicorn', p. 147. Philosophers, amongst others, both then and now, would strongly contest this assertion: but perhaps Orwell was referring colloquially rather than academically to 'philosophy' and 'logic'.
84 Crick, *Orwell*, pp. xvi, xvii.
85 Bowker, *Orwell*, p. 158.
86 Ibid., p. 53.
87 Crick, *Orwell*, p. 143.
88 See, for example, Larkin's poems, 'Going, Going', and 'Church Going'.
89 Crick, *Orwell*, p. 143.
90 Ibid., p. 142.
91 Bowker, *Orwell*, p. 124.
92 Orwell, 'Arthur Koestler', written in 1944 and included in *Critical Essays*, 1946. (The citation here is from Orwell, *Essays*, in which it is also included, pp. 268–78; p. 277.)
93 Crick, *Orwell*, p. 351.
94 Orwell, 'What Is Socialism?', *Manchester Evening News*, 31 January 1946, cited in ibid., p. 351.
95 Crick, *Orwell*, pp. 404–5. In the event there were two funerals: Anthony Powell and Malcolm Muggeridge arranged for a funeral service to be held at Christ Church in Albany Street, London. 'The congregation was a strange, heterogeneous assemblage, mostly comprising unbelievers and Jews, for whom the Anglican funeral service meant little … Muggeridge found it "a rather melancholy and chilly affair".' Bowker, *Orwell*, p. 415.
96 Hitchens, *Why Orwell Matters*, p. 160.

97 Bowker, *Orwell*, p. 428.
98 Orwell, 'Marx and Russia', *Observer*, 15 February 1948, cited in ibid., p. 429.
99 Hitchens, *Why Orwell Matters*, p. 163.
100 Ibid., p. 164.
101 Orwell, *New Leader*, 1947, cited in Shelden, *Orwell*, p. 468.
102 Bowker, *Orwell*, p. 430.
103 Woodcock, *The Crystal Spirit*, pp. 278–9.
104 Crick, *Orwell*, p. 406.

7

E.P. Thompson

Edward Thompson was a significant figure in the articulation and development of English radicalism in the second half of the twentieth century. He was primarily responsible for a decisive shift in English historiography to an emphasis upon 'history from below', with a new centrality given to the culture, activism and aspirations of 'the common people' in modern English history. Politically, after his full-hearted membership and activism in the Communist Party of Great Britain (CPGB – hereafter CP) for a formative period of his life – from 1942 until his high-profile resignation in 1956 – he was instrumental in establishing the 'first' New Left. He was, throughout his adult life, a peace campaigner and activist and he attained national pre-eminence in the 1980s through his leading role in the European Nuclear Disarmament (END) movement. Finally, his writing – both his academic, historical work[1] and his political and polemical essays and articles[2] – is of an outstanding intellectual quality.

Despite the range of these achievements – and he was in addition a literary critic (and a teacher of history and English literature), the author of a novel, a poet and a biographer – there was a unity and coherence to his intellectual and political life. The two continuing themes of Thompson's approach were his belief in the importance of *human agency* in the historical process; and, linked to this, his advocacy of *socialist humanism* as the keynote of progressive politics. The extent to which this politics was present and prominent in his CP years is an important, and somewhat neglected, aspect of Thompson's radicalism, and is discussed below. However, what is beyond question is that, from 1956, these were fundamental to both the theory and practice of his politics and writing in general, and his New Left and peace movement activism in particular.

As Perry Anderson has written in his perceptive study of Thompson's politics, '[t]he pivot of Thompson's construction ... is the notion of agency', side by side with his unbending emphasis upon the importance of empirical enquiry in the study of history.[3] Similarly, David Goodway has argued persuasively that Thompson's ideological perspective can be identified through the dichotomy he drew between 'Necessity' and 'Desire'. ' "Necessity" is Marxist economic determinism, the course of the productive forces and the relations of production in society.' Thompson, in contrast, emphasised 'Desire', defined as 'morality, conscience, human will and, what became for Thompson the defining term, "agency". Operating in tandem, [these two elements] together constitute "moral realism".'[4]

In Marx's famous formulation, that 'Men make their own history, but they do not make it just as they please; they do not make it under circumstances chosen by themselves, but under circumstances directly encountered, given and transmitted from the past', Thompson's emphasis, in all his academic work and political activism, at least after 1956, was consistently upon the first, 'agency', clause. It is in this context, too, that Thompson should be seen as a central figure in the development of cultural studies in Britain.[5] He rejected, as did others in the New Left, what was seen as the crude determinism of the 'base and superstructure' model, characteristic of Stalinist formulations of Marxist theory.

Thompson's ideological position therefore embodied some of the key themes of English radicalism: a strong, secularised egalitarian ethic, deriving essentially from a New Testament morality, and secondarily from English Romanticism; an empirical approach to historical analysis; a belief in the moral power and political efficacy of 'the common people' and their social movements; and an explicit identification with the historical reality and political importance of the English radical tradition.[6]

To this must be added, as noted, Thompson's organising concept of 'socialist humanism'. This became a particularly prominent theme in his work and politics after 1956: indeed, by the time of END in the 1980s, it had become the cornerstone of his 'Third Way' critique of the two super-powers, the USA and the USSR, and what he argued were their fatally flawed ideologies.[7] There were tensions in Thompson's conceptualisation of 'socialist humanism'. As Kate Soper has observed, 'it cannot be denied that a "socialist" recognition of the class-conditioned nature of experience and affectivity is in uneasy tension with Thompson's "humanist" appeals to a more universal and apparently "natural" moral sense'.[8]

At his most pessimistic, Thompson came to argue that the socialist project itself had failed not because of Stalin, Khrushchev or the contingent historical events of the twentieth century, or because of the faults, inadequacies or betrayals of socialist parties, but rather because, as Kate Soper has summarised his position, in some 'more collective, trans-class, even trans-historical sense', human nature has ' "betrayed" itself, and we are all – exploited and exploiters, manipulated and manipulators – to blame'.[9]

Such pessimism was closely related to his own disappointment at the collapse of the first New Left's project and his distaste for the abstract socialist theorising of the second New Left[10] (and for what he saw as the quasi-Trotskyist politicking and posturing of the Far Left in the anti-Vietnam War campaign). All this led him, partly through his own willed withdrawal,[11] to a politically lonely isolation. However, with the resurgence of the peace movement in the 1980s, and his leading role in END, Thompson's faith in socialist humanism reasserted itself. As Soper has concluded, despite its theoretical difficulties, Thompson's 'appeal to the moral subject, and to the power of concerted human action to make history, proved catalytic' in the turbulent years leading up to the dissolution of the Soviet model of communism in Eastern Europe and, subsequently, the Soviet Union itself.[12]

This humanist, Enlightenment perspective lies at the heart of English radicalism and is an effective counter to both the post-humanist quietism and the identity politics so dominant in the early twenty-first century. Before turning to his time in the CP and its significance, attention is turned to the important influence of Thompson's family background upon his intellectual and political development.

Family and early influences[13]

Thompson was born, the second of two sons, on 3 February 1924 to Edward John Thompson, formerly a Methodist missionary in India and, after the First World War, a part-time lecturer at Oriel College, Oxford (later, a Research Fellow in Indian history), and Theodosia (née Jessop), daughter of an American Presbyterian missionary. Both Thompson's parents were progressive, intellectual and increasingly anti-imperialist. Indeed, E.J. Thompson became disillusioned with both Methodism and Britain's imperial rule in India, and was an active, though ambivalent, advocate of Indian independence: Gandhi and Nehru were amongst the many visitors to the cosmopolitan Thompson household at Boar's Hill, Oxford.

Another and even greater influence upon Thompson was his older brother, Frank,[14] whom he admired and respected: more than that, he was in awe of him. Notwithstanding his early death, Frank remained an inspirational figure to Thompson for the rest of his life. Frank, who was intellectually outstanding both at Winchester and at university, became active in left-wing politics at Oxford and joined the CP, though he was never an orthodox, 'doctrinaire' Party member: he was, rather, a romantic idealist.

In many ways, then, both Thompson's parents and his brother were ideologically radical liberals rather than 'fully theorised' socialists. Thompson recalled his home as a place where 'the power of rhetorical persuasion and poetic imagination was not so much extolled as lived';[15] and which was 'supportive, liberal, anti-imperialist, quick with ideas and poetry and international visitors'.[16] Although he was later to become highly critical of Methodism, the cultural influence of his original background in this faith, and his education at Kingswood, his father's old Methodist school, were also significant.

In 1941, he gained a minor scholarship to Corpus Christi College, Cambridge, and was soon elected President of the University Socialist Club. In 1942 he, like his brother before him, joined the CP, a congenial home for left-wing radicals, now that the USSR was at war with the Nazis and a 'Popular Front' policy had been adopted. His Cambridge career was interrupted by his military service, which he spent largely in Italy as a tank-troop commander. His wartime experiences were rarely referred to directly in later life. But the war did confirm to him the truth of two of his fundamental beliefs: that war was an irrational and immoral affair; and that the linked causes of socialist transformation and peace movement activism were of paramount importance.

Although his main political formation was in the decade following the war, it is telling that, for the rest of his life, he referred to the years from the mid-1930s to the mid-1940s as 'the decade of heroes'. A part of the explanation for this lies in the profound effect upon him of the brutal murder of his brother Frank in 1944 by the right-wing Bulgarian government.[17] Subsequently, Thompson and his mother (his father had died in 1946), travelled to what was then Yugoslavia with the British Youth Brigade to help a team of peasants, workers, soldiers and students construct a 150-mile railway.[18]

After the war, Thompson returned to Cambridge, obtained a first-class degree in the Part 1 History Tripos, and was elected to a College Foundation Scholarship. He stayed on in Cambridge, not to complete Part 2 of the History Tripos, but to undertake largely undirected research in English literature and social history, the subjects which were to become the central concerns of his intellectual life. It was at this time, too, that he met Dorothy Sale (née Towers), his future wife, and a fellow modern historian and CP member.

Historian and adult educator

Thompson had had some experience of adult education during the war, through his work in the Army Bureau of Current Affairs. After the war, and back in Cambridge, he had undertaken some part-time teaching for the Workers' Educational Association (WEA). University adult education, with its 'semi-detached', quasi-autonomous relationship with the mainstream university, and its potential for direct contact with the working class and the organised labour movement, had a natural appeal for Thompson. He recalled years later that ' "I went into adult education because it seemed to me to be an area in which I would learn something about industrial England and teach people who would teach me" '.[19] He and Dorothy were also keen to avoid the 'Golden Triangle' of Oxford, London and Cambridge: Thompson was to remain a proclaimed man of 'the Provinces' and a critic of the 'Metropolitan elite'. His appointment, in 1948, as Staff Tutor (in effect, Lecturer) in the Department of

Adult Education and Extramural Studies at the University of Leeds, was thus an ideal post for Thompson. The West Riding of Yorkshire had a strong association with English working-class radicalism, and Leeds had a vibrant, expanding and intellectually stimulating extramural department.

For the next seventeen years, Thompson taught adult classes in both history and literature in a range of locations. It was from this background, and the interactions it produced with a variety of adult students, that Thompson developed, first, his lengthy, politically committed biography of William Morris (1955), and, in 1963, his most famous book, *The Making of the English Working Class*.

Through this latter, ground-breaking work, Thompson not only became the 'founding father of "history from below"', but gave a new and original primacy to the concept of 'class'. He treated class not as a given, a fixed sociological category, defined by a series of necessary characteristics, but rather as 'a dynamic, interactive process that "owes as much to agency as conditioning"'. Since class relations were 'constantly being made and remade by human agents, they had to be depicted in motion'.[20] Moreover, he argued, it was appropriate to refer to an emerging, single class, rather than a loosely linked collection of 'classes', because the experience of capitalism 'brought together a range of diverse trades and occupations, and gave them the chance to create a unified (if never uniform) response'.[21]

Trade unions, 'friendly societies', and other labour organisations gave expression to the developing culture of the new working-class community. For the working class, economic grievances and exploitation, and the growing *consciousness* of its own class position, were exacerbated by the harsh repression of the state. Material concerns were thus increasingly translated into broadly political forms.[22] The new working class was not only instrumental in its own 'making', it also consistently built upon the notion of the 'freeborn Englishman', a central, longstanding element in the tradition of English radicalism.

Over his seventeen years at Leeds, he had frequent disagreements with the Department's predominant culture, embodied in the educational concept of 'the liberal tradition', with its emphases upon 'objectivity', 'university standards' and the like. Thompson saw this culture as essentially inculcating conformism to the prevailing social democratic culture and the ideological assumptions which underlay it.[23] Thompson rejected this perspective and its assumed 'common sense neutrality'. In contrast, he saw adult education as a dialectical process with the tutor learning from the students with their varied life experience: ideally, there should be a symbiosis between abstract knowledge and lived experience. Whilst he certainly believed in the 'Enlightenment' values of a pedagogical methodology of objectivity and tolerance, he saw them as '*by-products*, not *aims* of education; nor were they appropriate in all situations'.[24] Thompson 'declared on more than one occasion that his aim was to make socialists, create revolutionaries and transform society'.[25]

Thompson took his teaching very seriously. Although he has been known largely for his academic and political writing, and his political activism, at Leeds he undertook a demanding teaching programme. He was an effective and committed tutor, as records from the time confirmed.[26] His writing, particularly *The Making of the English Working Class*, was based on his West Riding teaching interactions with his adult students,[27] and upon the dialectical educational process which he so enthusiastically advocated. Dorothy Thompson recalled, after his death, that he undertook ' "most of his historical research for his classes and only began to write it up when he was directly commissioned to do a book ... [W]riting was always second to teaching at that stage, except writing poetry." '[28]

Thompson thus worked hard and productively on both his research and teaching. However, this, he estimated later, occupied only approximately half of his time. The other half was devoted to his political work in the CP (he became an active member of the Yorkshire District Committee), and to his political roles as Chair of the Halifax Peace Committee, Secretary of the Yorkshire Federation of Peace Organisations and editor of the *Yorkshire Voice of Peace*. What was the nature of his CP involvement and how far was his ideological position in these years congruent with his post-1956 'socialist humanism' and New Left activism?

Thompson's 'communist years'

The CP had an ambivalent relationship with English radicalism. On the one hand, its central characteristics were predominantly 'Stalinist': that is, for almost all of its existence (until the 'Eurocommunist' years from the 1970s), it followed the erratic policy dictates of, first, Lenin and then Stalin and his successors. There was little if any democratic, intra-party discussion and debate. It also accepted without question both the 'democratic centralist' ideology of the bureaucratic Party machine, and the transparently false and evasive explanations of the atrocities committed in the name of communism by the leadership in the USSR and subsequently in the 'socialist' states of Eastern Europe.[29]

On the other hand, as John Saville, has argued, England 'is a very old country; there is a native radicalism among ordinary people which goes back a very long way, and the Communist Party ... grew out of these traditions: a source, no doubt, of both its strengths and weaknesses'.[30] It is clear that, from the outset, Thompson identified with this tradition and its culture and saw the CP as firmly within the fold.

However, the CP in Britain as a whole – and especially in England – was never a mass party, unlike its counterparts in most comparable Western European societies. The CP's membership, at its height in the Second World War, was approximately sixty thousand: for most of its existence it was considerably less. Although for some years it had significant influence in the trade union movement, it was never a major political force in England. However, its *intellectual* influence on English radicalism in the twentieth century was significant. For Thompson, the only one of those considered in this book to have a lengthy involvement with the CP, his 'CP years' were important for his subsequent intellectual and political development.

No definitive analysis can be made of Thompson's roles in and attitudes towards the CP from 1942 to 1956 until there is full access to his archival papers. Following his death in 1993, his widow, Dorothy, deposited his papers at the Bodleian Library, Oxford, with the stipulation that they should be embargoed for fifty years, that is, until 2043.

Two points are nevertheless beyond dispute. His break from the CP in 1956 was, for Thompson as for many others, traumatic and painful; his subsequent distancing from the Party was at first bitter but also, for several years, in some ways hesitant and partial. Secondly, his disillusion with the CP broadened eventually into a more or less complete disavowal of Marxism *per se*. (By the end of his life, he did not consider himself intellectually in any meaningful sense a Marxist.)[31]

The nature of his relationship with the Party during the years of his membership is more contentious, however. For these years we are reliant, at present, necessarily, on the following: the publicly available letters, articles and statements by Thompson during this period; his *post facto* recollections (and maybe rationalisations); the accounts of his CP contemporaries, notably those of his friend and fellow historian John Saville;[32] and the academic analyses of scholars in the field.

There was certainly, at the level of generality, as Efsathiou has argued, 'a specific continuity ... between Thompson's involvement in Popular Front politics, his activity in the British New Left, and his later work as the voice of European Nuclear Disarmament (END)'.[33] In my own previous work on Thompson, I have observed that Thompson was, from the outset, 'a Popular Front, social-movement man, a perspective in harmony with the eloquent "human agency" argument which permeates his historical as well as his political writing'.[34] It is also the case that, in his early CP years, he pursued assiduously a Popular Front policy through his editing of the *Yorkshire Voice of Peace*, where he regularly included articles from churchmen, Labour Party members and non-affiliated peace activists, whilst at the same time maintaining an orthodox 'CP editorial line' (for example, over the Korean war).[35]

The broader assertion that he was always a dissident, or quasi-dissident, communist, unhappy with the 'democratic centralism' of the Party, and its uncritical acceptance of the twists and turns of Soviet policies, is, however, more contentious. This was clearly how Thompson remembered, or chose to remember, his CP years, when he stated in a 1979 piece:

> Long before '1956' there were centres of 'premature revisionism' among Communist intellectuals and among others who resisted the didactic methods of the Party officers, the wooden economism of its politics and the correct pabulum offered as 'Marxism'. This incipient heresy was unfocused, lacking in articulation ... we identified our enemy far too loosely as 'King Street' – a bullying and bumbling bureaucracy rather than (as it was) a highly articulated Stalinist clerisy.[36]

In a lengthy and detailed analysis of such claims, however, John McIlroy has concluded that the 'available materials provide insufficient evidence ... that he was a dissident in this period. On the contrary: what we know plausibly points towards the suggestion that during the post-war decade he poured his formidable intellectual abilities, his impressive energies, his passion for humanity and his longing for a better world ... into prosecuting the cause of Stalinism which he identified with human progress'.[37]

McIlroy provides several examples from Thompson's writings at the time to substantiate this assertion. In 1947, for instance, despite the Bulgarian communists' decision that a democratic opposition was unacceptable, Thompson's enthusiasm for 'the new democracies' of Eastern Europe was undimmed. These were, he wrote, 'the most inspiring developments in the history of Man ... These are revolutionary changes. Human nature itself is being changed by human agency.'[38] He disparaged the numerous intellectuals of the Left in Britain, and elsewhere in the West, who were critical of the USSR: Arthur Koestler, Stephen Spender and, especially, George Orwell,[39] and 'insisted intellectuals in the Soviet Union and its dependencies had voluntarily embraced a people's culture ... "we have all become fuddled"', he wrote in 1947, '"and only a good dose of the free air of the People's Republics can clear our system ... This problem is largely solved by the March of history itself ... No climate could be more fertile for the creative imagination."'[40]

As the Cold War deepened, Thompson had no hesitation in supporting the USSR against what he saw as the aggressive imperialism of the USA and its allies, most notably Britain. (The Labour governments of 1945–51 pursued an unquestioning pro-USA policy, initially under the aegis of the longstanding anti-communist Ernest Bevin, the Foreign Secretary.)

Thompson's approach in the broad 'cultural field' was rather more nuanced. McIlroy claims that Thompson advocated 'socialist realism', in the context of the CP Journal *Our Time*. However, more sympathetic – and, in this field, more expert – critics, such as Andy Croft, the poet, publisher and CP member from 1983 until the Party's demise, emphasise rather Thompson's and others' advocacy of a more humanistic and critical socialist approach. There was, Croft maintains, an oppositional culture developing, albeit slowly and often in coded language, through the Party's journals, *Left Review* before the war, and *Our Time* in the post-1945 period. Eventually, this formed the basis of the dissatisfaction of many of the Party's intellectuals with the wider politics of the Party leadership. This came to a head in 1956.

However, it is equally true that Thompson did not demur when the Party leadership rejected, in 1952, his proposal that the journal, *Our Time*, should carry '"historical articles, polemic, reportage and human studies of life in socialist countries"'; and that writing should be included only if it were free of jargon, '"no matter if the writer was a member of the Central Committee"'.[41] Instead, the Party launched the '"Zdhanovite" *Daylight* journal, reminiscent of the proletcult of the Third Period'. Thompson did not hesitate to abide by the party's decision. '"*A party decision is a party decision, and of course now it must be operated loyally and enthusiastically*"' (my italics).[42]

This was a telling phrase. Thompson's attitude to the Party may have been critical in private. (Indeed, in this same letter, he went on to express regret and criticism at such arbitrary Party edicts.) But in public he remained a loyal Party member, accepting Party decisions and discipline without question.

It might be expected that the influential Historians' Group in the Party would be a focus for more critical perspectives. Not only were Thompson and his wife, Dorothy, members, as noted: other major historians were also active in this group, Christopher Hill and Eric Hobsbawm amongst them. Ground-breaking and original research was undoubtedly produced by members of this group; but it is also the case that, at least publicly, the group's members '"uncritically defended the Soviet Union and Stalin"'.[43] There may have been 'informal' criticisms voiced by group members: but the currently available Thompson papers do not give evidence of such dissent.

In 1957, Thompson recalled that he had been '"duped by the Rajik and Kostov trials, because I was a casuist here and perhaps an accomplice there. We were Communists, because we had faith in the fundamental humanist content of Communism and during the darkest years of the Cold War it was our duty to speak for this. I do not regret this, although I wish we had spoken more wisely and, therefore, to more effect."'[44] There is no evidence that, before 1956, he said or wrote anything critical of Stalinism in general or the show trials in particular.

There is more evidence of a similar nature, but enough has been said to indicate the nature of Thompson's perspectives in his CP years – although, as noted, any final judgement must await the release of Thompson's papers. There remains, however, the question of how much of Thompson's evolving 'socialist humanism' was evident in his first major book, *William Morris: Romantic to Revolutionary* (1955). Writing in 1980, one of the foremost Marxist critics of Thompson's perspective, Perry Anderson, claimed that Thompson's portrayal, in 1955, of Morris as a revolutionary socialist 'radically incompatible with the orthodox ethos of Stalinism' had 'to a considerable extent' prepared the ground for the 1956 break.[45] Similar arguments have been made by David Goodway[46] and Christos Efstathiou.[47]

Such arguments are certainly true at a level of generality. The very choice of Morris, and Thompson's emphasis upon his revolutionary socialist humanism, were evidence of this. '"With Morris moral weight and scientific analysis were complementary and inseparable."'[48] However, in the original, 1955 edition, Thompson was unequivocal in his orthodox CP assertion that '"Morris's moral criticism of society is not only entirely compatible with dialectical materialism ... it is also the theme of his most vigorous and original writings within the Marxist tradition"'.[49] Thompson went on to defend explicitly the 'base/superstructure' causative model that was to prove such a defining issue for the New Left in a few years' time. Morris '"did not make the mistake of giving precedence to moral factors as the agents of revolutionary change ... But, nevertheless he laid the greatest stress upon their agency ...

'Necessity' alone would impel spontaneous riot and class struggle wasteful and uncertain of success." '[50] Thus Thompson can be seen 'straining at the leash' of orthodoxy – but still bound by Party discipline to 'hold the line'. Also, in the 1955 edition, he was fulsome in his praise of the Soviet Union. Morris's utopian vision of 'A Factory as It Might Be' had, Thompson argued, been realised in the USSR: '"today visitors return from the Soviet Union with stories of the poet's dream already fulfilled ... today they have before them Stalin's blueprint of the advance to Communism"'.[51] Not surprisingly, Thompson's book was praised in the *Marxist Quarterly* by that guardian of Party orthodoxy, Page Arnot.[52]

By the time of the second edition of the Morris book, in 1976, Thompson's politics had changed radically. All passages such as those cited above were either deleted or drastically revised.

Viewed in retrospect, the tensions in Thompson's politics were thus apparent by the late 1940s or early 1950s. Indeed, such tensions may well have been present as early as 1945. In the Epilogue to his three-volume autobiography, the veteran communist Jack Lindsay recalled that, in November 1945, at a CP conference, there was a discussion of 'a lengthy document of mine on the nature of culture. Everyone condemned it but the young E.P. Thompson. (It defined culture as a form of production as against the notion that it was a part of a superstructure with a determining economic base.)'[53]

The picture is thus a complicated one. There is no doubt that, in his 'CP years', Thompson, believing that communism provided the best formation for bringing about human emancipation, abided loyally by Party discipline; it also seems to be the case that he, and others in the intellectual, 'cultural' group that constituted his closest colleagues and friends, harboured increasingly severe reservations about the Party leadership and its policy stances. However, they kept such misgivings largely to themselves.

The purpose of this lengthy discussion of Thompson's perspectives in the CP, in some of his most formative years – 1942 to 1956 – is not to seek to undermine his subsequent impassioned radicalism and his centrally important role in both the first New Left and the peace movement; still less is it intended to besmirch the integrity of a key figure in twentieth-century English radicalism. Rather, the intention is to illustrate the degree to which loyalty to a rigid ideology, and to the organisational representation of that ideology, can lead inexorably to support for morally and politically untenable positions.

Twenty-twenty hindsight is, of course, a convenient attribute. The ideological and political fallacies, and the persistent 'wishful thinking' of the CP's politics, were not apparent at the time; and the unfolding tragedy of the Stalinist and post-Stalinist eras could not, perhaps, have been foreseen. Moreover, for Thompson's generation, the crucial role of the Red Army in the defeat of Nazism, and the massive death toll suffered by the USSR, were of paramount importance and had an emotional as well as a political resonance. This contrasted, particularly forcefully for this generation, with the flaccid appeasement and weaknesses of the Western democracies in the 1930s when confronted with the threat of Nazism.

Many in the English radical tradition in the twentieth century espoused, at one time or another, the ideals and the political strategy and tactics of the CP, Pankhurst and Wilkinson, for example. But it became clear to almost all of them – and to many others – that the CP, as the Marxist-Leninist version of Marxism itself, was ultimately a dangerous cul-de-sac. In the final analysis, the CP had no viable place in English radicalism. Not only was its political potential always severely limited because of its inability to become a mass party of the working class: more fundamentally, its values and *modus operandi* were never congruent with the core values of English radicalism.[54]

Thompson's 'CP years', though important in understanding his overall politics and impact, should be regarded, as they were in the end by Thompson himself,[55] as politically mistaken. There is an irony in the vehemence with which, after 1956, Thompson denounced Stalinism. This sat oddly with his previous, wilful blindness to the iniquities of Stalin's USSR. As Anderson drily observed: 'Is the *official* announcement of Stalin's crimes [in Khrushchev's speech in 1956] then to mark the frontier between venial and mortal responsibility? The suggestion would seem to be that it was understandable to dismiss Trotsky and ignore Serge, but inexcusable not to heed Khrushchev or Mikoyan.'[56]

In 1956, perhaps belatedly, Thompson and many others (approximately seven thousand) came to the conclusion that the Party was no longer a politically or morally tenable organisation.

'1956', the first New Left and CND[57]

The year 1956 was a watershed year for the British Left in general, and for Thompson in particular. Khrushchev's speech at the Twentieth Congress of the CPSU, denouncing Stalin's crimes, provoked turmoil in the communist world. This culminated in the brutal repression of the Hungarian uprising in November *and* the refusal of the CPGB's leadership to permit full, open discussion and debate: as a result, Thompson and many others resigned from the Party. In the same year, the Suez crisis, precipitated by British and French military intervention in clandestine collaboration with Israel against a newly militant Egypt, created a mass protest across the centre and Left of British politics.

The first atmospheric testing of the British hydrogen bomb took place in 1957. The concerns over nuclear weapons testing, and their deleterious effects, and the associated demand for Britain to renounce nuclear weapons unilaterally as a catalyst to trigger multilateral disarmament, mounted through 1957. The result was the creation of the Campaign for Nuclear Disarmament (CND) in early 1958. Although other peace organisations had been active in the earlier 1950s, it was CND that became the focal point for a new mass movement.[58]

The two movements, the New Left and CND, were closely linked – though CND was both a much larger movement and far more diffuse ideologically. Not only were their objectives broadly similar, at least in terms of foreign and defence policies (discussed below), but their ethos and culture were highly congruent. Both movements were largely composed of idealistic, frustrated, and predominantly middle-class young people; neither had formal membership, nor constitutions (although later CND was to spend much time and effort developing a constitution, committee structure, standing orders and so on); there was very little by way of a formal, specific policy programme; and neither had any aspiration to develop into a 'vanguard party'.

After his resignation from the CP, Thompson continued for some years to describe himself as a 'dissident Communist', although repudiating his former adherence to Stalinist ideology. In November 1956, he argued that 'Stalinism is socialist theory and practice which has lost the ingredient of humanity. The Stalinist mode of thought is not that of dialectical materialism, but that of mechanical idealism ... from the fluid movement of Lenin's analysis of particular social realities, Stalin plucked axioms. Stalinism is Leninism turned into stone.'[59]

By 1957 Thompson was arguing that, in the current Cold War, both Western capitalism and Soviet communism were forms of self-alienation, 'commodifying' in their different ways human beings and reducing them to economic entities. 'Socialist humanism', he wrote in the summer of 1957, 'declares: liberate men from slavery to things, to the pursuit of profit or servitude to "economic necessity". Liberate man, as a creative being – and he will create, not only new values, but things in super-abundance.'[60]

Thompson's 'socialist humanism' was linked integrally to the 'Third Way' politics which the New Left and the radical wing of the peace movement advocated. The demand for unilateral nuclear disarmament, to break the escalation of the arms race, had to be accompanied, Thompson believed, by Britain's withdrawal from NATO *and* the development of a 'positive neutralist' foreign policy.[61] The objective, Thompson argued, was to champion 'a new internationalism [whose aim is not] that of the triumph of one camp over another, but the dissolution of the camps and the triumph of the common people'.[62]

Thompson's advocacy of Britain taking a 'moral lead' and creating political momentum through these policies, may be seen, in retrospect, as over-estimating Britain's prominence and influence as a world power. (His argument, in fact, has much in common, in this particular respect, with J.B. Priestley's original article in the *New Statesman*, 'Britain and the Nuclear Bombs', in November 1957, which was the immediate catalyst for the formation of CND.) However, it must be borne in mind that Britain at that time was one of only three nations to possess nuclear weapons and a disarmament initiative could thus, arguably, have had a significant impact. Less tangibly, only a decade since the end of the Second World War, Britain still had a self-image – on the Left as well as on the Right – of being a 'Great Power'. It is thus understandable that such perceptions were widely held at the time.

Thompson's continuing themes of human agency and Popular Front movements as the essential engines of progressive political change, thus came together in the developing campaign for nuclear disarmament and the 'organic' building of the New Left through its journals and through the network of New Left clubs. Thompson's early optimism about the potential of these twin movements was relatively short-lived, however. CND had scored a notable, if surprising, victory at the 1960 Labour Party Conference, where a vote in favour of unilateral nuclear disarmament had been passed, reflecting a wave of pro-unilateralist feeling in several of the large trade unions; however, for a variety of reasons,[63] it rapidly became clear that this policy commitment would be reversed (as it duly was, by a large majority, at the 1961 Conference). Although CND, and related movements,[64] continued to grow until 1963,[65] the movement lacked strategic direction and became increasingly fragile as its fundamentally incompatible constituent ideologies and groupings turned against each other.

The New Left 'coalition', in which Thompson 'played a pivotal role',[66] was equally subject to such dangers. The two journals of the New Left, *The New Reasoner* and the *Universities and Left Review*, merged in late 1959 to become *New Left Review* (*NLR*). As Peter Sedgwick has noted, the 'Communist tradition' of the *New Reasoner* group (and its predecessor, *The Reasoner*) 'brought into the fusion ... an explicit commitment to class-struggle, an iteration of the role of human agency as against impersonal historical process' and an adherence to a Labourist strategy.[67] The culture of the *ULR* group was very different. The editors were almost all recent Oxford graduates and in their twenties; they had no strong links to the labour movement; they were, generally, cultural and social theorists rather than historians; and, as Thompson wrote of the 'Aldermaston generation', they 'never looked upon the Soviet Union as a weak but heroic Workers' State; but, rather, as the nation of the Great Purges and of Stalingrad'.[68] Their central concerns were more with 'modern cultural themes'[69] than with the history and traditions of English radicalism.

The merger of the two journals was thus destined to be difficult. Relationships on the board were fractious and, after much strife, there was in 1963 a wholesale change in the journal's nature and purpose. Under the new young editor, Perry Anderson, and his 'team' (initially Robin Blackburn and Tom Nairn), *NLR* became a journal focused, firstly, upon bringing Western European Marxist theory to the British Left, and, secondly, upon 'Third World Marxisms'. This second New Left had no ambition to be linked with any radical social movement; and, indeed, Anderson, and others associated with the *NLR*, critiqued and rejected Thompson's 'socialist humanism', and attacked what they saw as his untheorised empiricism.

This was a bitter dispute, especially on Thompson's part. He felt betrayed and undermined, emotionally as well as intellectually and politically. He could, by common consent, be a 'highly temperamental and "difficult"' man to work with.[70] It was not until 1976 that Thompson became (partially) reconciled to Anderson, referring to him by then in an interview 'as a "comrade" with whom he did not wish to argue'; and later enthusing over 'Anderson's *Considerations on Western Marxism*, which he saw as a repudiation "of all that philosophical stuff Perry has been publishing in the *Review* for years"'.[71]

From the mid-1960s to the mid-1970s, Thompson effectively withdrew from public, political life. But he revisited, analysed and broadened the polemical debate with the 'structuralists' – proto-Stalinists he would claim in his more irritable moments. He wrote three wide-ranging, lengthy, somewhat obsessive – but brilliant – intellectual *tours de force*: *The Peculiarities of the English* (1965); *An Open Letter to Lesek Kolakowski* (1973); and *The Poverty of Theory: or an Orrery of Errors* (1978). In them all, he reasserted with passion his creed of 'socialist humanism', and celebrated the radical traditions and vibrancy of the 'common people of England'.

Despite the partial rapprochement noted above, the debate reached an acrimonious climax in the notorious confrontation between Stuart Hall, Richard Johnson and Thompson in December 1979, at St Paul's Church, Oxford, at the *History Workshop* conference.[72] Thompson accused his New Left colleagues of an obsessive concern with 'the minutiae of theory' and argued that they were too little concerned 'with big political issues like the erosion of civil liberties in Britain'.[73] It was not the content so much as the hostile *tone* of Thompson's bitter denunciations that so alienated many on the Left. The polemic was not all on one side, however: Hamilton noted correspondence between Tom Nairn and Jonathan Rée, editor of *Radical Philosophy*, in which Nairn referred to Thompson as similar to Enoch Powell and 'representative of "a village-idiot tradition" which was no longer "politically pressing"'.[74] The differences between Thompson, Saville (and the other ex-CP *New Reasoner* radicals) and Anderson and his colleagues were numerous, as noted earlier. But what irritated Thompson most, and provoked his scornful, dismissive polemic, was the abstracted, *haut en bas*, 'armchair theorising' of Anderson *et al*. It was clear that those around Anderson's *NLR* had no interest in, let alone commitment to, political *activism*. For Thompson, this was a shameful dereliction of socialist duty.

Thompson was not to participate in public political life, in any major way, until the 'second wave' of the anti-nuclear peace movement and his leadership role in END (see below). Nevertheless, he was a persistent and, as always, passionate defender of the fundamental civil liberties and free institutions of Britain which he saw as under threat from the state and from the bureaucratic and corporatist cultural control increasingly evident in the 1970s. In *Writing by Candlelight* (1980) he drew together a series of articles written in the 1970s and concerned in part with the erosion of academic freedom and the corporatist culture of the University of Warwick,[75] but largely with the 'State and Civil Liberties'. This illustrated his belief in the English radical tradition and the hard-won freedoms wrung from the state over the centuries. (Thompson's scholarly research on the detailed history of these developments has been influential: see *Albion's Fatal Tree* (1975) and *Whigs and Hunters* (1975)).

Despite his political quasi-isolation, Thompson thus remained consistent in his ideological belief in the moral potential of the 'common people' and the importance of defending the civil liberties achieved in Britain over the preceding two hundred years. He was also consistent in seeing these aims as best articulated through a series of 'Popular Front', social-movement, iterations.

Thompson and END[76]

The growing protests across Europe against NATO's proposed siting of cruise missiles in Western Europe[77] aroused Thompson's zeal. He saw END 'as a new kind of grass-roots, anti-nuclear pacifism':[78] but he also envisioned END, important though its substantive aims were, as a means of reviving a Popular Front strategy to resist the political establishment and its ideology on a wider front.[79] Thompson had a high-profile, pivotal role in the new 1980s movement, which was larger, more transnational and less tied to orthodox political parties of the Left, whether social democratic or communist, than had been the case in the anti-nuclear movement of the 1950s and 1960s.

The pamphlet *Protest and Survive*, which he wrote as a riposte to a letter in *The Times* from Michael Howard, Chichele Professor of the History of War at the University of Oxford, caught the public imagination.[80] Thompson rapidly became a figure of public prominence.

Although Thompson had been discussing, from the mid-1970s, with Ken Coates of the Bertrand Russell Peace Foundation (BRPF) amongst others, the possibilities of mounting a new trans-European campaign to protest against the curtailment of civil liberties and growing militarisation, nothing had materialised. but the NATO decision to deploy cruise missiles in Europe, *and* the attempts by the state to close down any debate on the issue, changed the political environment. Howard's rather bland call for extensive civil defence preparations to 'give protection to a substantial number of the population in the event of ... a "limited" nuclear strike'[81] seemed to many to symbolise the unthinking drift to nuclear war, and the unacceptable complacency of the political establishment.

In the autumn of 1981, an estimated five million people demonstrated in Europe against cruise missiles: before this, Thompson, jointly with Ken Coates, had launched the END Appeal (on 28 April 1980) which had laid the blame for the mounting crisis on *both* super-powers. Thompson, and others in the leadership,[82] were determined from the outset that the movement should not be seen, as some had seen CND, 'as the Kremlin's fifth column'.[83] The emphasis was upon opposition to the Cold War *per se*, 'not just nuclear weapons. END called for a transnational movement of citizens and made an explicit link between peace and democracy or human rights.'[84]

For Thompson, and most people in END, the emphasis was thus upon popular, social movement activism, rather than working through the formal political parties of the Left. Thus the Appeal called for activists to 'learn to be loyal, not to "East" or "West", but to each other, and we must disregard the prohibitions and limitations imposed by any national state'. The objective was a nuclear-free Europe 'from Portugal to the Urals'.[85] Thompson was insistent that the movement should be linked with dissident movements in Eastern Europe: he saw this as an essential element in undermining the Cold War culture that permeated the 'East' as well as the 'West'.

Here was one of the points of tension with Ken Coates and the BRPF. Coates was temperamentally committed to *realpolitik* and saw political advance as coming via the long march through the committees of labour movement and socialist organisations. He was impatient with the romanticism of Thompson's emphasis upon dissident movements in the East and he thus saw the focal point of END as being the organising of trans-European 'Conventions', bringing together the key political actors, and thus developing increasing pressure for a nuclear-free Europe.

When political change came, in the form of Gorbachev's radical reforms of the Soviet system, the disarmament agreements with Reagan and the subsequent upheavals in Eastern Europe, Coates saw them as, essentially, coming through the formal political system. Thompson, on the contrary, saw this as a movement *of the people*, uniting those of different cultures and beliefs in a fluid, popular and intense campaign for a new way of politics: an 'anti-politics', as George Konrad termed it.

Thompson developed his critique in his alternative Dimbleby Lecture, *Beyond the Cold War*, and in his article and subsequent book on 'Exterminism'.[86] He argued that there was a 'deep structure' to the Cold War, a mutually re-enforcing and relentless drive to an outcome of 'exterminism'. The two super-powers, Thompson argued, 'do not *have* military-industrial complexes: they *are* such complexes'.[87] There was a 'reciprocal logic of the opposed weapons systems';[88] and the 'ruling interests on both sides have become ideologically addicted, they need its continuance'.[89]

In his book *Zero Option*, Thompson reiterated his Popular Front perspective and argued for a broad alliance, to create 'the international elan to throw the cruise missiles and the SS-20s back'.[90]

The hegemonic 'common sense' of the two super-power systems had been strengthened by the Cold War. Significantly, non-alignment initiatives were greeted with hostility by *both* sides: the fate of Allende in Chile and Dubcek in Czechoslovakia, for example. Only through Popular Front alliances could such negative forces be defeated.

The movement must, therefore, Thompson argued, go behind the missiles to the Cold War itself: détente between nation-states had been superseded by a détente of peoples, working both to undermine state structures and to link, independently of the blocs, kindred spirits across the divide. Increasingly, Thompson saw the cause of peace and human rights as indivisible; and, as he had long believed, it was social movements of the 'common people' which would be the primary agencies of progressive change. As Mary Kaldor has argued, his stance in the 1980s was significantly different from his advocacy of positive neutralism in the 1950s and early 1960s. Whereas the latter had been 'about building a non-aligned bloc of nation states, END was about getting rid of alliances, building a bottom-up movement of European citizens. It was détente from below, or, in Edward's phrase, "citizens' détente".'[91]

Thus, Thompson argued, the revolutions which transformed Eastern Europe and the Soviet Union from the late 1980s were inspired not only through 'high politics' – the rise of Gorbachev, the economic problems of the Soviet system and so on – but through the popular movements for peace and civil freedoms. As Mary Kaldor recalled Thompson saying, 'history is made by the people but it is never subsequently told that way'.[92]

The Romantic radical

Eric Hobsbawm, probably the most celebrated twentieth-century British socialist historian after Thompson, remained in the CP from the early 1930s until its demise, towards the end of his long life. His politics thus differed from those of Thompson. Nevertheless, Hobsbawm judged Thompson to be both a brilliant and an important historian, and an admirable socialist radical. In his autobiography, *Interesting Times: A Twentieth-Century Life*,[93] Hobsbawm recalled Thompson's 'quite extraordinary gifts, not least the sort of palpable "star quality", which led every eye to turn towards his increasingly craggy good looks'. His ' "work combined passion and intellect, the gifts of the poet, the narrator and the analyst. He was the only historian I knew who had not just talent, brilliance, erudition and the gift of writing, but … genius in the traditional sense of the word." '. He also 'fitted the Romantic image of the genius in looks, life and work …'.[94]

However, there is something of a sting in the tail of Hobsbawm's assessment. Thompson had been 'showered by the fairies at birth with all possible gifts except two. Nature had omitted to provide him with an in-built sub-editor and an in-built compass'.[95]

This is a graphic and fair assessment of Thompson, who was, by any criterion, an outstanding figure. Intellectually brilliant, he was also one of the most charismatic and impressive public figures of the twentieth-century English Left, and a polemicist without modern equal. There was, though, substance to Hobsbawm's first caveat. To an almost absurd degree, Thompson's pen ran away with him – albeit to great effect. The almost one thousand pages of his classic *The Making of the English Working Class*, which focused on a short span of English history, began life as a (commissioned) textbook (originally to be approximately sixty thousand words) on 'Working-Class Politics, 1790–1920'. His *Open Letter to Lesek Kolakowski* ran to virtually a hundred pages; and his polemical essay against Althusserian structuralist Marxism, *The Poverty of Theory*, to over two hundred pages. Thompson's written style, indeed his whole persona, was the antithesis of the 'soundbite', 'Twitter' culture which so bedevils the early twenty-first century.

Hobsbawm's second caveat is more contentious. He implies that Thompson's lack of 'compass' led him into unprofitable diversions from his central scholarly work as a historian. (He refers specifically to the 'criminal' folly of 'controverting a thinker [Althusser] who would be dead as an influence in another ten years' time'.)[96] However, this argument perhaps fails to appreciate the unity and coherence of Thompson's intellectual and political work. He saw innovative, radical, scholarly work and political activism as an indivisible whole.

Thompson's political life was characterised by a series of, frequently bitter, fallings-out. The year 1956 was a defining moment for him: as David Goodway has commented, Thompson's 'great blind spot was his sentimental loyalty to pre-1956 Communism'.[97] He felt betrayed and rebuffed by the failure of the early New Left of which he had had such high hopes; and he resented, and was exasperated by, the exponents of the theoretically inclined *New Left Review* group around Anderson. He bore a long-term political grudge, as can be seen from his 'explosion' at the St Paul's Church meeting in December 1979, noted earlier. Even his closest friends and collaborators, John Saville and Ralph Miliband, found him 'difficult' at times. On the other hand, he could be kindness itself to younger scholars, and left-wing activists: and he had a warmth and friendliness, with an infectious sense of humour. In truth, he was an intense and passionate man: he took ideas, politics, literature and life itself seriously and his emotions were easily aroused. Thompson was a Romantic to his fingertips: his erudition and empathy with English (and European) literature was as great as his identity as a radical historian. In one sense, he was, as Andy Croft has observed, a 'poet manqué'.[98]

Thompson's Romanticism centred on the moral integrity and political potential of the 'common people' to continue the long struggle for emancipation and socialist values and freedoms that had been inherent in English radicalism for centuries, and found their counterparts in analogous struggles and social movements across the globe. Thompson's intellectual work and his political activism were indissolubly linked in his commitment to the English radical tradition; and his intellectual power, his vivid writing and charismatic campaigning had a profound impact on progressive politics in Britain and beyond in the second half of the twentieth century.

Notes

1   His most famous book is *The Making of the English Working Class* (London and New York: Gollancz and Vintage, 1963, subsequently published by Pelican, 1968). Other major historical works include: *William Morris: Romantic to Revolutionary* (Lawrence and Wishart, 1955; revised second edition, Merlin Press, 1976); *Whigs and Hunters: The Origins of the Black Acts* (London and New York: Allen Lane and Pantheon, 1975); *Customs in Common* (London and New York: Merlin Press and New Press, 1991); *Witness Against the Beast: William Blake and the Moral Law* (Cambridge: Cambridge University Press, 1993).

2 Thompson wrote a voluminous amount of political and polemical articles, books and pamphlets. Among the most significant are: his contributions to *The New Reasoner* and *New Left Review*; (ed.) *Out of Apathy* (London: Stevens and Sons / New Left Books, 1960); 'The Peculiarities of the English', in R. Miliband and J. Saville (eds), *Socialist Register 1965* (Merlin Press, 1965); *The Poverty of Theory and Other Essays* (London: Merlin Press, 1978); *Protest and Survive* (Nottingham: Spokesman Pamphlets 71, CND and BRPF, 1980); *Writing by Candlelight* (London: Merlin Press, 1980); *Exterminism and Cold War* (Verso and New Left Books, 1982); *The Heavy Dancers* (Merlin Press, 1985); *Persons and Polemics* (Merlin Press, 1994).

3 P. Anderson, *Arguments within English Marxism* (New Left Books and Verso, 1980), pp. 17–18.

4 D, Goodway, *Anarchist Seeds Beneath the Snow: Left-Libertarian Thought and British Writers from William Morris to Colin Ward* (Liverpool: Liverpool University Press, 2006), p. 276, citing Thompson, *William Morris* (1955), p. 838.

5 Thompson's work thus complemented that of other adult educators concerned with cultural studies, notably R. Hoggart, *The Uses of Literacy* (1957), and R. Williams, *Culture and Society* (1958). See also: T. Steele, *The Emergence of Cultural Studies 1945–65: Cultural Politics, Adult Education and the English Question* (Lawrence and Wishart, 1997), chapter 7.

6 See in particular, Thompson, 'Peculiarities of the English'. In this landmark article, a polemical and passionate response to Anderson's critique, Thompson gave his most succinct summary of his political and historical perspective. For Anderson, see: 'Origins of the Present Crisis', *New Left Review* 23 (January–February 1964), reprinted in P. Anderson and R. Blackburn (eds), *Towards Socialism* (Fontana and New Left Books 1965); and 'Socialism and Pseudo-Empiricism', *New Left Review* 35, 1966.

7 See R. Taylor, 'Thompson and the Peace Movement: From CND in the 1950s and 1960s to END in the 1980s', in R. Fieldhouse and R. Taylor (eds), *E.P. Thompson and English Radicalism* (Manchester: Manchester University Press, 2013), pp. 181–201; C. Efstathiou, *E.P. Thompson: A Twentieth-Century Romantic* (Merlin, 2015).

8 K. Soper, 'Thompson and Socialist Humanism', in Fieldhouse and Taylor, *E.P. Thompson and English Radicalism*, p. 126

9 Ibid., p. 131.

10 This was given its fullest articulation in his polemical essay, critiquing Althusserian, structuralist Marxism, in the title essay of Thompson, *The Poverty of Theory*.

11 He declined the invitation from Saville and Miliband to join them in editing the 'Socialist Register', 'the annual that would most closely follow the tradition of the NR (New Reasoner)', M. Newman, 'Thompson and the Early New Left', in Fieldhouse and Taylor, *Thompson and English Radicalism*, p. 174. See also, for more detail, M. Newman, *Ralph Miliband and the Politics of the New Left* (Merlin Press, 2002), pp. 115–20.

12 Soper, *Thompson and Socialist Humanism*, p. 138.

13 This section draws upon R. Fieldhouse, T. Koditschek and R. Taylor, 'E.P. Thompson: A Short Introduction', in Fieldhouse and Taylor, *Thompson and English Radicalism*, pp. 1–22.

14 See P.J. Conradi, *A Very English Hero: The Making of Frank Thompson* (Bloomsbury, 2012).

15 B. Palmer, *E.P. Thompson: Objections and Oppositions* (Verso, 1994), p. 25.
16 E.P. Thompson, *Beyond the Frontier: The Politics of a Failed Mission* (London and Stanford, CA: Merlin Press and Stanford University Press, 1997), p. 47.
17 See ibid., pp. 41, 84–6; and Conradi, *A Very English Hero*, pp. 291–324, 366, 369–70. Thompson maintained that his brother had been murdered with the connivance, for political reasons, of the British government. Conradi discusses the issues involved at some length, but remains agnostic. See also Fieldhouse and Taylor (eds), *Thompson and English Radicalism*, pp. 6–7.
18 E.P. Thompson, *The Railway: An Adventure in Construction* (British-Yugoslav Association, 1948); H.J. Kaye, *The British Marxist Historians* (Cambridge: Polity Press, 1984), p. 169.
19 R. Fieldhouse, 'Thompson: The Adult Educator', in Fieldhouse and Taylor, *Thompson and English Radicalism*, p. 26, citing M. Merrill, 'An Interview with E.P. Thompson', in MAHRO, *Visions of History* (Manchester: Manchester University Press, 1983), p. 12.
20 T. Koditschek, 'The Possibilities of Theory: Thompson's History', in Fieldhouse and Taylor, *Thompson and English Radicalism*, pp. 70–1.
21 Ibid., p. 72.
22 Thompson's subsequent historical research and publications concentrated largely upon the earlier part of this historical process and its antecedents in the eighteenth century. See, for example, *Whigs and Hunters*; *Customs in Common*; D. Hay, P. Linebaugh, J. Rule, E.P. Thompson and Cal Winslow, *Albion's Fatal Tree: Crime and Society in Eighteenth-Century England* (London and New York: Allen Lane and Pantheon, 1975); and a series of journal articles, including: 'Time, Work Discipline and Industrial Capitalism', *Past and Present* 38, 1967; and 'Eighteenth- Century English Society: Class Struggle without Class', *Social History* 3, No. 2, 1978.
23 See Fieldhouse, 'Thompson: The Adult Educator', *passim*.
24 Ibid., p. 32.
25 Ibid., p. 31.
26 See ibid., pp. 37ff.
27 *The Making of the English Working Class* was dedicated to two of his adult students, Joe and Dorothy Greenald.
28 Fieldhouse, 'Thompson: The Adult Educator', pp. 37–8, citing Leeds University Archive, Departmental Records: Adult Education Supplementary Papers, Dorothy Thompson to Andy Croft, 3 July 1995.
29 These were detailed not only by contemporary critics such as George Orwell and Arthur Koestler but also later by former communists such as Saville and Thompson himself.
30 J. Saville, 'The Communist Experience: A Personal Appraisal', in R. Miliband and L. Panitch (eds), *Socialist Register 1991* (Merlin Press, 1991), pp. 8–9.
31 Letter from Dorothy Thompson to the author, 2012.
32 Saville, an economic historian, based at the University of Hull, was eight years older than Thompson. Both were members of the CPGB Historians' Group (see below), as was Dorothy Thompson; but they were not close friends until 1956, when they decided to produce, first, *The Reasoner* and subsequently *The New Reasoner*, one of the central publications of the New Left. On Saville's view of Thompson, see J. Saville, 'Edward Thompson, the Communist Party and 1956', in R. Miliband and L. Panitch

(eds), *Socialist Register 1994* (Merlin Press, 1994), pp. 20–31; on Saville's own CP experience, see Saville, 'The Communist Experience: A Personal Appraisal', in Miliband and Panitch (eds), *Socialist Register 1991*, pp. 1–27.
33 Efstathiou, *Thompson*, p. vii.
34 Taylor, 'Thompson and the Peace Movement', in Fieldhouse and Taylor, *Thompson and English Radicalism*, p. 181.
35 Ibid., pp. 182–3.
36 J. McIlroy, 'Another Look at E.P. Thompson and British Communism, 1937–1955', *Labor History* (on-line Journal), 26 June 2017, p. 2, citing E.P. Thompson, 'Edgell Rickword [1979]', in Thompson, *Persons and Polemics*, pp. 236–43.
37 Ibid., p. 26.
38 Ibid., p. 7, citing E.P. Thompson, 'Comments on a People's Culture', *Our Time* (October 1947), pp. 234–8.
39 See his polemical essay on Orwell, 'Outside the Whale', in *Out of Apathy*; reprinted in *Poverty of Theory*, pp. 1–33.
40 McIlroy, 'Another Look', p. 7, citing Thompson, 'Comments on a People's Culture', pp. 35–8.
41 Ibid., p. 15, citing letters from Thompson to Emile Burns, 27 May 1952, and from Thompson to Margot Heinemann, 4 June 1952. Andy Croft has claimed, however, that '*Left Review* was not in any sense oppositional; it didn't need to be. The Popular Front years allowed and encouraged exactly those ideas that later became the source of critical and oppositional thinking inside the Party'. Letter to the author, 9 April 2018.
42 Ibid. (letter to Heinemann).
43 Ibid., p. 10, citing D. Dworkin, *Cultural Marxism: History, the New Left and the Origins of Cultural Studies* (Durham, NC, and London: Duke University Press, 1997), p. 21.
44 Thompson, 'Socialism and the Intellectuals' (1957), cited in McIlroy, 'Another Look', pp. 19–20.
45 Anderson, *Arguments within English Marxism*, p. 145.
46 Goodway, *Anarchist Seeds Beneath the Snow*, p. 277.
47 Efstathiou, *Thompson*, p. 53.
48 McIlroy, 'Another Look', p. 21, citing Thompson, 'The Making of William Morris', *Arena*, April–May, 1951, p. 26, note 14.
49 McIlroy, 'Another Look'. p. 22, citing Thompson, *Morris*, p. 832.
50 McIlroy, 'Another Look', pp. 21–2, citing Thompson, *Morris*, pp. 837–8.
51 McIlroy, 'Another Look', p. 23, citing Thompson, *Morris*, pp. 760–1.
52 R. Page Arnot, 'William Morris, Communist', *Marxist Quarterly*, October 1955, pp. 237–55.
53 J. Lindsay, 'Epilogue', in *Life Rarely Tells: An Autobiography in Three Volumes* (Penguin Books, 1982), p. 801. I am grateful to Andy Croft for drawing my attention to this quotation.
54 There have been many honourable and sincere Marxist socialists who remained committed to the CP through all its crises, and despite its manifest ideological and political problems. Two contrasting examples are the contributors, including Andy Croft, to: A. Croft (ed.), *After the Party: Reflections on Life Since the CPGB* (Lawrence and Wishart, 2012); and the noted historian Eric Hobsbawm, who joined the CP in the early 1930s and remained a member until the Party's demise.

55 By late May 1956, Thompson had come to regard the CPGB as analogous to the Roman Catholic Church, for so long the main adversary of English radicals. The CPGB leadership, he argued in a letter of May 1956, to Bert Ramelson, ' "have in fact been acting as High Priests interpreting and justifying the Holy Writ, as emanating from Stalin, rather than creative Marxists" '; he amplified this in a subsequent (1956) letter to George Matthews, arguing that, like the Roman Catholic Church, the CPGB ' "excommunicated heretics ... and sought to establish the truth or falsity of doctrines by referring to a self-consistent system of thought founded upon authority and Biblical texts, rather than by constant reference to the facts" '. Cited by McIlroy, 'Another Look', p. 24.

56 Anderson, *Arguments within English Marxism*, p. 117.

57 This section, and the following section on Thompson and the peace movement, draws heavily upon my previous publications on these themes: in particular, 'Thompson and the Peace Movement', in Fieldhouse and Taylor, *Thompson and English Radicalism*; *Against the Bomb: The British Peace Movement 1958–1965* (Oxford: Clarendon Press, 1988). There have also been, since Thompson's death, several books analysing in some detail these aspects of Thompson's life, work and significance: S. Hamilton, *The Crisis of Theory: E.P. Thompson, the New Left and Post-War British Politics* (Manchester: Manchester University Press, 2011); Efstathiou, *Thompson*, 2015; Dworkin, *Cultural Marxism*, 1997; Palmer, *Objections and Oppositions*, 1994.

58 See Taylor, *Against the Bomb*, for a detailed analysis not only of CND but of its predecessor bodies, in particular the NCANWT and the DAC, and of the later Committee of 100. See also J. Hinton, *Protests and Visions: Peace Politics in Twentieth Century Britain* (Hutchinson Radius, 1989); and Goodway, *Seeds Beneath the Snow*, chapter 12, pp. 260–87. For a sociological study of the nature and background of CND's supporters, see F. Parkin, *Middle Class Radicalism: The Social Bases of the British Campaign for Nuclear Disarmament* (Manchester: Manchester University Press, 1968).

59 E.P. Thompson, 'Through the Smoke of Budapest', *The Reasoner* 3, November 1956, p. 6.

60 E.P. Thompson, 'Socialist Humanism', *The New Reasoner* 1, Summer 1957, p. 143.

61 A fuller statement of the New Left's position on positive neutralism is contained in Peter Worsley's 'Imperialism in Retreat': '[Britain could] generate immense pressure, in alliance with India, Ghana, Yugoslavia and backed by the uncommitted countries, for world peace and active neutrality. And most of these uncommitted nations are countries which could, under such stimulus, move towards socialism ... not forming another frozen bloc, but trading and communicating freely, gradually breaking down the barriers on both sides.' In Thompson (ed.), *Out of Apathy*.

62 E.P. Thompson, 'The New Left', *The New Reasoner* 9, Summer 1959.

63 For a detailed discussion of the relationship between CND and the Labour Party and wider labour movement, see Taylor, *Against the Bomb*, pp. 19–72 and 275–315.

64 Principally, from 1957 to 1960, the Emergency Committee for Direct Action Against Nuclear War (DAC); and from late 1960, the Committee of 100. See ibid., on the DAC, pp. 115–89; and on the Committee of 100, pp. 190–274.

65 After Hugh Gaitskell's sudden death in January 1963, and the election of the wily and pragmatic Harold Wilson as leader of the Labour Party, the divisive 'nuclear issue' was by general consent put to one side as Labour unified in the lead-up to the 1964 general election.

66 Newman, 'Thompson and the Early New Left', p. 160.
67 P. Sedgwick, 'The Two New Lefts', in D. Widgery (ed.), *The Left in Britain 1956–1968* (Pelican, 1968), p. 135.
68 Thompson, Editorial, *The New Reasoner*, Spring 1958.
69 Efstathiou, *Thompson*, p. 84.
70 Newman, 'Thompson and the Early New Left', p. 160.
71 Interview with Merrill, cited in Hamilton, *The Crisis of Theory*, p. 157.
72 For an extended discussion of this event, and Thompson's part in it, see Hamilton, *Crisis of Theory*, pp. 173–9.
73 Ibid., p. 177.
74 Ibid., p. 166, citing J. Rée, 'E.P. Thompson and the Drama of Authority', *History Workshop Journal* 47, p. 216.
75 These articles were later developed into a book, *Warwick University Ltd.* (Penguin, 1970).
76 For further discussion, see Taylor, 'Thompson and the Peace Movement', in Fieldhouse and Taylor, *Thompson and English Radicalism*, esp. pp. 187–97; and Efstathiou, *Thompson*, pp. 116–65.
77 In November 1979, the *Guardian* reported that 'Britain would take the largest number of Cruise Missiles (160), followed by Italy (112), West Germany (96 plus 108 Pershings), Holland, and Belgium'. Efstathiou, *Thompson*, p. 131, citing *Guardian*, 14 November 1979.
78 Efstathiou, *Thompson*, p. 117.
79 This argument is developed in some detail in ibid., pp. 116–65.
80 Fifty thousand copies were sold in less than a year; a subsequent Penguin Special, centring on *Protest and Survive*, sold a further 36,000.
81 Michael Howard, letter to *The Times*, 30 January 1980.
82 The original 'Committee of Seven' in END were: Thompson, Coates, Peggy Duff, Stuart Holland, Mary Kaldor, Bruce Kent and Dan Smith. It soon attracted high-profile supporters from the European Left, including Professor Ulrich Albrecht, Claude Bourdet, Antonia Brouda and Jean-Pierre Vigier.
83 Mary Kaldor, in conversation with the author, 24 May 2012.
84 M. Kaldor, *Global Civil Society: An Answer to War* (Cambridge: Cambridge University Press, 2003), p. 60.
85 END Appeal, 'A Nuclear Free Europe', 1980.
86 E.P. Thompson, 'Notes on Exterminism, the Last Stage of Civilisation', *New Left Review* 121 (May–June 1980); reprinted in Thompson, *Zero Option* (London: Merlin Press, 1982), pp. 41–80; Thompson, *Exterminism and Cold War* (London: Verso and New Left Books, 1982); and Thompson, 'Beyond the Cold War', printed version of a lecture given on 26 November 1981, END, 1982.
87 Thompson, 'Notes on Exterminism', p. 64, citing C. Wright Mills, *The Causes of World War III* (New York: Simon and Schuster, 1958), p. 47.
88 Thompson, *Heavy Dancers*, p. 136.
89 Thompson, 'Beyond the Cold War', p. 19.
90 Thompson, *Zero Option*, p. 76.
91 Kaldor, in conversation.

92 Ibid.
93 Hobsbawm, *Interesting Times: A Twentieth-Century Life* (Allen Lane, 2002, paperback, Abacus, 2003).
94 Ibid., p. 215, citing Hobsbawm's Memoir of Thompson in *Proceedings of the British Academy* 90, 1995, pp. 524–5.
95 Hobsbawm, *Interesting Times*, p. 215.
96 Ibid.
97 Goodway, *Anarchist Seeds Beneath the Snow*, p. 285.
98 Andy Croft, in conversation with the author, February 2018.

8

Michael Foot

Throughout his long political life, Michael Foot[1] was unshakeably committed to his distinctive form of radicalism, which was intrinsic to his intellectual, cultural and journalistic persona. More than any politician of his time, Foot's absorption in, and deep knowledge of, the cultural and historical legacy of English radicalism determined his political outlook and his accomplished oratory.

'Foot's Liberalism went to the core of his being', according to his biographer, Kenneth O. Morgan; as Shirley Williams observed, he remained 'in some sense always a Liberal'.[2] This was confirmed by Barbara Castle: '"The Foot brothers all merge into one collective Foot type: rational, radical and eminently reasonable … they are natural Liberals."'[3]

Foot's cultural and literary heritage and his radical Liberal idealism stem from his strong family background. In common with the rest of his family, notably his father Isaac, Foot had a lifelong and '"inflexible loathing"' of the Tories, whom he regarded as 'incurable enemies of freedom'.[4] It was from this background that Foot developed his version of what Thompson described, as the English 'Liberty Tree'.[5] Foot's socialism was 'literary, cultural and humane, drawing heavily on traditions of protest and demands for democratic change'.[6]

The Foot family

Foot's family was large, all-embracing and self-referential. Isaac, his father, was a Methodist, a passionate Liberal and a West Country man whose tradition of Dissent he saw as dating back to Cromwell. Michael, born in 1913, was the fifth of seven children: their father is the subject of a memorable and warm portrait in Foot's book *Debts of Honour*.⁷ Isaac's devotion to books was legendary: his library numbered approximately sixty thousand volumes, most of them read and many of them annotated in some detail. Isaac's 'main influence on his sons and daughters, and especially on Michael, lay not in politics but in books'.⁸ He was, in Michael's words, 'a bibliophilial drunkard'.⁹ It was a very male-dominated household. Although Foot was devoted to his mother, and to his sisters, it was taken for granted that only the male members of the family should go on to have political careers.

Michael was a prodigious collector and reader of books, and a prolific writer. His 'habitual response to electoral setbacks was to write a book'.¹⁰ His first book, *Armistice 1918–1939*, was published in 1940, and, 19 books later, his last, *Isaac Foot: A West Country Boy – Apostle of England*, in 2006. He also maintained an active journalistic career for virtually the whole of his adult life until he assumed high government office. His output ranged from 'opinion pieces' to political and polemical writing, to serious review articles; and he was also, at various times, editor of *Tribune* and of the *Evening Standard*.

Foot's background thus combined an intellectual elitism with a very particular tradition of Dissent. It was an English and specifically Devonian tradition.¹¹ Although Foot jettisoned Christian beliefs relatively early¹² – and became opposed to religion in general and Christianity in particular – he retained a deep knowledge of the Bible and an affection for the ethos, and some aspects of the morality, of Dissenting Christianity. A favourite saying of all the Foots – 'pit and rock' – alluded to the passage in Isaiah: 'Look unto the rock whence ye are hewn and to the hole of the pit whence ye are digged.'

The Foots were, in some ways, adherents of the Puritan tradition. But this was emphatically not of the dismal, joyless variety. The Foot household 'was, like so many Puritan households, suffused with music and song'.¹³ Significantly, Foot entitled the chapter on his father in *Debts of Honour*, 'A Rupert for the Roundheads'.

All the Foot sons were privately educated but at appropriately Dissenting public schools. Michael attended Leighton Park School, a largely Quaker foundation, where there was no Officer Training Corps and where boys learned 'that war was not glorious but tragic, that internationalism was a nobler creed than patriotism, and that human beings had an equal value regardless of race or colour'.¹⁴

By the time Foot went up to Oxford, in October 1931, his character, interests and political and cultural orientations were well-established.

Oxford, Liberalism and his conversion to socialism

Foot was at Wadham as an Exhibitioner. He found Oxford, and especially his years at Wadham, '"the greenest and most gracious, the peerless and the most perfect in the whole green glory of Oxford"'.¹⁵ His Oxford years were 'enriching in every way'.¹⁶ He read PPE (Philosophy, Politics and Economics) but found only politics to his taste; it was largely due to a brilliant and helpful Keynesian economics tutor

(Russell Bretherton) that he coped with economics. But philosophy 'he found less than riveting, too abstract and detached from real life'.[17] His interests were political, historical and literary. This academic orientation was reflected in his subsequent political career: he never showed any aptitude for, or even much interest in, economic analysis and policy; nor did he ever develop a political philosophy.

It was not only in the academic context that Foot thrived in politics: he was President of the Liberal Club (it was not until 1934, a year after he left Oxford, that he made up his mind that he was a socialist and joined the Labour Party); and, in 1933, he became President of the Union: his 'brand of revivalist Liberal oratory swept opponents aside'.[18]

His adherence to core radical Liberal principles remained strong throughout his life: he was committed to human rights, tolerance, parliamentary democracy and religious, social and sexual liberation. Similarly, he was passionately opposed to censorship.

Although he became, soon after his time at Oxford, an increasingly left-wing socialist, communism never had any appeal for him, though he was attracted to aspects of Marxist analysis, particularly to the 'early Marx's' theory of alienation and the materialist conception of history. He was resolutely opposed not only to fascism and Nazism but also to the brutal and authoritarian Soviet regime: he was unusual on the Left in the 1930s in condemning from the start the Moscow show trials, especially that of Bukharin.

His longstanding involvement with India began at Oxford: he became friendly with Krishna Menon and contributed a chapter to the latter's book *Oxford and War* (1934); through Menon he met Nehru in 1938 and became a lifelong friend and supporter of the Congress Party's dominant family. Later, this led to a stubborn defence of Indira Gandhi's increasingly authoritarian rule, which was vehemently criticised by many on the Left, including that other enthusiast for India, E.P. Thompson.[19]

Foot formed an important friendship at Oxford with John Cripps, the son of the senior left-wing Labour politician, Stafford Cripps. Foot and the younger Cripps undertook a short debating tour in the USA in 1934. Although Foot had some interest in American popular culture, was enthusiastic about aspects of Roosevelt's 'New Deal' and had some acquaintance with American writers such as Emerson and Thoreau, he had little regard for the perceived relevance of Atlanticism and the proclaimed 'special relationship'. His was an inherently *English* radicalism and, although he was in some ways an ardent enthusiast for *European* culture, he was never attracted to American radical politics.

It was through Stafford Cripps that, uncertain of his future career, Foot took a post as Personal Assistant to Cripps's brother in Liverpool, a post he occupied, not very happily, for only nine months. It was also through Cripps that Foot met senior Labour figures, including Lansbury, Bevin and Aneurin Bevan, 'who was to shape his destiny for ever'.[20] In Liverpool, Foot's direct experience of working-class poverty and deprivation finally convinced him to move from the Liberal to the Labour Party. In a letter to his mother in March 1935, he wrote that '"in the present circumstances Liberalism offers absolutely no contribution to the problem of poverty which with peace is far and away the most important problem and that Socialism is the only solution"'.[21]

Foot's literary heritage

Before discussing Foot's early political career, and the nature of his radicalism, it is important to note briefly the formative influence of English literature and 'letters' upon his socialist perspective. More than any leading British politician of the twentieth century, Foot was 'a man of letters'.

Of Foot's twenty books, some were works of lasting intellectual or political significance: for example, *The Pen and the Sword: Jonathan Swift and the Power of the Press* (1957), and his two-volume hagiographic but brilliant biography of his great hero, Aneurin Bevan, *Aneurin Bevan 1897–1945* (1962) and *Aneurin Bevan 1945–1960* (1973).

Most of Foot's heroes were *outsiders* in one way or another: Swift, Disraeli, Charles James Fox and Beaverbrook, for example; and he had a particular affinity with idiosyncratic, Dissenting intellectuals of Irish extraction: not only Swift but Hazlitt and Burke. He had a great affection towards, and a deep knowledge of, the Romantic poets, especially Wordsworth, Coleridge and Byron. He drew inspiration too from the political, and literary, Puritanism of the seventeenth century: Cromwell and the Levellers, but also Milton, whom he could quote at length from memory. He described his greatest political hero, Aneurin Bevan, as a 'sensual Puritan': the same could be said of Foot himself. He had a love of the good things of life, 'wine and women' as much as literature and culture.

His literary canon was idiosyncratic but it defined an unmistakably English, radical, Protestant hinterland from which his passionate socialist convictions sprang. Erudite, rich in literary allusion and inspired by egalitarian, socialist values, Foot thus had an impregnable ideological framework for his day-to-day political concerns; and it ensured that, even in the most difficult circumstances – of which he experienced not a few – his resolution and commitment never faltered.

Early career: Labour and journalism

Now firmly in the Labour camp and, through Cripps, well-connected, Foot was selected, aged 22, as the Labour candidate for Monmouth in November 1935. Monmouth, the safest Tory seat in Wales, was unwinnable, but Foot fought a vigorous campaign and the Labour vote increased by three thousand. He had, he said to the *Western Mail*, '"enjoyed myself ... more than I can say"'.[22] However, he naturally now looked for a more promising seat and, in 1938, he was adopted as the candidate for Devonport, Plymouth, on his 'home patch'.

In the meantime, however, he needed to find work. He secured a post as a trainee on the *New Statesman*. Foot was never comfortable at the *New Statesman* and, in 1937, he left. (R.H.S. Crossman, later a valued colleague and friend on the Labour Left, succeeded him.) In 1937, Cripps, with financial backing from George Strauss, launched *Tribune*, the mouthpiece of the non-Marxist Labour Left from then on, with which Foot had a close involvement for decades. *Tribune*'s editor was William Mellor, an experienced, older left-wing journalist who had a long-term relationship with Barbara Betts (later, Castle). Foot had met Barbara Betts in 1935 and they had a lifelong, close political and personal, though non-sexual, friendship.

Foot soon became a central figure on the paper. In the first of many *Tribune* crises, in 1938, Mellor resigned, because Cripps proposed an agreement with Victor Gollancz, of the Left Book Club, to merge *Tribune* with the LBC in order to pursue a 'Unity Front', pro-Soviet policy. Cripps offered the editorship to Foot, who, to his credit, refused the offer, partly out of loyalty to Mellor, but more importantly because he was resolutely opposed to a pro-Soviet perspective. He also saw, with some insight, that Cripps, much as he liked and respected him, and greatly though he was in his debt in political terms, was 'a naïve and highly fallible messiah'.[23]

In 1938, Bevan introduced Foot to Lord Beaverbrook, who was 'immediately struck by him'.[24] This unlikely, but very close, 'almost filial', relationship became one of the most important in Foot's life. (The relationship is discussed below.) Foot benefited immediately from this new friendship: he was employed on Beaverbrook's *Evening Standard* at a salary of £450 a year. 'He had exchanged one patron for another, the erratic Cripps for the mercurial Beaverbrook.'[25] He thrived at the *Evening Standard*, working closely with the editor, Frank Owen. With the crisis of 1940, the paper 'entered upon its glory'; it was, as Foot claimed, ' "the flaming herald of the embattled city" '.[26] Foot wrote a series of trenchant editorials, centring on the absolute need to prosecute the war effort and not to contemplate any negotiated peace with the Nazi regime; and he also emphasised that the war must be seen as a democratic, 'people's war', fought on behalf of *all* the people of Europe, including those of Germany and Italy.

It was from this period that one of Foot's most famous books emerged, in extraordinary circumstances: *Guilty Men* (1940) was written in four days by Foot and three others, and was published by Gollancz, authored anonymously, and published in July, one month after the manuscript had been completed: it was a huge success. Despite a ban being imposed by W.H. Smith and Wymans, 217,000 copies were sold. Fifteen men were listed, with the supreme 'guilty man' being Chamberlain. It was 'the most influential wartime tract Britain had known for over two hundred years, and the best-selling ever', and added 'the sheen of patriotism to his socialism'.[27]

Foot had, in fact, a 'thoroughly good, comfortable war'.[28] (He had volunteered for active service but had been rejected because of his chronic asthma.) His reputation as a campaigning socialist and anti-fascist journalist was now established; and he was also 'manifestly a patriotic one'.[29]

Amongst his friends he could now number Orwell, Koestler, Hemingway and Dylan Thomas. He was a leading and well-paid public figure: by 1943, he was earning £4000 a year; this compared with salaries for an MP of £400, and a Permanent Secretary in the Civil Service of £3000.

His personal life also took a decisive turn for the better. He had always been shy and something of a loner, and often indeed lonely; he had suffered from asthma and eczema; and, although he had had several relationships, none had proved fulfilling and he had never married. This changed in 1944 when he met Jill Craigie, a radical, experienced film director with a strong cultural hinterland. From this time until her death in December 1999, they were inseparable and, as Morgan notes, for 'Michael, a romantic, passionate man, Jill was the perfect partner'.[30]

With the end of the war, Foot was keen to return to the political fray. In 1945, his parliamentary career began and was to become the centre of his political life until his eventual retirement from the House of Commons in 1992. Before considering this next phase of his life, attention is turned to two of the most important relationships of his life and their impact upon his politics.

Beaverbrook and Bevan

As Foot noted in his biography of Aneurin Bevan, he, Bevan, 'was never a hero-worshipper; but I was'.[31] His pantheon of heroes was a defining characteristic of Foot's life; but amongst these three stand out as 'father figures' as well as heroes: Isaac, his own father of course, as already discussed, Lord Beaverbrook and, above all, Aneurin Bevan.

The mutual liking that was immediately apparent between Foot and Beaverbrook is well-described in Foot's affectionate essay in *Debts of Honour*.[32] Beaverbrook was a 'rampaging individualist', a newspaper proprietor of decidedly right-wing, populist views, an active member of the Conservative Party and an 'appeaser' in the 1930s, who subsequently became a member of Churchill's wartime government. Foot claimed, none the less, that Beaverbrook was 'an instinctive radical ... in the true sense that he had an urge to get to the roots of the question and the will to wrench them up with both hands ... [his] radicalism was deep and abiding'.[33]

The real explanation for Foot's attachment to Beaverbrook lies in less directly political areas. Foot was captivated by the quality, the sheer brilliance of the conversations at the convivial weekend house parties which Beaverbrook gave at his country residence, Cherkley. Regular guests – almost all male – included Randolph Churchill, Bevan, Joseph Kennedy, H.G. Wells and many more: all exotic, opinionated, intelligent, argumentative and entertaining. Foot always revelled in such contexts: his later regular lunch gatherings at the Gay Hussar restaurant in Soho is a further example of his liking for such social, intellectual, convivial occasions.

Beaverbrook had 'charm' and 'audacity', two key qualities in those whom Foot admired and liked. And Beaverbrook in turn admired Foot's erudition, especially his 'feel for history and literature',[34] his irreverence and his ability to tell a good story. In the end, quite simply, they liked each other.

Yet it remains a strange relationship. In reality, there is no sense in which Beaverbrook was a 'true radical'. He was 'a buccaneering champion of the free market, along with tariffs within a protective imperial system';[35] he was foremost amongst the appeasers, as noted, and a warm supporter of the Irish-American US ambassador, Joseph Kennedy, who was implacably opposed to Britain and to the declaration of war on Germany in 1939; and he used his newspapers as vehicles for his eccentric right-wing views. Those who came close to Beaverbrook, including Foot and Bevan, were always 'in danger of becoming licensed rebels'.[36]

There can be no such equivocation about Foot's relationship with the greatest of all his heroes, Aneurin Bevan. For Foot, Bevan embodied all that was best about democratic socialism; equally important, he was the archetypal romantic, working-class socialist, steeped in the deep culture of the working-class community of South Wales, and a passionate and remarkable orator. The two men had much in common. They were both absorbed in understanding the sweep of historical events, especially revolutionary change, and the ideas underlying them; both too were shaped by books, not only those concerned with history and politics but also literature, poetry and the arts in general. Both too came from Methodist backgrounds, but had rejected religious belief; and both loved wine, whisky, good conversation and good food: they 'loved a good party', but they also revelled in the lonely quietness of the hills.

In terms of personal style, both men were informal in their dress, notoriously so, in Foot's case, when he became leader of the Labour Party in 1979. They both suffered from physical handicaps: Foot's asthma and eczema, and Bevan's stutter; but both overcame them to become superb orators and debaters. They 'rank among the few politicians who have been equally effective on the platform and in the House of Commons'.[37]

They were natural rebels, delighting in debate and controversy; and they disliked both dull politicians, like Attlee; and intolerant, bullying bosses like Bevin and Hugh Dalton.

The differences were: that Bevan was a senior and powerful figure in the Labour hierarchy, whilst Foot was, in 1945, a new, junior MP. Secondly, despite his erudition and easy relationship with intellectuals and powerful figures, Bevan remained true to his working-class roots and the community from which he came. Like many middle-class, left-wing socialists, Foot was somewhat in awe of this genuine proletarianism, which appealed to his romantic, idealistic view of the world.

Bevan was the defining political figure in Foot's life. He was more than Bevan's 'comrade. He would be his Boswell, his Engels, his John the Baptist, and of course his parliamentary heir.'[38] (Foot inherited Bevan's Ebbw Vale seat on the latter's untimely death in 1960: see below.)

Foot and Bevan did have a major falling-out over the unilateral nuclear disarmament issue in 1957 (discussed below). This was a painful period for both men; but, essentially, 'Foot's passionate admiration for this brilliant, articulate tribune ... was unshakeable'.[39]

Foot's biography of Bevan is a work of lasting importance.[40] It is not, in any conventional sense, a scholarly biography, although it does draw upon a wide range of original sources. Rather, it is 'a polemic, and hopelessly one-sided ... There is no criticism of Bevan at all.'[41] However, it paints a detailed and valuable picture of the Labour Left in the earlier part of the twentieth century and it is written with Foot's characteristic brilliance.

'Long after his death in 1960 Bevan remained the most important person in Foot's life, not excluding Jill. He was central to Foot's every crisis of conscience, the permanent sounding board for his socialist values'.[42]

Michael Foot in Parliament, 1945 to 1964: Bevanism, the Labour Left and peace politics

In the 1945 election, Michael's father, Isaac, and his brothers John and Dingle all stood as Liberal candidates. Labour's landslide victory – a 180 majority over the Conservatives and 146 overall – was a huge surprise, not least to the Foot family. Isaac, John and Dingle were all defeated whilst Michael was elected for Devonport with a majority of 2013. There was a 14 per cent swing against the Conservative, Hore Belisha.

He now came to revel in parliamentary life. He loved the intrigue, was an enthusiastic and notably able parliamentary performer, and rapidly became an expert in the arcane arts of parliamentary procedure, a skill which would stand him in good stead over the decades. He also rapidly found a congenial group of like-minded Labour Left colleagues: R.H.S. Crossman, Barbara Castle (whom he had known well before), Ian Mikardo, Tom Driberg, and J.P.W. Mallalieu amongst them. Such people constituted the 'soft Left'; there was also a smaller 'hard Left' group of 'fellow-travelling' MPs, including Konni Zilliacus, D.N. Pritt and John Platt-Mills.[43]

Foot's key campaigning issue, following his election, was his advocacy of a 'Third Force' in the postwar context. This was the theme of his maiden speech in Parliament, generally agreed to be an impressive debut. Replete with rhetorical flourishes and erudite allusions, Foot's essential message was absolutely clear:

> We have a conception of political liberty which our friends in Russia unhappily have not been blessed with. We have at the same time a conception of economic democracy ... which is unhappily not yet shared by the people of the United States ... It is this unique combination of treasures ... which gives to us the commanding position of leadership if we choose to exercise it ... may it not be our destiny as the freest and

most democratic and a Socialist power to stand between the living and the dead and stay the plague?[44]

Attlee was typically dismissive of such idealistic ambition: '"Very nice, no doubt. But there wasn't either a material or a spiritual basis for it."'[45] Bevin, predictably, was vehemently opposed to such dangerous flights of fancy. Foot was thus, despite his growing prominence, seen as something of an eccentric romantic, the personification of the rebel comfortable with the Labour Party as a party of protest, rather than a party of serious, responsible government. There was no prospect, at this stage, of governmental office.

Foot was involved in a series of Labour Left campaigns in the 1945–51 period. These included opposition to the terms of the US war loan; and campaigning for a peaceful resolution of the Israel/Palestine problem in the Middle East. Throughout his adult life, Foot was strongly pro-Israel – though less so after the Suez crisis in 1956. The plight of Germany in the aftermath of the devastation in the latter stages of the war, and the dangers of a rearmed Germany in the mounting Cold War, were major policy concerns. Foot played a central role in 'Save Europe Now', centring on the desperate condition of German refugees, especially children and young people. The SEN Committee, in addition to Foot, involved several figures later prominent in the Campaign for Nuclear Disarmament (CND): Canon Collins, Peggy Duff and Bertrand Russell.

The 'Keep Left' group, chaired by Ian Mikardo, emerged in the later 1940s to articulate the views of the 'soft Left'. Its 1947 pamphlet, written by Mikardo, Foot and Crossman, called for socialist planning, a 'Third Way' foreign policy and the withdrawal of troops from overseas territories and an end to conscription. For Foot, it was the 'moral leadership' that Britain could provide for a 'Third Force' that was the key policy – shades of the CND years to come.

However, perhaps surprisingly, Foot strongly backed the formation of NATO in 1949: it was 'as warmly applauded by Foot in *Tribune* as by the party mainstream'.[46] He ridiculed those who regarded the USA and the USSR as equally anti-democratic. Despite his antipathy to the USA and its political culture, he adopted, like Orwell, 'a regretful but firm anti-Communism'.[47]

There began in these years a deep division between Left and Right in the Labour Party, inextricably linked to the acrimonious personal competition for power between Bevan and Gaitskell. Although (largely) resolved by 1958–59, the rift persisted, albeit in somewhat different terms and contexts, for the remainder of the century. The bitterness of the Bevan–Gaitskell division had a visceral quality, matched in the twentieth century Labour Party only by the deep divisions caused by Ramsay MacDonald's 'treachery' in 1931. Such bitter divisions were to re-emerge in the later disputes between the Labour leadership and the 'Bennite' opposition (Chapter 11).

Foot was centrally involved in this dispute, in effect as Bevan's lieutenant. Bevan had always disliked Gaitskell: he felt that 'there was an ideological emptiness about [him]: "He's nothing, nothing, nothing".'[48] The feeling was mutual. The antipathy reached new heights when, as Cripps became terminally ill, Gaitskell was appointed to replace him as Chancellor of the Exchequer. There were clashes over German rearmament and over prescription charges, the latter seen by Bevan and the Left as the 'thin end of the wedge' in undermining the fledgling NHS; this was further exacerbated a little later by the government's decision to send troops to Korea and the implicit link between this decision and the cuts in public expenditure for the embryonic Welfare State.

On 22 April, Bevan, John Freeman and Harold Wilson resigned from the government. The divisions were now explicit. It was against this background that the 1951 general election resulted, despite Labour's largest ever popular vote (13,948,882), in a Conservative victory – 321 MPs, compared with Labour's 295. Thus began 13 years of Conservative rule.

In 1955, Bevan and the Left argued against nuclear 'first use': but Foot, like Castle (and indeed Jennie Lee, Bevan's wife and long-time Labour, and originally ILP, left-winger),[49] were always instinctive unilateralists who wanted Britain 'to renounce such weapons completely on moral grounds'.[50] Bevan, however, was never opposed on principle to nuclear weapons. At the time, such differences appeared to be nuanced and relatively minor. But by 1957 they had emerged as major, explosive and destructive.

Attlee resigned as leader in December 1955, following Labour's defeat in the May 1955 general election. In the ensuing election for party leader, Gaitskell defeated Bevan and Morrison by a comfortable margin.[51] This ended, in effect, 'Bevanism' as anything like a formal movement: it had had no coherent ideological position. Bevan, like Foot, never wrote or even enunciated a 'political philosophy': this is discussed below in more detail in relation to Foot's political position and legacy. The same applies to Harold Wilson, the erstwhile Bevanite. The failure to articulate such a critique is a significant failure on the part of the leaders of the Labour Left, first Bevan and later Foot. Beguiling phrases, political passion, and great oratory are, in the end, not sufficient: they have to be underpinned by a coherent political philosophy and strategy to be effective. This inadequacy on the Labour Left in this period contrasts with the rigorous revisionist position articulated by Anthony Crosland in his two seminal books *The Future of Socialism* (1956) and *The Conservative Enemy* (1962). The 'Gaitskellites manifestly had all the best tunes'.[52]

Of more immediate importance to Foot in 1955 was the loss of his Devonport seat by a tantalisingly close vote.[53] Nothing daunted, Foot soon plunged into the furore over the Suez debacle. Despite his strong pro-Israel sympathies, he had no hesitation in condemning the shambolic and disastrous invasion; and, with Mervyn Jones, he published a book, *Guilty Men, 1957: Suez and Cyprus*:[54] although it lacked the originality and sparkle of the 1940 polemic, it was nevertheless a powerful critique of the Eden government. Foot and Bevan remained close throughout the

Suez crisis, and the subsequent turmoil and anguish surrounding the brutal Soviet repression of the Hungarian uprising. All this changed in 1957, when the dispute over nuclear weapons emerged at the Brighton Conference of the Labour Party in November.

Britain's development of nuclear weapons became an issue of increasing concern in the mid-1950s, not only on the Labour Left but in progressive circles generally. The realisation that atmospheric nuclear tests were harmful to health 'was a new and horrifying discovery'.[55] Scientific evidence was mounting that radiation could cause a range of cancers, including leukaemia, and might well result in future generations of defective children. CND was inaugurated in January 1958.[56] There were other initiatives both nationally and locally, including the radical Direct Action Committee (DAC), the forerunner of the higher-profile Committee of 100, both of which were committed to non-violent direct action. But the mainstream of the emerging movement was clearly supportive of the Labour Party; and, certainly at leadership level, CND saw its role as essentially a pressure group to persuade public opinion, and thus the Labour Party in Parliament, to adopt a unilateralist nuclear defence policy.

Foot was centrally involved in this movement, becoming a leading member of the original Executive Committee of CND.[57] Bevan, similarly, until his 1957 Conference speech, also *appeared* to support this growing movement. Although he backed the original decision to proceed with the manufacture of the bomb, there are numerous examples of his declared support for unilateralism: and, at the National Executive Committee (NEC) discussions of the issue in the lead-up to the 1957 Conference, he was one of the signatories to a proposal that the Party should make the case ' "for stopping unilaterally the manufacture of nuclear weapons" ',[58] and he took a full part in the ensuing Committee debate. By the following NEC meeting, a few days later, he had completely changed his mind.[59]

Political calculation was very probably the motivation, but the sudden change of policy stance, the 'apostasy' as those on the Left saw it, the lack of any consultation, and even more the *manner* of the criticism of the unilateralist position, provoked a crisis on the Left. In memorably searing phrases Bevan denounced unilateralism as 'an emotional spasm'; and accused unilateralists of wanting to 'send a British Foreign Secretary ... naked into the Conference chamber'.

Foot, and almost all on the Labour Left, were appalled, angry and dismayed. Foot wrote an explicit denunciation of Bevan's position in *Tribune*; but for Foot the whole episode was devastating: 'his idol, his hero, his supreme fount of inspiration and hope, had betrayed the principles in which they all believed. It was easily the most wounding experience of Foot's life.'[60] Foot, out of Parliament, though 'depressed ... sad and forlorn',[61] threw himself (and *Tribune*) into anti-nuclear campaigning. Arguments raged between Foot and Bevan whenever they met: Bevan 'could not believe that it was beyond his power, for the first time in their long association, to bring Michael round to his way of thinking'.[62] The climax of their rift came in July 1958 when, after a reception at the Polish Embassy, and fuelled by alcohol, a supposedly reconciling nightcap at the Foots' house culminated in Bevan shouting at Foot '"You cunt! You cunt!"' and smashing one of Jill Craigie's Sheraton chairs on the floor, breaking its legs.

By the summer of 1959, passions had cooled somewhat and there was at last 'a proper reconciliation'.[63] Bevan agreed to speak on behalf of Foot at Devonport prior to the general election, called for 8 October 1959. Foot could have accepted a safe Labour seat (he was invited to seek selection for Aberavon); but Foot was loyal to Devonport, and anyway he was at heart a writer and journalist as much as he was a politician: 'it would have caused him no great unhappiness to spend the rest of his life preaching socialism, editing *Tribune* and writing books like *The Pen and the Sword*',[64] his work on Swift.

In the event, Bevan was unable to come to speak on Foot's behalf. The cancer that was to kill him had already taken hold. The election was a disaster for Labour. For the third consecutive time the Party faced defeat: the Conservatives gained 23 seats. Foot, as he had expected, lost Devonport but more heavily than anticipated: the sitting Conservative MP, a good constituency member, Joan Vickers, achieved a comfortable 6454 majority in a straight fight with Labour.

In the aftermath, Gaitskell attempted to shift the Party to the right at the Labour Conference. He proposed to revise Clause IV of the Constitution, which committed the Party to public ownership. Foot made an explicit attack on Gaitskell and his proposal, with his characteristic passion, and received an ovation. Bevan, however, in what proved to be his last major Conference speech, adopted a more conciliatory tone. But he was by now convinced that he would have to break with Gaitskell and resurrect the socialist principles that had guided his life. Foot later put on record a conversation he had had with Bevan over lunch in December 1959, in which he (Bevan) 'said that great upheavals would have to be faced if the Party was not to be twisted into a caricature of what a Socialist Party should be'.[65] However, there is likely to have been a measure of 'wish fulfilment' in Foot's account: he was emotionally committed to re-establishing the socialist credentials of his hero. It is anyway an open question, at best, whether Bevan could have gained the trust and support of his erstwhile colleagues on the left of the Party. The dismay, the anger and the disillusionment caused by his treachery, as it was perceived, ran deep.

Bevan's death on 6 July 1960, at the relatively early age of 62, was a blow from which Foot never fully recovered. His 'grief was profound and irremediable';[66] and it was tinged with guilt. 'It seems almost certain', he wrote, 'that the political agonies he had endured contributed to his physical destruction.'[67] Jennie Lee, Bevan's widow, was bitter in her condemnation. The '"wounds inflicted by the unilateral disarmers in 1957 and 1958 ... had done their deadly work. Until their attacks began, he never had so much as a stomach ache ... He did not die, he was murdered." '[68]

Nevertheless, Jennie Lee agreed to Foot writing Bevan's biography; and she supported his decision to seek selection for Ebbw Vale, Bevan's old seat. Foot was adopted, on the third ballot; and he won the by-election convincingly, with a majority of 16,729 in November 1960. He was to hold the seat until his eventual retirement from the Commons in 1992.

Foot became *de facto* leader of the Labour Left in the parliamentary party, a position he held until the 1970s when the twin processes of the rise of the 'Bennite' Left (see Chapter 11) and Foot's own rise to high governmental office arguably severely constrained, if never extinguished, his proclaimed radicalism. This is to anticipate, however.

Through 1959 and 1960, CND and the wider peace movement grew rapidly and culminated, at least as far as Labour activists were concerned, with the passing of an explicitly unilateralist resolution at the 1960 Labour Party Conference.[69] Foot was unequivocally an advocate of the moral case for unilateralism; he believed, like A.J.P. Taylor, James Cameron and J.B. Priestley amongst others, that by taking this moral initiative a process of multilateral disarmament *could* be kick-started and that Britain alone could give this moral lead, and save the planet from the dangers of nuclear war.

Gaitskell's argument in his speech at the Conference was, by common consent, shrewd and formidable (as discussed in Chapter 2). Gaitskell, in his concentration upon the issue of NATO, had identified a key weakness. Foot was always, at best, equivocal about NATO and, as will be recalled, had been an enthusiastic supporter of the organisation on its creation in 1949.

For a series of complex reasons,[70] the 1960 decision was reversed at the 1961 Conference. Gaitskell, and the centre Right, had made astute concessions to the unilateralist case, and his defence proposal, 'Policy for Peace', was adopted by the NEC. Foot, and still more Cousins and the Transport and General Workers' Union (TGWU), had been out-manoeuvred and Gaitskell's majority at the Conference was substantial.

From this time onwards, Foot's involvement in CND lessened, though for many years he was a familiar figure on the annual Aldermaston March. This 'distancing' was exacerbated by two developments in the peace movement. The mass campaign for civil disobedience launched by Bertrand Russell and others in late 1960[71] was not an initiative that Foot supported. He could see no justification for such illegal action, given that Britain had a well-established parliamentary democracy. For Foot, parliamentary sovereignty was a key value. Secondly, from 1961, many in CND were campaigning for independent pro-disarmament candidates to be put forward for election to Parliament. In 1962 a formal organisation, INDEC (Independent Nuclear Disarmament Election Committee), was created. Foot denounced 'the proposal to put up occasional independent CND candidates at by-elections, as "poison"'.[72] INDEC faded, for a variety of reasons, quite quickly; but the whole episode and the peace movement's more general emphasis upon extra-parliamentary action, further alienated Foot and other more mainstream Labour Left supporters.

When Gaitskell died, unexpectedly, in January 1963, Harold Wilson succeeded him as leader. Though hardly by this stage a man of the Left, Wilson was seen as both a capable and a canny politician and a leader more likely to accede to the policy proposals of the Left. *Tribune* and Foot backed his strategy. Foot continued to criticise Wilson's support of the British nuclear deterrent but, essentially, he and others on the Left closed ranks in the lead-up to the 1964 election.

Foot and the 1964–70 governments

One of Foot's biographers entitles the chapter on this period of Foot's life 'Towards the Mainstream':[73] this accurately reflects the reality. Indeed, for the remainder of his political career in Parliament, Foot became a leading player in the Parliamentary Labour Party and, in the 1970s, an absolutely central figure in the Labour governments of 1974–79. Politically, his days as a radical firebrand were, if not over, severely curtailed as the responsibilities of office and power increasingly dominated; or, if a more jaundiced view is taken, he began the process of 'selling out'. His trajectory does highlight the perennial dilemma of Labour Left socialism in reformist parties. Is the 'correct' course, to remain on the backbenches and to pursue an energetic oppositional approach; or is it rather, as in Foot's case (and indeed in Bevan's), to accept the compromises inherent in high office in the hope of making real progress in achieving socialist change? (This is a key issue and is returned to in the concluding chapter.)

For Michael Foot, there was never any question which of these positions he would adopt: he was, despite all the oppositional rhetoric and his passionate, moral beliefs, essentially a Labour loyalist. He never deviated from his belief in parliamentary democracy and the absolute need for Labour to strive for power through the existing electoral system.

The analysis of the remainder of Foot's career is dealt with relatively briefly here, as the focus of this study is upon his *radicalism*. Nevertheless, there are many important aspects of Foot's career in Parliament, from 1964 until his retirement, that throw light upon the nature of his radicalism and the dilemmas with which he, and the Labour Left in general, were faced.

There were several aspects of Foot's personal circumstances in the early to mid-1960s that had significant implications for his political life. Following Bevan's death, there was a series of further bereavements: in December 1960, Isaac, his father, died; in 1964, within a few days of each other, Nehru and Beaverbrook died; and, deeply upsetting, his troubled sister Sally, always a favourite sibling, was found drowned in the river below the caravan in which she lived. (Although the coroner returned an open verdict, it seems more than likely that she committed suicide.) In October 1963, Foot was severely injured in a car crash. For a few days it was thought that he might not survive. He emerged quite recovered – and, bizarrely, with his asthma and eczema cured, and his smoking habit terminated – but, from then on, not only did he always walk with a stick, his overall persona was of a man far older than his chronological years.

In the programmes and policies of Wilson's governments of 1964–66 and 1966–70, there was much that Foot found unacceptable; and he was a constant and articulate critic, especially of Wilson's support for the American involvement in the Vietnam War, denouncing it as 'shameful' and prophesying that it could 'never be brought to a successful conclusion'. Wilson wanted Foot to join his government but Foot declined: he had too many policy disagreements (over Rhodesia, and the East African Asians issue, as well as Vietnam, and domestically over incomes policy). However, although critical, he proclaimed fervently and repeatedly the importance of securing a successful Labour government.[74]

The catalyst for Foot's change, political transformation even, was his close relationship with Jack Jones, the new leader of the TGWU. Jones, an archetypal 'organic intellectual of the working class', had fought in the Spanish Civil War, and was an unswerving and able democratic socialist. Foot had never been close to the trade unions but, through Jones, he moved from being, in Morgan's somewhat overblown words, 'a patrician progressive, living in a world of humane middle-class intellectuals, to seeing himself as a tribune of the proletariat'.[75]

In the Shadow Cabinet, following Heath's surprise victory in the 1970 election, Foot became shadow spokesman on Fuel and Power, and in October 1971, shadow leader of the House of Commons. When Wilson returned to power in 1974, Foot became Secretary of State for Employment. (Jack Jones told Harold Wilson that Foot would be 'the ideal, perhaps the only, choice'.)[76] Foot was initially a nervous performer as a minister. He had become a natural protester and rebel, had no experience of political office and was 'by no means a natural master of detail'.[77] Foot's civil servants, originally sceptical, were generally enthusiastic about the new, unconventional, informal, sociable and unorthodox Minister; and Foot's speeches in the Commons were judged 'the most dazzling parliamentary performance in living memory' (*Guardian*) and he was seen as the 'superstar of the new Labour Cabinet … The extent of Foot's triumph is hard to overestimate' (*Sunday Times*).[78]

By far the most important issue for Foot, and indeed for the government's domestic policy agenda, was the 'Social Contract'. Although Foot and Healey, the Chancellor of the Exchequer, had disagreed over virtually every aspect of policy for twenty years, they worked well together over wage control and the implementation of the 'Social Contract'; similarly, Foot's relationship with Shirley Williams, as Minister of Consumer Affairs, was excellent. In the light of Foot's opposition (and threat to resign) over the issue of a statutory wages policy, Wilson dropped the idea; and Foot secured a deal with the trade unions, with Jack Jones's help. Foot's performance on this issue in the Commons and also at the Party Conference won unstinting praise from the press, as well as from his Labour colleagues.[79]

By the mid-1970s, therefore, Foot was firmly entrenched in the top echelons of the Party and the government. Following Wilson's surprise decision in March 1976 to stand down as Prime Minister and Party leader, Callaghan was elected leader and Foot became, in effect, Deputy Prime Minister.

Foot's position necessitated regular personal visits to the Queen. As a lifelong republican, this might have been expected to cause difficulties. However, his relations with the monarch were warm and cordial: a great dog lover, as was the Queen, he often took his dog with him and a bond was thus created. This is a good example of how his natural, human warmth, linked to his literary and historical erudition, almost always overcame any ideological differences. (His close friendship with Enoch Powell was perhaps a more dramatic such example.)

He also shared with the Queen a strong and romantic patriotism. His biographer recalls one telling example. In the summer of 1981, when Foot was Leader of the Opposition, the Queen indicated her irritation with King Juan Carlos of Spain, who had objected to the Prince and Princess of Wales calling in at Gibraltar in the royal yacht, *Britannia*, during their honeymoon. '"After all", declared the Queen, "it's my son, my yacht and my dockyard". After a period of silence, Foot burst out enthusiastically, "Your Majesty, Queen Elizabeth I could not have put it better".'[80] The firebrand rebel had moved a long way.

From 1974 to 1979, to the indignation of his left-wing colleagues, Foot remained loyal to Callaghan and refused to engage in any left-wing conspiracies to unseat him; indeed, Foot and Callaghan became very close and developed a strong personal bond. Similarly, as noted, despite their differences, Foot and Healey also became mutually respectful colleagues.[81] In the 1976 crisis over the International Monetary Fund loan, which entailed draconian public expenditure cuts, Foot's support of Healey (and Callaghan) was crucial. Foot's timely final intervention in Cabinet, urging all to keep together for the sake of the labour movement, was decisive. In Benn's view, Foot and his colleagues had given way to the Treasury.[82]

By early 1977, the government's position had become untenable. Foot was instrumental in securing the 'Lib–Lab' pact agreement. By background and temperament, there could have been no one better suited to securing a deal. Ironically, in one sense, Foot was returning to his earlier liberalism, and the pact saw a revival, albeit briefly, of the Progressive Alliance reminiscent, it could be argued, of the pre-1914 situation.

The ensuing turmoil over the so-called 'Winter of Discontent', following Callaghan's decision not to call an early election in the autumn of 1978, and the inability of the government to prolong wage restraint agreements with the unions, was a catastrophe for Labour. '"It was like being on board the sinking *Titanic* without the music"', in Bernard Donoghue's words.[83]

The final collapse of the Labour government came over the devolution proposals, on which Foot and John Smith had been leading, and for which Foot, almost alone in Cabinet, had considerable enthusiasm. Despite complex manoeuvring by Foot, using all his skills of persuasion and knowledge of Common procedures, Callaghan finally decided that he had no alternative other than to proceed with a confidence motion in the Commons. In the ensuing vote on 28 March 1979, the government was defeated by a single vote, 311 to 310.

The victory of Margaret Thatcher and the Conservative Party in the ensuing election on 3 May 1979 ushered in a new, extreme right-wing, neo-liberal era.

Although Callaghan continued as Leader of the Opposition for 17 months after Labour's defeat (to October 1980), his drive and enthusiasm had gone. It was, all in all, a dismal and depressing time for the Labour Party, not least because a bitter Left/Right rift erupted. The dispute centred initially on the demands of the Left, articulated through the CLPD (Campaign for Labour Party Democracy), for three constitutional changes to internal procedures, all of which aimed to increase the powers of party activists and trade unions, and correspondingly reduce the autonomy of the Parliamentary Labour Party (PLP).

Foot was wholly opposed to such proposals and deeply depressed by their acceptance. For him, socialism could come about only through persuading the population at large to elect a Labour government, and through the sacred (to him) procedures of parliamentary democracy. Moreover, Foot construed MPs' role in a Burkean way: they were representatives, not delegates, and their responsibility was to articulate views, in Parliament, on behalf of all their constituents and in accord with their own consciences. There could be no outside control by any third party: all the proposals of the Bennite Left thus smacked of an authoritarian mindset.

A leadership election in the Party took place in the autumn of 1980, following Callaghan's resignation. Denis Healey was clearly the front runner, with unparalleled experience of senior ministerial roles. But Healey was an abrasive figure, intellectually outstandingly able, but deeply divisive, arrogant and confrontational. He was not an easy man to like. Foot was genuinely reluctant to stand but he was persuaded that only he could prevent the Party tearing itself apart. In the event, on the second ballot, and to general surprise, Foot defeated Healey by 139 votes to 129. Healey was, to an extent, magnanimous: he immediately offered to serve as Deputy Leader: had he won Foot would have made a similar offer. Later, Healey wrote that Foot was 'a kindly and cultured man, as well as a brilliant orator, but he simply did not look like a potential Prime Minister; he had failed to command public respect as Leader of the Opposition'.[84]

It could be added that Foot was also an erudite and unusually *likeable* man; and a charismatic figure for many on the Left, particularly in social movements such as CND and the organisations campaigning against the Vietnam War. But Healey was right: Foot never seemed to himself or anyone else a potential Prime Minister. He was a figure from a distant Old Labour past: not only was he chronologically relatively old, he also appeared old-fashioned. His notoriously 'casual' clothes and appearance, and his generally eccentric, somewhat shambolic demeanour, made him look out of touch with the times. The right-wing press seized upon such episodes as his wearing an (alleged) 'donkey jacket' at the Cenotaph Remembrance ceremony, to question his suitability as Prime Minister, and by implication, in this particular instance, to accuse him of a lack of respect for the war dead, and a lack of patriotism.

His 'style' as Leader of the Opposition was one of tolerance and pluralism. 'People who worked with him repeatedly called him "a lovely man"'.[85] He was emollient, pleasant to everyone, unusually kind at a personal level to his staff, and modest in his habits. He had not a shred of pomposity or conceit.

It was, though, not a happy time for Foot, still less so for the Labour Party. The Party was divided, partly because of the continuing problems with the Bennite Left: Benn's decision to stand against Healey for the Deputy Leadership in 1981, which he came tantalisingly close to winning, and the continuing bitter divisions in the Party, brought great frustration to Foot as Leader. Even more serious, however, were the defections on the right of the Party: in early 1981, the 'Gang of Four' – Roy Jenkins, Shirley Williams, David Owen and Bill Rodgers – resigned from the Labour Party and launched the new Social Democratic Party (SDP). Twenty-eight Labour MPs (and one Conservative MP) joined the new party. Foot was particularly distressed to lose Shirley Williams, for whom he had great respect and affection. All in all, it was 'a massive blow'.[86]

In an interview with the *Daily Star*, Foot summed up 1981 in uncharacteristically negative terms: ' "This has been a deeply frustrating and wasted year, and it's largely our own fault." '[87] The following year, 1982, was to bring further trauma and division. In addition to the continuing problems in the Party, the Falklands crisis erupted in the spring. Foot saw the Argentinian invasion as unprovoked aggression, reminiscent of the fascists and Nazis in the 1930s. He had no hesitation in supporting the decision of the government to counter such action militarily. He *did* press for resolution of the conflict through diplomatic negotiations; and the Party's policy was to abstain on the vote on 20 May 1982 (33 MPs defied the whip and voted against the government: those who were front bench members were sacked); but Foot was clear that, should negotiations fail, military action would be justified. Healey was out of the country when the crisis arose. Had he been in Britain, he 'would have tried to moderate some of Michael's rhetoric'.[88] The Party was divided on the issue and many on the Left were strongly opposed to Foot's stance.

The Falklands campaign was presented, by Thatcher, as a great, patriotic triumph: the right-wing press went into jingoistic overdrive and her electoral position was greatly strengthened. Foot was not expected to win the 1983 election, nor did he himself privately envisage success. He campaigned vigorously, was greeted rapturously and with great affection by Labour supporters and appeared, as always, to enjoy the whole process of electioneering. However, he led not only a chaotic campaign but an explicitly old-fashioned one. Although he had been, earlier, a regular and successful television broadcaster, his declaratory, oratorical style did not suit the modern mass media context.

Added to this, the Manifesto, famously described by Gerald Kaufman as 'the longest suicide note in history', was an ambitiously socialist programme, not supported, indeed actively opposed, by several key members of the Labour leadership. The election results were little short of disastrous. Labour lost 60 seats. The new House had 396 Conservatives, 209 Labour and 26 Liberal/SDP MPs; the vagaries of the electoral system disguised to an extent the Labour Party's poor performance: the Liberals/SDP gained 26 per cent of the vote, Labour only 28.3 per cent, with the Conservatives on 43.5 per cent.

Rapidly, at the union leaders' instigation, Neil Kinnock was elected leader to replace Foot, easily defeating Roy Hattersley, who became his deputy. Foot's time as Labour leader, indeed as a leading Labour *figure*, was over. Before turning finally to a consideration of Foot's particular perspective on English radicalism and his contribution to the tradition, attention is turned to one key policy area (which has profound resonances for Britain in the last years of the second decade of the twenty-first century, in the context of 'Brexit'): the relationship of Britain with the European Economic Community (which developed subsequently into the European Union).

Foot and Europe

Foot and Hugh Gaitskell agreed about very few political issues, and disliked each other. But in their attitude to the EU/EEC, they were at one. Gaitskell advocated an economically and politically independent Britain, emphasising expanding trade and other links with the Commonwealth.

Foot was in many ways a true European. He and his wife, Jill, were devoted to Venice and, later, Dubrovnik. Some of the thinkers and writers to whom he was most committed were continental European rather than British: Montaigne, Heine, Stendhal and Silone, for example. Moreover, he was an internationalist and, in 1945, he had been a strong advocate of a united Europe as the central part of a 'Third Force' in international politics. Foot was also an admirer of Willi Brandt and François Mitterrand; and he was fully aware that all the major Western European socialist parties were in favour of the European Union. Yet he was, until the late 1990s,[89] a determined opponent of the EU/EEC.

There were essentially three reasons for Foot's opposition. First, he was a radical socialist and he saw the EU/EEC as 'a rich man's club', an organisation dedicated to the protection and extension of corporate capitalism. Membership of such an organisation would, he believed, make *impossible* socialist planning, the extension of public ownership, the development of the Welfare State and the creation of a more egalitarian society. Secondly, he had remained, since his days as a Liberal, an advocate of 'free trade', and he saw the EU/EEC as a protectionist cartel which would endanger the 'cheap food' policy which had to be central to any Labour government's policy programme.

The third reason, however, was the most important and went to the heart of Foot's radicalism. The sovereignty of Parliament was a non-negotiable political principle for Foot. He had always been, as noted earlier, a strong advocate of liberal democracy and its institutions, especially of Parliament, operating within a fully democratic system, with the accompanying freedoms which are central to liberalism and democratic socialism. For Foot, these freedoms, and the institutions within which they were embodied, would be threatened and undermined, perhaps fatally, by merging British sovereignty into a bureaucratic, remote and capitalist EU/EEC. Foot compared joining the EU/EEC 'to the shame of Munich'.[90]

Conclusion

It is a commonplace that all political careers end in failure: this is certainly true of Michael Foot. The Labour Party took many years to recover from the defeat of 1983 for which he must bear significant responsibility. Although his political career was effectively over, and although he became increasingly detached from the higher echelons of the Party under the leadership of Neil Kinnock and Roy Hattersley,[91] he remained an active MP[92] and a loyal member and supporter of the Party. In later years, he was an enthusiast for Robin Cook's 'ethical foreign policy'; and, whilst he was closer to Gordon Brown, his personal relations with Tony Blair were 'perfectly good, and with Cherie Blair better still',[93] at least until the Iraq war.[94]

Nevertheless, his formidable energies were devoted after 1983 largely to writing: from 1984 to 2006, he published no fewer than seven books, one at least of which, his study of Byron, was a work of considerable scholarship and lasting significance.[95]

Long and committed though his political career was, he was thus always equally attached to and defined by his literary and cultural heritage. He was an internationalist, but his was a very *English* internationalism. He thought of himself, with justification, as a citizen of the world: he was a lifelong friend and supporter of India and of Ireland and he was among the first to agitate for the humane treatment of German civilians and refugees after the war, and later for the admission to Britain of oppressed minorities, such as the East African Asians.

But he 'felt rooted in his England'[96] and drew his inspiration from *English* radicals-activists, historians, writers and politicians. Not for him the social and political theorising of France, Germany and Italy: he was at one with Orwell in his disdain for and suspicion of abstract theorising; and, for a widely read intellectual, he showed relatively little interest in European history and politics, and still less in those of the USA. He was an avid reader of Gibbon, Macaulay and Carlyle, and, like Thompson, he traced the lineage of English radicalism back to the Peasants' Revolt, the Levellers, Tom Paine and the Chartists. For Foot, twentieth-century radicalism in Britain, represented *inter alia* by Hardie, Lansbury and Bevan, was an extension of this radical crusade for social and political liberation.

Foot also had, as noted, a 'deep patriotic pride in English liberties and institutions',[97] especially to Parliament; and he believed in British 'exceptionalism'. Whilst he was in many respects a left-wing socialist – and had a long history as a rebel on the backbenches – he was also attached to a romantic version of what other socialists would identify as British imperialism (thus he celebrated not only Cromwell but also Francis Drake and Marlborough and the later Churchills);[98] and he was similarly 'bonded' with the public schools and with Oxford and Cambridge – a system of which he was of course a product.

Foot embodied a romantic, moral strand in English radicalism, attached to the 'empirical method' and to the importance of striving for liberation, equality and liberal enlightenment. He was the most intellectual and 'bookish' of twentieth-century British politicians but he did not apply his intellect to developing a political philosophy. His oratory, passion, humanity, and skills as a parliamentarian, were of the highest order. But he made no significant contribution to socialist thought. He, like Bevan, was always a practical politician, concerned more with 'means' rather than 'ends'. He remained, in the end, an articulate practitioner of the 'radical conscience' of the Left, always fighting the socialist, humanitarian battles, ever audacious and often courageous. Above all, it is agreed by almost everyone who knew and worked with him, that he was the kindest, warmest and most humane of men: a living exponent of the humanistic, radical creed in which he believed steadfastly throughout a long and active life.

Notes

1. Wherever possible, Michael Foot is referred to here as 'Foot'. When he needs to be distinguished from the numerous other Foots, his full name is given.
2. K.O. Morgan, *Michael Foot: A Life* (Harper Press, 2007; pb. edition, Harper Perennial Press, 2008). References are taken from the paperback edition, p.29; and ibid., p. 30, citing interview with Baroness Williams of Crosby (Shirley Williams), 1 November 2004.
3. M. Jones, *Michael Foot* (Gollancz, 1994, p. 31), citing Barbara Castle, *The Castle Diaries*, vol. 2, 1974–76, entry for 20 March 1975 (Weidenfeld and Nicolson, 1984).
4. Morgan, *Foot*, p. 33; Jones, *Foot*, p. 17.
5. E.P. Thompson, the title of Part One, *The Making of the English Working Class* (Gollancz, 1963; paperback edition, Pelican Books, 1968); see Chapter 7, this volume.
6. Morgan, *Foot*, p. 407.
7. M. Foot, *Debts of Honour* (Davies-Poynter, 1980).
8. Morgan, *Foot*, p. 9.
9. Jones, *Foot*, p. 14.
10. Morgan, *Foot*, p. 438.
11. His deep Devonian identity is reflected in his lifelong active support for Plymouth Argyle Football Club, at whose ground a stand is named in his honour.
12. At Oxford, he 'discarded all religious belief to become an agnostic humanist', Jones, *Foot*, p. 25.
13. M. Foot, *Debts of Honour* (Picador edition, 1981), p. 12.
14. Jones, *Foot*, p. 20.
15. M. Foot, *Loyalists and Loners* (Collins, 1986), cited in Morgan, *Foot*, pp. 24–5.

16 Ibid. (Morgan), p. 25.
17 Ibid., p. 26.
18 Ibid., p. 32. His brothers Dingle and John had also been Presidents of the Oxford Union; and his brother Hugh had been President of the Cambridge Union: a family record unlikely to be equalled.
19 See E.P. Thompson, *Writing by Candlelight* (Merlin Press, 1980), pp. 145–6.
20 Morgan, *Foot*, p. 40.
21 Jones, *Foot*, p. 38, citing letter from Foot to his mother, 5 March 1935.
22 Morgan, *Foot*, pp. 54–5, citing Foot in the *Western Mail*, 16 November 1935.
23 Ibid., p. 65.
24 Ibid., p. 66.
25 Ibid.
26 Jones, *Foot*, p. 81, citing Foot's entry on Frank Owen in the *Dictionary of National Biography*.
27 Morgan, *Foot*, p. 75.
28 Ibid., p. 88.
29 Ibid., p. 81.
30 Ibid., p. 104.
31 M. Foot, *Aneurin Bevan*, vol. 1, 1897–1945 (MacGibbon and Kee, 1962), p. 164, note.
32 Foot, *Debts of Honour*, chapter 4.
33 Ibid., p. 75.
34 Morgan, *Foot*, p. 67.
35 Ibid., p. 69.
36 Ibid., p. 70.
37 Jones, *Foot*, p. 40.
38 Morgan, *Foot*, p. 96.
39 Ibid.
40 Foot, *Bevan*, vol. 1, 1962; and vol. 2, *Aneurin Bevan 1945–1960* (Davies-Poynter, 1973).
41 Morgan, *Foot*, pp. 225–6.
42 Ibid., p. 96.
43 The only 'hard Left' figure at this time with whom Foot was on friendly terms was Harry Pollitt, the veteran Communist Party activist and official, and leader of the Party during the 1940s and early 1950s. This was due in no small part to Pollitt's determined advocacy of 'Popular Front' policies in the prewar period, despite the twists and turns of Stalinist foreign policy.
44 Jones, *Foot*, pp. 138–9, citing Foot's maiden speech in the House of Commons, 20 August 1945.
45 Ibid., citing Attlee's evidence to the Royal Commission on the Press, 1949.
46 Morgan, *Foot*, p. 125.
47 Ibid.
48 Ibid., p. 144, citing Foot, *Bevan*, vol. 2, p. 292.
49 On Jennie Lee, see the excellent biography by Patricia Hollis, *Jennie Lee – A Life* (Oxford: Oxford University Press, 1997).
50 Morgan, *Foot*, p. 158.

51 The figures were: Gaitskell 157, Bevan 70 and Morrison 40.
52 Morgan, *Foot*, p. 163.
53 The result in Devonport was: Conservative 24,821; Labour 24,721; Liberal 3100. Conservative majority 100.
54 M. Foot and M. Jones, *Guilty Men, 1957: Suez and Cyprus* (Gollancz, 1957).
55 Jones, *Foot*, p. 219.
56 For detailed analysis of the anti-nuclear peace movement from the mid-1950s to the mid-1960s, see R. Taylor, *Against the Bomb: The British Peace Movement 1958–1965* (Oxford: Clarendon Press, 1988).
57 See ibid., pp. 22ff; pp. 275ff.
58 Ibid., p. 279, citing NEC Minutes, October 1957.
59 The immediate cause of this change of heart was, almost certainly, a long night's discussion, lubricated by a plentiful supply of whisky, between Bevan and Sam Watson, the miners' leader.
60 Morgan, *Foot*, p. 175.
61 Ibid., p. 176.
62 Jones, *Foot*, pp. 229–30.
63 Morgan, *Foot*, p. 180.
64 Jones, *Foot*, p. 237.
65 Ibid., p. 243, citing Foot, *Bevan*, vol. 2, p. 651.
66 Ibid., p. 245.
67 Ibid.
68 Ibid., citing Lee, *My Life with Nye* (Cape, 1980), p. 252.
69 For detailed discussion of the lead-up to the 1960 Conference, the debate itself and the subsequent political struggle in the Party, see Taylor, *Against the Bomb*, pp. 289–307.
70 See ibid., pp. 298ff.
71 On the Committee of 100, see ibid., chapter 5, pp. 190–272.
72 Ibid., p. 84, citing P. Duff, *Left, Left, Left* (Allison and Busby, 1971), p. 195. On the INDEC initiative more generally, see Taylor, Against the Bomb, pp. 81–8.
73 Morgan, *Foot*, chapter 7.
74 In a debate with Tariq Ali and Bob Rowthorn, for example, he argued that the attempt to achieve socialism through 'battles on the streets' had resulted in the victory of Mussolini and Hitler. 'He urged socialists to model themselves on the Chartists. "Their great idea was by mobilising power outside Parliament to get real power inside."' Jones, *Foot*, pp. 311–12, citing a debate on 24 January 1969, and subsequent discussion in *Tribune*, 14 February 1969.
75 Morgan, *Foot*, p. 252.
76 Ibid., p. 283.
77 Ibid., p. 286.
78 Ibid., p. 294.
79 For details, see ibid., pp. 318ff.
80 Ibid., p. 334.
81 See D. Healey, *The Time of My Life* (Michael Joseph, 1989; pb. edition, Penguin, 1990).
82 Morgan, *Foot*, p. 346, citing Benn, *Against the Tide 1973–76*, 2 December 1976, pp. 673–4. See also Chapter 11 below on Tony Benn.

83 Morgan, *Foot*, p. 365, citing B. Donoghue, *Prime Minister* (Cape, 1977, p. 176).
84 Healey, *Time of My Life*, p. 499.
85 Morgan, *Foot*, p. 383.
86 Ibid., p. 395.
87 Jones, *Foot*, p. 481, citing interview in the *Daily Star*, 10 November 1981.
88 Healey, *Time of My Life*, p. 496.
89 By 1999, he was 'converted' to support for the EU, in part because of his admiration for European socialists, but specifically because of the increasing benefits accruing to workers and to the working class generally through the Social Chapter. See Morgan, *Foot*, pp. 470ff.
90 Ibid., p. 276.
91 He retained a close personal friendship, however, with Glenys and Neil Kinnock.
92 He was especially active in the protests against Serbian aggression, and in support of Croatia and other oppressed, emerging nations in the former Yugoslavia.
93 Morgan, *Foot*, p. 469.
94 Foot spoke, with his customary passion and eloquence, at the huge demonstration in London against the Iraq War on 15 February 2003.
95 The books were: *Another Heart and Other Pulses: The Alternative to the Thatcher Society* (Collins, 1984); *Loyalists and Loners* (Collins, 1986); *The Politics of Paradise: A Vindication of Byron* (Collins, 1988); *The History of Mr. Wells* (Black Swan, 1996); *Dr. Strangelove, I Presume* (Gollancz, 1999); B. Brivati (ed.), *The Uncollected Michael Foot* (Politicos, 2003); and, with Alison Highet, *Isaac Foot: A West Country Boy –Apostle of England* (Politicos, 2006).
96 Morgan, *Foot*, p. 490.
97 Ibid., p. 491.
98 Randolph Churchill, his Conservative opponent at several Devonport elections, was a close friend and a regular companion at Beaverbrook's table.

9

Joan Maynard

Joan Maynard was a relatively minor figure in the history of twentieth-century English radicalism. However, there are compelling reasons for including her here. The Labour Party since its inception has been very predominantly an urban party: the Conservatives, and to an extent the Liberals/Liberal Democrats, have been dominant in rural England. But the history of radicalism predates the industrial and urban age and the subsequent formation of the Labour Party, as was discussed in Chapters 1 and 2. A 'rural perspective' is thus important in the context of this study.

Joan Maynard identified passionately with the countryside and its people. As Frank Allaun, the veteran Left Labour MP, observed: '"She knew more about agriculture than any man or woman in the Labour Party."'[1] She was unique, on the Labour Left, not in her rural background but in having, at the core of her political being, rural concerns in general and the plight of agricultural workers in particular.

She was an admirer, though a critical one, of William Cobbett. In an essay she wrote when an adult student in a Leeds University and WEA Joint Tutorial Class, she identified his key qualities:

> I would put first his spirit of fearless independence, second he was a Countryman, who loved our beautiful Countryside, and the people who worked in it. This he demonstrated in a practical way by devoting so much of his life, and his great ability, in order that working people and particularly those in the countryside should share in the good life.[2]

She could have been describing herself and her political ideals and objectives.

Even when she became an MP, in 1974, for the quintessentially industrial safe seat of Sheffield Brightside, whose constituents naturally had quite other concerns,

Maynard continued to give prominence in Parliament and in her wider campaigning to rural issues.

Secondly, she had a wholly working-class background. She experienced real poverty in her childhood and, although clearly intelligent, diligent and enthusiastic, she nevertheless left school at 14. Not that she resented her relatively deprived early life. On the contrary, she 'thought herself blessed to have been brought up in the countryside, despite the severe financial hardship. She loved the freedom of the fields and woodlands and endless outdoor fun with school friends.'[3]

Finally, she was, as a woman Labour MP, one of a small band in Parliament: in 1974, when she was elected, there were only 18 Labour women MPs, 5 per cent of the PLP. Similarly, Maynard had been the only woman on the 14-member National Union of Agricultural Workers Union (NUAW) Executive. Although there had been a small number of women Labour MPs with working-class backgrounds – Ellen Wilkinson (Chapter 5) and Jennie Lee among them – all were graduates. Maynard alone could share fully the experiences and perspectives of the mass of working-class women. She identified with ordinary people, 'our people', and she had a strong belief in the innate goodness of human beings. It was capitalism that had perverted and defiled human values: the task was thus to liberate humankind by replacing the capitalist system, economically and culturally as well as politically, so that the fundamental human values of co-operation, fairness and above all care and consideration for others would prevail. The Dissenting tradition, which gave prominence to the 'love thy neighbour' ethic of the New Testament, lay at the heart of Maynard's politics.

Joan Maynard is thus a unique figure in twentieth-century English radicalism and represented an important ideological element in the broader tradition.[4]

Family background and values

Joan Maynard, born in 1921, was the youngest child of Matt and Effie, tenant farmers on 100 acres in North Yorkshire. Their tenancy was short-lived, however, as the farmer sold off the farm in lots to neighbouring farmers after the First World War. Matt Maynard briefly took a job as a salesman for a corn merchant; but he was not, in Joan Maynard's words, 'business-minded', and was dismissed in 1924. The family 'descended progressively into debt' and bankruptcy appeared imminent within a few years.[5] However, in 1936, through a friend, James Hutchinson, Maynard's parents obtained a let on a sub-Post Office in Thornton-le-Street, a hamlet near Thirsk. This provided some security; and in addition they managed to buy, on a 100 per cent mortgage, the 28-acre Post Office farm.

A key element in Joan Maynard's later development was her father's interest in literary and political issues. Even when really poor, the Maynard household was full of books, both serious literature and political books and pamphlets. From an early age, Joan joined her father and her older brother Edric in intense discussions of politics, particularly socialism, and the moral values which underpinned radical political beliefs.

The family were regular churchgoers, both Anglican and Methodist, but in her teens Joan ceased to attend church: ' "they say one thing on a Sunday but do something very different the rest of the week" '.[6] She never could abide hypocrisy and cant. It is important, however, to note that it was the Church as an organisation that she rejected: she remained committed to the Christian ethic of the New Testament and, almost certainly, retained a core of Christian spiritual adherence.

Her beliefs, though buttressed by socialist ideas and analysis, complemented later by aspects of Marxist theory, were fundamentally *moral* and were formed in the family home. Her core beliefs remained unchanged throughout her political life. She was outraged by *injustice* and *inequality*: capitalism was irrational, inefficient and anarchic but what she really objected to was its inherent unfairness, and the suffering which resulted for the mass of the working class.

In the countryside this unfairness manifested itself primarily through land ownership and the power and advantages that went with it, not least the tied cottage system, whose abolition was one of the main causes of Maynard's political life. Class conflict was central to her political perspective: there was 'our class' and 'the other class'; and you were either 'with us' or 'against us'. She expressed her concept of class division in her edited book, *A Hundred Years of Farmworkers' Struggle*:[7] 'Really it is four-cornered: The State, the Law, the Church and the Ruling Class, all united against the workers and all carried on the backs of the workers too.'

Her 'notion of class was more medieval than Marxist' and was based on her growing up on a smallholding in rural North Yorkshire. 'It was more akin to feudal serfdom than industrial manual labour.' Her pragmatic view of class was inclusive. She 'had no difficulty in including ... a variety of apparently middle class comrades ... *provided they supported her political struggles*'.[8]

Maynard's view of politics and the political struggle was Manichean: if you were on the side of the working class and were therefore by definition a socialist, she would give unconditional and unshakeable support. As already noted, if you were not 'with us', you were 'against us' and must be opposed. There were no grey areas, no room for 'complexity' or compromise. She was thus much more interested in *ends* than in means, and was always strongly in favour of working with other socialists, outside the Labour Party. Thus she had frequent comradely contact, from the mid-1950s onwards, with members of the Communist Party and wrote often for the *Daily Worker* and later the *Morning Star*. A typical piece in the *Daily Worker* in 1956 called for socialists and communists to get together ' "to talk things over ... How the Tories ... must laugh to see the working class movement split in this tragic way ... Our [that is, Labour Party socialists and the Communist Party] fundamental interests are the same. It is because I feel so strongly that I want to see an immediate end to bans and proscriptions in the Labour movement." '[9] Much later, she similarly opposed the expulsion from the Labour Party of 'Militant Tendency' supporters.

At the other end of the political spectrum, Maynard was quite happy, when a County Councillor in North Yorkshire, to collaborate with some of the North Yorkshire gentry if the occasion demanded: she 'appreciated their liberal, caring attitude towards the poor'.[10] This was the case, too, when Maynard was an MP and working on the national stage. Sir Richard Body, the Conservative MP who chaired the Agriculture Select Committee of which Maynard was an active and well-informed member, 'admired and valued Joan's hard work and integrity, "On agricultural issues Joan and I stood shoulder to shoulder. Joan was a good person. If you divide people into the net givers and the net takers in the world, she was one of the former. She was ahead of her time." '[11]

Maynard was no theoretician: she was a pragmatist to her fingertips. Socialism was so obviously right, morally and theoretically, that the task was to get on and achieve it, rather than worry away at the finer points of analysis and ideological dispute. One of her favourite maxims, directed often at academic friends and colleagues (including the author) in her inimitably friendly but firm manner, was to the effect that 'half an hour on the picket line is worth six hours in the library'. Thus the jibe in the Conservative press and elsewhere that she was 'Stalin's grandmother' was not only cheap but a total misunderstanding of her and her politics. Certainly she would co-operate with communists, as with other socialists, but she shared neither their sectarianism nor their concern with rigorous Marxist theorising.

She was always suspicious of leaders: her affinity was with the ordinary people, 'our people'; she was critical of hierarchies and the pomposity, self-aggrandisement and careerist ambitions which often characterised those achieving, or aspiring to, high office; and she was similarly suspicious of bureaucracy and obfuscation, both of which were endemic in the Labour Party, in the Union and in parliamentary culture and procedure.

However, such pragmatism never threatened her commitment to socialist objectives. An anecdote cited by O'Connor illustrated this perspective succinctly. As National Vice-President of the National Union of Agricultural Workers Union (NUAW, discussed below), one of Maynard's duties was to present long-service awards to retiring members. 'After one presentation she warmly praised the recipient's service and Socialism; one of his sons hesitated. "Well, the trouble is, Dad only ever sees one side of the question". "Aye", said Joan with feeling, "that's what I like about him".'[12]

The Union

The twin pillars of Maynard's politics were her commitments to the rural working class and the NUAW[13] and to the socialist Left of the Labour Party. It was the NUAW, however, that was always her emotional reference point. ' "The Union and Yorkshire – what could be dearer to my heart!" '[14]

She joined the NUAW in 1947, at the invitation of Jack Brocklebank, district organiser of the Union, who became a lifelong friend. From the outset, Maynard recognised the inherent difficulties that confronted farmworkers. Unlike most workers, those in agriculture worked in small numbers and often in close proximity to their employer. They were thus likely to lack the solidarity, strength and confidence which are enjoyed by many industrial workers and workers in the public services. However, as she observed in the 1970s, farming is 'becoming more and more big business... the boss becomes and *is* more remote, his interests are looked after by a manager who has a far more impersonal relationship with the men. This means that eventually in agriculture the relationship between worker and employer will become more like it is in industry.' Maynard campaigned tirelessly on the issue of the tied cottage system, as noted. ' "The tied cottage system has kept them [the farmworkers] quiet and it has held down wages in the industry." '[15] She argued that the power of the farmer over the farmworkers was insidious: whether or not it was exercised, the farmworkers were always aware that, if they 'stepped out of line', they might be evicted. In a fundamental sense, the farmworker was thus not a free citizen. The abolition of this iniquitous system was an issue to which she returned when she was an MP, as is discussed below.

Maynard, and a small group of other left-wing socialists, confronted a solidly right-wing union leadership. As Wilf Page, a Communist Party (CP) member and one of Maynard's comrades in the Union, observed: ' "The Executive was a very conservative force. The countryside is a very conservative force. They represented, really, the countryside... we were in advance – if I may use that term – of the people in the countryside." '[16]

She had a struggle to secure election to the Union National Executive, despite her unstinting and growing reputation. By 1958, Maynard, as delegate to the Yorkshire County Committee of the NUAW, was elected County Secretary. After much politicking, and despite the strong opposition of the NUAW leadership, Maynard was eventually elected as National Vice-President, and thus *ex officio* a member of the National Executive, in 1966, defeating three other strong (male) candidates. Achieving office in the Union did nothing to moderate Maynard's militancy. On the contrary, she used her new profile to oppose the Union leadership's timidity and refusal to confront and challenge the employers. In her view, the leadership was profoundly mistaken in its *de facto* acceptance of the structural inequalities in rural society; and she articulated forcefully her scepticism about the Agricultural Wages Board and its cautious approach to improving farmworkers' wages and conditions. She argued that only through industrial action, primarily selective strikes, could substantial wage increases be achieved. Moreover, Maynard advocated an increase in the basic wage rate, rather than in skilled workers' rates: *fairness*, as ever, was her criterion.

Maynard was heavily criticised at the Union Executive meetings for her confrontational style as well as her militant politics; worst of all, in the Executive's view, she criticised in public and explicitly the Union leadership and what she saw as its reactionary politics. She wrote regularly in the socialist press arguing for more radical policies. For example, in 1972, she wrote in the bulletin of the Institute for Workers' Control (IWC) that the leadership's conciliatory approach over wage negotiations should be abandoned. '"Where have we ever got by going round with a begging bowl? Nowhere! We have steadily over the years been losing the wages battle. A successful selective strike would do more good than years of talking."'[17] Similarly, at the 1966 Biennial Conference, she attacked the Executive Committee's 'sordid sell-out of our membership' on the issue of tied cottages.[18]

In such a context, it is not surprising that the leadership was determined to oust Maynard from the Vice-President post. This they accomplished at the 1972 Biennial Conference at Weymouth. A motion was put to Conference proposing the abolition of the post of Vice-President on the spurious grounds that the constrained finances of the Union required a reduction in the costs of the Officers. (As a lay member, Maynard cost the Union nothing but modest expenses.) The motion was carried, on a show of hands; and the call for a card vote was rejected by the Chair. It was altogether a shabby and acrimonious affair. Maynard was devastated: '"it was the worst blow I ever had, because the Union meant more to me than anything else; it was the saddest moment in my career. In my life."'[19] Even her election to the Labour Party's National Executive Committee (NEC) a few months earlier could not really compensate.

Maynard was, however, a resilient and determined woman. She continued campaigning on Union issues, undaunted by this setback. For example, at the Biennial Conference in 1976, Maynard proposed a motion, which was heavily defeated, calling for the Union's withdrawal from the Agricultural Wages Board (AWB). She pursued a similar course in Parliament, where by then she was an MP, through a private member's bill (an enabling bill) to provide for the conversion of the AWB to a statutory Joint Industrial Council. Also, after the 1976 Conference, Maynard and her 'coterie of Yorkshire supporters set up an undercover "Agricultural New Policy Discussion Group"',[20] whose purpose was to act as a network and pressure group to formulate left-wing policies on such issues as tied cottages, wages policy and the AWB, and plans for securing the election of a left-wing President of the Union, probably Maynard herself.

Maynard was indefatigable in pursuing the tied cottage issue, not only through the Union but through the Labour Party, inside Parliament and in the wider movement. At the 1965 Labour Conference, for example, she moved the resolution demanding that the Labour government should 'abolish the tied cottage system immediately'. She continued to argue the case at the 1968 Labour Party Conference and at the Trade Union Congress. On her election to Parliament in 1974, Maynard 'immediately contacted ten sympathetic Cabinet ministers to seek their support for getting abolition of the tied cottage legislation into the first session of Parliament and presented a petition with over 140 MPs' signatures to 10 Downing Street'.[21]

Her campaign achieved at least partial success in April 1976 when the government published a bill extending the Rent Act's security of tenure to workers living in agricultural tied cottages. Despite 'wrecking amendments' in the House of Lords, the Act came into effect on 1 January 1977. Maynard, although dissatisfied because outright abolition had not been accomplished, nevertheless acknowledged that farm workers now had the security of knowing that alternative accommodation would be provided if they were evicted.

Without Maynard's constant agitation this victory, partial though it was, would not have been achieved. As Audrey Wise, a close friend and fellow left-wing MP, put it: 'The Left didn't really take up rural issues, they did with the tied cottage, but they wouldn't have done without Joan.'[22]

Another cause central to her rural focus was her long campaign for land nationalisation. (It was this advocacy of land nationalisation which led Maynard to support, albeit briefly, Acland's Common Wealth Party.) As early as the 1952 Labour Party Conference, Maynard moved a resolution on this issue and two years later she proposed, at the Union's Biennial Conference that:

> This Conference believes that the nationalisation of land is essential for any real substantial increase in agricultural production because the scale of fixed capital investment required can only be undertaken by the state.

Tam Dalyell, in his affectionate obituary in the *Independent*, wrote that:

> Etched into my memory is the look of pained impatience on Hugh Gaitskell's face ... in Scarborough in 1958 ... at the Labour Party Conference Rural Areas debate on the policy document Prosper the Plough ... a striking jet-black-haired Yorkshire lass ... strode to the platform and with no inhibitions whatsoever harangued us all on the urgent need to nationalise the land – every arable acre of it. This was the perennial delegate from the Thirsk and Malton constituency, Joan Maynard.[23]

She continued to argue the case on every possible occasion until her retirement.

Roger Fieldhouse captures, in his recollection of his own involvement in the Union in North Yorkshire in the 1960s and 1970s, the central importance to Maynard of the Union and of rural workers' comradeship. In this period, Fieldhouse was invited as Tutor/Organiser for the Workers' Educational Association (WEA) in North Yorkshire, to Union District Committee meetings.

> These meetings, usually held in the back room of a country pub with a fire burning in the winter, were Joan's world ... The atmosphere was warm and, above all, comradely ... It was like travelling back in time with a copy of E.P. Thompson's *Making of the English Working Class* in one's pocket. It conjured up images of early trade unionism, Chartist meetings, the Tolpuddle Martyrs, Cobbett's *Rural Rides*, Tom Paine and back through the long tradition of English radicalism from Levellers and Diggers to John Ball and the Peasants' Revolt. It was this rural radicalism that formed Joan's political ideas and beliefs.[24]

As Chris Mullin wrote, in the *Guardian* on 24 September 2011, she was recalled with great affection in the Union: 'One of her union colleagues said of her: "I've been a member for 50 years and I've known all our leaders. In my opinion she is the greatest fighter the farm workers have produced."'

Politics

Maynard, brought up in a working-class socialist household and greatly influenced by her father and her older brother Edric,[25] was enthused by the famous Labour victory in 1945. However, she was attracted too by Sir Richard Acland and his Common Wealth Party: Acland was '"a true socialist"', she thought. Reflecting later on the 1945 government, Maynard's view was that, had Labour had the desire and commitment, a peaceful socialist revolution could have been achieved: '"the Tories were reeling. They didn't reel for long."'[26] For her, nationalisation should be the initial key policy objective for socialist governments: and she always maintained that Attlee and his government failed this test.

In January 1946, Maynard and her brother Edric attended a meeting in Thirsk, chaired by Jack Brocklebank, and it was agreed that Thirsk and Malton Labour Party should be established. Although she had no knowledge of committee procedures, Maynard became Secretary. As always, she worked extraordinarily hard, recruiting, organising and generally proselytising for the cause in her local community. In August 1946 she was elected to the Thirsk and Malton Divisional Party and subsequently to its Executive: in 1949 she was appointed Press Officer.

In July 1950, aged 29, Maynard became the youngest JP in the North Riding. She saw her role as a magistrate in political and moral terms: '"I tried to leaven the bread. I tried to get the other magistrates to see that the people were usually there because of the circumstances under which they had been brought up ... I always tried to vote against anybody being sent to prison."'[27]

Maynard stood as a Labour candidate for Thirsk in the North Riding County Council election in April 1952. Although she lost, she made her mark through tireless campaigning and her passionate advocacy of socialist policies; in May she was successful in the Rural District Council election; and in 1955 she *did* win a seat on the County Council, with a majority of 144. Maynard always rejected the notion that the County Council was 'unpolitical'; and she had no time for so-called 'Independents'. Politics, at local as at national level, was always about class struggle: 'our class' against 'the other class'.

She campaigned vigorously on a range of local issues: housing and rents, old people's homes, school education and so on – all from a solidly socialist perspective. Maynard was widely respected as a local councillor. Charlie Pattison, a Thirsk jeweller, was typical: '"She is one of the few politicians that I could say I would put my hand in the fire for her honesty. There are very few of those."'[28]

Conscious as she was of the limitations of her own educational opportunity, Maynard was especially concerned with education in the broader struggle for fairness, equality and the building of a vibrant, informed democracy. She was thus a keen advocate of comprehensive schooling and also of the abolition of fee-paying schools. Liberal adult education was of particular importance for Maynard, not only in terms of her political philosophy of citizenship but personally, for her own development. In 1945, she saw an advertisement for a WEA evening class on 'Social History through Literature', which she joined, and thus began a long and close association with adult education, particularly the WEA and the University of Leeds's Department of Adult and Continuing Education. Through the WEA she learned that there was more than one kind of democracy. ' "There isn't just political democracy, putting a cross on a ballot [paper] every four or five years, there's also economic democracy ... I began to realise that a very small number of people own the real wealth in society and the majority of people didn't own very much at all. Nevertheless, the majority were the people who created the wealth for the minority; those ideas have never left me." '[29]

Maynard subsequently organised reading groups on economic and political issues, and attended WEA summer schools in her holidays.

Keen advocate though she was of liberal adult education, Maynard had no qualms about co-opting adult education in the service of the wider socialist movement. At the time of the 1964 general election, Roger Fieldhouse was Tutor/Organiser for the WEA in North Yorkshire. 'Officially I was meant to be neutral [but] there was no chance of my being neutral on Joan's watch. She kindly but firmly explained that my role was to outline the various issues and make it clear that everyone should vote Labour.'[30]

From the outset, she was strongly opposed to the right-wing national leadership of the Labour Party. When Labour lost the 1959 election, she argued that it was because the Labour Party had been apologetic about nationalisation and cautious in its overall approach. She was appalled at Gaitskell's (unsuccessful) proposal to abolish the 'Clause IV' commitment to public ownership, and his defiance of the 1960 Conference vote for unilateral nuclear disarmament.

At the local and regional level, Maynard was engaged in constant skirmishes with the Labour Party bureaucracy over her confrontational politics and her frequent articles and speeches for 'far Left' organisations and publications. One of her great qualities was that she could not be intimidated: she treated everyone in the same way and spoke the truth as she saw it. She was that rare human being: someone who genuinely regarded all people as equal.

Her principled activism had not gone unnoticed at national level. Nevertheless, it was a remarkable achievement for her to be elected to Labour's NEC, in the Women's Section, in 1972. The base for her support was the Thirsk and Malton Constituency Labour Party (CLP), a large proportion of the CLP votes nationally, but also, crucially, the bloc votes of three big trade unions. In the event, Maynard beat the popular Eirene White by only 105,000 votes, a very narrow margin. (She even had the support of her own union: her typically wry comment was that her '"Union were quite glad to unload me on the Labour Party NEC, anything to get me out of their hair ... they saved the day really"'.)[31]

On the NEC, she pursued vigorously a range of socialist policies. In an interview with the *Morning Star* on 7 October 1972, she said that these included '"fighting against any kind of incomes policy under capitalism, pressing for equal pay and opportunity for women, and putting the farm workers' point of view, in particular an end to the tied cottage system. I will continue to work for the party to adopt Socialist policies as quickly as possible. I have never believed in consensus politics."'[32] There was much more in the same vein.

Left-wing colleagues urged Maynard to stand for Parliament but she was reluctant: her priority, as always, was the Union and she wanted to concentrate upon fighting Bert Hazell for the Union presidency in 1974. However, she was increasingly conscious of her multiplicity of roles and the danger that, despite her best efforts, she might fulfil none of them properly.[33] In the end, she decided that, having been the Party agent for 21 years, she '"would have a go"'.[34]

After a few unsuccessful attempts for adoption by CLPs – at Chester-le-Street and Newcastle East – and turning down an informal approach from Lincoln, she was selected for the safe Labour seat of Sheffield Brightside, defeating among others David Blunkett. Despite the ousted previous MP for the constituency, Eddie Griffiths, standing as 'Independent Labour', and a 'dirty' campaign, Maynard was elected and served as MP for the constituency until her retirement in 1987. Many left-wing socialists, when elected to Parliament, become disengaged from their constituents and the wider labour movement: they become 'incorporated' into the strong culture of Parliament, its deeply rooted assumptions and procedures and its overall mystique.[35] Arguably, this applies especially to Labour MPs from a working-class background. There was never the slightest danger that Maynard would succumb to the lure of Parliament. In an article entitled 'My advice to new Members of Parliament', she wrote:

> Politically, remember it's not our place, it's not geared for our benefit. All its traditions are alien to working class people ... their system waters ... down (proposed legislation), it works for them not for our people. Political power resides in the Commons, but real power, economic powers, still reside in the hands of those who own the land, money, and what's left of the commanding heights of our industry. When a Labour Government is in power the economic power outside Parliament exerts control, and has always done so.[36]

She thus had no illusions about Parliament and adopted, in effect, a Marxist analysis of Parliament's place in the contemporary capitalist socio-economic structure, a perspective articulated in particular by Ralph Miliband.[37] Maynard differed, at least in emphasis, from Miliband, however, in that she believed that Parliament 'could be made to work for us, but so far we have never had a Parliamentary Labour Party, as a majority, prepared to make the House of Commons work more democratically and in the interests of working class people'.[38]

Although the abolition of the tied cottage system and related rural issues were the focus of Maynard's concerns as an MP, she was also a conscientious and effective constituency MP. This was in part because of her natural rapport with working-class people and her inherent warmth; and also because, although at the outset she knew little of the industrial world, her constituents' problems were familiar: health, education, jobs, money worries, housing and so on. She also had an excellent team working with her in the constituency. But in terms of *issues*, over and above her rural concerns, one stood out: the mounting crisis over Ireland.

Ireland

At first sight, it is hard to see why Maynard felt so passionately about Ireland. She had no Irish connections, and had no firmly held religious views, sectarian or otherwise, apart from her general adherence to the moral radicalism of the New Testament; and she had little knowledge or understanding, certainly at the outset, of the complexities of Irish history and culture. The explanation, however, as always with Maynard, was straightforward. When she first visited Northern Ireland in 1979 as a member of a three-woman delegation of the National Assembly of Women, she began to learn how the nationalist population was discriminated against. 'It really shook me … I suppose it's because I could never bear injustice – and I saw the terrible injustice of what was going on – that [is why] I became committed to the Irish cause'.[39]

Similarly, she was horrified by what could be done under the Special Powers Act; she believed that the inequalities were so glaring that they could only be maintained by force. The ultimate aim, therefore, must be the reunification of Ireland. It was thus two of Maynard's key values – her fundamental, moral rejection of both *injustice* and *inequality* – that underlay her passionate commitment to the Irish nationalist cause.

She quickly established a rapport with the few other left-wing Labour MPs who supported the Irish nationalist movement, in particular Martin Flannery and Jeremy Corbyn: 'Jeremy was probably one of the very best MPs – he was wonderful on Ireland, and Benn of course.'[40] This small group of MPs were vociferous in their rejection of various iterations of the Prevention of Terrorism Act. In her view, it was not about the prevention of terrorism: 'it was really about terrorising Irish people in this country and collecting information. They could hold people for a week without ever charging them; it's scandalous.'[41] In 1982, 52 Labour MPs voted against the Act, defying the Whips: by March 1983, the PLP official 'line' was to vote against, thanks in large part to the effective campaigning of the left-wing group.

Maynard was closely involved with the 'Troops Out' movement, formed in 1973; her concern with civil liberties also led her to back the National Council for Civil Liberties (NCCL), now 'Liberty', whose Chief Executive was the subsequent Labour Cabinet Minister Patricia Hewitt.

As Chris Mullin recalled at a Memorial Meeting for Maynard in 1998, as a 'politician Joan was fearless. If she thought a cause was right, she did not sit around calculating the effect on her opinion poll rating. She spoke up.' She voted against the Prevention of Terrorism Act, 'not because she was soft on terrorism – on the contrary – but because she believed the Act to be an affront to liberty'.[42]

Maynard called repeatedly for the withdrawal of British troops and for negotiations to begin with the objective of creating a united Ireland. Others in the Labour Party disagreed strongly, including not only Labour Northern Ireland Ministers Roy Mason and Merlyn Rees, but also left-wing colleagues and friends, such as Hans Breitenbach of York Fabians. In October 1975, the Labour Party established a Northern Ireland study group and Maynard was included as a member, despite opposition from her Labour and Conservative critics. The group was irreconcilably divided from the outset, with the trade union members particularly opposed to 'nationalist' arguments. (In Maynard's view, this was because their Northern Ireland members were overwhelmingly from the Protestant community.) Maynard was central to the growing opposition to government policy in Northern Ireland and to the demand for a change of policy to resolve the deteriorating situation: she organised petitions, led demonstrations, asked numerous questions in the House of Commons and generally campaigned tirelessly.

The change of government in 1979 brought no change in Labour's bipartisan policy on Northern Ireland: Maynard regarded this as a 'real conspiracy' between the two parties. Although there were mounting calls from the Left to end this consensus, the bulk of the Labour Party could not be convinced. Maynard was probably right in her observation that '"most people in the labour movement, sadly, just think it is such a difficult issue that they hope it will go away"';[43] this distancing was exacerbated by fear of reprisals and death threats.

Maynard and others established the Labour Committee on Ireland. This acted as an effective pressure group on the leadership throughout the 1980s. In June 1980, the Labour NEC passed a resolution, by 11 votes to 8, stating that: 'The NEC is implacably opposed to the programme and methods of terrorism. Equally however we are opposed to repression and torture in the prisons of Northern Ireland.' The climate of opinion in the Party, if not the leadership, was slowly changing, in part because of the constant campaigning of Maynard and her colleagues.

Following the Conservative election victory in 1983, when Sinn Fein's Gerry Adams won the Belfast West constituency, Jeremy Corbyn invited Adams to visit the House of Commons. This visit caused predictable uproar and Maynard was one of the few MPs to give public, unqualified support to Corbyn. The relationship between Corbyn and Maynard was close: he respected her as someone ' "who had radical views on international issues and who was prepared to see Ireland as an international issue"'.[44]

There continued to be immense pressure on Maynard, from the media, from the Labour leadership and in the House of Commons to denounce the IRA as terrorists. This she conspicuously refused to do, arguing that such condemnations only fuelled the intransigence on both sides and made a political settlement impossible. She was, though, unequivocal in *distancing* herself from the IRA. In the House of Commons she declared that: '"I repeat what I have said before, that I am not in favour of violence here or anywhere else. I have certainly never been and am not a supporter of the IRA or any other warring groups in that unhappy country."'[45]

Typical of her pragmatic approach, Maynard spent a lot of time and effort publicising the wrongful convictions of Irish prisoners in Britain, campaigning for better prison conditions for Irish political prisoners and trying to arrange support for their families. There are numerous examples of gratitude from those who benefited from her campaigning. Sister Sarah Clarke, working from a convent in North London and campaigning on these issues, and author of *No Faith in the System*,[46] was unstinting in her praise. Unlike other MPs, including Clarke's own, Maynard ' "always took the right step. She was a lovely lady ... I just admired her, that she had that courage. She knew awful things were happening and she was prepared to listen." '[47]

It was through Maynard that Chris Mullin was able to make contact with the 'Birmingham Six' and subsequently the 'Guildford Four' and with Sister Sarah. The three of them, and a little later Jeremy Corbyn, led the eventually successful campaign for the release of all those wrongly convicted of terrorist atrocities. In March 1991, the Campaign Group of Labour MPs agreed the following early day motion: 'This House wishes to put on permanent record its gratitude, admiration and respect for the untiring work of Mr. Chris Mullin, a member of this House, who inspired by Joan Maynard, former MP, has worked unceasingly to prove the innocence of the Birmingham Six, and by doing so, played a central role in their release.'[48]

Maynard's long campaign on Ireland was one of her most notable achievements. It is not only that, in the light of subsequent events, her perspective proved to be vindicated: it is also that she was unshakeable in her beliefs and commitments, despite being in a tiny minority, and suffering from vicious and continual criticism. As always, for Maynard the undoubtedly complex issues could be reduced to a few fundamental facts. Ireland had been colonised by the British; injustice, exploitation and discrimination had been evident for many years; and there would never be peace in Ireland until unification was achieved and the British withdrew.

Coming home

Maynard decided in 1985 that she would not stand again at the next general election. Her decision was based primarily on her domestic, family commitments: her sister

Elsie, who was suffering from Alzheimer's disease, returned from the USA to be near her; and her brother Rowie was becoming increasingly frail.[49] Maynard always took her family responsibilities very seriously: in addition to her numerous public and political roles, she had acted as a 'carer' for much of her adult life. The moral code which lay at the heart of her radicalism permeated her whole life, the personal as well as the political.

There were, however, ancillary reasons. Although she had been extremely diligent in her national role as an MP and a member of the NEC – and much else – she '"was never taken over by the place"' (the House of Commons),[50] like so many others. Moreover, she was never at home in London: she was not a 'city person'. '"I was looking forward to retirement because I love the countryside. I was looking forward to coming back here to live."'[51] A final reason was that she was becoming tired as she got older: in her view, to be a good MP was an extremely arduous full-time job, seven days a week, often for 12 or more hours a day. Ever pragmatic, she thought that all MPs should stand down in their mid-60s.

However, her return to North Yorkshire did not mean an end to political activism. She immediately became involved in a large array of organisations, including standing for election to the Parish Council. The former MP and prominent NEC member swapped these national roles for a place on Sowerby Parish Council. This typified Maynard's politics: there was not a shred of pomposity or self-aggrandisement in her character. For her, the struggle for socialism took place on many fronts, all of them important.

She chaired Thirsk Local Labour Party and she and a group of socialists established the North Yorkshire Campaign Group, members of which met in each other's houses on Saturday mornings; she resumed her activism with the Union and she became involved too, through her sister's illness, with the local branch of the Alzheimer's society; she joined the Yorkshire Rural Community Council and was elected vice-chair; she campaigned against the proposed east coast pylon corridor and became a member of the Rural Arts Conservation Committee. The list extended beyond this, but gives a flavour of her continuing activism.

This chapter has focused, necessarily, on Maynard's politics and the mainsprings of her radicalism. However, important aspects of Maynard's personality were not directly political. She was an environmentalist before her time, with a deep appreciation of the natural world and the importance of preserving Britain's countryside. Her biographer recounts a countryside walk she took with Maynard two years before she died. Munching apples bought from a local orchard, Maynard said: '"Fruits of the earth, Kristine."' This was 'an expression of reverence, for Nature, for the natural world, for human endeavour'.[52] Her other enthusiasms included her garden and Yorkshire cricket: she reminded people that Thomas Lord (founder of the famous cricket ground, Lord's, in London) was a Yorkshireman. And finally, she had a great sense of fun and loved a good joke, often at her own expense.

At her funeral in 1998 – she died of cancer on 28 March 1998 – many people, including comrades and opponents, both local and national, paid generous tribute to her. On her tombstone is inscribed: 'Steadfast in her beliefs: a True Socialist'.

Contribution to English radicalism

Maynard was firmly in the English radical Dissenting tradition. Buttressed as it was by some elements of class analysis theory, the core of her beliefs was moral. She had direct experience in her social milieu of the inequity and unfairness of capitalism and she devoted her life to the struggle to mitigate its unjust effects and in the longer term to replace it with a fully socialist system. It was, similarly, a combination of an *a priori* belief in the innate goodness of ordinary human beings and her lived experience that led her always to be suspicious of leaders and to trust rather in the good sense of the people. In that fundamental sense she was a true democrat. The importance she attached to education was in part because, through her own experience, she realised the key role a liberal education, in the broader sense, could make to personal development. But even more fundamentally she believed that only through a full and intellectually rigorous education, especially in history and the social sciences, could an informed citizenry create a vibrant, participatory democracy.

Thus, she was not anti-intellectual, far from it; but her emphasis was always upon activism, particularly collective action, to try to confront the multiple injustices meted out by the system and indeed directly by 'the other class' against 'our class'.

Everything, for Maynard, was seen and analysed through the lens of *class*. Whilst this gave a sure, simple and clear basis for Maynard's essentially moral socialism, it did lead at times to a somewhat rigid and reductive politics. A particularly prominent example of this was her perspective on feminism. She had ' "never been a very strong feminist" '. For her, the struggle for equality for women was essentially a ' "part of the struggle for Socialism against capitalism, which is an exploiter of men, and of course even bigger exploiter of women who are less well organised" '. She was in favour, of course, of equal pay ' "and everything like that – equal opportunities" '.[53] And she had no hesitation in backing controversial 'women's issues', such as the right to abortion and opposition to the 'strip searching' of Irish women prisoners in British jails. But she was never interested in women MPs, or any other group of activist women, organising *as women*. As Wilf Page, her CP comrade in the Union, observed, ' "I think it's the last thing Joan would want to do – get a woman's movement going." '[54] Jeremy Corbyn recalled that she was always opposed to women-only shortlists for the selection of Parliamentary candidates. ' "I would argue for it and she against. Her view would be that you fight the class fight and that the class fight comes first." '[55]

Audrey Wise was surely right in her claim that Maynard ' "would be discriminated against because she was a Socialist – and perhaps in Joan's case mostly because she was a Socialist, but she would have been affected, whether she knew it or not, by the discrimination against women"'.[56] But Maynard would not, or could not, acknowledge this. Like Jennie Lee, she always considered herself a socialist who just happened to be a woman.

She learned through her adult education involvement, and from her political comrades in the Union and the labour movement, about some aspects of Marxist analysis – in particular the historical materialist thesis that claims that exploitation and inequality are necessarily and structurally inherent in the capitalist system. But Maynard was never a thoroughgoing Marxist or materialist; her roots lay in the radical Dissenting tradition, as noted, and especially in its *rural* articulation. As Thompson noted in *The Making of the English Working Class*,[57] and as Maynard's biographer argues, Nonconformism and particularly Methodism was often an explicitly oppositional force in rural areas. Methodists held that the fruits of the earth are God's gift to all people, the poor as well as the rich.

The labour movement, and English radicalism generally, is permeated with Nonconformist, Dissenting morality. Many Labour leaders have been Christian Socialists: Keir Hardie, Arthur Henderson and George Lansbury among them. (The name of Maynard's home in Sowerby was 'Lansbury House'.) Few, though, have had both a rural and a working-class background. Maynard's roots were deep in this tradition and her involvement in later years with the evangelical Christian preacher Neville Knox should be seen in this light. (She attended regularly religious meetings at Knox's home.) Far from being a 'late conversion', this involvement was an indication of her lifelong spiritual, moral commitments. For Maynard, as for many from this Dissenting, radical tradition, her religion and her politics were inextricably linked. Of course, Maynard gave overwhelming emphasis in her life to her political commitments: but the moral, social and religious underpinnings were always there.

Maynard was undoubtedly a dogmatic, outspoken and at times confrontational politician; and she was clearly and explicitly on the far Left of the Labour Party and the wider labour movement. As Roger Fieldhouse has observed, this approach resulted in her believing that 'the ends justified the means' and thus in her 'supporting some rather unpleasant things: but she believed this was necessary'.[58] Given these characteristics, it is hardly surprising that she had many enemies, not only in the Tory press, but in her own Union and in the PLP. What *is* surprising is that she was so admired, respected and liked by many across the political spectrum. In his obituary, Tam Dalyell, the veteran Labour MP, recalled a conversation with Sir Robin Turton MP, then 'Father of the House' and a quintessentially 'high Tory'; Turton's long-time opponent in the safe Conservative seat of Thirsk and Malton had been Joan Maynard. Turton stated: 'Actually, I like and respect her. She is politically utterly Utopian and I might think quite dotty. But she is a good-mannered woman, a kind woman and well thought of by people who regard her views with anathema.'[59]

As Chris Mullin recalled at her memorial meeting, 'she retained the respect of persons of all political persuasions ... she was a politician who radiated integrity'.[60] And, as he wrote later, 'Despite her strong opinions, she was a kind and gentle woman, respected by all who knew her'.[61]

Maynard's profound faith in the capacity of ordinary people, working together, to build a new socialist society was at the core of her political beliefs; and her rural background, knowledge and perspective brought a distinctive and necessary dimension to twentieth century English radicalism and its commitment to bringing about a new social order.

Note

I am especially grateful to Roger Fieldhouse, a close friend and colleague of Joan Maynard's, for his advice and insights in relation to this chapter.

Notes

1. Frank Allaun, MP, cited in Kristine M. O'Connor, *Joan Maynard: Passionate Socialist* (Politicos, 2003), p. 249.
2. Ibid., p. 26.
3. Ibid., p. 6.
4. John Morrison, who worked for many years in North Yorkshire, has pointed out that Joan Maynard 'was not alone ... There were ... thousands of unsung rural radicals. I met some of them at NUAW branch meetings which I attended once a month.' Letter to the author, 20 November 2019.
5. O'Connor, *Maynard*, pp. 3–6.
6. Ibid., p. 11.
7. Joan Maynard (ed.), *A Hundred Years of Farmworkers' Struggle* (Nottingham: Institute for Workers' Control (IWC), n.d. (c. 1974)), p. 4.
8. Roger Fieldhouse, in a note to the author, 23 May 2017.
9. 'Don't Make the Tories Laugh', *Daily Worker*, 2 June 1956, cited in O'Connor, *Maynard*, pp. 79–80.
10. Fieldhouse, note to the author.
11. O'Connor, *Maynard*, p. 252, citing the *Guardian*, 18 July 1987.
12. O'Connor, *Maynard*, p. 120.
13. The National Union of Agricultural Workers was founded in 1920; this changed in 1968 to the National Union of Agricultural and Allied Workers Union; and in 1982 it became the Agricultural and Allied Workers Trade Group of the Transport and General Workers' Union. For the remainder of this chapter the NUAW is referred to as 'the Union'.
14. Maynard, 'The Land Worker', August 1969, cited in O'Connor, *Maynard*, p. 48.
15. Maynard, *Farmworkers' Struggle*, pp. 3–4.
16. Page, cited in O'Connor, *Maynard*, p. 107.

17 IWC Bulletin, 1972, No. 10, p. 51, cited in *ibid.*, p. 129. Maynard was a leading member of the IWC and chaired its meetings.
18 Fieldhouse, note to the author.
19 Maynard, cited in O'Connor, *Maynard*, p. 131.
20 Fieldhouse, note to the author. Roger Fieldhouse was the convener of this group.
21 Ibid.
22 O'Connor, *Maynard*, p. 236.
23 Dalyell, obituary, *Independent*, 29 March 1998.
24 Fieldhouse, note to the author.
25 Her older brother Edric was a great influence on Maynard. He moved to London in 1936, worked in a bookshop and studied part-time with a view to entering academic life. 'Joan longed for the day he would become a professor' (O'Connor, *Maynard*, p. 13). Edric was not only left-wing, he was also a pacifist, and passionate about art and music. He became friendly with the composer and pacifist Michael Tippett and, after the war, when he was a conscientious objector, he was preparing for the university entrance examination when he was struck down with peritonitis and died.
26 Maynard, cited in O'Connor, *Maynard*, pp. 30–1.
27 Fieldhouse, note to the author.
28 O'Connor, *Maynard*, p. 102.
29 Ibid., p. 21.
30 Fieldhouse, note to the author.
31 O'Connor, *Maynard*, p. 134.
32 Ibid., p. 135.
33 At this stage she was not only an active and well-known member of the Labour Party's NEC, and active in the NUAW: she was also a Parish and Rural District Councillor, contesting county council elections, a magistrate, and the Labour Party agent in one of the largest constituencies in the country. She also had domestic responsibilities.
34 O'Connor, *Maynard*, p. 137.
35 For the classic account of this process, from a Marxist perspective, see R. Miliband, *The State in Capitalist Society* (Weidenfeld and Nicolson, 1969).
36 Maynard, 'My advice to new Members of Parliament', Joan Maynard Papers, n.d., cited in O'Connor, *Maynard*, p. 154.
37 See Miliband, State in Capitalist Society; and Miliband, *Parliamentary Socialism*, second edition (Merlin Press, 1973).
38 Maynard, 'My advice', cited in O'Connor, *Maynard*, p. 154.
39 O'Connor, *Maynard*, p. 168.
40 Ibid., p. 169.
41 Ibid., p. 174.
42 Chris Mullin, former MP, Maynard's Memorial Meeting, 1998.
43 Maynard, cited in O'Connor, *Maynard*, p. 184.
44 Corbyn, cited in ibid., p. 191.
45 Maynard, February 1984, cited in ibid., p. 193.
46 Sister Sarah Clarke, *No Faith in the System* (Cork: Mercier Press, 1995).
47 Ibid., p. 36, cited in O'Connor, *Maynard*, p. 197.
48 Cited in ibid., p. 200.

49 Elsie died on 25 February 1990, and Rowie on 6 May 1993.
50 Maynard, cited in O'Connor, *Maynard*, p. 295.
51 Ibid., p. 292.
52 Ibid., p. 257.
53 Ibid., p. 286.
54 Page, cited in ibid., p. 286.
55 Corbyn, cited in ibid., p. 287.
56 Wise, cited in ibid., p. 288.
57 E.P. Thompson, *The Making of the English Working Class* (Gollancz, 1963).
58 Roger Fieldhouse, in conversation with the author, October 2017.
59 Tom Dalyell, MP, obituary of Joan Maynard, *Independent*, 29 March 1998.
60 Mullin, Memorial Meeting, 1998.
61 Mullin, *Guardian*, 24 September 2011.

10

Stuart Hall

Stuart Hall, uniquely amongst those considered in this book, was arguably not a twentieth-century 'English radical' at all; his inclusion here could thus be seen as questionable. He was born in Jamaica and spent his childhood and adolescence in Kingston. His memories and experience of these formative years 'guarantee that I shall be Jamaican all my life, no matter where I am living'.[1] When he came to study in Oxford in 1951, he 'never had any aspiration to be English, nor have I ever become English ... it felt as if the British were a quite different, and foreign, race'.[2] Nor, despite his living in England for the rest of his life (he died in 2014), and marrying an English woman, Catherine Barrett, in 1964, did this perspective change. Decades later, he observed that: 'Indeed I feel less English now than when I first arrived'.[3]

However, there are several powerful reasons for his being seen as a key figure in the development of English radicalism in the later twentieth century. First, his self-identity was essentially 'diasporic'; he occupied a 'third space', neither Jamaican nor English. His intellectual and political energies, and considerable abilities, were devoted in part to analysing both the 'colonial experience' and culture, and the ways in which both anti-colonial, anti-racist politics and analysis, and wider socialist praxis could be articulated in Britain. He also lived at a time when Britain's Empire was rapidly disintegrating and when, correspondingly, Britain was becoming a far more multicultural society. 'You could say I have lived, metaphorically speaking, on the hinge between the colonial and post-colonial worlds ... I have belonged, in different ways, to both at different times of my life, without ever being fully of either.'[4] The complex problematic of the 'end of Empire', anti-colonialism, multiculturalism and their relationship to a New Left socialist politics has been of critical importance in late twentieth-century English radicalism. Secondly, Hall played a pivotal role in the development of the post-1956 New Left. Although he had profound differences with E.P. Thompson (discussed below), for Hall, as for Thompson, '1956' was a defining year: 'I was formed as one of the last colonials, and politically I was a child of 1956: of Suez and Hungary, of the collapse of the Communist dream, of the Cold War and of post-war decolonization, and thus of an earlier [i.e. than 1968] and very different kind of "New Left."'[5]

Thirdly, and a part of his New Left involvements, Hall played an important, though controversial, policy-making role in the Campaign for Nuclear Disarmament (CND). Fourthly, the emphasis upon the *cultural* dimensions of the socialist project was central to the post-1956 New Left. Hall, as well as British intellectuals of an earlier generation (Thompson, Raymond Williams and Richard Hoggart), was an innovative and influential cultural studies theorist, and was more attuned than his older colleagues to the new theorists of postmodernism and post-colonialism.

Finally, Hall's contentious analyses of the cultural and political phenomenon of 'Thatcherism' and how the Left, in this context, had to redefine itself, had intellectual and political resonance.

The analysis which follows looks in turn at each of these facets of Hall's contributions to English radicalism.

The complexities of Hall's diasporic identity: Jamaica and Oxford

Hall's background in Jamaica was relatively privileged. His family was from the Jamaican middle class, clearly not a part of the upper echelons but with a strong sense of their social standing. His father was an accountant with the United Fruit Company; and his mother, who had been in effect adopted by her uncle, a prosperous and prominent lawyer, whose forebears had been involved in the slave trade, was a dominant presence in the Hall household. Like many Jamaicans of her class and time, she was almost obsessively Anglo-centric, with a romanticised vision of England and English society and culture.

Hall, like his mother, was (dark) 'brown' rather than 'black', an important social indicator in the middle-class Jamaica of the time. (There existed, as Hall recalled, 'what Freud calls "the narcissism of minor differences"'.) His was a comfortable, loving home: yet his family 'wasn't my world. I fundamentally didn't belong to it'; his adolescence was 'a process of disenchantment and disaffiliation ... I felt like a sort of internal exile'.[6]

Hall's intellectual and social – and emotional – development was conditioned by the cultural and political dominance in Jamaica of England as the imperial power. (Although Hall acknowledged the complexities involved in the distinctions between 'Englishness' and 'Britishness', he was clear that it was very predominantly England and English culture that was the prevailing force in Jamaican life and in his own formation.) The curriculum at his elite school, Jamaica College, was Anglo-centric in the extreme. In the arts, there was a focus upon *English* literature; and in the study of history, a parallel emphasis upon an English, 'Whig interpretation of history', approach. The cultural 'message' was thus clear: the steady progress of (European) civilisation from the Enlightenment onwards had reached its pinnacle in the artistic and philosophical achievements in Western (by implication, largely English) society in the nineteenth and twentieth centuries.

He thus came to Oxford in 1951 both well-versed in the intellectual antecedents and the cultural determinants of England and Englishness, *and* very conscious of his essential *difference*, as a 'coloured' colonial. He was, from the outset, deeply anti-colonial and critical of the assumptions of the 'liberal' school of England's world role. 'Whenever the British began to imagine themselves as lovers of liberty they also conceived of themselves, at one and the same time, as the imperial lords of humankind'.[7]

Hall at this time had read some Marx but was not in any full sense a Marxist. Marx and orthodox Marxism failed to address, in his view, both the theoretical issues of race and ethnicity, and the practical, political phenomenon of racism and cultural prejudice in Western societies. (At this stage, Hall, like most activists on the Left, had little appreciation of 'gender issues'.) If Hall's attitude to Marx and Marxism was ambivalent, his antipathy to Oxford, or at least its predominating culture, was unconditional. 'The Oxford of the 1950s was dominated by "Hooray Henries" ... attempting to relive *Brideshead Revisited* ... Its atmosphere was relentlessly masculine and ... sexist.' It was characterised by the 'upper middle-class English male commanding attention to confidently expressed banalities as a sort of seigneurial right'. Hall found the 'ethos of Oxford Labour politics' equally distasteful. It 'was unremittingly white and English, in its deepest sensibilities. The Labour Party group ... I found peculiarly off-putting. I couldn't stand its combination of Puritanism, Fabian self-righteousness and a studied yet simultaneously unconscious commitment to the protocols of Oxford's England.'[8]

Such perceptions reinforced his opposition to colonialism and the values 'it harboured in its bloodstream: servitude, poverty, patriarchalism, class inequality and racialized difference ... but also cultural colonization, all the petty humiliations of daily life'. Even more importantly, it generated the 'silences, unconscious evasions and disavowals, the self-deceiving double-talk of colonial discourse itself, which so often masks its hidden presences with absences, gaps and silences, making them simultaneously both knowable *and* unspeakable for those living them'.[9]

His antipathy to Oxford was exacerbated by its conservatism in relation to his subject specialism, English literature. Oxford's snobbish and reactionary rejection of F.R. Leavis and the new thinking around the journal *Scrutiny* was, for Hall, 'the start of a lifelong intellectual disengagement from Oxford and all that it stood for'.[10] However, although Hall found little to engage him in his college, Merton, or the wider University, a little later he did find his milieu in a group of other 'outsiders' (students from the West Indies, the USA, Canada, Australia and elsewhere). In this group, he engaged in reading and discussing Caribbean and other 'colonial' novels and poetry, in playing jazz and in frequent visits to the avant-garde cinema.

The dramatic political events of 1956– the disastrous and bungled Anglo-French/Israeli Suez escapade; and the Soviet repression of the Hungarian uprising – solidified and gave expression to Hall's already embryonic New Left stance. 'These events signalled that the dream of Soviet Communism was dead; but so too was the illusion that Western imperialism was either finished or that it was benign.'[11]

Hall and the New Left

The debacle of Suez deepened and strengthened Hall's opposition to British imperialism. It 'underlined the enormity of the error in believing that lowering the Union Jack in a few ex-colonies necessarily signalled the "end of imperialism" or that the real gains of the welfare state and the widening of material affluence meant the end of inequality and exploitation'.[12]

Similarly, the crushing of the Hungarian uprising destroyed, for many, the last vestiges of belief in the Soviet Union, and more generally the Marxist-Leninist model of revolution, as representing a truly socialist vision. Unlike Thompson, Saville and other Marxists of the older generation, Hall and his Oxford radical colleagues had never had any illusions about the Soviet Union. Thus Hall was 'strongly critical of everything I knew about Stalinism ... and could not fathom the reluctance of the few Communists I met to acknowledge the truth of what was by then common knowledge about its disastrous consequences for Soviet society and Eastern Europe'.[13]

The year 1956 thus had led Hall to advocate a position of 'positive neutralism', aimed at bringing together 'Third World' leaders such as Nehru, Nkrumah and Sukarno. In retrospect, such a politics appears overly optimistic, if not naive. As Hall reflected several decades later, all this 'came to grief on the rocks of the remorseless politics of international polarization, on the nuclear arms race, as well as the conflicts within the decolonization movements themselves ... We didn't foresee at all how the global imperatives of the Cold War would overwhelm the liberatory promise of decolonization.'[14]

If, politically, a new, 'Third Way', positive neutralism lay at the heart of the New Left, in terms of its policy stance, it was the primacy given to the place of *culture* in radical politics that was the distinctive emphasis in Hall's and the *Universities and Left Review's* (*ULR's*) New Left underpinning political theory. The key question for Hall was ' "What did culture – so long relegated to a subordinate sphere of interest – have to do with"' processes of historical change, the phenomenon of the Cold War and indeed the broad issue of the transition from a capitalist to a socialist society?[15]

Hall always accepted, in general terms, the orthodox Marxist 'materialist conception of history' and the centrality of class conflict within capitalist societies. However, he was highly sceptical, at the very least, about Marxist intellectual 'traditionalism'; and the tenor of his prose, and his wide-ranging intellectual and political preoccupations, indicate perhaps that such avocations of 'the true socialist faith' were little more than paying lip service to the fundamentals.

This may be somewhat speculative. But what is clear is that Hall was vehement in his belief in the (post-1956) New Left formation: 'I've stayed consistently identified with this political moment ... It is who I am politically', as he reflected several decades later.[16] Similarly, he stated that: 'I was never an economic reductionist. Never. I was never an orthodox Marxist. I was always a heterodox Marxist'.[17]

Most of the Oxford founders of *ULR* had no background in and little affinity with the English labour movement, its traditions, preoccupations and priorities. The contrasts with the *New Reasoner* New Left were thus marked. (On the latter, see E.P. Thompson, Chapter 7.) Hall, and most of the other leading figures in the *ULR* New Left, were social scientists, broadly defined. This contrasted with the ex-Communist Party (CP) *New Reasoners*, most of whom were historians and well-versed in English radical history, most notably Thompson and John Saville. Unlike the *New Reasoners*, who had retained their CP antipathy, as much emotional as political, to the USA, the *ULR* group were 'attracted by the vitality of American popular life, indeed to the domain of mass culture itself'.[18]

In 1958, Hall wrote a radically revisionist article in *ULR*, detailing what he perceived to be this changed social and political environment.[19] He argued that the steadily increasing (relative) prosperity of most people, including the working class, in the 1950s, accompanied by high levels of employment, had enabled new spending habits. Newly acquired domestic interests – 'home-making', 'interior decoration' and leisure pursuits generally – were accompanied by increasingly suburban and 'new town' living environments. There was an accompanying growth in the sales of domestic consumer 'white goods'. Equally important, he argued, 'the nature of work itself, the rhythm and skills involved, have changed out of all recognition'.[20]

The dominance of a consumerist culture, where most people, including workers in traditional working-class occupations, saw themselves as 'consumers' rather than 'producers', buttressed bourgeois, individualist cultural conceptions. The traditional labour movement and working-class *alternative* culture – a society based upon a communal and co-operative ethic – was under severe pressure. (Hoggart's definitive study of working-class community, *The Uses of Literacy*, published in 1957, had made this argument forcefully, albeit in a different, and non-Marxist, tone.)[21] Such trends in society were exacerbated, Hall argued, by the large numbers of people now employed in the lower levels of management and administration. Often, the social and working environment led to those in this position developing an at least partial identification with the firm itself; they were thus 'drawn into the whole ideology of big corporation businesses'.[22] Moreover, commodities 'have accumulated a *social value* ... They have become insignias of class and status ... Capitalism is now a system based upon consumption.'[23]

This was producing an atomised, individualistic society, where old patterns of working-class collectivism, and community solidarities were dissolving. This did not herald, he emphasised, the end of class inequalities and class conflict: capitalism remained by definition an inegalitarian, unjust and rapacious system. But it did change fundamentally the nature of the class structure of society: and socialists had to understand, confront and learn how to oppose this new social reality.[24] The result of these changes, Hall argued, had been a pervasive alienation. Unless and until the capitalist system and its accompanying culture could be overthrown, advance towards a socialist system would not be possible.

Such revisionist arguments[25] challenged the dominant perspectives of English radicalism in the late twentieth century and had implications for both its political analysis and its strategic position. Class structures and class relationships *have* changed; moreover, the increasing fragmentation and complexity of society, the diversity and fluidity of occupational employment structures, and of ethnicity, have given rise to new forms of radical activism. Changing conceptions of gender, 'second wave' feminism, the importance of environmental issues, and the changes in the perceptions and actuality of women's roles in society, have added a further dimension to late twentieth-century English radicalism (Chapter 2).

Hall had little patience with the 'hard Left', whose advocates regarded such revisionist thinking with hostility, and saw it as a distraction from 'the real struggle'. For Hall, socialist politics had to engage with the 'world as it is', not as 'theory' says it should be. Hall was here, as elsewhere, a proponent of praxis and always saw this as the keynote of meaningful, effective political action. His engagement with a variety of social movements, ranging from CND to the feminist movement, bears testament to this.

Thompson's criticism, however, Hall took more seriously. For Thompson, Hall's approach lacked a proper 'sense of history' and tended to 'view working people as the *subjects* of history … as *victims* of alienation … [there was] a tendency to assert the absolute autonomy of cultural phenomena without reference to the context of class power: and a shame-faced evasion of that impolite historical concept – the class struggle'.[26] This was a familiar polemical argument of Thompson's deployed against 'non-historians'.[27] In response, Hall argued that Thompson had, to an extent, missed the point of his argument: it was concerned, as reflected in the very title of his article, with 'not the fact, but the *sense*, of classlessness'.[28] It was '"an admittedly impressionistic excursion into the field of working class *psychology*"'.[29]

The restraint evident in Hall's response to Thompson's polemical, somewhat aggressive, critique reflected both his respect for the older man *and* his sense of remaining still something of an outsider to the British Left. Personally, Thompson was, Hall recalled many decades later, both friendly and considerate. 'I sometimes think of their [Edward and Dorothy Thompson's] house in Halifax. How they held everything together was a mystery … Catherine and I used to go and visit Edward and Dorothy at their cottage in Wales. They were very kind to us, even though I found them a formidable couple.'[30]

However, in Hall's view, although Thompson was 'committed to the cause of colonial liberation ... I didn't feel that he had a sense of what colonialism was and how it operated. He was very English in his imagination, in the fibre of his being. He didn't connect with my preoccupation about racial identity,'[31] Moreover, Hall did not feel confident enough to engage in scholarly debate with the Thompsons about British history. In some ways, he remained in awe of both Edward and Dorothy. He certainly regarded Thompson as a brilliant academic.[32] But, as he recalled, '[o]urs was always a tense relationship, in spite of our closeness, and it became more tense as time went on'.[33]

Their relationship was certainly strained when Hall became editor of *New Left Review* (*NLR*) in 1960, the new journal resulting from the coming together of *ULR* and the *NR*.[34] Hall was, he recalled, a 'neophyte' among the experienced and formidable radicals of the older generation, notably Thompson and Raymond Williams. 'Editorial boards were a nightmare for me. I'd indicate the possible contents of the next issue and then hold up my hands before the storm broke, and the fathers spoke!'[35] Hall nevertheless genuinely regarded Thompson and Williams as 'my fathers'.[36]

John Saville, who became chair of the editorial board in June 1960, was Hall's 'salvation ... He protected me from the wrath that began to emanate from Halifax.'[37] As the New Left began to decline in 1961, the movement held an acrimonious 'Way Forward' conference in July. By the end of 1961, it had become clear to Hall, and to most of the members of the original board, that the journal, in its present form, was no longer viable and, in 1962, Hall resigned as editor.[38]

By 1963, the *NLR*, under the editorship of Perry Anderson, embarked on a new course, as 'an internationally renowned organ of Marxist scholarship, but it never constructed – or attempted to construct – a political or social movement of the kind sought by the early New Left'.[39] It was, as Hall generously recalled, '[n]ot at all the aspiration of the previous New Left, but a great project nonetheless'.[40] Moreover, Hall admired Anderson's intellectual prowess, though they were markedly different in temperament, interests and objectives. For Hall, Anderson was an intellectual of the highest order. 'If you have the kind of Eton education that he did, you just know things that ordinary human beings don't know. He is very, very clever.'[41]

By 1964, therefore, this 'key, frenetic phase' in Hall's life had come to a close.[42] However, Hall's activist role in a movement to which he contributed a great deal – CND – should be noted before moving on to other aspects of his wide-ranging contributions to English radicalism.

Hall and CND[43]

CND was central to Hall's politics, as indeed it was to Thompson's (Chapter 7). His involvement also had a very direct personal impact upon Hall's life: it was on the 1962 Aldermaston March that he met his future wife, Catherine Barrett.

Hall, like all those centrally involved in the first New Left, was wholly committed to CND's central, unifying demand for Britain to rid itself, unilaterally, of nuclear weapons as a catalyst to achieve more general nuclear disarmament. But Hall, ever the political pragmatist and undaunted by adopting controversial, revisionist perspectives, also saw his role as that of a strategic political educator. Perceptively, he saw the essential dichotomy in the movement: between the elite leadership group – essentially the CND Executive Committee,[44] '"people who knew how to lobby, how to influence people in the Labour Party and/or Government"'[45] – and the mass movement, which focused on large-scale street protests, notably the annual Aldermaston March, to build public pressure for changes in policy.

There was thus a sharp division between the elite, pressure-group conception of the campaign leaders – figuratively, the 'Front of the March', as Hall put it – and the mass movement, the 'Back of the March'. The former saw the issue of the bomb, critically important as it was, as a single issue, a mistaken policy in what was otherwise a reasonably well-organised and acceptable society. In sharp contrast, the mass movement, 'enormously varied though its ideology was, saw the bomb as the final, absurd, and obscene product of a society which was based on irrational if not insane assumptions'.[46]

Hall was a supporter of the latter perspective. For him, the key concomitant of the unilateralist demand was British withdrawal from NATO and the adoption of a positive neutralist foreign policy. In his CND pamphlet, 'NATO and the Alliances', Hall argued that Britain must build on unilateralism to '*use that renunciation as a political lever ... The point would be that Britain, disencumbered of both Bomb and Alliances,* would then be free to act as a rallying point outside both nuclear alliances – the Warsaw Pact and NATO' to encourage others 'to join an offensive for disengagement and disarmament'.[47] This controversial policy stance became CND policy in 1960.

Hall also supported the initiative to put forward independent nuclear disarmament candidates at both by-elections and general elections, as did Thompson. But the opposition from the predominantly 'Labourist' CND leadership was too strong for this to make much progress.[48]

However, it was in late 1962, with the CND policy statement, 'Steps Towards Peace', that Hall made his most significant, and controversial, contribution to CND. As always, Hall was determined to be politically realistic, no matter how revisionist the policy was taken to be. The movement, following the Cuban Missile crisis and its successful resolution, was in a difficult position. Averting what had seemed to be a real possibility of full-scale nuclear war produced both enormous relief *and* the realisation that whatever Britain or other middle-ranking powers might do would make little difference.

Hall also realised, unlike many in the movement, not only that CND had lost the argument in the Labour Party in 1961 but that this position was highly unlikely to be reversed. It was thus necessary, however unpalatable, to reconstruct CND policy in order to 'keep the issue alive, on the front bench as well as the back bench'.[49] The new proposals restated the unilateralist commitment, and the accompanying demands for the removal of US bases and the cessation of nuclear weapons tests; and, in the original draft (by Hall), there were added only three further demands: the withdrawal of nuclear weapons from all territories outside the USA and the USSR, a test ban treaty and a new, higher priority for the UN. As Peggy Duff argued, the damaging impact of the final version of 'Steps Towards Peace' resulted from the insistence of the Executive Committee and CND Council that 'almost all the policy of CND with only one exception, withdrawal from NATO' should be included. 'It was this that did the damage, for "Steps Towards Peace" came to be seen in the campaign as a deep-laid plot to drop the issue of NATO.'[50]

The reaction in the movement was that 'Steps Towards Peace' signified a retreat from the 'purity' and radicalism of CND's policy stance and muddied the waters, giving the impression of CND returning to conventional politics with its complexities and compromises. It was a 'profound psychological blow' to the movement.[51]

In retrospect, Hall (and indeed Canon Collins, the CND Chairman) acknowledged that the 'Steps Towards Peace' initiative had been a mistake: '"in terms of the psychology of the movement the 'Steps Towards Peace' proposals were a very bad mistake – *very* bad ... in terms of the mass movement it was a very bad judgment ... it was not defensible"'.[52]

Hall's role in CND was therefore significant. But in retrospect his position can be seen, as he acknowledged, as ultimately ill-judged. Nevertheless, his determination to confront the 'world as it is', to engage in dispassionate, committed strategic thinking, however 'counter-cultural' in movement terms, commanded respect at the time: and, with hindsight, can be seen as, at the very least, 'a good fault'. Moreover, it has to be noted that, in 1960–62, he was not only young (28 to 30), and still something of an outsider to the complex world of English radicalism, but he was also extremely busy with his New Left activities, to say nothing of his full-time teaching job. His achievements and commitment in this period were remarkable.

Hall and cultural studies

Arguably, the most important intellectual contribution made by Hall to late twentieth-century English radicalism was his pioneering role in the foundation and development of cultural studies as an academic field. Hall readily acknowledged the influence and importance of his precursors in the older generation of English radicals: Thompson, of course, and Hoggart too; but in particular, Raymond Williams. He was unstinting in his admiration of Williams, both as an intellectual and as a man: he was 'a wonderful thinker ... The more excited Raymond became, the quieter he grew ... Temperamentally they [Williams and Thompson] were opposites ... I found Raymond incredibly approachable ... much closer to my own formation than Edward ever had been.' (Hall recalled that, some time after the early

New Left days, 'Thompson made it clear that he hated Cultural Studies',[53] despite arguably being one of its formative influences if not founders.) Nevertheless, and acknowledging this intellectual debt, Hall claimed that 'it's not wrong to suggest that cultural studies began here [in the *ULR*]'.[54]

In 1964, Hall's career and life took a new and decisive direction. He and his wife, Catherine, moved to Birmingham, and Hall took up a post at the University to work with Richard Hoggart in the newly established Centre for Contemporary Cultural Studies (CCCS) and he remained there, becoming Director in 1972, until he moved, as Professor of Sociology to the Open University in 1979. Throughout his time at Birmingham, and subsequently at the OU, where he remained until his retirement in 1998, cultural studies was the focus of his academic concerns.

Since the early days of the New Left, the domain of culture had always been at the forefront of Hall's intellectual identity and at the heart too of his analytical framework. However, it was not until his move to Birmingham that cultural studies became formally, so to speak, his academic home. As Brian Meeks has written, Hall's methodology 'might be described as an approach that never abandons a materialist reading of history, yet always seeks to explain material forces as operating through social and cultural categories, which possess their own dynamic and establish their own inner mechanics of operation'.[55]

Hall's range of concerns in the field was wide-ranging: youth culture; the significance of popular culture and modern media in the current social consciousness; issues of racial and ethnic identity, and racist and anti-racist politics; gender and sexuality as well as class; and the complexities of Marxist, and post-structuralist and postmodern, theorisations of cultural studies.[56] Hall's eclecticism and his consistent determination to examine, in the cultural and radical political context, whatever at any given time constituted the current preoccupations of the serious media and the 'thinking public' could be, and was, easily caricatured. Terry Eagleton, for example, in a 1996 article in the *London Review of Books*, entitled 'The Hippest', described Hall as '"the Left's finest instance of the strategic intellectual, the theorist as mediator and interventionist, broker and communicator, bringing the more arcane flights of Frankfurtian or Post-Structuralist theory to bear on questions of voting patterns and televisual imagery, racism and youth culture. Nimble, mercurial, and timelessly up-to-date, he has nipped from one burningly topical issue to another, turning up wherever the action is, like a cross between a father figure and Mr. Fixit."'[57]

Although there was some truth in this, in reality Hall's approach was consistent with his earlier political radicalism. He was intent upon analysing the world 'as it is' (or at least as he perceived it to be), from a radical political perspective. How could and should the Left respond to the new challenges and complexities of late capitalism? Hall played a key role in broadening the analysis, and in exploring which 'agency' (or agencies) were best equipped to achieve radical change. The reorientation towards social movements, identity politics and the *fluidity* of English radical politics in the late twentieth and early twenty-first centuries owed much to Hall's interventions – in both academic and political contexts.

Hall drew on diverse radical theories. Indeed, it could be argued that this 'theoretical mix' bordered at times on incoherence. In varying contexts, Hall's theoretical analysis was influenced *inter alia* by Althusser, Derrida, Foucault and postmodernism in general; post-colonial theorists such as Fanon; 'second wave' feminism; and Gramsci – all in addition, again *inter alia*, to radical theorists of an earlier generation, not only Williams but Lukács, Benjamin and, of course, Marx. The complexity of Hall's theoretical position is not the focus for this chapter: here, rather, the concentration is upon the relationship between Hall's interventions and the development of English radicalism in the late twentieth century.[58]

Hall came to place an even greater emphasis than in his earlier New Left days upon *culture* as a determining factor in radical political analysis. Thus, in 1987, Hall observed that ' "while not wanting to expand the territorial claims of the discursive infinitely, how things are represented and the "machineries" and regimes of representation in a culture do play a *constitutive*, and not merely a reflexive, after-the-event, role. This gives questions of culture and ideology, and the scenarios of representation – subjectivity, identity, politics – a formative, not merely an expressive, place in the constitution of social and political life." '[59] Thus, 'cultural politics … should be seen as central to social transformation'.[60] Hall was critical of the Left, including sections of the New Left of both the 1956 and 1968 generations, as ' "still waiting for the old identities to return to the stage. It [the orthodox Left] does not recognise that it is in a different political game" '.[61] And, he reiterated, emphasising the point, that radicals should ' "remember that questions of culture are not superstructural to the problems of economic and political change; they are constitutive of them!" '[62]

Although he had by this stage rejected, at least implicitly, the 'Marxist positioning of class as central and as able to constitute a "master-narrative" ',[63] he continued to maintain that his position was founded in Marx's *Capital*, and indeed declared that: ' "I remain Marxist" '.[64] This eclecticism is not so much an indication of ideological confusion as of Hall's predisposition to use various theorists to facilitate his analysis of *particular* problems in *particular* circumstances in order to move forward to an informed position of political activism. In the end, in theoretical terms, he was, as he reflected, ' "closer to being wholly a Gramscian than anything else, but this is because … we have re-invented Gramsci … a Gramsci that is in touch with Marx's questions but gives culture more seriousness" '. As Hall himself acknowledged, his theoretical eclecticism had been a source of criticism in some quarters and praise in others; however, he disagreed: ' "I don't think it's either; I think [it's] just how I am – *I never have been wholly anything*" ' (my italics).[65]

Hall's perspective on both the origins and the subsequent nature of cultural studies has certainly been challenged. Tom Steele argues that cultural studies did not spring 'fully-armed from the side of a university department of English … the project of cultural studies more properly belongs to the experimentation, interdisciplinarity and political commitment of adult education immediately before and after the Second World War'.[66] It was in the interaction between university adult education tutors – such as Thompson, Hoggart and Williams – and their local, adult communities that cultural studies emerged, organically. The abstracted academicism of Hall and other New Left theorists led, it was argued, to a 'dogmatic insistence on separating contemporary cultural studies from the political economy of culture'.[67]

In his work on Raymond Williams,[68] Jim McGuigan emphasises that Williams shared this perspective. In March 1986, Williams 'insisted that cultural studies emerged from classes on literature, history and current affairs with mature students … originally located in adult education, developed through the old polytechnics and colleges of education'. Williams saw Hall's approach as '"a very academicized kind of literary or intellectual history"'.[69] He regarded this perspective as confining cultural studies to a '"bureaucratized"' formation, and '"the home of specialist intellectuals"', who were reviving '"the simpler kinds (including Marxist kinds) of structuralism … The whole project was then radically diverted by these new kinds of idealist theory."'[70]

Such criticisms shaded over into a sharper critique of Hall's (and Hobsbawm's) revisionist political arguments concerning the nature of the Left in the era of Thatcherism. However, before considering this aspect of Hall's contribution to English radicalism, some discussion of his interventions on the cultural analysis of race, racism and the colonial experience, is essential. This had particular resonance in England in the second half of the twentieth century, given the 'end of Empire' and the influx of large numbers of Afro-Caribbean and Asian immigrants. With his Jamaican background, and his personal, emotional understanding of the conflicted identity of such immigrants, he was able to make a unique contribution in this area.[71] (However, this focus was intertwined with issues of gender and feminist perspectives which he saw as being of central importance. He also acknowledged that he and the large majority of the early New Left activists had been characterised by 'a profound unconsciousness' over issues of gender.)[72]

Hall was insistent that there was not an 'essentialist racism', rather many, often interconnected racisms. The culture of slavery had emasculated both men and women and subjected them not only to economic hardship and total subservience but to a systematic destruction of their self-respect. However, when slavery was eventually abolished, 'the idealized, gendered norm … sanctioned the virtue of patriarchal authority within the family'. The 'respectable, nonconformist supporters [of abolition] took it to represent the *restoration* of the properly virtuous gender roles which the plantation, during its long history, had degraded. A common conviction rested on the assumption that enslavement had debased womanhood.' The paradox, after abolition and emancipation, was that, with men working away from the home, Jamaican society became '"matrifocal"'. Yet, when the man *was* at home, he 'exercised authority, received the lion's share of food and enforced sexual discipline'.[73]

This was, Hall argued, 'a degraded inheritance' from colonialism in Jamaica (and elsewhere in the West Indies), which transferred itself to the West Indian community in Britain, and became more marked, negatively, in the tense social environment of the 1940s and 1950s. Afro-Caribbean men frequently showed 'casual aggression and violence' towards both women and male homosexuals; 'and the more calculated exercise of male power through the means of rape'. Related to this, the 'dangers perceived in relations between black men and white women go to the heart of race in Britain in the 1940s and 1950s. The erotic element proved the combustible factor in the racial imaginary ... Racial and sexual fears conjoined, each feeding off the other.'[74]

Race had played, Hall argued, 'a historically determining role in the self-definition of Britain as a nation'.[75] 'There was, in the one register, the endless invocation of the civilizing mission and of the duty to advance the empire at a moderate, gentlemanly pace towards its own transcendent abolition. And in a separate register the colonial masters repeated their conviction that it was their duty to administer their unbridled authority wherever they deemed it necessary. Seemingly opposites, over time each voice combined with and came to exist inside the other.'[76] Thus, in complex ways, the racist hostility found in Britain amongst a significant section of the indigenous white population towards Afro-Caribbean men had its roots in the experience of colonialism and slavery in Jamaica and elsewhere in the West Indies.

For Hall, race always appears '"in a formation, with other categories and divisions" of class, gender and ethnicity';[77] he thus saw cultural conceptions of race, in their socio-historical context, as being of determining significance. 'Identity needs to be thought of "as contradictory, as composed of more than one discourse, as composed always across the silences of the other" rather than as "a sealed or closed totality".'[78] His analysis of racism is not that of 'a single phenomenon marching unchanged through time, but [of] different racisms that arise in specific historical circumstances, and their effectiveness, their ways of operation'.[79]

Hall's contribution in this area to English radicalism thus had several dimensions. First, he placed the cultural at the centre of his explanatory framework and emphasised the ways in which *cultural* analysis was essential in a variety of contexts, but not least in the formulation of a radical politics relevant for the late twentieth century. Secondly, his conceptualisation of race and racism in the context of British (principally English) colonialism and its specific historical evolution in Jamaica and the wider West Indies illuminated the situation of both the ethnic minority communities in Britain and the attitudes and ideological approaches of the indigenous, white population of the UK to the influx of black and brown immigrants from the late 1940s onwards. Third, he insisted that the centrality given by 'traditional' socialists to the old, rigid (and seemingly unchanging) categories of social class was no longer applicable. His theorisation of the contemporary, complex social structures played a major role in the reorientation of the Left to new and complex realities, and forced the Left to confront uncomfortable political choices. Whilst retaining an adherence to Marxism (especially in its Gramscian variant), he insisted that the complexity of multiple identities must be taken into account in strategies of resistance to capitalism.

Hall and the conceptualisation of Thatcherism

Of equal importance in the development of English radicalism in the late twentieth century was Hall's analysis of 'Thatcherism' and his – again revisionist (and controversial) – argument about the appropriate response of the Left. Much of this debate centred on the pieces he, and others, in particular Eric Hobsbawm, wrote in the journal *Marxism Today*.[80]

Thatcherism, Hall argued, represented 'the decisive break with the postwar consensus, the profound reshaping of social life'.[81] Thatcherism was, for Hall, 'an attempt to achieve hegemony for a distinct set of ideas, and [was] a response to an organic crisis of the social-democratic consensus of post-war Britain'.[82] It was a confident, assertive and profoundly *ideological* response to the interlocking crises of the British economy and the British state, which had been developing since the 1970s. The manifest failures of the Wilson and Callaghan governments to deal with the economic and social tensions of the late 1970s, culminating in the so-called 'Winter of Discontent' in 1978–79, were combined with a series of 'moral panics', exacerbated by the right-wing tabloid press, to produce a real sense of crisis.

Thatcherism's response was to forge a new authoritarian populism, which brought together 'the liberal discourses of the "free market" and economic man and the organic conservative themes of tradition, family and nation, respectability, patriarchalism and order'. This was set in a context of a perceived crisis of identity, in racial, gender and sexual, as well as changing class, terms, 'precipitated by the unresolved psychic trauma of the "end of empire"'. Hall argued that this perspective was combined culturally in Thatcherism with a form of '"regressive modernization" – the attempt to "educate" and discipline the society into a particularly regressive version of modernity by, paradoxically, dragging it backwards through an equally regressive version of the past'.[83]

Thatcherism managed 'to articulate a new form of common sense'.[84] The populist achievement was to articulate 'a set of beliefs which had considerable popular resonance, appealing to ... a mentality of independence, holding on to one's assets and feeling hostile to paternalistic state power and opposing it by a sense of ... "standing on one's own two feet"'.[85] Substantial sections of the traditional working class, and of the growing lower middle class, were convinced by this ideological combination, buttressed by a series of popular measures, such as the sale of public 'council housing', a low-tax regime and a 'crack down' on the trade unions (culminating in the miners' strike in 1984–85). In addition, Thatcher herself made great nationalist capital from the Falklands War, cementing her image as a forceful, determined leader and rekindling the quasi-dormant imperial yearnings of the more conservative elements in British society (to be found not only in supporters of the Conservative Party but also in large sections of the working class).

Thatcherism also appealed to corporate capital and her governments gave consistent priority to the interests of business (especially finance capital), and reinforced this ideologically by adopting a crude utilitarianism and vocationalism in education, at both school and further and higher education levels. In true populist mode, Thatcherism attacked some of Britain's traditional institutions, especially those with a liberal, progressive ethos, such as the universities and the BBC, 'substituting a brash market-oriented modernity'.[86]

In Hall's view, Thatcher's 'hegemonic project', whose elements included among other thngs the privatisation programme and the assault on local democracy, especially the Greater London Council, was crucially dependent upon its *cultural* dimensions: 'its construction of the respectable, patriarchal, entrepreneurial subject with "his" orthodox tastes, inclinations, preferences, opinions and prejudices ...; its rooting of itself inside a particularly narrow, ethnocentric and exclusivist conception of "national identity"; and its constant attempts to expel symbolically one sector of society after another from the imaginary community of the nation'.[87]

Hall, as noted earlier, adopted a Gramscian framework for the analysis of Thatcherism. In addition to the prominence given to the cultural dimensions of the hegemonic project, Hall employed Gramsci's concept of the 'war of position' (in contrast to the 'war of manoeuvre').[88] In his view, the Labour Party, the labour movement and the wider socialist community had failed to engage with the new social and political realities.

Thatcherism succeeded in capturing the 'high ground' of British political culture by, in Andrew Gamble's words, formulating a politics and a society characterised by ' "the free market and the strong state" '.[89] The forces of the Left were still engaged with the 'all-or-nothing, class-against-class scenarios of the "war of manoeuvre" ' which continued to dominate the 'the political imagination of the left'.[90] While Thatcher and her allies saw the need for a radically new political reorientation, 'the Left in Britain was blind to the need to establish a counter-hegemonic ideology'.[91] However, in Hall's view, it was '[p]aradoxically, the "party" of history and change [that] seems paralysed by the movement of history and terrified of change'.[92]

Hall saw insoluble contradictions for the parliamentarist Labour Party, or any other social democratic party organisation. There were a whole series of difficult, if not impossible, 'squaring of circles' to be accomplished; but, centrally, it was the longstanding problem of a social democratic party, once in government, having to find 'solutions to the crisis which are capable of winning support from key sections of capital, since its solutions are framed within the limits of capitalist survival. But this requires that the indissoluble link between party and class serves both to advance and to discipline the class and the organizations it represents

... at key moments of struggle ... [Labour is] by definition "on the side of the nation" *against* "sectional interests", "irresponsible trade-union power", etc., i.e. against the class.'[93]

The result was that Labour, by the time of the zenith of Thatcherism in the 1980s, could 'be represented as undividedly part of the power bloc, enmeshed in the state apparatus, riddled with bureaucracy, in short, as "with" the state; and Mrs. Thatcher, grasping the torch of freedom ... who is ... out there, "with the people"'.[94] It was thus that Thatcherism came to be seen as radical; and the Labour Party, conversely, as the old, outdated defender of the *status quo*.

This revisionist perspective was strongly contested by others on the Left. In McGuigan's view, Hall, and *Marxism Today* and its 'New Times' thesis, were 'an accommodation to defeat, [a] sad recollection of past hopes and pessimism concerning future possibility'.[95] In addition, because of Hall's exclusive concentration upon the role of culture in the social process, he virtually ignored the crucial role of political economy; and, linked to this, his analysis implicitly 'isolated national politics from overwhelming international developments in terms of political economy'. In the final analysis, for McGuigan, Hall's 'position in the adjacent fields of cultural research and politics represented little more than a multicultural version of social democracy'.[96]

Ralph Miliband was equally scathing in his 1985 article 'The New Revisionism in Britain'.[97] He argued that the revisionists' arguments 'constituted a retreat from socialist positions',[98] and rejected Hall's argument that 'class' was no longer a primary determinant in the political process. For a variety of reasons, including its reliance on the sale of its labour power and its low-income status, the new social class formations 'remained as much the "working class" as its predecessors'. Moreover, 'no other group was remotely capable of mounting an effective and formidable challenge to the existing structures of power and privilege'. Gender and ethnic identity had not superseded class as determinants of disadvantage: on the contrary, they *complemented* it. Miliband also disputed Hall's revisionism in relation to the state. The power of the dominant class and its allies, Miliband argued, 'could only be overcome by an effective state'.[99]

There is force in such criticisms. Despite later disavowals, Hall's revisionism came close to facilitating, intellectually, the rise of New Labour. And such arguments contributed to the virtual collapse of the socialist Left during the 'Blair years'.

Conclusion

Stuart Hall made striking and important contributions to English radicalism. He combined a subtle, deeply personal, analysis of race and racism, and the 'problematic' of the way forward for the British radical Left. As has been noted, he always thought of the early New Left as expressing most accurately his political position and he embraced the humanistic socialism of that movement and combined it with his increasing concentration upon the centrality of cultural analysis to the socialist project.

He was very different in style and ideological substance from the older generation of the New Left. In contrast to the rather 'tweedy' personas of Thompson, Miliband et al., Hall was not only of a different ethnicity and generation but was, in Eagleton's words, '"a Marxian version of Dorian Gray, a preternaturally youthful character whose personal style evokes a range of faded American epithets: hip, neat, cool, right-on"'.[100] More importantly, Hall played a key role in developing a more fluid, responsive ethos on the English radical Left, which has had to adjust to a rapidly changing political environment: the restructuring of social class; the collapse of Soviet communism and the general decline of the 'established' Left across Europe; and the rise of social movements, identity politics and multiculturalism. Hall took full account of the importance of the colonial experience both on the ethnic minorities in Britain *and* on the indigenous white population and its culture. Distinctively, Hall analysed these social phenomena through the powerful lens of his own Jamaican heritage and socialisation.

Although Hall was a prolific writer, and was at ease with academic, theoretical discourse, he was at heart an advocate of praxis, of bringing cultural and political analysis to bear upon political activism. Moreover, as he observed, a 'lot of people always find me talking easier to get hold of than me writing. I have an easier relationship with talking, lecturing and so on!'[101] More than that, Hall 'always thought of [himself] as an educator'. It was no accident that he completed his career at the Open University: he was, amongst many other professional and personal attributes, an adult educator. 'I get the greatest pleasure out of those moments when from a different place and with a different experience you can open a door ... you can give them the handle of a concept with which they can go back to their own experiences and cut into different links.'[102] (In this commitment to adult education he shared common ground with some of the prominent New Leftists of the older generation: Thompson, Williams and Hoggart amongst them.)

His commitment to praxis was linked to his persistently revisionist approach both to theory and to radical political objectives and how to achieve them. Despite his engagement with abstract radical political theory, he was essentially, as noted, a pragmatist; and he was repeatedly courageous in confronting established political positions and the often intimidating and 'senior' individuals who were attached psychologically as well as politically to them. For example, his disagreements with Thompson and others in the early New Left; his advocacy of controversial policy stances in CND; his attacks on traditionalist Labour Left positions; and his critique of Thatcherism. This is not to claim that he was, by any means, always correct: he acknowledged in hindsight that his perspectives had sometimes been mistaken (for example, over his 'Steps Towards Peace' initiative in CND). But his revisionist, pragmatic approach contributed significantly to the development of English radicalism in the later years of the twentieth century and the first decade of the twenty-first.

However, his emphases upon 'identity politics', and his espousal of essentially destructive and negative revisionism in relation to the position of the Left in the Thatcherite era, contributed to the Left's problems in the 1990s and early 2000s. Politically, his most important contributions were twofold: to emphasise the *complexity* of class structure in modern Britain, and the centrality of gender, ethnicity and the importance of the 'colonial experience' for both ethnic-minority communities and the wider society; and, secondly, to acknowledge the critical importance of social movements in the development of English radicalism.

It was in part his continuing status and self-perception as a quasi-outsider to British society, despite his living in England from 1951 until his death in 2014, that enabled him to be a distinctive, positive and empathetic critic of contemporary English society. His own position exemplified his argument that 'identity' was no longer, if it ever had been, a uniform, single entity. Like so many others in the globalised modern world, Hall had a range of identities. The title of his memoir/autobiography indicated one key aspect of this multiple identity. He was, indeed, a *Familiar Stranger*, in both England and Jamaica; and he lived, and his theoretical and political positions were formed, on the basis of a *Life Between Two Islands*.[103]

Hall's contributions to English radicalism have been universally acknowledged; and he remained one of the outstanding and original intellectuals and activists on the Left over several decades, and was a tireless and effective proponent of what might be termed 'a revisionist praxis'.

Notes

1 S. Hall (with B. Schwarz), *Familiar Stranger: A Life Between Two Islands* (Milton Keynes: Allen Lane, 2017), p. 10.
2 Ibid., p. 14.
3 Ibid., p. 210.
4 Ibid., p. 11.
5 Ibid., p. 45.
6 Hall, in ibid., pp. 97, 57.
7 Ibid., p. 180.
8 S. Hall, 'The "First" New Left: Life and Times', in Oxford University Socialist Discussion Group (eds), *Out of Apathy: Voices of the New Left 30 Years On* (Verso, 1989), p. 19. And see Hall, *Familiar Stranger*, p. 253.
9 Hall, *Familiar Stranger*, pp. 21–2.
10 Ibid., p. 223. His postgraduate study of Henry James, an unlikely choice, was justified by Hall because of James's status as a 'cultural comparativist', looking intelligently at England as an outsider. Hall retained a lifelong interest in and respect for James.
11 Ibid., p. 243.
12 Hall, 'The "First" New Left', p. 12.
13 Ibid., p. 16.
14 Hall, *Familiar Stranger*, p. 232.

15 Ibid., p. 243.
16 Ibid.
17 Michael Rustin, '"Working from the Symptom": Stuart Hall's Political Writing', in B. Meeks (ed.), *Culture, Politics, Race and Diaspora: The Thought of Stuart Hall* (Kingston and London: Ian Randle Publishers and Lawrence and Wishart, 2007), p. 121, citing Hall, 'Politics, Contingency, Strategy', *Small Axe* 1, 1996.
18 Hall, *Familiar Stranger*, p. 245.
19 S. Hall, 'A Sense of Classlessness', *Universities and Left Review* (*ULR*) 5, Autumn 1958, pp. 26–32.
20 Ibid., p. 26.
21 R. Hoggart, *The Uses of Literacy* (Chatto and Windus, 1957; pb. Pelican, 1958).
22 Hall, 'A Sense of Classlessness', p. 27.
23 Ibid., p. 29.
24 Hall's perspective thus differed sharply from the Labour revisionists of the 1950s, notably Anthony Crosland, whose classic study *The Future of Socialism*, 1956, provided the intellectual foundation for Gaitskell and the Labour Right.
25 'Revisionism', a term used by Hall himself to describe his positions on various contentious issues, is used here in a neutral, not a pejorative, sense.
26 E.P. Thompson, 'Commitment in Politics', *ULR* 6, Spring 1959, p. 51. Samuel, too, was critical of Hall's approach. See R. Samuel, 'Class and Class Consciousness', *ULR* 6, Spring 1959, pp. 44–50.
27 The most celebrated, and still pertinent, exchange on analogous themes is P. Anderson, 'Origins of the Present Crisis', *New Left Review* (*NLR*) 23, reprinted in P. Anderson and R. Blackburn (eds), *Towards Socialism* (Fontana and New Left Books, 1965); 'Socialism and Pseudo-Empiricism', *NLR* 1:35, January–February, 1966; and E.P. Thompson, 'The Peculiarities of the English', in R. Miliband and J. Saville (eds), *The Socialist Register 1965* (Merlin Press, 1965), reprinted in Thompson, *The Poverty of Theory and Other Essays* (Merlin Press, 1978).
28 D. Scott, *Stuart Hall's Voice: Intimations of an Ethics of Receptive Generosity* (Durham, NC: Duke University Press, 2017), p. 72.
29 S. Hall, 'The Big Swipe', *ULR* 7, Autumn 1959, p. 50, cited in ibid., p. 73.
30 Hall, *Familiar Stranger*, pp. 263–4.
31 Ibid.
32 In Hall's view, Thompson was 'a brilliant social historian. *The Making of the English Working Class* is a wonderful, wonderful book'. Ibid.
33 Ibid.
34 Hall was reluctant to take on the role of editor and did so only because Thompson refused, and nobody else volunteered.
35 Hall, *Familiar Stranger*, p. 264.
36 Ibid., p. 265.
37 Ibid., p. 264.
38 Following Hall's resignation, a short-lived editorial triumvirate assumed responsibility (Perry Anderson, Denis Butt and Samuel). The latter two resigned in March 1962, following heavy criticism from the board, and in the light of increasing debts. Thompson persuaded Anderson to continue as editor. *NLR* began a new, very different, but, in

its own terms, successful life. It has continued as a respected theoretical journal of the intellectual international Left.
39 M. Newman, 'Thompson and the Early New Left', in R. Fieldhouse and R. Taylor (eds), *E.P. Thompson and English Radicalism* (Manchester: Manchester University Press, 2013), p. 60.
40 Hall, *Familiar Stranger*, p. 266.
41 Ibid.
42 Ibid.
43 For details of the British anti-nuclear peace movement of the late 1950s and early 1960s, see R. Taylor, *Against the Bomb: The British Peace Movement 1958–1965* (Oxford: Clarendon Press, 1988). On Hall's involvement in CND, see especially pp. 45–6, 54–6, 328–9, 334–5.
44 The CND Executive Committee was chaired by Canon Collins and its members were almost all Labour Party members or supporters. Most, too, were prominent members of the English, upper-middle-class metropolitan 'liberal establishment'. They included Jacquetta Hawkes, A.J.P. Taylor, Michael Foot and James Cameron. For details of the CND leadership, see Taylor, *Against the Bomb*, pp. 22ff.
45 Hall, in conversation with the author, April 1978, in ibid., p. 45.
46 Taylor, *Against the Bomb*, p. 47.
47 Hall, 'NATO and the Alliances', CND pamphlet, Spring 1960, cited in ibid., p. 55.
48 The organisation formed to put this policy into practice – INDEC, the Independent Nuclear Disarmament Election Committee – had a short and largely unsuccessful existence. For details, see Taylor, *Against the Bomb*, pp. 84–6. Hall became a member of the INDEC board.
49 Hall, in conversation, *Against the Bomb*, p. 92
50 P. Duff, *Left, Left, Left* (Allison and Busby, 1971), p. 204, cited in Taylor, *Against the Bomb*, p. 93 (footnote).
51 Taylor, *Against the Bomb*, p. 94.
52 Hall, in conversation, in ibid., p. 95 (footnote).
53 Hall, *Familiar Stranger*, p. 265.
54 Ibid., p. 241.
55 Meeks, 'Introduction: The Return of the Native Son', in Meeks (ed.), *Culture, Politics, Race and Diaspora*, p. xiv.
56 Hall published widely, largely in academic journals and left-wing political publications. Bibliographies are given in Hall, *Familiar Stranger*, and in Meeks, *Culture, Politics, Race and Diaspora*.
57 T. Eagleton, 'The Hippest', *London Review of Books* 18, No. 5, 1996, reprinted as 'Stuart Hall' in Eagleton, *Figures of Dissent* (Verso, 2003), pp. 207–15, cited in Scott, *Stuart Hall's Voice*, p. 25.
58 On Hall's cultural theory, see C.W. Mills, 'Hall's Changing Representations of Race', in Meeks, *Culture, Politics, Race and Diaspora*, pp. 120–48; L. Grossney, 'Stuart Hall on Race and Racism: Cultural Studies and the Practice of Contextualism', in Meeks, *Culture, Politics, Race and Diaspora*, pp. 98–119; D. Morley and Kuan-Hseng Chen (eds), *Stuart Hall: Critical Dialogues* (New York, 1996); and C. Rojek, *Stuart Hall* (Cambridge: Polity Press, 2003).

59 Hall, 'New Ethnicities', in Morley and Chen, *Stuart Hall*, p. 443, cited in Mills, 'Changing Representations of Race', p. 131.
60 Mills, 'Changing Representations of Race', p. 131.
61 S. Hall, 'Old and New Identities, Old and New Ethnicities', in L. Black and J. Solomos (eds), *Theories of Race and Racism* (London and New York: Routledge, 2000), cited in Mills, *Changing Representations of Race*, p. 133.
62 S. Hall, 'Subjects in History: Making Diasporic Identities' in W. Lubiano (ed.), *The House that Race Built: Black Americans, US Terrain* (New York: Pantheon Books, 1997), cited in Meeks, *Culture, Politics, Race and Diaspora*, p. 135.
63 Meeks, *Culture, Politics, Race and Diaspora*, p. 133.
64 Hall, 'Old and New Identities', p. 68, cited in ibid., p. 134.
65 Hall, 'Politics, Contingency, Strategy', pp. 151–2, cited in Mills, 'Changing Representations of Race', pp. 137, 141.
66 T. Steele, *The Emergence of Cultural Studies 1945–65: Cultural Politics, Adult Education and the 'English Question'* (Lawrence and Wishart, 1997), p. 9.
67 Ibid., p. 206, referencing the argument made by J. McGuigan, *Cultural Populism* (Routledge, 1992).
68 J. McGuigan, draft manuscript for a forthcoming biography of Raymond Williams. I am grateful to Jim McGuigan for permission to quote from this draft.
69 Ibid., chapter 9, citing Williams, *The Politics of Modernism: Against the New Conformists* (Verso, 1989). p. 155.
70 Williams, *The Politics of Modernism*, p. 157.
71 McGuigan's view, according to Tom Steele, is that Hall's particular focus upon issues of race and identity, was 'a fairly late comer in his political trajectory, at the same time that he was standing back from issues of social class'. Letter from Tom Steele to the author, 2 March 2019.
72 Hall, 'The "First" New Left', p. 38. However, he noted that Thompson was more sensitive than most to gender issues, probably due, he thought, to Dorothy's influence.
73 Hall, *Familiar Stranger*, p. 87.
74 Ibid., pp. 88, 181.
75 As he noted, Peter Fryer had demonstrated that, contrary to popular belief, 'brown' and 'black' immigration to Britain had long been a significant element in urban social environments, especially London. P. Fryer, *Staying Power: The History of Black People in Britain* (originally published in 1984; new edition, Pluto Press, 2018), p. 180 (*Familiar Stranger*).
76 Hall, *Familiar Stranger*, p. 180.
77 Mills, 'Changing Representations of Race', p. 130, citing Hall, 'New Ethnicities', 1987, pp. 442–4.
78 Ibid., pp. 132–3, citing Hall, 'Old and New Identities', p. 49.
79 S. Hall, 'Epilogue: Through the Prism of an Intellectual Life', in Meeks, *Culture, Politics, Race and Diaspora*, p. 281.
80 On Eric Hobsbawm, see his autobiography, *Interesting Times: A Twentieth-Century Life* (Allen and Unwin, 2002; pb. Abacus, 2002). Hall's book *The Hard Road to Renewal* (Verso, in association with *Marxism Today*, 1988) was composed largely of pieces from *Marxism Today*.

81 Hall, *Hard Road to Renewal*, p. 2.
82 J. Schwarzmantel, *Gramsci's Prison Notebooks* (The Routledge Guides to the Great Books) (Abingdon: Routledge, 2015), p. 286.
83 Hall, *Hard Road to Renewal*, p. 2.
84 Schwarzmantel, *Gramsci's Prison Notebooks*, p. 286.
85 Ibid., p. 287.
86 Ibid.
87 Hall, *Hard Road to Renewal*, p. 8.
88 Gramsci defined the 'war of manoeuvre' 'as a 'frontal attack on the state'. Historically, this had been, variously, the mass strike, 'permanent revolution', or other forms of insurrectionary strategy. He saw this perspective as 'not relevant to the situation of advanced or complex modern democracies, and hence doomed to defeat'. In contrast, the 'war of position' was defined as a 'protracted struggle in and through the institutions of civil society, perhaps as preparation for a final direct assault'. However, as Schwarzmantel observes, it 'is not entirely clear what a war of position would involve, as a practical political strategy'. Schwarzmantel, *Gramsci's Prison Notebooks*, pp. 205–8.
89 A. Gamble, *The Free Economy and the Strong State: The Politics of Thatcherism* (Basingstoke: Macmillan, 1994), cited in ibid., p. 287.
90 Hall, *Hard Road to Renewal*, p. 7.
91 Ibid., p. 9, cited in Schwarzmantel, *Gramsci's Prison Notebooks*, p. 288.
92 Hall, *Hard Road to Renewal*, p. 11.
93 Ibid., p. 46.
94 Ibid., p. 52.
95 McGuigan, draft manuscript.
96 Ibid.
97 R. Miliband, 'The New Revisionism in Britain', *New Left Review* 150, March–April 1985.
98 Newman, *Miliband*, p. 281.
99 Ibid., pp. 282–4.
100 Eagleton, 'The Hippest', cited in Scott, *Stuart Hall's Voice*, p. 24.
101 b. hooks and s. hall, *Uncut Funk: A Contemplative Dialogue* (London and New York: Routledge, 2018), p. 48.
102 Ibid., p. 104.
103 Hall reflected towards the end of his life that he 'couldn't physically return [to Jamaica] because it would not be a return … it is so different from what I think of as where I began'. Ibid., p. 126. In the end, and indicative of the importance of his personal, family life, Hall indicated that 'home is where love is'. Ibid., p. 124.

11

Tony Benn

From the 1970s until his death in 2014, Tony Benn was by far the most prominent English radical. 'By the early twenty-first century few people could remember a time when Tony Benn was not playing a leading role in politics. Only the Queen had been longer in public life and was still active in 2011.'[1]

He had had a continuously high political profile ever since his election to Parliament in November 1950 at the age of 25; he was an MP for 47 years in all, retiring in 2001, famously stating that he was resigning from Parliament in order to spend more time on politics. Able parliamentarian though he was, it was his talents as a communicator and a populariser of socialist beliefs that brought him to public prominence. From early in his career, he was a regular and popular contributor to political programmes on radio and television; and, against the spirit of the times, he was regularly able to command large audiences at public meetings and political demonstrations.

Peter Jenkins, the *Guardian* political commentator (and no friend of Benn's), wrote in a review in 1981 that there were three phases in Benn's political career: first, the 'young Benn, with his prefect's chin, boy-scout keenness and pipe-smoking *gravitas*, [who] would have done for the hero of an Ealing comedy'. Then there was 'middle Benn, the new computer-speak, managerial whizz-kid politician of the Technological Sixties ... At around that time he told me at a party about how he had opened a file on the giant hogweed which, according to the newspapers, was advancing on the West End from Kew Gardens. That was Benn the mad boffin ... Late Benn dates from 1968, when ... he was "into" revolutionary sociology and radical theology.'[2]

Caricature though it was, there is some truth in this description. Benn's political perspectives *did* change markedly through his long years at the heart of Labour politics, as did his, often obsessive, enthusiasms. Broadly speaking, Benn, like his father, became progressively more left-wing as he got older. (He 'immatured with age', in Harold Wilson's memorable phrase.)

However, his commitment to radical political change, centred on the extension of democratic structures and processes, and upon attaining greater justice and fairness, and thus social equality, never faltered. He saw democracy and socialism as essentially coterminous. His socialism was founded on *moral* precepts, rather than theoretical analysis; and this morality was based upon his English Christian Dissenting Nonconformism. Although he and his wife Caroline, who was from a broadly similar American Christian background, both eventually rejected the theological aspects of Christianity, Benn adhered absolutely and to the end of his life to the moral imperatives of his Dissenting Christian background.

In his long ministerial career, Benn had some practical achievements (but arguably more failures). But his considerable legacy lies not so much in legislative and constitutional advances but rather in his lasting influence upon the political and social perspectives of large numbers of people. His mother instilled in him in childhood the distinction 'between the kings of Israel who exercised power and the prophets of Israel who preached righteousness, and I was brought up to believe in the prophets rather than the kings'.[3] In one of his rare lectures on Marx and Marxism – for a lifelong, leading socialist he was remarkably little acquainted with the writings of Marx or later Marxists – he argued that Marx is often seen, and by implication *should* be seen, ' "as the last of the Old Testament prophets" '.[4] Whatever the truth of this observation, Benn himself can be seen as a late twentieth-century exemplar of this approach.

His Englishness was as central to his personality and beliefs as was his socialist radicalism: and they were inextricably connected. The long history of the Benn family, and also of his mother's family, in radical politics, their Dissenting religious beliefs and their upper-middle-class Victorian values and lifestyle – 'austerity lightened by my father's sense of fun'[5] – were central to Benn's politics.

It is thus with a discussion of Benn's family and its influence upon his politics that this analysis begins.

Family and early life

Benn, born in April 1925, was the second son of William Wedgwood Benn (later Lord Stansgate) and Margaret Benn (née Holmes). Both Benn's grandfathers had been MPs and had supported radical causes. Benn's father was elected as a radical Liberal MP in 1906, and was, at 28, the youngest member of the House. From the outset, William Benn espoused radical causes: amongst them, Home Rule for Ireland, the creation of the Jewish homeland, the legal protection of trade union funds and opposition to the Boer War. He always loathed war and was under no illusions about its horrors and the sufferings inflicted upon innocent people.[6]

After Lloyd George, whom William Benn believed to be unprincipled and not a true Liberal, became leader of the Liberal Party, Benn joined the Labour Party, was elected MP for North Aberdeen in 1928, and became Secretary of State for India in MacDonald's ill-fated 1929 government. After losing his seat in 1931, he returned to Parliament in 1937 as MP for Gorton, Manchester. He became a peer, at Churchill's request, in 1941.

Michael Benn, Tony's older brother, who had been intending to become a clergyman, was killed in the war and it thus fell to Tony Benn to inherit the title on his father's death in late 1960. He wished to renounce the peerage in order to continue his political life in the House of Commons, and the constitutional issues arising brought Benn into the political limelight (as discussed below).

Benn's father was one of the main influences on his political beliefs and career. As he recalled many years later, ' "I was, and still am, greatly influenced by my father's ideas and by his example. I am profoundly grateful to have started my life with, and learned my politics from, such a teacher, such a father and such a friend." '[7]

His mother was an almost equally important influence, especially in her religious beliefs (discussed below). From a Scottish, radical liberal and Nonconformist background, she was as a young woman rebellious and independent-minded. She was a lifelong feminist, supported the suffrage campaigns and was a campaigner for the ordination of women.

Benn's parents married in 1920, when William Benn was 43 and Margaret only 23. 'It was a genuinely happy childhood ... International affairs were given an urgency for the children, imbibing them with a sense of world community which would never leave them.' The family culture was centred on politics and religion, which were 'the constant subject of discussion'.[8] The rather Victorian, Gladstonian ethos of his childhood was carried through into Benn's own family. The 'Benn brand', as his biographer has it, embodied 'courtesy ... sobriety, tolerance of difference and commitment to public service'. All the Benns, whatever their political and other differences, have believed in and practised 'integrity and hard work'.[9]

Yet Benn's childhood, and in many respects his subsequent development, was also narrow and somewhat philistine. He recalled in old age that during his 'childhood and growing up, no attempt was made to develop the artistic, musical and literary side of life, and that became a serious disadvantage as I got older'. And, he recalled, 'I was never a great reader at school and cannot remember many books being read to me as a child'.[10] Similarly, he was, by his own admission, not an 'intellectual' and had read little history or political theory (and few of the world's great novelists, poets and dramatists). It was Walter Padley, the trade union leader, for example, who in the early 1960s 'introduced Tony Benn to the Levellers and Diggers ... with whom Benn's expensive education had not acquainted him'. His interest in these early English radicals 'was fired, though he was not to incorporate their rhetoric into his own until the 1970s'.[11] And it was not until Caroline, his wife, presented him at Christmas 1976 with a copy of *The Communist Manifesto* that he had read any of Marx and Engels's work.[12]

It was from this somewhat eccentric and rarefied family environment that Benn embarked upon his teenage years at Westminster School. The family lived at what is now Millbank, and Westminster was thus his '"local school … I walked there and back every day"'.[13] It was hardly surprising, therefore, that his mother recalled many years later that he '"has only ever wanted to be in Parliament. It was his only ambition. He used to go to the House of Commons when he was a little boy and sit in the Strangers' Gallery and watch the debates."'[14]

From Westminster he went up to New College, Oxford, to read PPE (Philosophy, Politics and Economics). He achieved a 'safe second' in 1948 – war service from 1943 having interrupted his studies[15] – but spent more time at the Oxford Union, researching and writing his speeches, than he did at his studies. Benn became President of the Union in 1947 and it was through the Union that he met Anthony Crosland and subsequently Roy Jenkins and Hugh Dalton. As a result of his Union presidency, he, Kenneth Harris and Edward Boyle were invited to undertake a speaking and debating tour of the USA. Harris recalled that, before they went, Benn's '"abilities were considerable … but [his speeches] were heavy, they could bore people. After America he was brilliant."'[16]

His trip to America had a far more profound impact than this upon his life, however. It was here that he met, and shortly after married, Caroline Middleton de Camp.[17] They were to remain very close and brought up a family of four children, Hilary Benn following the family tradition and becoming a prominent Labour MP and Cabinet Minister. At her death, on 22 November 2000, Benn wrote in his *Diary* that she had been his '"best friend and inspiration … the finest person I ever met in the whole of my life"'.[18]

After a brief spell working for the BBC as a producer on the North American Service, Benn was selected-against stiff opposition-for Stafford Cripps's seat, Bristol South-East. (Cripps had to retire in October 1950 because of deteriorating health.) 'To his amazement, Benn was selected'.[19] He was elected with a comfortable majority (though less than Cripps's) on 30 November 1950: his parliamentary career had begun.

Religion

Before moving on to discuss Benn's Westminster career, attention should be turned briefly to the critical importance of religion in Benn's overall ideological perspectives. Mention has already been made of his parents' strong Nonconformist religious convictions. For Benn, both religious and secular belief systems (communism, fascism) have entrenched *authority* at their heart. For Dissenters, such authority structures have to be challenged. *All* people have 'a direct line to the Almighty' and they do not 'require a bishop to mediate concerning what to believe and what to do'.[20] Benn saw an indissoluble connection between New Testament teaching and socialist politics. 'The idea of Heaven on Earth – or justice in practice – was an integral part of the dissenting tradition and of the trade union movement.'[21]

Initially, Benn was 'as devout as could be'.[22] However, over the years, his faith changed, almost imperceptibly. Partly because of his understanding of the advances in science, but predominantly because of 'the nature of the Church', Benn gradually adopted a more agnostic, humanist position. He thought the Church sought 'to use the teachings of the Bible to justify its power structures in order to build up its own authority'.[23]

Typically, therefore, even religious belief and its attempts to address the most fundamental questions about human life and the existence or otherwise of a deity, were reduced by Benn to essentially *political* questions of power relationships in the Church. Almost as an afterthought, it seems, he added that he found the notion of original sin to be 'deeply offensive', and the resurrection and proclaimed divinity of Jesus to be problematic, and in the end rationally untenable; nor did he retain a belief in the immortality of the soul. 'I see Jesus ... as one of the greatest teachers, along with Moses and Mohammed ... My doubts are about the risen Christ and not about the importance of Jesus. Christians claim to have founded a Church in Jesus's name, and my doubts are about this institution rather than about the teachings he left behind.' In the end, he came to believe, with Tom Paine, that: ' "My country is the world and my religion is to do good" ... I have evolved from being a devout boy, through doubt and distrust in religious structures, to acceptance of the lessons the great religious teachers have taught.'[24]

The moral teachings of the Bible remained the absolute foundation of his radical politics. Despite all the marked changes in his political outlook in his long career, this belief never wavered.

MP in the 1950s and 1960s

The focus here is upon Benn's contributions, in the first period of his parliamentary career, to the development of English radicalism. The details of his wide range of ministerial roles are not analysed in any depth.[25]

His maiden speech, in February 1951, set the tone for his future prominence. Defying convention, Benn spoke on a highly controversial subject, the desirability of having a nationalised iron and steel industry. He 'spoke with grace, wit and skill';[26] the compliments on his speech came not only from his Labour colleagues but from the Conservative opposition and the press. Even as a new MP, he had no hesitation in speaking his mind on a series of moral issues: however, his 'public morality never ceased to enrage his opponents but, more importantly for his own career, it also appalled his supporters'.[27]

Benn rapidly became a familiar presence on television but especially, in these early years, on BBC Radio. He was a regular panellist on the popular *Any Questions?*

programme, which had an audience of 16 million by 1953. The producer, Michael Bowen, recalled that ' "Tony Benn was such an *Any Questions?* person. He was our automatic choice as the Labour MP on the panel. He built himself up as the star Labour man." '[28]

At this stage of his career, he was not on the left of the Party. In the acrimonious debate on Gaitskell's 1951 budget, for example, in which it was proposed to impose charges on dental treatment and on the provision of spectacles, Benn abstained; nor did he oppose rearmament or support, in the later 1950s, the Campaign for Nuclear Disarmament (CND). More generally, he did not back the 'Bevanites' in the bitter divisions of the 1950s. As he later recalled, he 'stood in the middle ground ... "I didn't burn any bridges." '[29] When Attlee resigned from the leadership of the Party in 1955, Benn voted for Gaitskell.

Meanwhile, he was building a solid reputation in his Bristol constituency as well as in Parliament. A key aspect of Benn's personality and of his politics was his real affection for 'ordinary people'. He was a genuinely kind and considerate man, and in that sense his passionate commitment to democracy, to involving as many people as possible in community discussions and decision-making, was sincere, and fundamental to his politics. It was the personal surgery meetings, Benn told a politics seminar at the London School of Economics in February 1952, that was ' "the side I prefer" '. And his mother, admittedly not an objective commentator, recalled that he had ' "a pastoral soul. He enjoys his surgery work even more than he enjoys the parliamentary work." '[30]

His assiduity certainly yielded results in Bristol South-East in the 1951 general election, where he achieved one of the highest votes – 30,811 – that he ever received. However, nationally the Labour Party lost power, with the Conservatives gaining a majority of 17. Thus began 13 years of Tory rule, ended only by Harold Wilson's narrow election victory in 1964.

Building on his already considerable media profile and ability, Benn helped Gaitskell prepare for his first television broadcast. Dalton noted in his *Diary* that he had spent two days preparing a party political broadcast ' "with the help of Tony Benn (very useful, moves through life like a cat, attractive, has reserves and sense of humour, *but not quite to be trusted*)" ': a caveat that was to be echoed repeatedly throughout Benn's career (my italics).[31]

In this 1951 Parliament, Benn concentrated especially upon foreign, mainly colonial, affairs. This was, he recalled, partly because of his father's influence: ' "I had anti-imperialism in my bloodstream ... the old left-liberal position." '[32] A second issue of concern to Benn, and many others, was the realisation of the threat of a catastrophic nuclear war. Benn was one of the prime movers behind the formation of the H-Bomb National Committee (with Richard Acland, Fenner Brockway, Anthony Greenwood and Donald Soper). Unlike the others, however, Benn was not at this stage a unilateralist, and he abstained on the Defence White Paper in February 1955. Benn's concern was, characteristically, more with the *secrecy* and lack of parliamentary consultation over the development of the H-Bomb than with the issue *per se*.

The year 1955 saw the Conservatives returned with a larger majority of 58 and Benn's vote, though he was comfortably re-elected, fell significantly, in part because of boundary changes. When the Suez crisis erupted in 1956, Benn supported Nasser's seizure of the Canal and was highly critical of the government's rash and, as it proved, disastrous decision to invade Egypt, with the French. When Gaitskell finally decided to move a motion of censure on the government and to launch a national campaign, Benn was again called in to help prepare Gaitskell's television broadcast. Gaitskell signed his script and gave it to Benn, inscribing it: ' "A thousand thanks" '. Later, he wrote effusively: ' "If it was effective this was largely due to you, both for the general plan you suggested and for much of the drafting." ' However, this contrasts with an entry in Gaitskell's *Diary*: ' "Tony Benn, although talented in many ways, a good speaker and a man of ideas, had extraordinarily poor judgment. He is the last person in the world I would go to for advice on policy." '[33]

Whilst Suez was an unmitigated political disaster, and brought down the Prime Minister, Anthony Eden, for Benn 'Suez had been all gain ... It brought together all his skills as a broadcaster, as a speaker, as a political organiser. He had emerged as a champion of morality ... He was factually accurate, he was dignified and he was gracious to his opponents.'[34] As a result, Gaitskell made him a junior minister in the Defence Department, though he resigned soon after over the nuclear weapons issue. Meanwhile, his television career developed and he was a regular presenter and participant in current affairs and political programmes.

After Labour lost the 1959 election badly – the Conservatives emerged with a 100-seat majority – Benn, again re-elected for Bristol South-East, was elected to the National Executive Committee (NEC) at the Party Conference later that year. As Michael Foot wrote in his highly critical appraisal of Benn: 'No one in Labour Party history – not even Herbert Morrison in his heyday – applied his mind and energies more assiduously to the work of the Executive.'[35] Another of Benn's attributes was his unlimited capacity not only for *hard* work but for what others would see as grindingly *dull*, detailed committee business. Parallel to this, Benn built an enormous archive, including his well-known political diaries, over his long career.[36]

His rising profile in the Party was confirmed when Gaitskell appointed him, at 34, as Shadow Transport Minister. Energetic and enthusiastic, Benn was full of bright ideas many of which were adopted by subsequent governments: the introduction of seat belts, harsher penalties for drunken drivers, the MOT road safety test for older cars and analysis of the causes of road accidents.

However, his confidence in Gaitskell was shattered by the latter's speech on the nuclear issue at the 1960 Conference.[37] It was not Gaitskell's stance on the nuclear issue *per se* which alienated Benn, but once again his determination that there must be full democracy in the Party. Gaitskell's insistence that the Party Leader, in conjunction with the PLP, and not the Party Conference, should determine Party policy, ran counter to Benn's democratic principles.

Following the untimely death of Bevan in 1960, Harold Wilson became *de facto* leader of the Labour Left. Benn voted for Wilson when he stood unsuccessfully against Gaitskell for the leadership in late 1960.[38]

On 16 November 1960, Lord Stansgate (William Benn) died, aged 83. Benn inherited the title and was thus automatically debarred from being an MP. Benn immediately began a long, ingenious and relentless campaign for a new Act of Parliament which would permit him, and other peers, to renounce their titles. Despite his ineligibility for the Commons, he persuaded his Constituency Labour Party to back him in the by-election: he secured a resounding victory on 18 April 1961. (His majority was over 13,000.) After numerous court battles, debates in Parliament and complex negotiations with leading politicians of both parties, the Act enabling peers to renounce their titles was passed by Parliament in July 1963. His campaign received prominent, and largely favourable, coverage in the press and on the broadcasting media. His public profile was considerably enhanced.

Edward St Clair, the Conservative who had replaced Benn as MP for Bristol South-East, resigned. At the subsequent by-election Benn was opposed only by Edward Martell, a right-wing maverick: Benn won by 20,313 votes to Martell's 4834.

Benn returned to the Commons as MP on 24 October 1963. When Labour assumed office in late 1964, Wilson appointed him Postmaster General. He had responsibility for a range of services: amongst them not only the Post Office network but the Post Office Savings Bank, all television and radio, and telephones. One-third of a million workers were employed. However, the service was inefficient and morale was low. Benn introduced some radical reforms. He raised the pay of postmen and postwomen; he increased the price of postage stamps and introduced the differential first- and second-class system; and he streamlined management structures. He made several mistakes[39] and not a few enemies amongst his senior political colleagues, notably George Brown; but by 1965–66 he had turned a deficit into a profit of £40 million.

It is notable, from the perspective of his impact upon radicalism in Britain in the 1950s and 1960s, that he took no part in the two most prominent extra-parliamentary mass movements of the period: CND and the associated peace movement organisations; and the movement of opposition to the Vietnam War. This is in sharp contrast to his high-profile activism from the 1970s onwards. On the other hand, he was consistent in his support of progressive civil liberties issues: he campaigned and voted for the abolition of capital punishment, for the legalisation of male homosexuality for consenting adults and for anti-racist causes.

Benn displayed in these years some of the personal characteristics which were both strengths and weaknesses. His energy, innovatory policy thinking and commitment were notable attributes. But he appeared, to many colleagues, increasingly to be a 'loner', obsessive and generally oblivious to others' interests and sensibilities.

There was about him, too, a stubbornness. Dick Crossman, at least initially a friend and colleague, noted in his *Diary* that ' "there is an odd harshness about him which makes him sometimes unattractive as a colleague ... although I doubt whether he is a believer, he has at times a kind of mechanical Non-conformist self-righteousness about him which seems to come out even more strongly in office" '.[40]

One of the paradoxes about Tony Benn, especially later in his career when he became almost idolised by many on the left of the Party and by many people in the wider community, was the persistent, and near-universal suspicion and hostility of his senior colleagues. (This issue is returned to in the Conclusion to this chapter.)

After Labour was returned with a majority of 96 at the 1966 election, with Benn securing a handsome victory in Bristol South-East, he remained for a few more months as Postmaster General. He had been a success, and Wilson regarded him as a ' "very good Postmaster General" '.[41] When Frank Cousins resigned from the government in July 1966, Wilson had no hesitation in appointing Benn as Minister of Technology.

This was, in many ways, the perfect role for him. Benn had a lifelong love of gadgets; he was a proficient user of new technology from its earliest years and he became a tireless advocate of its beneficial potential. (There was an irony, some decades later, in juxtaposing the supposedly 'trendy' and youthful Tony Blair, with his enthusiasm for, but low levels of skill in actually using, IT, with the now elderly and seemingly old-fashioned Tony Benn, who was nevertheless a highly competent user of the new IT systems.)

However, despite all the rhetoric and the 'grandstanding', Benn's term of office at 'Mintech', as he dubbed it, was a failure. 'With all the power, all the talent and all the money of Mintech, what did it achieve? Depressingly little.'[42] British manufacturing industry continued to decline; Concorde was an expensive failure; Benn's various initiatives – at Upper Clyde Shipbuilders, for example – all failed, some disastrously so. Moreover, he became increasingly unpopular with his colleagues. Benn described his erstwhile friend Crossman, in 1968, as ' "an incredibly inadequate man, like Hugh Dalton" ';[43] Crossman, in turn, in his *Diary* for 1976, although acknowledging that Benn was ' "brilliant at public relations and has enormous drive and ambition and even imagination" ', claimed that he ' "refuses to face the real difficulties because *he has a second rate intellect*" ' (my italics).[44] There is some truth in this rather brutal assessment. The political perspectives and policies of Wilson's Cabinet can be, and were, criticised. But there can be no doubt of the high intellectual calibre and intelligence of many of its members: Roy Jenkins, Anthony Crosland, Dick Crossman, Denis Healey and Wilson himself. In this company, Benn was intellectually, if not politically, a lightweight; and he emerged from this period both diffident *and* determined to pursue his political ambitions. From the late 1960s he turned his energy and enthusiasm towards the goal of securing the Party leadership. By the summer of 1971, Benn could record in his *Diary* that he had ' "decided I would like to be leader rather more consciously" '.[45]

His biographer accurately observed that what Benn, with his 'temperament, with his mixture of high ideals, showmanship and diffidence ... most wished to happen would be that his admiring colleagues would thrust the crown upon him'. This was always a vain hope. Thus, the 'path Benn now took was more common: he established the leadership in his sights, and looked to ways which would propel him towards it'.[46]

At the 1970 election, where Edward Heath gained an unexpected victory, with 330 seats to Labour's 287, Benn's majority was reduced to 5688 (only partly because of boundary changes). But the scene was now set for the next, and markedly different, phase of Benn's political career.

MP from 1970 to 2001

Benn began to embrace increasingly radical, left-wing positions. He advocated workers' control of industry, which he argued was an extension of his commitment to socialist democracy. He differentiated workers' control and industrial democracy from nationalisation. As he put it in his memoir: the 'programme of socialism is sometimes associated with nationalisation. Nothing could be further from the truth ... The idea of socialism is of common ownership and that things are best done by cooperation.'[47] He had, however, backed Barbara Castle's ill-fated 'In Place of Strife' proposals in 1969. This was partly out of loyalty to Castle, but also because, at that stage, he took the orthodox centrist view that 'unregulated strikes' were detrimental to the efficacy of British industry. Whatever the rights and wrongs of this position, it is another example of Benn's policy volatility.

When John Davies, the Conservative Industry Minister, announced the closure of UCS (Upper Clyde Shipbuilders) in the Commons on 29 July 1971, Benn described the decision as '"a major tragedy ... and it has been introduced by you without one single word of regret"'.[48] When the UCS workers occupied the shipyard, Benn marched in the crowd of seventy thousand in protest.

It was also at this stage that Benn became a high-profile critic of the European Economic Community (hereafter, Common Market). Benn's position on whether or not Britain should be a member of the Common Market changed markedly over his years in Parliament. Originally, in the early 1960s, he had opposed British membership because, he argued, it would exacerbate Cold War thinking, and would impede, if not prevent, Britain's ability to undertake socialist planning in economic policy as this would be decided largely in Brussels. The Common Market was, in effect, a 'rich man's club'. However, by 1967, he had become strongly in favour. Barbara Castle recorded in her *Diary*, in April 1967, that in a Cabinet discussion, Benn had made '"a passionate speech in favour of a technologically united Europe"'.[49] Benn confirmed, many years later, that this had been his view: '"at that time [he thought that] the only way you could deal with multinational companies was by multinational political structures"'.[50]

Benn has the dubious distinction of being the originator of the proposal for a referendum on British membership of the Common Market. When Heath, always an enthusiast for Europe, became Prime Minister in 1970, it was clear that British entry into the Market was his political priority. The Labour Party was divided on the issue. Although Benn still, at this stage, backed entry, he argued, on democratic principle, that only a referendum could ensure that the people had a proper decision-making role. Initially, he was the only member of the NEC to vote in favour of a referendum. However, by March 1971, the Shadow Cabinet had been persuaded to support the idea. (Wilson, and others, realised that the referendum proposal could prevent a serious split in the Labour ranks.)

By 1974, Benn had changed his mind – yet again. In part, this was because of his experience as a minister, when he had had direct experience of working with the 'Brussels bureaucracy', and he claimed that, as an elected politician, he was ' "a slave … in Brussels, and I loathed it when I saw what it was about" '.[51] This change of view, which was to be his permanent position on the Common Market/EU issue, resulted also from his general shift to the left, which meant he was mixing in politically more anti-Common Market circles, and from his belief in the importance of 'sovereignty'. On this latter issue, he had a somewhat different perspective from his fellow Labour left-winger Michael Foot. (The contrast between the two is discussed below.)

In July 1974, Benn finally declared publicly that he was opposed to Britain's entry into the Common Market. In a letter to his constituents, he argued that entry ' "would make the United Kingdom into one province of a Western European state'; and that the Common Market ' "degraded parliamentary democracy" '.[52]

Given the division of opinion in the Cabinet, and the wider Party, Wilson had no alternative but to allow Cabinet members to campaign for the 'No' side in the referendum, which was held on 5 June 1975, even though the government's policy was to remain in the Market. Benn was joined in his opposition by, amongst others, Michael Foot and Barbara Castle.

The 'No' campaign was an uneasy alliance between the minority Left of the Labour Party and the minority Right of the Conservative Party. As commentators subsequently observed, any cause which was backed by Benn, Enoch Powell and the Communist Party was, by definition, for many voters, a cause which must be opposed.[53] Benn was undoubtedly the major figure in the 'No' campaign, attracting large crowds at rallies and public meetings, and often receiving a standing ovation. By the end, he was exhausted and, as so often, exhilarated to the point of hysteria by his reception. It was all to no avail: the 'Yes' campaign triumphed with 17 million votes, as against the 'No' campaign's 8 million.

Benn continued, undaunted, to oppose the Common Market, and still more the subsequent European Union. Later in life his position had, if anything, hardened. The EU, he argued, 'is a carefully constructed medium for eliminating all democratic influences hitherto exercised by the electors in the member states; it presents this as a triumph of internationalism, when it is a reversal of democratic gains made in the previous hundred years'.[54]

The Common Market was by no means the only area of policy where Benn, in the 1970s, moved decisively to the left. After Labour's narrow election victory in February 1974, Wilson – who by now was exasperated by Benn and his 'loner' determination to strike attitudes publicly and not to accept Cabinet 'collective responsibility' – nevertheless appointed him as Secretary of State for Industry. Energetic as always, Benn set about establishing the National Enterprise Board (NEB), and gave government backing to a number of worker co-operatives. Reappointed to Industry following the October 1974 election, he introduced the Industry Bill, aiming to extend the nationalisation programme, protect vulnerable industries and, through public subsidy, rebuild them into profitable concerns. Not only did this relatively radical measure face severe opposition from political opponents, the press and the employers, even the trade unions were lukewarm. Jack Jones, leader of the TGWU, for example, '"felt he was with us but not of us ... He never seemed to be attuned to the trade union outlook."'[55]

The Bill was subjected to such heavy amendments in Committee that it emerged emasculated; these manoeuvrings were in all probability backed if not engineered by Wilson himself. Benn became increasingly isolated in the Cabinet where the levels of distrust and hostility rose: his persistent 'grandstanding' in pursuit of his leadership ambitions alienated almost all his senior colleagues. He was widely seen as inappropriately ambitious and careerist.

His fifteen months at Industry produced several innovative initiatives, but few if any successes. After the referendum on the Common Market in June 1975, Wilson, angered by Benn's persistent disloyalty and by his high profile in the 'No' campaign, demoted him to Secretary of State for Energy. Benn contemplated resigning but did not do so. In the end, Benn reasoned that being given a different Cabinet job was not a resigning issue.

When Wilson resigned, to general surprise, in March 1976, Benn stood in the leadership election. He was badly defeated. In the first ballot he received 37 votes, compared with 90 for Michael Foot, 84 for Jim Callaghan and 56 for Roy Jenkins. In the second ballot he voted for Foot. Undaunted as always, Benn threw himself into his new role, where he achieved far more than he had at Industry. The key issue was North Sea oil. With Benn as Minister, 25 per cent of North Sea oil was secured for public ownership within five years. Whilst British manufacturing industry continued its seemingly inexorable decline, North Sea oil was a large-scale and successful development, yielding significant financial benefits to the economy. Benn again proved himself to be an efficient and diligent administrator. The other major issue in his ministerial brief was nuclear power. Benn mastered the complexities of this new technology and was in a position to take informed decisions on policy development: but, overall, he was opposed to a further extension of nuclear power.

At the same time that he was immersing himself in this demanding ministerial brief, Benn, with his advisers, especially Francis Cripps, developed what became known as the Alternative Economic Strategy (AES). Rather than accepting the traditional capitalist remedies for Britain's serious economic problems, the AES recommended: selective import controls, the development of the NEB, and severe controls on the finance sector and its institutions. Whilst this was rejected, with some irritation, by Callaghan (it was '"quite unacceptable ... I don't see why you wrote it"'),[56] it attracted wide support amongst the rank and file of the labour movement.

Given its small majority, and with further losses through by-elections, the government's position became untenable. The 'Lib–Lab' pact came into existence in 1977 (though the Liberals withdrew support in early 1978). Benn opposed the pact; and he also supported the right of 'Militant' supporters to be members of the Labour Party. Although he certainly did not accept a Trotskyist analysis, he claimed that the Labour Party was 'a broad Church' and that, on democratic grounds, all shades of socialist opinion should be accommodated. It is not unduly cynical, however, to surmise that political calculation and the need to build his base of support in the Party were also important factors in his stance.

The government staggered from crisis to crisis, culminating in the so-called 'Winter of Discontent' in 1978–79, and the fall of the government became inevitable. On 28 March 1979, the government was defeated on a 'no confidence' motion (by 1 vote). In the ensuing general election in May 1979, the Conservatives won 339 seats to Labour's 269. (Benn's majority fell to 1890.) The long dominance of Margaret Thatcher began.

The two years or so following this serious electoral defeat saw the high point of Benn's challenge for the Labour leadership, and thus for a radical shift to the Left. Ostensibly, the initial battle in the Party centred on three structural issues: the mandatory reselection of MPs; the NEC having the final decision on the contents of the Party's manifesto; and the composition of an 'Electoral College' for choosing the Party leader. Benn, of course, was in favour of all three 'reforms', the first two of which were backed by Conference in 1979, whilst it was decided that the third was to be delegated to a Party Commission of Inquiry. (Eventually, with Benn's backing, the College was established with the trade unions having 40 per cent of the vote and the PLP and the Constituency Labour Parties 30 per cent each.)

The 1980 Labour Conference marked the pinnacle of Benn's command of the Party: his 'crowning achievement'.[57] Motions were carried calling for the removal of all nuclear bases, including the Americans', from Britain, and for withdrawal from the Common Market. Philip Whitehead wrote that: '"He seemed to be everywhere, addressing fringe meetings three at a time ... and mixing a potent brew of instant socialism from the platform"'.[58] Benn demanded a new Industry Act, to introduce common ownership, industrial democracy and controls on capital; and he called for the abolition of the House of Lords. He gave 'what he believed was the best speech of his life' in support of the NEC controlling the drafting of the Manifesto. His speeches here, and at fringe meetings, were 'rapturously welcomed' by the Conference: but he was 'execrated' by the PLP.[59]

Benn, who spoke on the eve of the Conference's closure, in favour of Irish unity, noted in his *Diary*: '"I think I have now reopened every issue that the establishment wants to keep closed – the Common Market, defence policy, economic policy and Northern Ireland."' With his usual optimism he added that: '"All these issues will mature and develop and in time they will come right"'.[60]

When Callaghan resigned as leader after the 1980 Conference, Benn had to decide whether to stand again for the leadership. He was now the undisputed leader of the Left: and he had facilitated, and on occasion led, a radical shift to the left in the wider Party (with a loyal, if small, number of supporters in the PLP, amongst whom, from 1983, was Jeremy Corbyn). However, the leadership election would be held under the 'old' rules, not through the Electoral College.[61] He thus decided not to stand: he would have been badly beaten. In the event, Foot (139 votes) narrowly defeated Healey (129 votes): Healey immediately accepted the Deputy Leadership.

Benn had delayed announcing his decision to stand for the *Deputy* Leadership until after the defectors to the SDP (Social Democratic Party)[62] had made their position public. He was urged, from all sides of the PLP, not to stand. In particular, Michael Foot, as Leader, pleaded with him not to do so. It would, Foot argued, further split the Party at a particularly vulnerable time. Relations between Foot and Benn in effect broke down from this point onwards (as is discussed below).

Healey did not especially want the job of Deputy Leader: he had, again with some justification, felt that he was the most able and experienced of Labour's senior figures and that he should have been elected Leader. He viewed the job as 'disagreeable and … in itself was not worth having. I felt, however, that it was essential to deny it to Tony Benn. If he had been Deputy Leader there would have been a haemorrhage of Labour defections to the SDP both in Parliament and in the country. I do not believe the Labour Party could have recovered.'[63]

Everyone was aware that this election was a proxy for the Leadership itself. For a variety of reasons, not least his age, Foot would not be Leader for long and, if Benn won the Deputy Leadership, he would be in prime position to become Leader in the near future. The result was desperately close: Healey won by 0.85 per cent. Joe Ashton, a colleague and friend of Benn's, but who abstained, tellingly remarked that, with Livingstone in London, Hatton (of 'Militant') in Liverpool, and Scargill in the National Union of Mineworkers, we '"were going down a road which was leading nowhere. And if Benn had become deputy leader it would have given a tremendous boost to the Owen mob [i.e. SDP]. That's what they wanted. That was the main reason I didn't vote for him. Without Healey there to give us a bit of stability and pull towards the middle we'd have finished in third place [i.e. in the general election]."'[64]

After his defeat, Benn became marginalised in the PLP: the Left was in retreat. The 1980s, however, saw a new wave of social movement activism: Benn was by now fully supportive of CND, the 'Greenham Women' and other similar progressive movements. His focus became increasingly *extra*-parliamentary.

When the Falklands crisis erupted, Benn, if not a lone voice, was certainly in the minority when he opposed Thatcher's invasion force and argued rather for the UN to take responsibility for resolving the dispute with Argentina. Although the Labour Conference in 1982 reaffirmed its commitment to unilateral nuclear disarmament and to the renationalisation of corporations privatised by the Conservatives, the Party generally moved to the centre, if not the Right. Benn was ousted from the Chair of the Home Policy Committee, his main 'power base' in the Party structure; he was also removed from nine key Party committees.

The harshest blow, however, was his defeat in Bristol. The Boundaries Commission abolished his Bristol South-East constituency. He could have secured a safe seat elsewhere but he was determined to stay and fight in the far less winnable Bristol East constituency. In the June 1983 general election, the Conservatives, riding on the wave of the Falklands 'victory', won a substantial majority, with 42 per cent of the vote. It was the worst Labour result since 1931. Benn performed very creditably in his new constituency – but he lost by 1790 votes. In the aftermath of the election, Foot resigned as Leader and Kinnock easily won the leadership election.

Benn was adopted as the Labour candidate for Chesterfield, following Eric Varley's resignation, and was elected MP in March 1984. Benn vigorously defended the miners in the bitter strike of 1984–85. He became so emotionally committed to the strikers' cause that, in the view of his biographer, his political judgement deserted him. His call for a general strike 'to protect free trade unionism' was politically unrealistic and unhelpful. He had always tended to romanticise the working class, and his excitability at this crucial period for the Left led to a (temporary) cooling with some of his major allies.

Benn had never believed Kinnock to be a man of the Left. In his view, the Party under Kinnock's leadership was offering not an alternative to capitalism but a promise to make it work a little more humanely. From this time onwards, Benn concentrated even more upon extra-parliamentary initiatives, in addition to carrying out assiduously his constituency duties. For example, he launched the Community Defence Campaign, using the tactics of the miners' strike to back other workers such as teachers, and print and hospital workers. He also established an International Committee to foster links with radicals in South Africa, El Salvador and elsewhere; and he instigated the 'Chesterfield Declaration', which set out an ambitious socialist programme, and which led to a Conference of socialist activists from the Labour Party and other socialist organisations in October 1987. (This became an annual event, and similar conferences and meetings were held in other Northern cities.)

In both the PLP and the Party at large, the British Left was in retreat. Benn lost badly when he stood again for the leadership in 1988; and, by 1989, only he and

Dennis Skinner remained as Left representatives on the NEC. As Benn's reputation and influence declined in the PLP, and to an extent in the wider Party, so his standing in the country increased. He called for civil disobedience against the poll tax; he opposed eloquently the Kuwait war in 1990–91; he undertook a widely publicised visit to talk with Saddam Hussein, and he opposed the West's sanctions and subsequent air strikes. He 'fulfilled his function as conscience of the nation. Few agreed with him one hundred per cent, but few felt there was no truth at all in what he was saying.'[65]

He was in some senses 'a man of the times'. Despite being in many ways an old-fashioned, almost Victorian, upholder of Nonconformist moral values, he was also a feminist, a steadfast opponent of war and latterly – convinced by his son, Hilary – a vegetarian. He was, moreover, as noted, an early advocate and practitioner of new technology and all its 'gadgets'.

Benn continued energetically, almost manically, to produce a string of somewhat grandiose and impractical – if arguably sensible – proposals. For example, he introduced in June 1981 his 'Commonwealth of Britain' Bill, which proposed, *inter alia*: the abolition of the monarchy; an elected president; an elected second chamber to replace the House of Lords; equal numbers of men and women MPs; votes at 16; the disestablishment of the Church of England; and the end of British jurisdiction in Northern Ireland.[66] His ideas were generally well-received, not least because they stood no chance of being adopted. Benn became, in the popular mind, a likeable British eccentric, harmless as long as he was nowhere near power.

The 1990s were a miserable decade for Benn. Politically, the rise of New Labour represented everything he disliked in the modern Labour Party (although he maintained close personal relationships with Tony, and particularly Cherie, Blair). Personally, the decade saw the death, not only of his mother, in 1991, but also of several good friends, including Joan Maynard, Jo Richardson, Ralph Miliband, Ian Mikardo and Eric Heffer. Worst of all, his wife, Caroline, was diagnosed with breast cancer in August 1995 and died in October 2000. Benn's own health was also a cause for concern: amongst other things, he had been diagnosed with leukaemia in 1989, and his condition slowly worsened.

His parliamentary career ended on 11 May 2001. A few years earlier, he recorded somewhat ruefully in his *Diary* that he ' "realised that the life I have led – just parliament, constituency, public meetings and the family – is a very narrow life" '.[67]

He continued to be active in public life, becoming a prominent opponent of the wars in Afghanistan and Iraq. In 2003, for example, he addressed 142 political meetings and made 385 broadcasts. He also began his well-attended public meetings, often in theatres, billed as 'An Evening with Tony Benn'. The attendances were remarkable: 1700 in Sheffield; 1800 in Bristol; over two nights in Edinburgh, 3600. He also produced a series of 'music and readings' with the folk singer Roy Bailey, in which Benn read quotations from the Peasants' Revolt and the English Civil War, and finishing with extracts from the Labour Party's 1945 Manifesto and the

'Greenham Women'. A record of 'Tony Benn's Greatest Hits' was produced; and eight volumes of his voluminous *Diaries* had, by the middle of the decade, sold in excess of a hundred thousand copies.

Benn had thus become by this stage a national figure, known to almost everyone and with a proven national appeal. However, there was an irony in the fact that, as his national profile grew, he became ever further distanced from the centres of power. There is some truth in Benn's typically pithy observation: ' "It's the same each time with progress. First they ignore you, than they say you're mad, then dangerous, then there's a pause and then you can't find anyone who disagrees with you." '[68]

As late as 2005, at the Labour Conference, Benn addressed five meetings a day. The strain proved too much and he collapsed. After a pacemaker was fitted he did reduce his level of activism but was still a frequent media presence. He died aged 88 in 2014.

Michael Foot and Tony Benn

As a footnote to this discussion, it is instructive to compare the approach to the socialist strand of English radicalism of Michael Foot and Tony Benn. They appeared to have much in common, in terms of both background and ideological perspective. Both came from notable English radical, and politically formidable, families, immersed in radical Liberal and Labour politics. And both had a powerful socialisation into the Dissenting, Nonconformist Christian tradition. Both men had fathers who influenced them greatly, and had ancestors active in public service, often as MPs. Both went to Oxford and became Presidents of the Oxford Union. Both, too, became prominent figures on the Left of the Labour Party and both were hailed as great orators and parliamentary performers. Yet they cordially detested each other. In Benn's case this is not so surprising: he was alienated, eventually, from virtually all his senior colleagues. With Foot, however, such enmity was unusual, although not unique. (He also detested Hugh Gaitskell.) Foot was, whatever his faults, almost universally regarded as not only a good man but an extremely likeable person.

A part of the reason for this antipathy originated in what might be termed politely, Benn's political volatility – although it is also true that he was consistent in his adherence to his lifelong core *values*. Foot was a leading, and loyal, member of the Bevanite Left, and frequently rebelled against the Party leadership. In contrast, in his early years in Parliament, Benn was close to Gaitskell and adopted a centrist, pro-EEC, pro-NATO position: and he continued to adhere to this centrist position under Wilson's leadership. 'Foot profoundly distrusted his younger colleague, and his suspicions were widely shared on the Labour front bench.'[69]

On Benn's side, he was disgruntled that Foot did not support him in his campaign for the reform of the House of Lords in 1969. In his *Diary*, he wrote that he thought of Foot as '"a conservative of the Left"'.[70] It is also clear that Benn was intimidated by Foot's literary scholarship and his status as an intellectual authority on some of the major figures of English radicalism. Moreover, Benn was surprisingly ill-informed on English history, political theory and much else.

According to Kenneth Morgan, whereas Foot's socialism was parliamentary and Aristotelian, Benn's was 'populist yet in some ways Platonic… but his vision lacked the historical grounding of Foot's'.[71] On the other hand, Foot was notoriously vague on specific policy proposals – or any blueprint for a future, long-term, socialist plan – whereas Benn certainly had a multiplicity of detailed policy proposals. 'His vision of a socialist Britain was futuristic… his focus, unlike Foot's, is on ends rather than means.'[72] Benn 'tried to be at one and the same time a technocrat and a populist. He advocated both centralism and localism, a kind of mixture between Jean Monnet and Jean-Jacques Rousseau… While always stimulating, he was often inconsistent.'[73]

Benn and Foot also differed in their conception of the role of Parliament. For Foot, Parliament was the heart of modern democracy, to be protected at all costs. For Benn, Parliament was only one aspect, albeit an important one, of the wider struggle for socialist democracy. Benn increasingly believed that the rank and file of the Party, and the wider public, were the essential elements in a 'fluid popular front, where the official Labour leadership would rapidly be superseded… Benn's party was the priesthood of all believers'; and, Morgan continues, somewhat extravagantly, that Benn's vision was 'an extension of the Congregationalism of his father and his forebears, with groups like Militant as the new Anabaptists'.[74]

Despite Benn's romanticised appeals to the history of English radicalism, Morgan is surely correct in his assertion that Benn's socialism 'is not really historical at all… It is curiously abstract, focusing on structures and mechanics, and unrelated to the political antecedents.'[75] Nor is his socialism 'literary' or 'cultural'. His 'bleak analysis seems… peculiarly mechanical, even bloodless, curiously lacking in humanity for so personally charming and cultured a man'.[76]

Both Benn and Foot were 'profoundly English, each a patrician rooted in his time. Indeed, there was an insularity about both… Both were products of a native radical tradition imbibed from their Liberal fathers. Neither had many close associations with Continental or Third World socialists… Neither was pro-American… Foot versus Benn was, by extension, Voltaire versus Rousseau.'[77]

Both stood outside the mainstream, and neither, despite all their political activism, eloquent oratory and remarkable energy, had decisive impact on the development of English parliamentary socialism in the 1990s and 2000s. 'New Labour' was an anathema to both of them. However, the entirely unexpected consequence of the turmoil in the Labour Party, following the 2008–9 economic crisis, was the rise to power in the Party of the archetypal 'Bennite' Jeremy Corbyn.

Conclusion

Benn was undoubtedly a major figure, and a major influence, well beyond the mainstream Labour constituency, in the development of late twentieth-century English radicalism. His idiosyncratic, if not eccentric, conceptualisation of popular radicalism, based upon the moral precepts of English Nonconformism (albeit in secularised form), struck a chord with large numbers of people. Increasingly unpopular, and distrusted, though he may have been in the PLP, he was an immensely successful and high-profile media (and mass-movement) figure. This was in no small part due to his natural talent as a communicator. From his earliest days in Parliament, Benn was able to craft the presentation of radical ideas in a popular, accessible and appealing style. He was not only eloquent and entertaining, he was self-deprecating and naturally witty: even his fiercest enemies – and there were many of them – could not deny his oratorical and 'modern media' abilities.

He was also remarkably energetic and diligent. Few could match his consistent levels of activism, which spanned many decades. Similarly, his persistent optimism and self-confidence, despite repeated setbacks, were notable. (However, it is instructive to note that he, like his father, was subject on occasion to depression: 'I too have periods of depression when I wonder if I have ever done anything worthwhile.')[78] There was much in his personality that was obsessive: he was a driven man. Although he showed little sign of 'careerism' in his early adult life, he became increasingly convinced that it was his political duty – or destiny – to lead the Party and the British people into the new socialist society. There was thus a strong Messianic streak to his personality.

He succeeded in presenting socialist ideas in demotic form through the popular media in a unique and appealing style. Benn enjoyed a media profile and a high degree of public and largely positive recognition unmatched by any other left-wing politician. These were no small achievements. As his biographer has accurately observed, at the heart of Benn's socialism was his belief in democracy. He often referred to his friend Reinhold Niebuhr's saying: '"Man's capacity for evil makes democracy necessary, man's capacity for good makes democracy possible."'[79]

He believed passionately in the innate good sense, and moral probity, of ordinary people, provided they exercised their freedom to create a fair and just economic and social system. To try to achieve this, he consistently – or at least consistently from the 1970s – challenged 'authority' in all its guises. 'With calmness, politeness and eloquence he repeated the message of popular democracy ... He gave people faith in their own power to bring about change.'[80]

However, it is striking that, given his long and varied ministerial career, and his immense energy and commitment, to say nothing of his notable talent for administration, management and innovatory policy proposals, his achievements were relatively modest. His 'loner' personality, his political volatility, and latterly his perceived 'naked ambition', all led to a near universal lack of trust among his senior colleagues. Moreover, he had very few supporters on the backbenches of the PLP. It is significant, too, that in his long parliamentary career he became alienated from all the leaders of the Party (with the partial exception of John Smith): Gaitskell, Wilson, Callaghan, Foot, Kinnock and Blair.

Benn was unusual in his total dedication to politics alone. This may well have originated in his family background and upbringing where, as noted earlier, his mother recalled that politics was the sole topic of conversation. Unlike most of his senior colleagues – Healey and Foot, for example – Benn had no 'hinterland', apart from his immediate family. This may account, in part, for his obsessive temperament.

Although he was neither an intellectual nor a theorist, he had no hesitation in seeking 'ideas from people like [Ralph] Miliband and Leo Panitch, who liked and respected him'.[81] His influence on political radicalism in the country at large was profound. He also continued to inspire a small but determined minority on the Left of the Labour Party through the years of New Labour dominance. The resultant resurgence of the Left in the Party, following its defeat in the 2010 general election, owes much to the influence and example of Tony Benn.

Benn was a man of many paradoxes. He was personally kind, courteous and polite, and he genuinely liked ordinary people and had the ability to express his views in a direct and appealing way. But he was also an ambitious and somewhat 'slippery' politician. He was old-fashioned and rooted in his parents' Nonconformism, but also modern, 'technology savvy', and a lover of gadgetry. He was a populariser and 'a man of the people', but also a 'loner', isolated politically and personally from his colleagues. Confident, witty and seemingly at ease though he was, he was also diffident and subject on occasion to depression.

Whatever his weaknesses and eccentricities, however, few have had a greater influence upon twentieth-century English radicalism.

Notes

1. J. Adams, *Tony Benn: A Biography* (Macmillan, 1992), revised pb. edition (Biteback Publishing, 2011). Quotations in this chapter are taken from the pb. edition, p. vii.
2. P. Jenkins, 'Post-Bourgeois Man', Review of *Arguments for Democracy* and *Manifesto*, *London Review of Books*, 1 October 1981.
3. T. Benn, *Dare to Be a Daniel: Then and Now* (Hutchinson, 2004), pb. edition (Arrow Books, 2005). Quotations in this chapter are taken from this pb. edition, p. 5.
4. R. Winstone (ed.), *The Best of Benn: Speeches, Diaries, Letters and Other Writings* (Hutchinson, 2014), pb. edition (Arrow Books, 2015). Quotations in this chapter are taken from this pb. edition, p. 174.
5. Benn, *Dare to Be a Daniel*, p. 3.
6. Nevertheless, although aged 37 and an MP, and thus exempt from war service, he joined the army and was awarded the DSO and the DFC. In the Second World War, by then in his sixties, he again saw active service.

7 Adams, *Tony Benn*, p. 158, citing interview with Benn, 27 November 1989.
8 Ibid., p. 11.
9 Ibid., p. 495.
10 Benn, *Dare to Be a Daniel*, pp. 118 and 100.
11 Adams, *Tony Benn*, p. 147.
12 Ibid., p. 368. Caroline Benn had decided that 'he had better know some Marxist theory ... He read it on Boxing Day, realising how much he had in common with the Marxist analysis of the structure of society'.
13 Ibid., p. 15.
14 Ibid., p. 10, interview, Lady Stansgate.
15 Benn noted that for ' "the serving officers it was a war against Germany ... For me it was a war against fascism." ' Ibid., p. 32, citing interview with Benn, 12 September 1989.
16 Ibid., p. 48.
17 Caroline de Camp had a first-class degree from Vassar and had won a postgraduate fellowship to study for a PhD at Columbia University on seventeenth-century English literature. However, after she and Benn married, on 17 June 1949, she abandoned her plans, moved to London and registered for a PhD at University College, London.
18 Adams, *Tony Benn*, p. 468, *Diary*, 23 November 2000.
19 Ibid., p. 65.
20 Benn, *Dare to Be a Daniel*, p. 5.
21 Ibid., p. 7.
22 Ibid., p. 10.
23 Ibid., p. 13.
24 Ibid., p. 16.
25 For the details of Benn's parliamentary career, see Adams, *Tony Benn*, chapters 6 to 37.
26 Ibid., p. 72.
27 Ibid., p. 74.
28 Ibid., pp. 75–6, citing interview with Michael Bowen, 15 June 1989.
29 Ibid., p. 84, citing interview with Benn, 25 September 1989.
30 Ibid., p. 81, interview, Lady Stansgate.
31 Ibid., pp. 87–8, citing Hugh Dalton, *The Political Diary of Hugh Dalton 1918–40, 1945–60* (Cape, 1986) (my italics).
32 Ibid., pp. 91–2, citing interview with Benn, 27 November 1989.
33 Ibid., pp. 122, 114.
34 Ibid., p. 127.
35 M. Foot, *Loyalists and Loners* (London: Collins, 1986), chapter on Benn, 'Brother Tony', p. 111.
36 The Benn archive was given to the British Library.
37 On the 1960 Conference and the nuclear issue, see M. Foot, *Aneurin Bevan*, vol. 2, 1945–1960 (Davis-Poynter, 1973); and R. Taylor, *Against the Bomb: The British Peace Movement 1958–1965* (Oxford: Clarendon Press, 1988), pp. 293–8.
38 Gaitskell received 166 votes and Wilson 81.
39 For example: his 20 per cent pay rise for postal workers breached Brown's incomes policy; he did not have the new stamps available when he increased postal charges; and, unrelated to his ministerial duties, he missed a crucial vote in the Commons, which

contributed to the government's defeat on the issue concerned. See Adams, *Tony Benn*, pp. 230ff.
40 Adams, *Tony Benn*, p. 252, citing R.H.S. Crossman, *The Diaries of a Cabinet Minister*, vol. 1 (1975).
41 Ibid., p. 257, citing A. Bourne, *Tony Benn* (1983). Benn reflected, many years later, that '"of all the departments I worked in, the one I liked the most was the Post Office … I liked the people, the inspiration, its history"'. Ibid., citing interview with Benn, 12 June 1990.
42 Adams, *Tony Benn*, p. 296.
43 Ibid., p. 266, citing Benn's *Diary*, 22 November 1968.
44 Ibid., pp. 265–6, citing Crossman's *Diaries*, vol. 2, 1976.
45 Ibid., p. 304, citing Benn's *Diary*, 22 May 1971.
46 Ibid.
47 Benn, *Dare to Be a Daniel*, p. 270.
48 Adams, *Tony Benn*, p. 310, citing Benn, *Diary*, 2 August 1971.
49 Ibid., p. 269, citing Castle, *Diaries*.
50 Ibid., p. 270, citing interview with Benn, 25 September 1990.
51 Ibid., p. 319, citing ibid. (Benn interview).
52 Ibid., p. 352.
53 See, for example, D. Childs, *Britain Since 1945: A Political History* (1979, seventh updated edition, Routledge, 2012).
54 Benn, *Dare to Be a Daniel*, p. 189.
55 Adams, *Tony Benn*, p. 341, citing interview with Jack Jones, 8 March 1991.
56 D. Powell, *Tony Benn: A Life* (London: Continuum, 2001), p. 73.
57 Adams, *Tony Benn*, p. 389.
58 Ibid., citing Philip Whitehead, *The Writing on the Wall* (1985).
59 Adams, *Tony Benn*, p. 390.
60 Ibid., p. 391, citing Benn, *Diary*, 2 October 1980.
61 Had Callaghan delayed his resignation until January 1981, the new Electoral College system would have come into force, and Benn would have stood a reasonable chance of being elected Leader.
62 The 'Gang of Four' – Shirley Williams, David Owen, Roy Jenkins and Bill Rodgers – eventually announced the formation of the SDP in March 1981. At this point, 13 Labour MPs and 1 Conservative MP defected to join the new Party.
63 D. Healey, *The Time of My Life* (London: Michael Joseph, 1989), pb. edition Penguin Books, 1990. Quotations in this chapter are taken from the pb. edition, p. 482.
64 Adams, *Tony Benn*, p. 401, citing interview with Joe Ashton, 26 February 1991.
65 Ibid., p. 448.
66 The list of proposed reforms did not include introducing a proportional representation electoral system. Benn believed that this would increase the power of the Party leaders and break the direct link between MPs and their constituents.
67 Adams, *Tony Benn*, p. 469, citing Benn, *Diary*, 7 January 1998.
68 Cited by Brian Brivati, Obituary of Benn, *Guardian*, 14 March 2014.
69 K.O. Morgan, *Michael Foot: A Life* (Harper Press, 2007), pb. edition (Harper Perennial, 2008). Quotations in this chapter are taken from the pb. edition, p. 397.

70 Ibid., p. 396, citing Benn's *Diary*, 16 April 1969.
71 Ibid., p. 403.
72 Ibid., pp. 403–4.
73 Ibid., p. 404.
74 Ibid., p. 407.
75 Ibid.
76 Ibid. However, as has been argued in this chapter, although Benn certainly had personal *charm*, he had little *cultural* hinterland, as he reflected ruefully in old age.
77 Ibid., pp. 408–9.
78 Benn, *Dare to Be a Daniel*, p. 65.
79 Adams, *Tony Benn*, p. 495.
80 Ibid.
81 Note from Mike Newman to the author, 5 November 2018.

12

Nicolas Walter

Anarchism, in the sense of a formal political movement, was not a major force in English radicalism in either the nineteenth or the twentieth century. This is in marked contrast to several other societies, where anarchists have often been prominent and important: in Russia (especially in the nineteenth century and in the years leading up to the 1917 Revolution and the years immediately afterwards), France, Spain (especially in the 1936–39 Civil War), Italy, and several South American countries.

However, the *intellectual* influence of anarchism, and its ideas and moral aspirations, have had a profound impact upon the left-wing culture in Britain. George Woodcock, a theorist and historian of anarchism, claimed that the English 'Diggers' of 1649 were the first recognisable anarchists in modern English history: 'their leader Gerrard Winstanley was nothing more or less than an anarchist'.[1]

The broader *libertarian* influences have been even more important. In his major study of anarchist and left-libertarian thought in twentieth-century Britain, David Goodway has convincingly argued for the inclusion in this tradition of, among others, William Morris, Edward Carpenter, Oscar Wilde, George Orwell and E.P. Thompson, as well as avowed anarchists such as Herbert Read and Alex Comfort.

Almost all twentieth-century anarchists, in England as elsewhere, have been socialists and often communists – in the pure, 'non-Marxist' sense. What is it, then, that is distinctive about anarchism? As Nicolas Walter, the focus for this chapter, argued: 'Like liberals, anarchists want freedom; like socialists, anarchists want equality.' But neither is sufficient. 'We are liberals but more so, and socialists but more so … The essence of anarchism, the one thing without which it is not anarchism, is the negation of authority over anyone by anyone.'[2] Anarchists thus emphasise one of the core *a priori* values of English radicalism: freedom of thought, speech and assembly.

Freedom and equality for anarchists are not contradictory but complementary: they are in practice the same thing. The fatal flaw in socialism has been its theoretical and practical reliance upon the state, the ultimate representation in modern societies of 'authority'. The state 'is a cause as well as a result of the class system, and a classless society which is established by a state will soon become a class society again'.[3] Although, as Goodway observes, anarchism is 'notorious for its diversity',[4] what 'connects almost all of these into a coherent political stance is unremitting hostility to the State and parliamentarianism, employment of direct action as the means of attaining desired goals, and organization through co-operative associations, built and federated from the bottom upwards. Of these it is the first that is entirely distinctive to anarchism.'[5]

The state is anathema to anarchists for a number of reasons. First, and most obviously, the state by definition curtails the freedom of the individual, and the wider society, through a series of controlling, often repressive, institutions. Whilst this has been especially marked in authoritarian states – not least in the supposedly communist states – such institutions also curtail freedom in Western liberal democracies. Secondly, both the political and bureaucratic structures of the state systematise and perpetuate inequality; and they provide a subtle and comprehensive means, primarily in Western societies, of *legitimising* culturally the existing order.[6] Thirdly, it is nation states which wage war and that were therefore responsible for the killing of millions of people in the twentieth century. The main users of bombs and violence have been not anarchists but governments.

Anarchists are by no means all pacifists: they support, in certain circumstances and usually reluctantly, the need for violence in civil wars and other civil conflicts. But they *do* always oppose wars waged by nation states. Moreover, they believe, in the words of the old anarchist slogan, that 'War is the health of the state'.[7] It is in times of war that the state can mobilise most easily the support of the population, curtail civil freedoms and centralise power.

Whereas socialists, whether social democrats or Marxists, have the objective of *capturing* the state (and perhaps democratising its structures), anarchists aim for its *overthrow*. 'The idea of libertarian revolution – of rebellion or insurrection – is that there is no distinction between ends and means, because *means are ends*.'[8] This is one of the theoretical objections to Marxism held by anarchists: the short- to medium-term necessity for 'the dictatorship of the proletariat', through the 'vanguard party', as argued for and practised by the Bolsheviks, was not only denied by anarchists, it was held to be inherently catastrophic and self-defeating. Such 'means', the institutions and cultures developed to oppose the current system, prefigure future structures, and thus led to the disasters of Stalinism. The anarchist way was not to rely on 'someone else', or some higher authority, to take action, or to assume responsibility, but for people to assume responsibility for themselves, hence their advocacy, for example, of workers' control in industry. As Alex Comfort, a leading anarchist voice in mid-twentieth-century Britain, argued: '"We may not be able to prevent atrocities by other people, but we can at least decline to commit them ourselves ... this revolution is something no party or government is going to do for you. *You have to do it yourself, beginning tomorrow*"' (my italics).[9] A continuing theme is thus *disobedience* – to authority in general and the state in particular.

> We have one enemy, irresponsible government ... Wars are not deplorable accidents produced by the perfidy of degenerate nations – they are the results of calculated policy ... Atrocities are not only the work of sadists ... they are the result of obedience, an obedience which forgets its humanity. We will not accept that obedience. The safeguard of peace is not a vast army, but an unreliable public ... The only way to stop atrocities is to refuse to participate in them.[10]

The fault line between socialists and anarchists is deep-rooted. Within a few years of the formation of the First International in 1864, there were divisions between the Marxists and the mutualist supporters of Proudhon, 'reinforced by other libertarians as anarchist movements began to form also in Switzerland, Spain and Italy'.[11] There ensued a clash, partly political and partly personal, between Marx and Bakunin and by late 1870 both Marx's International and the 'anti-authoritarian' International had collapsed. Such divisions persisted and deepened with the formation of the Second International in 1889 and led, in 1896, to the permanent exclusion of anarchists from the organisation.

Anarchism flourished as a radical, mass social movement in societies with despotic or centralising states, often dominated culturally by an ultra-reactionary Roman Catholic Church, and where the emerging opposition centred on authoritarian, Marxist-Leninist Communist Parties. In contrast to such societies, the 'liberal, minimal statism of Britain ... was situated in a world apart from these turbulent and sanguinary histories'.[12]

With Franco's victory in the Spanish Civil War, following on from the defeat – and often liquidation – of anarchists in Fascist Italy and Nazi Germany in the 1920s and 1930s, and earlier in the USSR, anarchism as a major political force was very much a minor presence in the second half of the twentieth century in Europe. Nevertheless, as noted at the outset, there was, not least in Britain, 'a distinguished minority intellectual, overwhelmingly literary, anarchist – and rather broader and still more distinguished libertarian – tradition'.[13]

In the late twentieth century Britain, the only directly political arena in which anarchists played a significant role was the anarcho-pacifist movement of the late 1950s and early 1960s, which mobilised substantial sections of the population, especially the young, against nuclear weapons and the preparations by the British state for nuclear war. Nicolas Walter played a prominent role in this movement, and wrote extensively and authoritatively about anarchist theory, strategy and tactics in this context. Attention is now turned to an examination of Walter's contribution in this and related fields, and to his articulation of the libertarian strand in English radicalism.

Nicolas Walter

Walter was born in 1934, into a Dissenting family with strong anarchist connections.[14] One of his grandfathers, S.K. Radcliffe, was a radical atheist, who wrote the history of the South Place Ethical Society in London; he was a freelance journalist and lecturer, who was a 'liberal rationalist' rather than a socialist. He was, recalled Kingsley Martin on his death, '"meticulous about accurate detail ... I have always regretted that I did not send [him] the manuscript of each of my books before publication; instead of awaiting his inevitable list of errors."'[15] This was a trait inherited by his grandson.

Walter's other grandfather was Karl Walter, an American anarchist and journalist, who had known Peter Kropotkin and Edward Carpenter. After a period in Italy, when he became a fascist sympathiser, he returned to London and to his erstwhile anarchist beliefs.

Walter's father, W. Grey Walter, was a leading neurologist, for many years Director of the British Neurological Institute in Bristol, and a member of the prestigious BBC TV *Brains Trust* panel. Nicolas's mother, Monica, had been a dancer at Sadler's Wells; after his parents divorced, he was brought up by his mother and her second husband, A.H.W. (Bill) Beck, who became a Professor of Engineering at Cambridge.

During his two years' National Service, Walter learned Russian, which led to his later writing authoritatively on Russian history, politics and literature. In 1954, he went up to Exeter College, Oxford to read Modern History. As an undergraduate, Walter was a left-wing Labour Party supporter but, on his return to London in 1957, where he worked initially as a schoolteacher, he rapidly became involved with the New Left, began visiting the 'Freedom' bookshop and contributed to *Freedom*, the anarchist newspaper.

As an anarchist and supporter of the mass movement against nuclear weapons, he wrote a letter to *The Times* in late 1960 defending the newly created Committee of 100, established to develop a campaign of mass civil disobedience as a counter to the increasingly constitutionalist, Labour-supporting Campaign for Nuclear Disarmament (CND).[16] He was consequently invited to become a founder member of the new organisation. As he was to write, overly modestly, in a postscript to *Nonviolent Resistance*: '"I was never at all important in the Committee of 100, but it was very important to me."'[17]

Walter's involvement in the peace movement, and the ways in which he analysed its relationship with anarchist theory and practice, are considered below. Although the peace movement, and associated activities, occupied much of Walter's time and energy in the 1960s, he was by profession a journalist. He became Deputy Editor of

Which? (1963–65), then Press Officer for the British Standards Institute from 1965 to 1967, and in 1968 chief sub-editor at the *Times Literary Supplement* (*TLS*). This latter was a post to which he was 'ideally suited and which he relished'. He had a rich store of anecdotes about 'life at the TLS – such as the peculiarities of another staff member, Martin Amis ...'.[18]

He resigned, however, from the *TLS* on the typically arcane grounds of his disapproval of the *TLS* changing from anonymous to signed reviews. He then became editor of the *New Humanist* (1975–85) and subsequently Director of the Rationalist Press Association (RPA), a post he held until his retirement in 1999. He was thus able to pursue to the full the other major preoccupation of his life – rationalism and atheism – in addition to his anarchism.

He was an indefatigable writer of letters to the (serious) press: by 1994 it was estimated that he had written about fourteen thousand letters to newspapers and periodicals, of which about two thousand had been published.

Walter could be 'awkward'; and he was certainly a stickler for factual accuracy and syntactical correctness. He was a formidable debater and polemicist; and he was a fierce reviewer.[19] But, though he may have been too acerbic at times, he was usually correct in his critique; and his writing was always thoroughly researched, factually accurate and clearly expressed.

Walter was a courageous, principled and powerful advocate of his beliefs. He was plagued by ill-health following a bout of cancer in 1974; eventually he was confined to a wheelchair and, in 2000, his cancer returned. Contrary to David Goodway's account,[20] he did not commit suicide, but died in a Milton Keynes hospice on 7 March.[21] His 1996 BBC World Service talk 'Facing Death' was a fitting and moving testimony to his unbending humanism.[22]

Walter's writings and activism illustrate and articulate the important contributions that anarchism has made to English radicalism in the twentieth century.

The anti-nuclear peace movement

Writing in 2006, Goodway claimed that 'the most original, creative anarchist thinking over the last seventy years has been within anarcho-pacifism. In an increasingly violent world ... non-violent tactics have the most to commend them.'[23] In Britain, it was primarily in the Committee of 100 that such politics was put into practice. As well as being a prominent activist in the Committee, Walter was arguably its foremost theorist.[24]

For Walter, the Committee of 100 was 'basically a crank organisation dressed up in respectable clothes'; and it belonged 'not to the tradition of majority revolution but to the tradition of minority dissent'.[25] Walter emphatically rejected the politics, and accompanying strategy, of the mainstream movement, which was to work in and with the official labour movement. The Committee, Walter believed, should reject the 'conventional wisdom' of how democracy operates – elections, representative assemblies and so on. He defined democracy rather 'in terms of face-to-face liberty, equality and fraternity'.²⁶ Most anarchists are, ideologically, communists, in the 'pure', non-Marxist sense, as noted: but they see the struggle not as centred on class conflict but as essentially between the protection and extension of individual freedom, on the one hand, and the repressive, authoritarian 'Warfare State', on the other. In the nuclear age, this wider struggle was focused upon building militant movements to oppose militarism and the build-up of nuclear weapons arsenals by the state.

Walter argued that, 'once you start protesting against the Bomb rather than against class oppression or personal violence, you find yourself opposing all war and the whole Warfare State. And when socialists start opposing war as such and pacifists start opposing the State as such, their separate paths lead directly to non-violent anarchism'; and, he continued, somewhat optimistically, that political energy and commitment would begin 'to flow rapidly away from the socialist and pacifist movements into the new unilateralist movement'.²⁷

Similarly, Walter argued, the history of pacifism demonstrated that, as Randolph Bourne put it in 1918: ' "We cannot crusade against war without crusading implicitly against the State". Pacifism is ultimately anarchism, just as anarchism is ultimately pacifism.'²⁸ The unfortunate result of the formation of the Peace Pledge Union in the mid-1930s was 'to drive the religious pacifists and the political anti-militarists apart'.²⁹ Only the development of 'non-violent resistance' could bring these two traditions together. (For Walter, the real history of pacifism should be seen as 'the way saints and heretics defended the doctrine of Christ against the Church'.)³⁰

The development of the non-violent resistance movement in Britain was pioneered by the Gandhian 'Direct Actionists' of the late 1940s and early 1950s. In 1949, some members of the PPU formed a Non-Violent Commission, and from this 'Operation Gandhi' emerged in 1951. This developed into the Emergency Committee for Direct Action Against Nuclear War (DAC), formed in 1957, organiser of the first Aldermaston March in 1958 and precursor of the far larger, more 'constitutionalist' and predominantly 'Labourist' CND.³¹

However, the pacifism of the DAC, radical though it was, was not enough for Walter and the anarchists and associated radicals of the Committee of 100. Citing Étienne de la Boétie, Walter argued that it was disobedience that was the key to liberation: ' "Resolve not to obey, and you are free." '³² The power of 'authority', more particularly the state, collapses if people *en masse* simply refuse to obey – as Gandhi showed to such effect in the struggle for Indian independence. It is but a short step from this position to active (non-violent) resistance. Alex Comfort, whom Walter regarded as the leading theorist of the new pacifism, and a lifelong anarchist,³³ argued, in 1946, that: ' "Objection is not enough … You do not want objection, you want resistance, ready to adopt every means short of violence to destroy and render useless the whole mechanism of conscription" '³⁴ and the associated culture of modern societies.

This consistently anti-authoritarian, anti-state perspective, with its political priority of the widest possible liberty for both the individual and society, is a centrally important strand in English radicalism. Of those considered in this book, several have been sceptical, at best, of orthodox socialism and its main political vehicle in twentieth-century Britain, the Labour Party. They have either, like Thompson and Sylvia Pankhurst, been advocates of popular social movements or, like Bertrand Russell, George Orwell and Stuart Hall, have seen radicalism in a much broader, *cultural* framework. But the importance and moral priority of liberty have been accepted by all those encompassed in the tradition of English radicalism. It is this attachment, almost on *a priori* grounds, to libertarian values, which was one of the main reasons for the failure of Marxism, and still more the Marxism-Leninism of the Communist Party, to achieve mass support in Britain.

However, it has been only the advocates of anarchism, who have taken this commitment to liberty to its extreme; and it is, as noted earlier, their total rejection of the state, and its accompanying bureaucracies, that is, in practical political terms, anarchism's most distinctive feature. And it is here that anarchists' critics have found grounds for their accusations of impracticality and political naivety. However, anarchists have not been opposed to organisation *per se*. In his book *About Anarchism* Walter argued that anarchists 'actually want much more organisation, though organisation without authority ... it actually works best without authority'. Anarchist organisation would be 'fluid and open'. Because all organisations tend towards both oligarchy and bureaucracy, anarchists believe that it is crucial to prevent the emergence of a ruling group, 'the rule of the few', and rigid structures.[35]

Walter put these principles into practice in the Committee of 100 in the early 1960s and its cognate organisations. He showed himself to be an able organiser, especially in the 'Spies for Peace' episode (discussed below). Indeed, his whole professional career exemplified his talents as an organiser, as well as an intellectual theorist, historian and political activist.

Walter attended the inaugural meeting of the Committee of 100 on 22 October 1960 and remained an active member until June 1961, when he 'resigned because of disagreement with its rhetoric and tactics, which [had] worried me from the beginning'.[36] He nevertheless remained active and, by the end of 1961, he had been arrested half a dozen times. He also remained a member of the London Committee of 100 (by far the largest and most important of the 13 Regional Committees) from 1 April 1962 until the summer of 1965, and wrote numerous articles, in both socialist and other radical journals, and in the *Guardian*, on nuclear disarmament and 'radical protest' issues.[37]

By early 1963, Walter had become frustrated with what he saw as the Committee of 100's unimaginative approach and its 'obsessions with non-violence, openness, symbolic actions, arrests, names, respectability, and so on'.[38] Walter became increasingly influenced by the Solidarity group, which had become a more significant force in the Committee.[39] However, 'as a dedicated anarchist who at that time was also a pacifist he was remote from their Trotskyist origins and continuing Marxist perspectives'.[40] The conclusion Walter came to at this time, was that '"we must attempt to hinder the warfare state in every possible way"'.[41] This meant, in effect, that he and a select group of other anarchist, or anarchist-inclined, young activists determined to take subversive action. The result was the 'Spies for Peace' episode of activism: at the time (1963), a spectacularly successful symbolic action, which attracted national media and political attention.[42] Walter and his wife, Ruth, were members of the small, London-based group: but the key people, according to Goodway, were Solidarity activists.[43]

The intention of the 'Spies' group was to expose what they saw as the hypocrisy of the state by ascertaining, clandestinely, as much detail as possible of the preparations for the eventuality of nuclear war by the government and the state authorities. Such plans, they were convinced, correctly, would centre on the provision of protected underground bunkers in which selected ministers and key elite bureaucrats could survive the war's devastating aftermath. The 'Spies' were, it was argued, 'dangerous because they question the basic assumption of all bureaucracies: that the State knows best. Such thinking threatens the Russian rulers as much as it does our own.'[44]

The group located RSG (Regional Seat of Government) 6 at Warren Row, near Reading, and, on 16 February 1963, visited the premises. Finding them unlocked, they gathered what papers they could and left. Revisiting the site on 23 February, the group picked the lock and took copies of official papers. After 'lying low' for a while to ensure that they were not under suspicion, the final version of the document, *Danger! Official Secret*, was compiled and about two thousand copies sent to peace activists likely to be on the Aldermaston March at Easter; and a further one thousand copies to national newspapers, a list from *Who's Who* and selected ministers and MPs. 'The typewriter was thrown into a river outside London, and – as a last act of political malice – the cardboard boxes were left in dustbins outside the old *Daily Worker* office in Farringdon Street.'[45]

On the Aldermaston March, several hundred marchers diverted from the official route, despite the best efforts of Peggy Duff, CND's Organising Secretary, to dissuade them, and a brief vigil and demonstration took place. Press coverage was extensive: virtually every national newspaper carried prominent accounts of the revelations. For a while, government security 'D' Notices restrained the press from publishing full details of the RSGs; but, on 19 April, full information was reported in the *Daily Telegraph*. *Private Eye* published a parody, and the BBC's *That Was The Week That Was* also publicised the event.

The anarchists were triumphant. As *Anarchy* put it: 'total damage to the State resulting from this demonstration: Damage to State property two pounds; Damage to State's image (already pretty fly-blown): immeasurable'.[46] Other actions followed, in London, in Cambridge and at Dover Castle; and, in September 1963,

Walter published a Solidarity pamphlet, *The RSGs 1919–1963*, giving the full historical background of the RSG system.[47]

Although the group subsequently attempted to broaden its activities to expose the emergency government system that lay behind the RSG structure, the security systems proved too complex and efficient to be penetrated. After several largely unsuccessful attempts, the group decided to disband in late 1964.[48] The members were never identified by the authorities.

Walter and the other members of the group took part in a series of later demonstrations,[49] and Walter was arrested and prosecuted for his disruption of the service at Brighton Methodist Church which took place during the Labour Party Conference in 1966 and at which George Brown and Harold Wilson were speaking. Walter and Jim Radford were each sentenced to two months' imprisonment in Brixton.

The 'Spies for Peace' episode illustrated both the strengths and the weaknesses of the anarchist perspective on the peace movement and its strategy. On the one hand, it was, within its own terms, a resoundingly successful example of 'propaganda by the deed'; it gave the ailing Committee of 100 a new lease of life and it strengthened the Committee's libertarian wing; and it was organised and implemented, with remarkably limited resources, effectively and efficiently. On the other hand, however, the notion that it heralded the birth of a new 'mass revolutionary movement' was illusory: the Committee of 100 was smaller, weaker, and less effective than it had been in 1961, and the movement generally was in steep decline. Moreover, nothing was more likely to alienate working-class industrial militants, let alone the working class *en masse*, than clandestine sabotage activity;[50] and without mass working-class involvement there was no prospect of any meaningful revolutionary movement. In the end, this dramatic example of anarchist activism further divided and weakened a movement already disintegrating.

Despite repeated attempts to revivify the Committee of 100, it was clear by 1964, as *Freedom* argued, that the necessarily 'limited existence' of such movements had, for the Committee, come to an end. It took a further four years, but, in September 1968, the Committee of 100 finally dissolved. Radical protest politics in Britain was now dominated by the anti-Vietnam War movement and, to an extent, by the neo-Trotskyism of '1968' and after.

Walter, always a realist as well as an indefatigable campaigner, warned as early as 1962 that, although the movement was vibrant and growing, it was still far from a mass movement with revolutionary potential: 'the people who came forward to help the Committee were still largely the same *déracinés*, middle-class intellectuals and bohemians who had dominated the unilateralist movement all along, and frighteningly few of those who didn't come forward were even sympathetic. *We may be a happy few, but we are still only a few*' (my italics).[51]

The anarchists' hopes and dreams for the Committee of 100 always far outran any potential that the Committee had for wholesale transformation. Walter realised this but, typically, it did not prevent him continuing the struggle. He realised that '[t]oo many people who support the Committee ... suffer from a delusion of grandeur';[52] but he also maintained that, in the broader context, 'anarchism is indeed a beautiful dream, but not therefore just an impossible utopia. It is a perfectly good answer to most political questions; the final – and fundamental – question is whether people really want it.'[53] He spent most of his life trying to persuade people that they *should* 'really want it': and he acted with great courage and integrity to try to realise this objective.

Rationalism and atheism

Rationalist and atheist beliefs are important elements in twentieth-century English radicalism. Many of those considered in this book vehemently rejected religious belief, although most of them had been brought up in strongly Christian, usually Nonconformist or 'low' Church Anglican, environments. These include Bertrand Russell, E.P. Thompson and Michael Foot. In all cases, however, their moral code and the implicit political values derived to an extent, usually a large extent, from this Christian background.

Nicolas Walter's background was significantly different. Several of his immediate forebears had been prominent and articulate rationalists, as well as anarchists, as was noted earlier. Like many avowed atheists, Walter had a deep knowledge and understanding of religion, especially Christianity. His book *Blasphemy* illustrates this aspect of his intellectual and philosophical stance.[54]

As Walter noted, anarchists 'have traditionally been anti-clerical, and also atheist ... The slogan, "Neither God nor master", has often been used to sum up the anarchist message.'[55] There have been anarchists who were Christian believers, notably Tolstoy; and for this minority, their egalitarian, pacific Christianity was inextricably connected to their anarchist beliefs. There have also been Christian/Anarchist movements, the Catholic Worker movement in the USA in the 1930s being the most significant. But these have been a minority, increasingly so as the secularism of the twentieth century came to characterise majority culture, in the West at least.

Walter's objection to religion was partly on philosophical grounds; but essentially his target was the authoritarian and obscurantist *Church* rather than Christianity *per se*. (As he noted in his book on blasphemy, 'two of the most significant figures in our civilisation – Socrates and Jesus – were put to death for blasphemy'.)[56] The rejection of 'divine authority encourages the rejection of human authority'.[57]

As the power of the Church steadily declined through the twentieth century, so anarchists' hatred of religion has similarly declined, and 'most anarchists now think of it as a personal matter'.[58] Anarchists believe that people should be free to believe and act as they wish, with three provisos: first, that there should be freedom of thought and expression in the wider society; secondly, that everything is 'open to question and criticism, however unpleasant or unfair';[59] and thirdly, that people's beliefs and practices should affect only themselves. In this context, then, anarchists adopt a classic Millite liberal position on issues of individual freedom of thought and action. The contemporary view of religion's place in a free society is encapsulated in Walter's phrase that there must be 'freedom from as well as freedom for religion'.[60]

Despite the increasing secularism of the age, however, the *cultural* power of Christianity remains considerable in Western societies, especially the USA. Even in Western Europe, the hierarchical, usually reactionary, perspectives and structures of the orthodox Churches exercise considerable influence. After his years of intense peace movement activism, Walter was able to turn his attention mainly to campaigning for a secularist approach. This 'one-time choirboy'[61] became, in 1975, as noted earlier, editor of the RPA's journal, the *New Humanist* and subsequently, in 1985, Director of the RPA. He continued there until his retirement at the end of 1999.

In these roles, he was a persistent, vigilant advocate of the rationalist position, always emphasising the essential libertarianism of the RPA's stance, and warning of the continuing dangers of Christian dogmatism and prejudice. He published a range of pamphlets and articles, ranging from the scholarly to the polemical, on themes and issues relating to the RPA's stance, and to the wider anarchist movement.

He retained his humanist atheism to the end. Writing to the *Guardian*, replying to an article about dying without the comfort of religion, he wrote: 'Religion may promise life everlasting, but we should grow up, and accept that life has an end as well as a beginning ... Mortality is inevitable, but morbidity is not.'[62]

Conclusion

It remains to make some final observations on the part that anarchism has played in twentieth-century English radicalism, and to discuss the extent to which its influence has been, arguably, rather less than might have been expected.

The first and most obvious point to make is that anarchism's defining beliefs in the freedom of the individual and the complementary civil freedoms in the wider society are also core values of English radicalism. These affinities are deep-rooted, predating the modern socialist movement. Anarchist, or more generally libertarian, thinkers and activists have been prominent in English radicalism since at least the eighteenth century, and arguably much earlier (as was discussed in Chapters 1 and 2 of this book).

One ideological result of the priority given to freedom has been the unbending hostility of anarchists to Marxism-Leninism as a theory and to Communist Parties as political organisations. All anarchists agree with Bakunin's claim that 'socialism without liberty is tyranny'.[63] A graphic example of this perspective has been the condemnation by anarchists of the notorious Bolshevik suppression of the Kronstadt uprising in 1921. This incident, though long ago and, in the sanguinary history of the twentieth century, of relatively minor importance, has been a symbolic issue on the Left.⁶⁴ Whilst virtually all communist (and Trotskyist) writers defended the suppression, on the not unreasonable grounds of the desperate plight of the fragile, early Bolshevik regime, anarchists have roundly condemned not only the action itself but even more importantly the ideological stance underpinning it. Trotsky, like Bukharin, acknowledged that the Kronstadt sailors were ' "our blind sailor comrades" ', and described the suppression as a ' "tragic necessity" '.⁶⁵ But he had no doubt about the absolute need for suppression.

For anarchists, this approach is an anathema. 'It is action, more than anything else, which reveals the true nature of human beings.'⁶⁶ Walter argued that the importance of Kronstadt is not that it was a ' "betrayal of the revolution" … but that it was indeed a "tragic necessity", a symptom of the underlying chronic illness of authoritarian socialism – the fact that it is objectively, practically, essentially counter-revolutionary'.⁶⁷

This unshakeable anarchist belief in the absolute connection, morally and politically, between means and ends lies at the heart too of English radicalism and its moral and pragmatic culture. This is discussed in the final chapter of this book. ⁶⁸

The anarchist opposition to the state, whilst not taken to the extreme even by the more libertarian figures considered in this study – such as Orwell and Thompson – has also been a prominent feature of the English radical tradition, with its emphasis upon social movements and democratic egalitarianism, and its scepticism about parliamentary democracy and the supposed neutrality of the state institutions.

Why, then, has anarchism not had more support in twentieth-century English radical circles? David Goodway, a leading libertarian intellectual, has put forward three convincing reasons for this relative failure. Firstly, anarchism has not offered intellectuals 'the social and political rewards which other forms of socialism did'. There have certainly been few if any positions of power or influence available to anarchists in the pursuit of the attainment of the 'free society' which they have advocated. Secondly, 'anarchist movements have tended to be exceptionally hostile not only towards the middle classes in general, but also bourgeois intellectuals'. Finally, and in my view most significantly, 'anarchism does not afford the theoretical and mental satisfactions that Marxism especially, but also reformist socialism, have done. It does not fetishize theory or cleverness or intellectual ability. Its appeal has been as much, if not more, emotional than rational.'⁶⁹

A fourth reason may also be suggested. Anarchism has had a persistently negative image in the popular consciousness, forever identified with shadowy figures using terror –usually bombs – against innocent people. This derives in part from the portrayals of anarchists in novels such as Conrad's *The Secret Agent* and, much later, Lessing's *The Good Terrorist*. However, this negative image also emanates from the, not wholly illusory, links that are perceived to exist between anarchism and the far Left terrorist organisations of the Angry Brigade, the Red Army Faction and the Baader-Meinhof group.

There are two important caveats, however, to this argument. The first is that, as Herbert Read noted in the 1940s, there are often to be found '"in unexpected places"' intellectuals who are '"fundamentally anarchist in their political outlook, but who do not dare to invite ridicule by confessing it"'.[70] Moreover, there are numerous writers, intellectuals and academics who can be broadly described as left-libertarians, some of them, such as Orwell and Thompson, considered in this book.

The second caveat is illustrated by the very different, but definitely anarchist, perspectives of Colin Ward – probably as well known as those of Nicolas Walter.[71] Ward, an architect and town planner, believed that anarchism, far from being an abstract, speculative theory of an imagined future, was '"rooted in the experience of everyday life, which operates side by side with, and in spite of, the dominant authoritarian trends of our society"'.[72] So, the embryonic anarchist society is already here '"in the interstices of the dominant power structure"'.[73] Thus some sort of anarchist society will – or could – come about not through 'climactic revolution ... but rather a prolonged situation of dual power in the age-old struggle between authoritarian and libertarian tendencies, with outright victory for either tendency most improbable'.[74]

Anarchism has been very much a minority movement-and indeed a much misunderstood and misrepresented ideology and practice – in twentieth-century Britain, on the Left as much as on the Right. But its influence has been considerable, and beneficial, for English radicalism. Its emphases upon the central importance of freedom – of thought and expression, and of political and religious belief – untrammelled by authoritarian interference and control, have been key cultural components of the radical tradition.

Similarly, its insistence that means cannot be separated from ends, and that *actions* are at least as important as theories, has been a salutary reminder of the dangers of many forms of socialist ideologies and movements. And finally, its opposition to the state, in an increasingly collectivist, as well as capitalist corporate, age has been a necessary corrective to the dominant strands of both Marxism and social democracy.

In Nicolas Walter, anarchism had both a profound thinker and theorist, who wrote with accuracy and verve of the tradition of which he was a part; and he was a tireless and courageous activist for the causes and the politics in which he believed.

Notes

1 G. Woodcock, *Anarchism: A History of Libertarian Ideas and Movements* (Harmondsworth: Penguin, 1963; revised editions 1975, 1986), cited in D. Goodway (ed.), *Nicolas Walter: The Anarchist Past and Other Essays* (Nottingham: Five Leaves, 2007), p. 24.
2 N. Walter, *About Anarchism* (Freedom Press, 1969, revised edition, 2002), pp. 29–32.
3 Ibid., p. 37

4   This diversity encompasses, as Goodway notes, the egoism of Max Stirner, the individualism of many American anarchists, the mutualism of Proudhon, the collectivism of Bakunin, the communism of Kropotkin and the revolutionary trade unionism of the syndicalists. D. Goodway, *Anarchist Seeds Beneath the Snow: Left-Libertarian Thought and British Writers from William Morris to Colin Ward* (Liverpool: Liverpool University Press, 2006), p. 3.
5   Ibid.
6   See R. Miliband, *The State in Capitalist Society* (Weidenfeld and Nicolson, 1969).
7   First used by Randolph Bourne, 'The State', in Bourne, *War and the Intellectuals: Essays, 1915–1919* (New York: Torchbooks, 1964), cited in Goodway, *Anarchist Seeds*, pp. 203–4.
8   N. Walter, 'Damned Fools in Utopia', originally published as a pamphlet by Nonviolence 63 (1963), reprinted in D. Goodway (ed.), Nicolas Walter, *Damned Fools in Utopia and Other Writings on Anarchism and War Resistance* (Oakland, CA: PM Press, 2011), p. 40. This contrasts with the view of others discussed in this book, notably Joan Maynard and Tony Benn, that frequently the ends *do* justify the means.
9   A. Comfort, *The Pattern of the Future* (1949), cited in ibid., p. 41.
10 A. Comfort, *Peace and Disobedience* (London: Peace News, 1946), pp. 6–7, cited in Goodway, *Anarchist Seeds*, p. 245.
11 Goodway, *Anarchist Seeds*, p. 6.
12 Ibid., p. 10.
13 Ibid.
14 For details of Nicolas Walter's biography, see Introduction, Goodway (ed.), *Anarchist Past*; see also obituary, Donald Rooum, 'Nicolas Walter', *Guardian*, 13 March 2000.
15 Goodway, *Anarchist Seeds*, p. 9, citing Kingsley Martin, obituary of S.K. Radcliffe, *New Statesman*, September 1958.
16 On the anti-nuclear peace movement in general, see R. Taylor, *Against the Bomb: The British Peace Movement 1958–1965* (Oxford: Clarendon Press, 1988); and on the Committee of 100 specifically, see pp. 190–272.
17 Goodway, *Anarchist Past*, p. 11, citing Walter, 'Postscript, 1979', *Studies in Nonviolent Resistance: Men Against War* (Nonviolence 63, 1963).
18 Goodway, *Anarchist Past*, p. 13.
19 I have personal experience of his reviewing acerbity. As David Goodway has recalled: 'One of the most excoriating reviews I have ever read was Nicolas's demolition in *Peace News* of Richard Taylor's first, co-authored book on the nuclear disarmament movement, *The Protest Makers* (1980).' As Goodway goes on to note, Walter was considerably more generous in his review of *Against the Bomb* (1988), describing it as 'excellent'. Nevertheless, the relevant point is, as Goodway notes, that Walter's criticisms of *The Protest Makers*, were, as I acknowledged, 'entirely justified'. Goodway, *Damned Fools in Utopia*, p. 10.
20 Goodway, *Anarchist Past*, p. 17.
21 Correspondence between the author and Christine Walter (Barrett), Walter's second wife, 9 August 2018.
22 N. Walter, *Facing Death*, BBC World Service Talk, printed in *Freethinker*, July 1996, reprinted in Goodway, *Anarchist Past*, pp. 287–8.
23 Goodway, Introduction, *Anarchist Seeds*, p. 14.

24 However, the ideologically creative, somewhat mysterious Ralph Schoenman, who became Bertrand Russell's secretary, also played a key role, both as an analyst and as a tactician. On Schoenman, see Taylor, *Against the Bomb*, pp. 210–16. The organisation Solidarity (Solidarity for Workers' Power to give the full title), although neither anarchist nor orthodox Trotskyist, also exercised an important role in the Committee of 100 from 1962–63 onwards. Its leading figure was Christopher Pallis. The group was associated with the French movement Socialisme ou Barbarie. Solidarity produced some striking, well-researched and original pamphlets on controversial topics; for example: 'The Kronstadt Commune'; 'Socialism or Barbarism'; 'Paris May '68'; and 'Hungary '56'. On its role in the Committee of 100, see Taylor, *Against the Bomb*, pp. 249–54; and D. Goodway (ed.), *For Workers' Power: The Selected Writings of Maurice Brinton* (Oakland, CA: AK Press, 2004). 'Maurice Brinton' was one of several pseudonyms used by Christopher Pallis. See also Goodway, 'Christopher Pallis', in *Anarchist Seeds*, pp. 288–308.
25 Walter, in Goodway (ed.), *Damned Fools in Utopia*, pp. 25, 29.
26 Ibid., p. 33.
27 Ibid., p. 32.
28 Ibid., p. 56.
29 Ibid., p. 59.
30 Ibid., p. 52.
31 On the DAC, see Taylor, *Against the Bomb*, pp. 115–89.
32 Walter, in Goodway (ed.), *Damned Fools in Utopia*, p.60.
33 On Comfort, see Goodway, *Anarchist Seeds*, chapter 11, pp. 238–59. Walter regarded Comfort as '"the true voice of nuclear disarmament, much more than Bertrand Russell or anyone else"'. Goodway (ed.), Walter, *Anarchist Past*, p. 11, citing Walter, 'Disobedience and the New Pacifism', *Anarchy*, No. 14 (April 1962), p. 112.
34 Comfort, cited in Walter, 'Nonviolent Resistance', in Goodway (ed.), Walter, *Damned Fools in Utopia*, p. 63.
35 Walter, *About Anarchism*, pp. 38–9. However, even some of those sympathetic to anarchism see this position as inherently problematic. John Quail, for example, in his book *The Slow Burning Fuse: The Lost History of British Anarchism* (Paladin Books, 1978), argued that the anarchist movement grows in times of '"popular self-activity, feeds it and feeds off it, and declines when that self-activity declines"'. However, he maintains that there is a paradox because 'anarchists have no strong institutional structure which could ensure permanent survival on its own, but if they had such a structure they would cease to be anarchist'. Walter, 'Community and Commitment: John Quail's *The Slow Burning Fuse*', in Goodway (ed.), Walter, *Anarchist Past*, p. 183.
36 Walter, 'An Autobiographical Note', *Studies in Nonviolence* 5, April 1979, in Goodway (ed.), Walter, *Damned Fools in Utopia*, p. 17. For discussion of the difficulties over strategy and tactics in the Committee of 100, see Taylor, *Against the Bomb*, pp. 282ff.
37 See Walter, 'An Autobiographical Note' for details.
38 Walter, 'Beyond Counting Arses', in Goodway (ed.), *Damned Fools in Utopia*, p. 97.
39 See note 25 above.
40 Goodway (ed.), Introduction, Walter, *Anarchist Past*, p. 12. However, as Goodway notes in his Preface to *Damned Fools in Utopia*, Ruth Walter 'objected strongly to my

describing him at the time of his association with the Solidarity group as a "pacifist". She points out that, while both of them were committed to non-violence as a means to certain ends, they didn't regard it as the only way of attacking the State and hence – unlike the pacifists – see non-violent direct action as "a kind of religion". They both disagreed politically with the pacifists in the Committee of 100 who (like Read) believed property should never be damaged, the Walters advocating instead the use of wire-cutters to cut the fences enclosing airbases' (p. ix).

41 Walter, 'Beyond Counting Arses', p. 98.
42 For detailed discussion of the 'Spies for Peace', see Taylor, *Against the Bomb*, pp. 257–66; *Inside Story* 8, 9, March–April and May–June 1973; Natasha Walter, 'How My Father Spied for Peace', *New Statesman* Essay, 2003; 'The Spies for Peace Story', *Anarchy* 29, No. 3, 1963, pp. 197–229.
43 David Goodway, in conversation with the author, 1 May 2018.
44 'The Spies for Peace Story', p. 197.
45 *Inside Story* 8.
46 'The Spies for Peace Story', p. 202.
47 Walter, 'The RSGs 1919–1963', Solidarity pamphlet 15, 1963.
48 For details of this last phase of activity, see Taylor, *Against the Bomb*, pp. 262–3.
49 These protests included: a further demonstration at Warren Row; the revival of the pirate radio 'Voice of Nuclear Disarmament'; the production of fake US dollars bearing slogans against the Vietnam War; and the Greek Embassy demonstration and occupation in April 1967. For details, see ibid., pp. 263–4.
50 In contrast, the morally inspired Gandhian Direct Action of the DAC struck at least some sort of chord with the ILP/pacifist Left tradition in the labour movement.
51 In Goodway (ed.), Walter, *Damned Fools in Utopia*, p. 28.
52 Ibid.
53 Walter, 'Godwin and Anarchism', *Freedom*, March 1966, reprinted in Goodway (ed.), *Anarchist Past*, p. 49.
54 Walter, *Blasphemy: Ancient and Modern* (Rationalist Press Association, 1990).
55 Walter, *About Anarchism*, p. 42.
56 Walter, *Blasphemy*, p. 14.
57 Walter. *About Anarchism*, p. 43.
58 Ibid.
59 Walter, *Blasphemy*, p. 95.
60 Ibid.
61 D. Martin, Obituary, *New York Times*, 19 March 2000.
62 D. Rooum, Obituary, *Guardian*, 13 March 2000.
63 Walter, 'Kronstadt', *Anarchy*, second series, No. 2, March 1971, reprinted in Goodway (ed.), *Anarchist Past*, p. 153.
64 The Bolsheviks brutally crushed the revolt of the Kronstadt sailors, who had been staunch comrades-in-arms during the Revolution and who were protesting not only at their near-starvation living conditions but also at what they saw as the betrayal of the egalitarian ideals of 1917. On the background to this complex series of events, and for a guide to further reading, see Walter, 'Kronstadt', in Goodway (ed.), *Anarchist Past*. pp. 136–53.

65 Ibid., p. 142.
66 Ibid., p. 152.
67 Ibid., p. 153.
68 This has not been the view of all those within the English radical tradition, however (see note 9 above). The perspective that prioritises 'ends' is encapsulated, at its crudest, in the oft-quoted observation of Stalin, that 'you can't make an omelette without breaking eggs'.
69 Goodway (ed.), Introduction, *Anarchist Seeds*, p. 8.
70 H. Read, *Annals of Innocence and Experience* (Faber and Faber, second edition, 1946), p. 134, cited in ibid.
71 On Colin Ward, see C. Ward and D. Goodway, *Talking Anarchy* (Nottingham: Five Leaves, 2003); K. Warpole, Obituary, Colin Ward, *Guardian*, 22 February 2010; Goodway, *Anarchist Seeds*, Colin Ward, chapter 14, pp. 309–25.
72 C. Ward, *Anarchy in Action* (Allen and Unwin, 1973, second edition, Freedom Press, 1996), p. 137, cited in Ward and Goodway, *Talking Anarchy*, p. 10.
73 Ibid., Ward and Goodway.
74 Ibid., p. 11.

13

A distinctive politics?

By the early twenty-first century, it was clear that, in the Western world, the age of 'the grand narratives' had ended. In the increasingly secular societies of the West (with the partial exception of the USA), religious narratives have little purchase in either philosophical or political contexts. Even less germane to contemporary political culture is orthodox (Marxist-Leninist) communism: virtually no one now adheres to any form of 'vanguardism', at least in its original, Leninist form.

The same cannot be said of liberalism and socialism, the two ideologies which have dominated progressive thought in the West since the later eighteenth century. They have both, however, in different ways and for different reasons, emerged battered, diminished and less confident in their ideological perspectives and assertions, after the challenges, reversals and defeats of recent decades (that is, from the 1970s to the 2010s).

However, it is also the case that capitalist orthodoxies, and their underpinning ideologies, have failed consistently in political as well as in economic terms. Levels of support for established political parties and ideas have decreased markedly in all Western societies; and, correspondingly, cynicism about and disillusion with the 'political class' have increased to levels unprecedented in modern times.

In many ways, this is a difficult context for taking forward the values and practices of English radicalism. These are not 'good times' for the Left. However, in my view, the politics and culture of English radicalism have rarely been more relevant and important for our society. Progressive politics and the established ideologies which have in the past been the vehicles for their articulation are threatened by the prevailing political culture in Britain as elsewhere. The values, strategies and overall approach of the radical tradition, which, as argued throughout this book, both underlie and are wider than the formal organisations of the Left, need to be reasserted vigorously.

This chapter thus recapitulates, briefly, the main themes of the English radical tradition as articulated in the twentieth century, and then addresses the following issues. First, what have been its strategies for political advance: how has the vexed question of 'agency' been addressed? Secondly, how do these perspectives relate to the climate of 'populism' and 'identity politics' in the early twenty-first century? And finally, as we enter the third decade of the twenty-first century, how is English radicalism positioned? and what are the challenges to be faced?

Themes

In Chapter 1 of this book, I argued that the values and beliefs of English radicalism in the twentieth century have centred, first, upon *freedom* – of thought and speech, assembly and personal lifestyle; and, second, upon *equality* – economically and materially, but also politically and socially. These values and beliefs have been buttressed by a belief in 'the common people' and in the priority that must be given to creating and developing an informed, participative and tolerant democracy. For such a democracy to develop and flourish, English radicals have had a strong commitment to justice and the rule of law. At a rather different level, there has been too a commitment to the provision of mass, popular critical education. A politically literate and involved citizenry is a key characteristic of a fully democratic, radically inspired society. There can be no 'short cuts', no bypassing democratic assent, if viable and sustainable radical change is to be secured.

A distinctive element in English radicalism has been the centrality given to extra-parliamentary, popular social movements. This is not to say that involvement in parliamentary and other orthodox institutions has been precluded for all those in this tradition: but it is to emphasise that *popular mobilisation* has always been held to be an essential element in the struggle for radical change.

As these case studies have shown, all those espousing English radicalism have held to these values, to the ethos of extra-parliamentary protest, and, in many instances, to the secularised Nonconformist moral code that underlay them. This politics has been articulated through the formal political process, but the focus has been particularly both upon the generalised struggle for socialist and libertarian change, and upon key 'issue' movements: for peace, for feminism, for anti-colonialism and anti-racism, and for environmentalism. All those leading figures analysed in this book have been involved in one or more of these movements. Similarly, all have been in their various ways ideologically 'English' in their cultural perspective. Yet this 'Englishness' is not straightforward for radicals.

A complex of reasons underlies the increasing unease and confusion over the whole notion of 'Englishness' in the early twenty-first century. First, there remains at the heart of the rhetorical conception of 'Englishness' the idealised *rural* society of pre-industrial times. H.V. Morton's 1927 book *In Search of England*, a popular classic for many years, exemplified this view: '"The village and the English countryside are the germs of all we are and all we have become ... as long as one English field lies against another there is something left in the world to love". Morton saw the agricultural workers as "the salt of the earth" and a kind of well of virtue and character from which the nation received constant refreshment.'[1] Whilst such sentiments find echoes in modern English radicalism – in Joan Maynard's attachment to a very different conception of rural society, for example (Chapter 9) – such a perspective is at heart conservative in nature. Moreover, there is a tension in the persistence of this attachment to a mythologised rural arcadia, in the context of an increasingly urbanised (and suburbanised) society.

Secondly, the decline of the cultural influence of the Church of England has undermined the 'common core of nationhood'.[2] Even more importantly, the virtual demise of the British Empire by the second half of the twentieth century destroyed the perception of a global English national hegemony.[3] This decline has led, arguably, to a 'loss of pride in English nationalism and to anger, ugliness and insularity'.[4]

Thirdly, the increasing disparity between 'the global mega-city of London with its south-eastern hinterland, and almost all other parts of the British Isles' has resulted both in growing support for the national movements in Scotland and Wales, and in tensions within England.[5]

Finally, the culture of 'Englishness' has been defined historically essentially in terms of social class hierarchies and the accompanying class-consciousness which permeates all sections of English society.[6] English radicals have abhorred such class divisions and the inequalities and sense of deference that they have engendered: but, at the same time, they have been uneasy about the shift in the late twentieth and early twenty-first centuries away from class-consciousness and class-based politics. Instead, there has been a foregrounding of a variety of other personal and group characteristics: these include gender, sexual orientation, ethnicity and regional identity. (Both 'populism' and 'identity politics' are discussed below.)

This has presented problems for English radicalism, not least because of the prevalence of nationalistic, xenophobic and populist trends in working-class, as well as middle-class, English culture. This can result, as Margaret Canovan has observed, in the clearly untenable position whereby radicals claim in effect that: '"*We* are in charge of humanity. *We* will consider authorising you to run your own affairs, provided we are convinced that you will do it in our way, not in yours."'[7]

There is thus a tension in English radicalism's proclaimed commitment to the ideals of democracy and a belief in the sanctity of the 'will of the people'; and its realisation that its ideological position is rejected by at least a minority of those whose interests and values it purports to represent. But perhaps this is hardly surprising, given the intense 'class conditioning' that contemporary capitalist culture inculcates.[8]

At all events, it has to be acknowledged that English radicalism's distinctive analysis and prescription necessarily involve taking forward values and policies which, whilst they are supported and embodied by social movements, and to an extent by political parties, of the Left, are frequently at odds with the prevailing culture.

It has thus been an *oppositional* force, while at the same time having at its core many of the values and characteristics of English culture *per se*, as detailed in the case studies which form the main concern of this book.

As has been implicit in the foregoing chapters, it is my belief that English radicalism does indeed constitute both a *distinctive* and an *important* politics. Its discrete components are arguably unexceptional: commitments to each of 'freedom', 'equality', 'secular moralism', 'social movements' and so on can be readily identified in other political formations. But its distinctiveness lies in bringing together the various elements into a coherent whole, resulting in a position which is 'greater than the sum of its parts'.

Whilst the coherence and general characteristics of the tradition in the twentieth century were clear, there remained tensions and conflicts, both theoretical and practical. Not least amongst these have been issues of strategy and 'agency': how best – and legitimately – can the objectives of radical change be achieved? Attention is thus turned to the various strategic positions taken by the leading figures discussed in this book.

Strategies

Those espousing progressive politics in twentieth-century England were confronted by a powerful conservative culture. There are no 'easy' strategies for achieving progressive change in such a context. Right-wing social democrats in Britain (and elsewhere) argued that, in the prolonged, Keynesian-induced postwar period of economic expansion and the accompanying social welfarism, the 'old contradictions' of the capitalist system had been transcended. Theorists such as Anthony Crosland argued that, in part because of the separation of ownership and control, and the linked development of a new, efficient managerialism, Britain and other Western societies were becoming post-capitalist in nature. Thus, persistent, gradual reformism could produce an equitable, civilised, democratic and prosperous society.[9]

This position, which in various forms has dominated Labour Party ideology from the 1950s to the early 2000s, was rejected by all those espousing English radicalism. Those discussed in this book who held to a parliamentarist strategy argued that capitalism, far from being superseded, had become in the twentieth century *more* exploitative and untenable at both national and global levels. (For those who had little faith in the parliamentary road such social democratic arguments were even more strongly rejected.)

English radicals were equally opposed – though for quite other reasons – to revolutionary, insurrectionary strategies. This was so partly on grounds of practicality: given Britain's, and especially England's, long history of relative political and cultural stability, and the failure of communist or other extreme ideologies to gain significant support, politically or philosophically, no such movement had any chance of success in the twentieth century. This became even more apparent after the international collapse of communism in the 1990s. However, such perspectives were also rejected by English radicals on principled grounds. Early in the century, some had been attracted, briefly, to the Communist Party or other revolutionary, or quasi-revolutionary, organisations. But all came to believe in broad terms in the necessity for both democratic, majority support for egalitarian restructuring *and* in 'gradualism' in some form.

Many twentieth-century English radicals – not all of them parliamentarians – have believed in working through the established institutions of the orthodox Left, in particular the trade unions and Parliament, to achieve a radical transformation. They have argued that, through long years of struggle and social, economic and political progress, democratic institutions *have* been established; and they have contrasted this with the clearly undemocratic nature of such institutions in earlier years. In the twentieth century, or at least after universal adult suffrage was attained in 1928, democratic institutions were at least potentially capable of delivering real, radical reform.

However, what distinguishes *all* those espousing English radicalism has been their commitment also to *extra*-parliamentary activism. Even Michael Foot, the ultimate parliamentarian, was an indefatigable Aldermaston Marcher and notable orator at countless political protests over decades; and he acknowledged that: ' "No left MP can be effective if there is no mass opposition outside Parliament" '.[10] The relationship between parliamentary left activism and extra-parliamentary movements relates to the 'classic' problem for left reformists in the Labour Party. As Ralph Miliband and others have argued convincingly,[11] the Party has been dominated by 'parliamentarism' and thus seemingly trapped in a system where the culture, assumptions and accompanying institutions preclude fundamental structural change, or at least make the attainment of such change extremely difficult. Added to this, the powerful economic interests of national, and increasingly international, capital are inherently opposed to such political radicalism. The strategic options for the left-wing MP, committed to the English radical agenda and values, were severely constrained, given that the Party has for most of its existence been dominated by the Right. Either, as with Michael Foot, compromises are made in order to obtain some power and thus purchase upon policy, but at the price of at least a degree of 'incorporation'; or, as with Frank Allaun, Ian Mikardo and many others, political integrity is maintained at the cost of remaining on the backbenches and relatively distant from power and influence. Most if not all have thus acknowledged that parliamentary politics has, for radicals, to be accompanied by a mass extra-parliamentary movement for change, if there is to be any chance of success.

For others within the English radical tradition, established – indeed, establishment – institutions such as Parliament were a part of the *problem* rather than vehicles for achieving radical, structural change. At the most extreme, anarchists like Nicolas Walter saw radical direct action not only as the *means* for attaining meaningful change but as prefiguring the future social structures of a radically reformed society. The 'mainstream' of English radicalism, so to speak, saw extra-parliamentary, popular mass movements as the *central focus* for their politics, whilst not dismissing entirely other, more orthodox, means to take forward progressive change. Bertrand Russell, for example, whilst politically essentially a liberal internationalist, and implicitly accepting in principle the existing institutional structures, nevertheless vehemently advocated civil disobedience in pursuit of what he believed to be the overriding issue of the avoidance of a catastrophic nuclear war in the late 1950s and 1960s. Whilst this danger has by no means disappeared, the ending of the Cold War lessened political tensions. However, a similar sense of international crisis is mounting in the twenty-first century over climate change and general environmental catastrophe. Analogous civil disobedience movements, with similar political justifications of existential urgency, are developing.

Extra-parliamentary mass movements, motivated by moral, progressive concerns, involve direct democracy and, by definition, ensure that the 'common people' are engaged participants in the political process, and can build both the culture and the structures of a reformed social system through their social movement activism. However, as noted, political structures remain elitist and hierarchical, and inequalities of wealth and power persist. In short, the conservative political culture remains dominant. In such a context it is hard, *though never impossible*, for extra-parliamentary movements to make a real and sustained impact.

There are additional problems inherent in seeing such movements as the harbingers of fundamental restructuring. As Frank Parkin demonstrated in his study of the anti-nuclear peace movement,[12] most of these movements attract predominantly middle-class support, and they are concerned with issues of moral (or other) principle. They are, in Parkin's sociological terminology, 'expressive'. In contrast, movements which attract working-class support, tend to be 'instrumental': that is, they centre on demands for a beneficial change in material circumstances for working people. For English radicalism, a tradition which centred its culture and its strategy on the 'common people', and, for some advocates, upon a *socialist* transition, the predominance of *middle-class* activism has clearly constituted a tension, if not an anomaly.

Moreover, such movements are inherently fragile coalitions. Although they can potentially attract support from a wide range of constituencies, their supporters often differ fundamentally on most other ideological questions. Problems arise when ambitious objectives fail to be realised: ideological differences then come to the fore, and such movements often disintegrate, at least temporarily. The history of peace movements, and to an extent of feminist movements too, is illustrative of these problems.

There are also tactical problems with social movement strategies. If 'barricades in the street' and a commitment to violent confrontation are ruled out, as they must be for both practical and principled reasons, for those espousing English radicalism, then such movements are confronted with difficult tactical decisions. Large, peaceful demonstrations can only take the cause forward for a time. Even with radical civil disobedience campaigns, such as those conducted by the Committee of 100 in the early 1960s, there quickly arises the question of 'what next?' Some, such as Ralph Schoenman, advocated an insurrectionary, though non-violent, tactic of 'paralysing the state' through filling the jails with protesters and instigating wholesale, mass non-cooperation with the state and civil authorities.[13] However, few supported such extreme positions, in part because such a perspective was impractical, but also because it was alien to the prevailing political culture.

Of course, an alternative is to pressurise the existing political system: but this too was very often rejected by social movement activists as they argued, as noted, that political parties were a central part of the *problem*, not the potential solution.

There is no single 'silver bullet' solution to this conundrum. The fundamental position for those advocating such change has been, as noted, to *focus* upon social movement activism, but to complement this with a range of other political involvements. For some, this has involved parliamentary or other party political activism; others have concentrated more upon 'civil society' engagement of various sorts. All have advocated using to the full the public forums available in a (relatively) free society for the discussion of political issues: the press and broadcasting media, supplemented in the twenty-first century by social media. If sufficient pressure can be brought to bear through increasing public concern over a specific issue, or series of issues, at least some reformist progress can be made. (Contemporary, twenty-first century examples in England include the partial success of various environmental campaigns: the 'Extinction Rebellion' protests against the growing crisis of global warming and climate change; the anti-fracking protests; and the movements against urban pollution. And, at a different level, the mass protests against Blair's policy on the Iraq war, which played a part in his political demise; and, at the time of writing, the mass protest against the Conservative government's policy on the EU, following the 2016 referendum, which has been one factor in the chaotic politics surrounding this issue in 2016–19.)

The political context for English radicalism in the early twenty-first century has been made considerably more complex because of the rise to prominence, nationally and internationally, of two separate but powerful political phenomena: 'populism' and 'identity politics'. There are good reasons not only to be wary of 'populism' but to question its conceptualisation. The term itself may obscure more than it illuminates. 'Populism' is normally described as 'a strategic approach that frames politics as a battle between the virtuous, "ordinary" masses and a nefarious or corrupt elite'.[14] There is thus a seductive, Manichean tendency in populism, a reductive, binary view of 'good' (the people) versus 'evil' (the elite). 'Populism', of various types, was a constant in politics in the twentieth century (Peronism in Argentina, for example). But what is new in the twenty-first century is its militancy and even more its seeming ubiquity.

Several problems arise, in the context of progressive politics in England, with the populist perspective. First, it is, as noted, binary, simplistic and reductive. Secondly, overwhelmingly it has led to the rise to power, in societies across the world, of grossly reactionary, xenophobic and dangerous leaders – most notably, in the West, Donald Trump, in the USA; but also Erdoğan in Turkey, Orbán in Hungary, Babis in the Czech Republic and many more. Thirdly, it legitimates a series of prejudiced, often racist, sentiments (and actions). Finally, it elides – illegitimately – very different ideologies and political formations.

The root causes of populism have been, first, the manifest failures of capitalism to produce a viable social and economic environment for the mass of the population of any given country. Gross inequalities have been all too apparent. As Chantal Mouffe has argued, in the British context, the finance sector has been overwhelmingly – and disastrously – dominant. Successive governments have pursued an ideological 'slash and burn', neo-liberal policy of savage cuts to the public and welfare sectors, accompanied by privatisation and the 'out-sourcing' of public services. This has led to increasing inequality and real hardship and poverty for large numbers of people – principally the working class and 'the already disadvantaged … but also a significant part of the middle classes, who have become poorer and more insecure'.[15]

Secondly, there has been a growing antipathy towards the 'political class' as a whole: this has been exacerbated by a febrile mass media, both the right-wing red-top press and social media platforms.

The dangers of right-wing populism in this context have been all too obvious; but, tempting though it may be, Chantal Mouffe argues that they cannot be countered simply by 'demonisation', by denouncing the Trumps of this age as quasi-fascists, or as symptoms of 'a kind of moral demise'. For her, the only solution is a 'left populism', not based on the 'Fordist working class' but rather built by creating a 'bond between social movements and a new type of party to create a "people" fighting for equality and social justice', and putting centre stage concerns with sexism, racism and "quality of life" issues'.[16]

'Left populism', defined in this way, has much in common with the social movement politics espoused by English radicalism in the twentieth century, although, for many, such a perspective is erroneous in its cavalier downgrading or even dismissal of 'class politics'. The fundamentals of a (libertarian) Marxist analysis of class relations and class conflict remain as true of twenty-first-century capitalism as they were in the twentieth century.

A different but related issue arises for English radicalism in the form of 'identity politics'. As was discussed in Chapter 10 in the context of Stuart Hall's radicalism, and as was evident in much of 'second wave' feminism, such a politics had a significant place in English radicalism in the later twentieth century. Hall's work in particular has had an influence on the foregrounding of issues of political and social identity– and especially of ethnicity (and the problems of racism in modern Britain) – in the contemporary profile of English radicalism. Whether this is an appropriate development of English radicalism in a new, multicultural context, or a distortion and undermining of the tradition, remains an open question. What is beyond doubt is that such identity considerations have made the definition and articulation of English radicalism in the early twenty-first century both more complex and more multifaceted. Such perspectives have certainly gained increasing traction in the early twenty-first century. James Meek, writing in the *London Review of Books*, has argued that identity politics cannot be dismissed 'as a self-indulgent distraction'. The 'extreme fluidity of capital, cultures and people ... has created today's multi-axis politics' and has led to the foregrounding of race, gender and sexual orientation in radical political culture.[17]

Few if any of the twentieth-century English radicals discussed in this book would dissent from such sentiments, but most would insist that such issues are complementary to the main focuses of concern. Within a capitalist society, based upon structural class divisions, these remain, first, the struggles for achieving the freedoms and equality referred to at the outset, within a framework of radical, secular moral values; and secondly, the creation of a social environment characterised by a humanist, Enlightenment approach, including crucially a tolerance of, and empathy with, a range of political and cultural traditions.

Challenges and prospects

The historical and political roots of English radicalism lie deep in the culture of the society. Its influence and importance have been profound. Its moralism, centred on but not confined to, a secularised Nonconformist Christianity, has given prominence to the social-justice, caring aspects of the Christian moral code, and emphasised the intrinsic equality of all men and women. Originally, such egalitarian, social justice precepts were based upon the Christian, Protestant belief system; in the twentieth century this was replaced, at least implicitly, for most people by a humanist frame of reference.

There has been an evocation of Enlightenment values, including the embracing of the empirical scientific method and the quest for a human-centred, and humanist, pursuit of knowledge in a context of freethinking, rational enquiry. This has been linked to the pragmatism – and a degree of scepticism about 'theory' – that has characterised British culture more generally.

A central theme of this book has been the importance of social movements in the development of English radicalism, and within that the emphasis upon the 'common people' and their potential as agents of social change. Such movements have formed the core, the very essence, of English radicalism in the twentieth century, as has been discussed in all the earlier chapters. This is evidence of the tradition's commitment to democracy – 'no short cuts' to radical objectives – and to (libertarian) anti-elitism. Extra-parliamentary protests continue to be a key part of the democratic process. In Chapter 7, on E.P. Thompson, I cited his observation, made in the context of the upheavals in Eastern Europe from the late 1980s, that 'history is made by the people but it is never subsequently told that way'.[18] Similarly, writing of the huge march on 23 March 2019, demanding a 'People's Vote' (second/third referendum) on the 'Brexit' issue, Tim Adams, in the *Observer*, wrote that 'this march mattered in the simple and fundamental way that mass movements always matter: as a reminder to those who make decisions in their name that democracy is not a settled state, but a shifting expression of collective will'.[19]

There is no doubt, however, that there have also been many problematic areas in twentieth-century English radicalism. The inherent fragility of issue-based social movements has been noted, as have the intractable problems of 'parliamentarism', to use Ralph Miliband's formulation. The question of 'agency', of how democratic, radical change can be achieved, remains a contentious and difficult problem. Closely related to this, issues of 'means and ends' have been approached very differently by those discussed in this book. Left-wing socialists, such as Joan Maynard and Tony Benn, have focused upon 'ends', and have been somewhat cavalier about the 'means' employed to attain their objectives. At the other extreme – and to my mind more persuasively – libertarians and anarchists, such as Nicolas Walter, have argued that 'means' *determine* 'ends'; and that, in the final analysis, 'means' can indeed *become* 'ends'. There has been, within English radicalism, an intellectual and political confusion and incoherence on this central issue.

There are further, general, problems in the tradition. The absence of a clear and cogent theoretical analysis has weakened English radicalism's strategic position; for example, the Labour Left's inability to mount a theoretically robust counter to Crosland's revisionism weakened further its already subordinate position in the Labour Party. In the extra-parliamentary context, the incoherence and fragility of social movements resulted, at least in part, from their confusions over social theory.

There have been tensions too over English radicalism's relationship with questions of national identity and the issue of nationalism. English radicals in the twentieth century have, on the whole, been intensely patriotic: Bertrand Russell, George Orwell, E.P. Thompson, Joan Maynard, Michael Foot and Tony Benn, for example. However, they were all at pains to differentiate sharply between their patriotism and the xenophobic nationalism which has been evident in Britain, both on the Right and in many working-class communities – and indeed in some sections of the labour movement. As Stuart Hall argued convincingly, residual problems of racism, xenophobia and a generally insular perspective have persisted, reflecting in part the post-colonial legacy of Empire.

There has been a series of historical and political conjunctures and issues which have undermined English radicalism's coherence in this area. Since 1945, Britain has in effect 'lost the Empire' but has lived with the cultural aftermath of the 'colonial experience', and its economic and social consequences – not least, the large increase in immigration from former colonies in Asia, Africa and the Caribbean. The chapters on Sylvia Pankhurst, George Orwell, E.P. Thompson and especially Stuart Hall discussed some of these issues. As noted, English radicalism has been far from exempt from insular attitudes and has found it difficult to cope with and adjust to a multicultural, ethnically diverse conception of radicalism.

The continuing, and in some ways increasing, dominance of the Right, culturally as well as politically and economically, is not a weakness of English radicalism *per se*. But it is perhaps the largest single political problem which has to be confronted. To the persisting inequalities in British society exacerbated by several years of 'austerity', has to be added the pervasive, and culturally pernicious, influence of the new social media. The explosion of powerful multinational IT companies has been accompanied by an extension of crass commercialism. Moreover, all this has taken place in a global context where any alternative conceptualisations of social reality often struggle to be heard.

The challenges facing English radicalism in the twenty-first century are thus formidable, as they have been in preceding centuries. But the humanistic, morally based principles of English radicalism survive: and, with future generations being increasingly well-educated and internationally informed, its relevance and purchase upon continuing struggles and campaigns are assured.

Let the closing sentiments be those of William Morris, a great English radical of the nineteenth century, and one of E.P. Thompson's heroes:

> if these hours be dark, as indeed they are, at least do not let us sit deedless, like fools and gentlemen, thinking the common toil not good enough for us, and beaten by the muddle; but rather let us work like good fellows trying by some dim candle-light to set our workshop ready against tomorrow's daylight.[20]

Notes

1 J. Black, *English Nationalism: A Short History* (Hurst and Co., 2018), pp. 128–9.
2 Ibid., p. 142.
3 Ibid., pp. 134ff.
4 B. Maye, Review, *Irish Times*, 13 October 2018.
5 A. Niven, '"Englishness" was never enough to build a nation on', *Guardian*, 20 November 2019.
6 A. Aughey, *The Politics of Englishness* (Manchester: Manchester University Press, 2007), pp. 111ff.
7 M. Canovan, 'Sleeping Dogs, Prowling Cats and Soaring Doves: Three Paradoxes in the Political Theory of Nationhood', *Political Studies* 49, No. 2, p. 209, cited in ibid., p. 113.

8 R. Miliband, *The State in Capitalist Society* (Weidenfeld and Nicolson, 1969), *passim*.
9 See A. Crosland, *The Future of Socialism* (Cape, 1956).
10 M. Foot, 'Credo of the Labour Left', *New Left Review* 49, May–June 1968, p. 27, cited in S. Hannah, *A Party with Socialists in It: A History of the Labour Left* (Pluto Press, 2018), p. 242.
11 R. Miliband, *Parliamentary Socialism* (Merlin Press, second edition, 1973).
12 F. Parkin, *Middle Class Radicalism: The Social Bases of the British Campaign for Nuclear Disarmament* (Manchester: Manchester University Press, 1968).
13 See R. Taylor, *Against the Bomb: The British Peace Movement 1958–1965* (Oxford: Clarendon Press, 1988), pp. 210–16.
14 M. Rice-Oxley and A. Kalia, 'What is populism and why is it such a potent force?', the *Guardian*, 3 December 2018.
15 C. Mouffe, 'Populists are on the rise but this is a moment for progressives too', the *Guardian*, 10 September, 2018.
16 Ibid.
17 J. Meek, Review article on books by Mark Lilla, *London Review of Books*, 30 November 2017. (Meek was referring specifically to the USA, but the point applies more generally to Western societies.)
18 Mary Kaldor, in conversation with the author, 24 May 2012 (see p. 134 above).
19 Tim Adams, the *Observer*, 24 March 2019.
20 William Morris, 'The Art of the People: An Address', 1879. Extract from the text of a lecture delivered by Morris to the Birmingham Society of Arts and School of Design. 19 February, 1879. Published by the Society.

Select bibliography

Original sources – details of interviews, private papers and correspondence, and private or draft research materials – are given in the References to each chapter. What follows here is a listing of the main secondary sources (books and articles) consulted for this study. The place of publication is London unless otherwise stated.

Adams, J. *Tony Benn: A Biography* (Macmillan, 1992; pb. Biteback Publishing, 2011).
Alexander, B. 'George Orwell and Spain', in C. Norris (ed.), *Inside the Myth: Orwell: Views from the Left* (Lawrence and Wishart, 1984).
Anderson, P. *Arguments within English Marxism* (New Left Books and Verso, 1980).
Anderson, P. 'Origins of the Present Crisis', *New Left Review* 23, January–February 1964, reprinted in P. Anderson and R. Blackburn (eds), *Towards Socialism* (Fontana and New Left Books, 1965).
Anderson, P. 'Socialism and Pseudo-Empiricism', *New Left Review* 35, 1966.
Anderson, P. and Blackburn, R. (eds), *Towards Socialism* (Fontana and New Left Books, 1965).
Aughey, A. *The Politics of Englishness* (Manchester: Manchester University Press, 2007).
Bartley, P. *Ellen Wilkinson: From Red Suffragist to Government Minister* (Pluto Press, 2014).
Bartley, P. 'Ellen Wilkinson (Red Ellen): From Suffragist to Government Minister', *Theory and Struggle*, Journal of the Marx Memorial Library, No. 117, 2016.
Beer, S.H. *Modern British Politics* (Faber and Faber, 1965; reprinted, 1971).
Beers, L. *Red Ellen: The Life of Ellen Wilkinson, Socialist, Feminist, Internationalist* (Cambridge, MA: Harvard University Press, 2016).
Benn, T. *Arguments for Democracy* (Cape, 1981; pb. Penguin, 1982).
Benn, T. *Dare to Be a Daniel: Then and Now* (Hutchinson, 2004; pb. Arrow Books, 2005).
Blake, R. *The Conservative Party from Peel to Thatcher* (Fontana Books, 1985).
Bowker, G. *George Orwell* (Little, Brown, 2003).

Brivati, B. (ed.), *The Uncollected Michael Foot* (Politicos, 2003).
Bullock, J. and Pankhurst, R. (eds), *Sylvia Pankhurst: From Artist to Anti-Fascist* (Basingstoke: Macmillan Academic, 1992).
Callaghan, J. *British Trotskyism: Theory and Practice* (Oxford: Blackwell, 1984).
Callaghan, J. 'Engaging with Trotsky: The Influence of Trotskyism in Britain', in E. Smith and M. Worley (eds), *Against the Grain: The British Far Left from 1956* (Manchester: Manchester University Press, 2014).
Ceadel, M. 'The Peace Movement Between the Wars: Problems of Definition', in R. Taylor and N. Young (eds), *Campaigns for Peace: British Peace Movements in the Twentieth Century* (Manchester: Manchester University Press, 1987).
Chase, M. *Chartism: A New History* (Manchester: Manchester University Press, 2007).
Clark, R. *The Life of Bertrand Russell* (Weidenfeld and Nicolson, 1975).
(Sister) S. Clarke, *No Faith in the System* (Cork: Mercier Press, 1995).
Coates, D. *The Labour Party and the Struggle for Socialism* (Cambridge: Cambridge University Press, 1975).
Coates, D. (ed.), *Paving the Way: the Critique of Parliamentary Socialism. A Socialist Register Anthology* (Merlin Press, 2003).
Collini, S. *Absent Minds: Intellectuals in Britain* (Oxford: Oxford University Press, 2006).
Colls, R. *George Orwell: English Rebel* (Oxford: Oxford University Press, 2013).
(Canon) L.J. Collins, *Faith Under Fire* (Leslie Frewin, 1966).
Connelly, K. *Sylvia Pankhurst: Suffragist, Socialist and Scourge of Empire* (Pluto Press, 2013).
Conradi, P. *A Very English Hero: The Making of Frank Thompson* (Bloomsbury, 2012).
Crick, B. *George Orwell: A Life* (Secker and Warburg, 1980; pb. Penguin, 1982).
Crick, B. (ed. and Introduction), *Orwell: Essays* (Penguin, 1994).
Croft, A. (ed.), *After the Party: Reflections on Life Since the CPGB* (Lawrence and Wishart, 2012).
Davis, M. *Sylvia Pankhurst: A Life in Radical Politics* (Pluto Press, 1999).
Derry, J.W. *The Radical Tradition: Tom Paine to Lloyd George* (Macmillan, 1967).
Dodd, K. (ed.), *A Sylvia Pankhurst Reader* (Manchester: Manchester University Press, 1993).
Duff, P. *Left, Left, Left* (Allison and Busby, 1971).
Dworkin, D. *Cultural Marxism: History, the New Left and the Origins of Cultural Studies* (Durham, NC, and London: Duke University Press, 1997).
Eagleton, T. 'The Hippest', *London Review of Books* 18, No. 5, 7 March 1996.
Eagleton, T. *The Illusions of Postmodernism* (Oxford: Blackwell, 1996).
Eagleton, T. *Figures of Dissent* (Verso, 2003).
Efstathiou, C. *E.P. Thompson: A Twentieth-Century Romantic* (Merlin Press, 2015).
Eglin, J. 'Women and Peace: From the Suffragists to the Greenham Women', in R. Taylor and N. Young (eds), *Campaigns for Peace: British Peace Movements in the Twentieth Century* (Manchester: Manchester University Press, 1987).
Egner, R. and Dennon, L. (eds), *The Basic Writings of Bertrand Russell 1903–1959* (Allen and Unwin, 1961).
Fieldhouse, R. *A History of Modern British Adult Education* (Leicester: NIACE, 1996).
Fieldhouse, R. and Taylor, R. (eds), *E.P. Thompson and English Radicalism* (Manchester: Manchester University Press, 2013).

Fieldhouse, R. 'Thompson: The Adult Educator', in R. Fieldhouse and R. Taylor (eds), *E.P. Thompson and English Radicalism* (Manchester: Manchester University Press, 2013).

Fieldhouse, R., T. Koditschek and R. Taylor, 'E.P. Thompson: A Short Introduction', in R. Fieldhouse and R. Taylor (eds), *E.P. Thompson and English Radicalism* (Manchester: Manchester University Press, 2013).

Foot, M. *Debts of Honour* (Davies-Poynter, 1980).

Foot, M. *Loyalists and Loners* (Collins, 1986).

Foot, M. *Aneurin Bevan*, 2 volumes (MacGibbon and Kee, 1962; Davies-Poynter, 1973).

Foot, M. 'Credo of the Labour Left', *New Left Review* 49, May–June 1968.

Foot, M. and Jones, M. *Guilty Men, 1957: Suez and Cyprus* (Gollancz, 1957).

Fryer, P. *Staying Power: The History of Black People in Britain* (1984; new edition, Pluto Press, 2018).

Goldman, L. *Dons and Workers: Oxford and Adult Education Since 1850* (Oxford: Oxford University Press, 1995).

Goodway, D. (ed.), *For Workers' Power: The Selected Writings of Maurice Brinton* (Oakland, CA: AK Press, 2004).

Goodway, D. *Anarchist Seeds Beneath the Snow: Left-Libertarian Thought and British Writers from William Morris to Colin Ward* (Liverpool: Liverpool University Press, 2006).

Goodway, D. 'The Spanish Civil War – The Case of George Orwell', in D. Goodway, *Anarchist Seeds Beneath the Snow: Left-Libertarian Thought and British Writers from William Morris to Colin Ward* (Liverpool: Liverpool University Press, 2006).

Goodway, D. 'Christopher Pallis', in D. Goodway, *Anarchist Seeds Beneath the Snow: Left-Libertarian Thought and British Writers from William Morris to Colin Ward* (Liverpool: Liverpool University Press, 2006).

Goodway, D. (ed.), *Nicolas Walter: The Anarchist Past and Other Essays* (Nottingham: Five Leaves, 2007).

Goodway, D. (ed.), *Nicolas Walter: Damned Fools in Utopia and Other Writings on Anarchism and War Resistance* (Oakland, CA: PM Press, 2011).

Hall, S. 'A Sense of Classlessness', *Universities and Left Review* 5, Autumn 1958.

Hall, S. 'The Big Swipe', *Universities and Left Review* 7, Autumn 1959.

Hall, S. 'NATO and the Alliances', CND Pamphlet, Spring 1960.

Hall, S. 'Conjuring Leviathan: Orwell on the State', in C. Norris (ed.), *Inside the Myth: Orwell: Views from the Left* (Lawrence and Wishart, 1984).

Hall, S. *The Hard Road to Renewal* (Verso, 1988).

Hall, S. 'The "First" New Left: Life and Times', in Oxford University Socialist Discussion Group (eds), *Out of Apathy, Voices of the New Left 30 Years On* (Verso, 1989).

Hall, S. 'New Ethnicities' (1987), in D. Morley and K. Chen (eds), *Stuart Hall: Critical Dialogues in Cultural Studies*, 1996.

Hall, S. 'Politics, Contingency, Strategy', *Small Axe* 1, 1996.

Hall, S. 'Subjects in History: Making Diasporic Identities', in W. Lubiano (ed.), *The House that Race Built: Black Americans, US Terrain* (New York: Pantheon Books, 1997).

Hall, S. 'Old and New Identities, Old and New Ethnicities', in L. Black and J. Solomos (eds), *Theories of Race and Racism* (London and New York: Routledge, 2000).

Hall, S. 'Epilogue: Through the Prism of an intellectual Life', in B. Meeks (ed.), *Culture,*

Politics, Race and Diaspora: The Thought of Stuart Hall (Jamaica and London: Ian Randle Publishing and Lawrence and Wishart, 2007).

Hall, S. with Schwarz, B. *Familiar Stranger: A Life Between Two Islands* (Milton Keynes: Allen Lane, 2017).

Hamilton, S. *The Crisis of Theory: E.P. Thompson, the New Left and Post-War British Politics* (Manchester: Manchester University Press, 2011).

Hannah, S. *A Party with Socialists in It: A History of the Labour Left* (Pluto Press, 2018).

Harrison, J. *Early Victorian Britain* (Fontana Books, 1979).

Harrison, S. *Sylvia Pankhurst: A Maverick Life 1882–1960* (Arun Press, 2003).

Healey, D. *The Time of My Life* (Michael Joseph, 1989).

Highet, A. with Foot, M. *Isaac Foot: A West Country Boy - Apostle of England* (Politicos, 2006).

Hinton, J. *Labour and Socialism: A History of the British Labour Movement 1867–1914* (Brighton: Wheatsheaf Books, 1983).

Hinton, J. *Protests and Visions: Peace Politics in Twentieth-Century Britain* (Hutchinson Radius, 1989).

Hinden, R. (ed.), *The Radical Tradition, Twelve Essays on Politics, Education and Literature* (Allen and Unwin, 1964).

Hitchens, C. *Why Orwell Matters* (New York: Basic Books, 2002).

Hobsbawm, E. *Interesting Times: A Twentieth-Century Life* (Allen Lane, 2002; pb. Abacus, 2003).

Hoggart, R. *The Uses of Literacy* (Chatto and Windus, 1957; pb. Pelican, 1958).

Hollis, P. *Jennie Lee – A Life* (Oxford: Oxford University Press, 1997).

Holton, S. *Feminism and Democracy: Women's Suffrage and Reform Politics in Britain, 1900–1918* (Cambridge: Cambridge University Press, 1986).

Holton, S. 'In Soulful Wrath: Suffrage and Militancy and the Romantic Feminism of Emmeline Pankhurst', in H. Smith (ed.), *British Feminism in the Twentieth Century* (Aldershot: Edward Elgar, 1990).

Holton, S. 'The Making of Suffrage History', in J. Purvis and S. Holton (eds), *Votes for Women* (New York and London: Routledge, 2000).

hooks, b. and hall, S. *Uncut Funk: A Contemplative Dialogue* (London and New York: Routledge, 2018).

Ingle, S. 'A Note on Orwellism', *Political Studies*, xxviii, No. 4, December 1980.

Jacob, A. 'Sharing Orwell's "Joys" – But Not His Fears', in C. Norris (ed.), *Inside the Myth, Orwell: Views from the Left* (Lawrence and Wishart, 1984).

Jenkins, P. 'Post-Bourgeois Man', Review of Tony Benn, *Arguments for Democracy* and *Manifesto, London Review of Books*, 1 October 1981.

Jones, M. *Michael Foot* (Gollancz, 1994).

Kaye, H.J. *The British Marxist Historians* (Cambridge: Polity Press, 1984).

Kingsley Kent, S. 'Gender Reconstruction after the First World War', in H. Smith (ed.), *British Feminism in the Twentieth Century* (Aldershot: Edward Elgar, 1990).

Koditschek, T. 'The Possibilities of Theory: Thompson's History', in R. Fieldhouse and R. Taylor (eds), *E.P. Thompson and English Radicalism* (Manchester: Manchester University Press, 2013).

Liddington, J. *Respectable Rebel: The Life and Times of Selina Cooper 1864–1946* (Virago, 1984).

Liddington, J. and Norris, J. *One Hand Tied Behind Us: The Rise of the Women's Suffrage Movement* (Virago, 1978).
Maccoby, S. *The English Radical Tradition 1763–1914* (Allen and Unwin, 1957).
Maccoby, S. *English Radicalism: The End?* (Allen and Unwin, 1961).
McIlroy, J. 'Another Look at E.P. Thompson and British Communism, 1937–1955', *Labor History* (on-line journal), 26 June 2017.
Martin, D. and Rubinstein, D. (eds), *Ideology and the Labour Movement* (Croom Helm, 1979).
Maynard, J. (ed.), *A Hundred Years of Farmworkers' Struggle* (Nottingham: Institute for Workers' Control, n.d., c.1974).
Meehan, G. 'British Feminism from the 1960s to the 1980s', in H. Smith (ed.), *British Feminism in the Twentieth Century* (Aldershot: Edward Elgar, 1990).
Meek, J. Review article on books by Mark Lilla, *London Review of Books* 39, No. 23, 30 November 2017.
Meeks B. (ed.), *Culture, Politics, Race and Diaspora: The Thought of Stuart Hall* (Jamaica and London: Ian Randle Publishers and Lawrence and Wishart, 2007).
Meeks, B. 'Introduction: The Return of the Native Son', in B. Meeks (ed.), *Culture, Politics, Race and Diaspora: The Thought of Stuart Hall* (Jamaica and London: Ian Randle Publishers and Lawrence and Wishart, 2007).
Meyers, J. *A Reader's Guide to George Orwell* (Thames and Hudson, 1975).
Miliband, R. *The State in Capitalist Society* (Weidenfeld and Nicolson, 1969).
Miliband, R. *Parliamentary Socialism: A Study in the Politics of Labour* (second edition, Merlin Press, 1973).
Miliband, R. 'The New Revisionism in Britain', *New Left Review* 150, March–April 1985.
Mills, C.W. 'Hall's Changing Representations of Race', in B. Meeks (ed.), *Culture, Politics, Race and Diaspora: The Thought of Stuart Hall* (Jamaica and London: Ian Randle Publishers and Lawrence and Wishart, 2007).
Moorehead, C. *Bertrand Russell: A Life* (Sinclair and Stevenson, 1992).
Morgan, K. *Labour in Power 1945–1951* (Oxford: Oxford University Press, 1984).
Morgan, K. *Labour People: Leaders and Lieutenants, Hardie to Kinnock* (Oxford: Oxford University Press, 1987).
Morgan, K. *Michael Foot: A Life* (Harper Press, 2007).
Morley, D. and Chen, K.-H. (eds), *Stuart Hall: Critical Dialogues in Cultural Studies* (Routledge, 1996).
Mouffe, C. 'Populists are on the rise but this is a moment for progressives too', *Guardian*, 10 September 2018.
Nairn, T. 'The Nature of the Labour Party', in P. Anderson and R. Blackburn (eds), *Towards Socialism* (Fontana and New Left Books, 1965).
Newman, M. *Ralph Miliband and the Politics of the New Left* (Merlin Press, 2002).
Newman, M. 'Thompson and the Early New Left', in R. Fieldhouse and R. Taylor (eds), *E.P. Thompson and English Radicalism* (Manchester: Manchester University Press, 2013).
Norris, C. (ed.), *Inside the Myth: Orwell: Views from the Left* (Lawrence and Wishart, 1984).
O'Connor, K.M. *Joan Maynard: Passionate Socialist* (Politicos, 2003).
Orwell, G. *Down and Out in Paris and London* (Gollancz, 1933).
Orwell, G. *Burmese Days* (Gollancz, 1934).

Orwell, G. *The Road to Wigan Pier* (Gollancz, 1937).
Orwell, G. *Homage to Catalonia* (Secker and Warburg, 1937).
Orwell, G. *Coming Up for Air* (Gollancz, 1939).
Orwell, G. *Animal Farm* (Secker and Warburg, 1945).
Orwell, G. 'Anti-Semitism in Britain', *Contemporary Jewish Record*, April 1945.
Orwell, G. 'Politics and the English Language', *Horizon*, 1946, reprinted in B. Crick (ed.), *Orwell: Essays* (Penguin, 1994).
Orwell, G. 'The Prevention of Literature', *Polemic*, No. 2, January 1946, reprinted in B. Crick (ed.), *Orwell: Essays* (Penguin, 1994).
Orwell, G. 'Why I Write', *Gangrel*, No. 4, Summer 1946, reprinted in B. Crick (ed.), *Orwell: Essays* (Penguin, 1994).
Orwell, G. *The English People* (Collins, 1947).
Orwell, G. *Nineteen Eighty-Four* (Secker and Warburg, 1949).
Orwell, G. *The Collected Essays, Journalism and Letters of George Orwell*, 4 volumes, edited by S. Orwell and I. Angus (Penguin, 1968).
Orwell, G. 'The Lion and the Unicorn: Socialism and the English Genius', reprinted in B. Crick (ed.), *Orwell: Essays* (Penguin, 1994).
Oxford University Socialist Discussion Group (eds), *Out of Apathy: Voices of the New Left 30 Years On* (Verso, 1989).
Palmer, B. *E.P. Thompson: Objections and Oppositions* (Verso, 1994).
Parkin, F. *Middle Class Radicalism: The Social Bases of the British Campaign for Nuclear Disarmament* (Manchester: Manchester University Press, 1968).
Perry, M. *'Red Ellen' Wilkinson: Her Ideas, Movements and World* (Manchester: Manchester University Press, 2014).
Pierson, S. *Marxism and the Origins of British Socialism: The Struggle for a New Consciousness* (Ithaca, NY, and London: Cornell University Press, 1973).
Priestley, J.B. 'Britain and the Nuclear Bombs', *New Statesman*, 2 November 1957.
Pugh, M. 'Domesticity and the Decline of Feminism', in H. Smith (ed.), *British Feminism in the Twentieth Century* (Aldershot: Edward Elgar, 1990).
Pugh, M. *The March of the Women: A Revisionist Analysis of the Campaign for Women's Suffrage, 1866–1914* (Oxford: Oxford University Press, 2000).
Purvis, J. and Holton, S. (eds.), *Votes for Women* (New York and London: Routledge, 2000).
Quail, J. *The Slow Burning Fuse: The Lost History of British Anarchism* (Paladin Books, 1978).
Rice-Oxley, M. and Kalia, A. 'What is populism and why is it such a potent force?', *Guardian*, 3 December 2018.
Richards, V. 'Orwell the Humanist', in Freedom Press, *Orwell at Home (and among the Anarchists)* (Freedom Press, 1998).
Ricks, T. *Churchill and Orwell: The Fight for Freedom* (Duckworth, 2018).
Rojek, C. *Stuart Hall* (Cambridge: Polity Press, 2003).
Rose, J. *The Intellectual Life of the British Working Classes* (New Haven, CT, and London: Yale University Press, 2003).
Rowbotham, S. 'The Women's Movement and Organizing for Socialism', in S. Rowbotham, L. Segal and H. Wainwright (eds), *Beyond the Fragments: Feminism and the Making of Socialism* (Merlin Press, 1979).

Rowbotham, S. 'Foreword', in B. Winslow, *Sylvia Pankhurst: Sexual Politics and Political Activism* (UCL Press, 1996).
Russell, B. *The Practice and Theory of Bolshevism*, 1920 (reprinted, Allen and Unwin, 1962).
Russell, B. *What I Believe*, 1925; (new edition, Routledge Classics, 2004).
Russell, B. *Education and the Social Order* (Allen and Unwin, 1931).
Russell, B. *The Autobiography of Bertrand Russell*, 3 volumes (Allen and Unwin, 1967. 1968, 1969).
Rustin, R. ' "Working from the Symptom": Stuart Hall's Political Writing', in B. Meeks (ed.), *Culture, Politics, Race and Diaspora: The Thought of Stuart Hall* (Kingston and London: Ian Randle Publishers and Lawrence and Wishart, 2007).
Ryan, A. *Bertrand Russell: A Political Life* (New York and London: Hill and Wang; Penguin, 1988).
Samuel, R. 'Class and Class Consciousness', *Universities and Left Review* 6, Spring 1959.
Saville, J. 'The Communist Experience: A Personal Appraisal', in R. Miliband and L. Panitch (eds), *Socialist Register 1991* (Merlin Press, 1991).
Saville, J. 'Edward Thompson, the Communist Party and 1956', in R. Miliband and L. Panitch (eds), *Socialist Register 1994* (Merlin Press, 1994).
Schoenman R. (ed.), *Bertrand Russell: Philosopher of the Century* (Allen and Unwin, 1967).
Schwarzmantel, J. *Gramsci's Prison Notebooks* (Abingdon: Routledge, 2015).
Scott, D. *Stuart Hall's Voice: Intimations of an Ethics of Receptive Generosity* (Durham, NC: Duke University Press, 2017).
Sedgwick, P. 'The Two New Lefts', in D. Widgery (ed.), *The Left in Britain 1956–1968* (Pelican, 1968).
Sedgwick, P. 'George Orwell: International Socialist: The Development of Orwell's Socialism', *International Socialism Journal*, 1969.
Shaw, M. 'War, Peace and British Marxism 1895–1945', in R. Taylor and N. Young (eds), *Campaigns for Peace: British Peace Movements in the Twentieth Century* (Manchester: Manchester University Press, 1987).
Shelden, M. *Orwell: The Authorised Biography* (Heinemann, 1991).
A. Sked and C. Cook, *Post-War Britain: A Political History* (Penguin, 1979).
Soper, K. 'Thompson and SocialistHumanism', in R. Fieldhouse and R. Taylor (eds), *E.P. Thompson and English Radicalism* (Manchester: Manchester University Press, 2013).
'The Spies for Peace Story', *Anarchy* 29, No. 3, 1963.
P. Stansky and W. Abrahams, *The Unknown Orwell* (Constable, 1972).
Steele, T. *The Emergence of Cultural Studies 1945–65: Cultural Politics, Adult Education and the 'English Question'* (Lawrence and Wishart, 1997).
Stradling, R. 'Orwell and the Spanish Civil War', in C. Norris (ed.), *Inside the Myth: Orwell: Views from the Left* (Lawrence and Wishart, 1984).
Tawney, R.H. 'British Socialism Today', *Socialist Commentary*, June 1952.
Taylor, D.J. *Orwell: The Life* (Chatto and Windus, 2003).
Taylor, R. 'CND and the 1983 Election', in I. Crewe and M. Harrop (eds), *Political Communications: The General Election Campaign of 1983* (Cambridge: Cambridge University Press, 1986).
Taylor, R. *Against the Bomb: The British Peace Movement 1958–1965* (Oxford: Clarendon Press, 1988).

Taylor, R. 'Thompson and the Peace Movement: From CND in the 1950s and 1960s to END in the 1980s', in R. Fieldhouse and R. Taylor (eds), *E.P. Thompson and English Radicalism* (Manchester: Manchester University Press, 2013).

Taylor, R. and Steele, T. *British Labour and Higher Education 1945–2000: Ideologies, Policies and Practice* (Continuum Studies in Educational Research, 2011).

Taylor, R. and Young, N. (eds), *Campaigns for Peace: British Peace Movements in the Twentieth Century* (Manchester: Manchester University Press, 1987).

Tholfsen, T. *Working Class Radicalism in Mid-Victorian England* (Croom Helm, 1976).

Thompson, E.P. *William Morris: Romantic to Revolutionary* (Lawrence and Wishart, 1955; second revised edition, Merlin Press, 1977).

Thompson, E.P. 'Commitment in Politics', *Universities and Left Review* 6, Spring 1959.

Thompson, E.P. (ed.), *Out of Apathy* (Stevens and Sons, 1960).

Thompson, E.P. 'Outside the Whale', in Thompson (ed.), *Out of Apathy* (Stevens and Sons, 1960; reprinted in Thompson, *The Poverty of Theory and Other Essays* (Merlin Press, 1978).

Thompson, E.P. *The Making of the English Working Class* (Gollancz, 1963; Pelican Books, 1968).

Thompson, E.P. 'The Peculiarities of the English', in R. Miliband and J. Saville (eds), *Socialist Register 1965* (Merlin Press, 1965); reprinted in Thompson, *The Poverty of Theory and Other Essays* (Merlin Press, 1978).

Thompson, E.P. *Warwick University Ltd.* (Penguin, 1970).

Thompson, E.P. *The Poverty of Theory and Other Essays* (Merlin Press, 1978).

Thompson, E.P. 'The Poverty of Theory', in Thompson, *The Poverty of Theory and Other Essays* (Merlin Press, 1978).

Thompson, E.P. *Protest and Survive* (Nottingham: Spokesman Pamphlets 71, CND and BRPF, 1980).

Thompson, E.P. 'Notes on Exterminism, the last Stage of Civilisation', *New Left Review* 121, May–June 1980; reprinted in Thompson, *Zero Option* (Merlin Press, 1982).

Thompson, E.P. 'Beyond the Cold War', Lecture, 1981; reprinted by END 1982.

Thompson, E.P. *Exterminism and Cold War* (Verso and New Left Books, 1982).

Thompson, E.P. *Zero Option* (Merlin Press, 1982).

Thompson, E.P. *The Heavy Dancers* (Merlin Press, 1985).

Thompson, E.P. *Writing by Candlelight* (Merlin Press, 1980).

Thompson, E.P. *Persons and Polemics* (Merlin Press, 1994).

Thompson, E.P. *Beyond the Frontier: The Politics of a Failed Mission* (London and Stanford, CA: Merlin Press and Stanford University Press, 1997).

Tombs, R. *The English and Their History* (Allen Lane, 2014).

Vallance, E. *A Radical History of Britain* (Little, Brown, 2009; pb. Abacus, 2010).

Vernon, B. *Ellen Wilkinson 1891–1947* (Croom Helm, 1982).

Walter, Natasha, 'How My Father Spied for Peace', *New Statesman* Essay, 2003.

Walter, Nicolas, *About Anarchism* (Freedom Press, 1969; revised edition, 2002).

Walter, Nicolas, *Blasphemy: Ancient and Modern* (Rationalist Press Association, 1990).

Walter, Nicolas, 'Postscript, 1979', *Studies in Nonviolent Resistance: Men Against War, Nonviolence* 63, 1963; reprinted in Goodway, *Anarchist Past*. (For both N. Walter, *Anarchist Past*, and N. Walter, *Damned Fools in Utopia and Other Essays*, see D. Goodway (ed.).)

Walter, Nicolas, 'Orwell and Anarchism', in Freedom Press, *George Orwell at Home (and among the Anarchists)* (Freedom Press, 1998).
Walter, Nicolas, *The RSGs 1919–1963*, Solidarity pamphlet 15, 1963.
Walter, Nicolas, 'Kronstadt', *Anarchy* second series, No. 2, March 1971; reprinted in Goodway, *Anarchist Past*.
Walter, Nicolas, 'Disobedience and the New Pacifism', *Anarchy*, No. 14, April 1962; reprinted in Goodway, *Anarchist Past*.
Walter, Nicolas, 'Facing Death', BBC World Service talk, reprinted in Goodway, *Anarchist Past*.
Ward, C. *Anarchy in Action* (Allen and Unwin, 1973; second edition, Freedom Press, 1996).
Ward, C. 'Orwell and Anarchism', in Freedom Press, *George Orwell at Home (and among the Anarchists)* (Freedom Press, 1998).
Ward, C. and Goodway, D. *Talking Anarchy* (Nottingham: Five Leaves, 2003).
Ward, K. and Taylor R. (eds), *Adult Education and the Working Class: Education for the Missing Millions* (Croom Helm, 1986; second edition Routledge, 2012).
Watson, G. *The English Ideology: Studies in the Language of Victorian Politics* (Allen Lane, 1973).
Webb, R. *Modern England from the Eighteenth Century to the Present* (Allen and Unwin, 1969).
Widgery D. (ed.), *The Left in Britain 1956–1968* (Pelican, 1968).
Wilkinson, E. *The Town that Was Murdered: The Life Story of Jarrow* (Left Book Club, Gollancz, 1939).
Williams, R. *Orwell* (Fontana Modern Masters, 1971).
Williams, R. *Keywords: A Vocabulary of Culture and Society* (Fontana Books, 1976; second edition, Flamingo, 1983).
Winslow, B. *Sylvia Pankhurst: Sexual Politics and Political Activism* (UCL Press, 1996).
Winstone R. (ed.), *The Best of Benn: Speeches, Diaries, Letters and Other Writings* (Hutchinson, 2014; pb. Arrow Books, 2015).
Wood, A. *Bertrand Russell: The Passionate Sceptic* (Allen and Unwin, 1961).
Woodcock, G. *The Crystal Spirit* (Cape, 1969).
Woodcock, G. *Anarchism: A History of Libertarian Ideas and Movements* (Harmondsworth: Penguin, 1963; revised editions, 1975, 1986).
Young, N. 'War Resistance and the British Peace Movement Since 1914', in R. Taylor and N. Young (eds), *Campaigns for Peace: British Peace Movements in the Twentieth Century* (Manchester: Manchester University Press, 1987).

Index

Acland (Sir) Richard 31, 172–3, 212
adult education 77, 90, 121–3, 166, 174, 196, 201
   see also Leeds, University of; National Council of Labour Colleges; Workers' Educational Association
agnostics/agnosticism 3, 22, 41–3, 210–11
Aldermaston March 31–2, 154, 191–2, 235, 237, 251
Allaun, F. 166, 251
Allen, C. 28–9, 45, 77
anarchism/anarchists 7, 11, 47–8, 82–3, 106, 230–42
Anderson, P. 10, 119, 126, 128, 130–1, 135, 191
Asquith, H.H. 62, 71
atheism/atheists 3, 22, 41–3, 239–40
Attlee, C.R. 65, 75, 87–9, 148, 150

Beaverbrook (Lord) Max 145–9, 155
Beers, L. 80–1, 88
Benn, C. (née Caroline Middleton de Camp) 208–10, 222
Benn, H. 210, 222
Benn, M. (née Holmes) 208–9
Benn, T. Chapter 11 *passim*, 7–8, 10–11, 84, 176, 256
   communicator 207, 210–13, 215, 222–3, 225
   Nonconformism 3–4, 208, 210–11
   renunciation of peerage 214
Benn (Lord Stansgate) W. 208–9, 214
Bertrand Russell Peace Foundation (BRPF) 49–50, 132–4
Betts, B. *see* Castle, B.
Bevan, A. 7, 9, 89, 98, 144, 146–9
Bevin, E. 148, 150
Blair, E. *see* Orwell, G.
Blair, T. 161, 215

British Broadcasting Corporation (BBC) 9, 70, 100, 199, 210–12, 234, 237
British Socialist Party (BSP) 29, 65
Brocklebank, J. 170, 173

Callaghan, J. 157–8, 218–20
Cambridge University 121
Campaign for Nuclear Disarmament (CND) 31–3, 47–8, 128–32, 150, 152, 191–3, 201, 212, 214, 221, 233, 235
Castle, B. 58, 142
Catholic/Catholicism *see* Roman Catholic/Roman Catholicism
Chartism 20
Christian/Christianity 3–4, 22, 28, 41–3, 109–11, 167–8, 208, 210–11, 239–40, 255
Churchill (Sir) Winston 67, 83, 87–8, 92
Coates, K. 132–4
Cobbett, W. 166, 172
Collins (Canon) L.J. 47–8, 150, 193
Comfort, A. 230, 232, 235
Committee of 100 32, 47–8, 233–9
Common Wealth Party 31, 172–3
Communist Party of Great Britain (CPGB/CP) 56–7, 65–7, 77–9, 100, 118–20, 123–8, 168, 188–9
Corbyn, J. 176–8, 180, 220, 224
Corio, S. 65, 67–8, 70
Craigie, J. 147, 149, 153, 160
Crick, B. 97, 100, 103, 106–7, 111–12
Cripps, S. 144, 151
Croft, A. 125, 135
Crosland, C.A.R. 4–5, 250
Crossman, R.H.S. 215

Daily Worker/Morning Star 168, 175, 237
Dalton, H. 148, 212, 215
Dalyell, T. 172, 181
Democratic Federation *see* Social Democratic Federation (SDF)
Diggers 16, 172, 209, 230
Direct Action Committee (DAC) 32, 47, 235
Dissenters *see* Nonconformism
Duff, P. 48, 150, 193, 237

Eagleton, T. 194, 201
East London Federation/East London Federation of Suffragettes (ELFS) 61–4
Emergency Committee for Direct Action *see* Direct Action Committee (DAC)
Ethiopia 63, 68–70
European Nuclear Disarmament (END) 32, 118–19, 124, 132–4
European Union (EU)/ European Economic Community (EEC) 160–1, 216–18, 253
Extramural *see* adult education

Falklands War 159, 199, 221
feminism/feminists 23–7, Chapter 4 *passim*, 75–6, 80–2, 180–1
Fieldhouse, R. 172, 174, 181–2
Foot, I. 142–3, 149, 155
Foot, M. Chapter 8 *passim*, 3–4, 7, 11, 21–2, 32–3, 213, 217, , 223–4
Freedom, anarchist newspaper 233, 238

Gaitskell, H. 32, 150–1, 160, 174, 212–14, 223
Gandhi, M.K./Gandhian 45, 47–8, 120, 235
Goodway, D. 10, 106, 119, 135, 230–1, 234, 241
Gramsci, A./Gramscian 195, 198–9
Guild Socialism 40, 50, 75, 77–9

Hall, C. (née Barrett) 185, 190–1
Hall, S. Chapter 10 *passim*
  colonialism/anti-colonialism 8–9, 185–8, 196–8
  cultural studies 193–8
  CND and New Left 131, 185–6, 188–93
  Thatcherism 198–200
Hardie, K. 29, 57–8, 63, 71
Healey, D. 156–9, 220
Hinton, J. 31–3
Hitchens, C. 100, 104, 108, 111
Hobsbawm, E. 134–5, 198
Holton, S. 23–4, 56

'identity politics' 254–5
Independent Labour Party (ILP) 21, 27–9, 57–9, 65, 75, 84, 93, 103, 107
Independent Nuclear Disarmament Election Committee (INDEC) 154
Institute for Workers' Control (IWC) 21, 171
Ireland (Republic of) 8, 176–8

Jarrow/Jarrow March 8, 80, 84–6
Jones, M. 156, 218

Kaldor, M. 133–4
Kirwan, C. 111–12
Koestler, A. 110–11, 125
Kronstadt uprising 240–1

land nationalisation 16, 172
Leeds, University of 121–3, 166, 174
Levellers 16, 172, 209

McGuigan, J. 196, 200
McIlroy, J. 124–8
Magna Carta 14–15, 17
Marx/Marxism 3, 5, 26–7, 29–30, 37, 39–40, 119, 123–9, 144, 187–91
Marxism Today 198, 200
Maynard, J. Chapter 9 *passim*
  feminism 180–1
  Ireland 176–8
  Parliament 175–6, 179
  religion 167, 180–1
  rural interests 166–76, 249
Miliband, R. 7, 10, 22, 135, 175, 200–1, 226, 251, 256
Morgan, K.O. 76, 142, 147, 224
Morris, W. 122, 126–7, 230, 257
Mouffe, C. 254
Mullin, C. 173, 177–8,182

National Council of Labour Colleges (NCLC) 77, 90
National Union of Agricultural (and Allied) Workers' Union (NUAW/NUAAW) 167, 169–73, 175
National Union of Distributive and Allied Workers (NUDAW) 79–80, 83 4
National Union of Women's Suffrage Societies (NUWSS) 23–7, 60, 77
Nehru, J. 82, 120, 144, 155, 188
New Left 32, 119–20, 126, 128–32, 185–6, 188–202
New Left Review 130–2, 191
New Reasoner 130–1, 189–91
No Conscription Fellowship (NCF) 28–30, 44–5
Nonconformism/Nonconformist 3–4, 22, 27–8, 50, 109–11, 142–3, 180, 208, 210–11, 223–6, 255
North Atlantic Treaty Organisation (NATO) 31, 129, 132, 150, 154, 192–3

Open University 194, 201
Orwell, G. Chapter 6 *passim*, 7–8, 11, 15, 22–3, 125
  anarchism 106, 230, 241–2
  Christianity 109–11
  communism/communists 98, 102–4, 107
  essayist 99, 108
  Labour Party 101, 106–7
  patriotism 104–5

O'Shaughnessy, E. 100
Owen, R./Owenism 5, 19–20
Oxford University 120, 143–4, 187–8, 210, 223, 233

Page, W. 170, 180
Paine, T. 17, 172, 211
Pankhurst, C. 24, 29, 58–67
Pankhurst, E. 24–5, 27, 29, 56–67
Pankhurst, R. 57–60
Pankhurst, R.K. 57–8, 65
Pankhurst, S. Chapter 4 passim, 8, 11, 22, 27, 29
Peace Pledge Union (PPU) 30, 45, 235
Peasants' Revolt 14– 15, 172
populism 253–4
POUM 82, 107
Priestley, J.B. 129, 154

Queen Elizabeth II 157, 207

Rationalist Press Association (RPA) 234, 240
Regional Seats of Government (RSGs) 237–8
Roman Catholicism/Roman Catholics 4, 15, 110, 232
Rowbotham, S. 27, 57
Russell (Earl) Bertrand Chapter 3 passim
 peace 43–9
 politics 39–41, 252
 social and ethical issues 41–3
Ryan, A. 38–9, 46, 50

Saville, J. 123, 135, 188–9, 191
Schoenman, R. 48–9, 253
Sheppard (Revd.) D. 30, 45
Smyth, N. 62, 67–8
Social Democratic Federation (SDF) 21, 24, 29
Social Democratic Party (SDP) 159–60, 220
socialist humanism 119–20, 123, 128–32, 200
'Solidarity (for Workers' Power)' 236–7
Spain/Spanish Civil War 82–3, 107, 230, 232
'Spies for Peace' 236–9
Steele, T. 195–6
suffragettes *see* Women's Social and Political Union
suffragists *see* National Union of Women's Suffrage Societies

Tawney, R.H. 3, 5, 17, 22, 78, 90, 92
Thatcher, M./Thatcherism 91, 158–9, 198–200

Thompson, D. (née Towers) 121, 123–4, 126, 190–1
Thompson, E.J. 120
Thompson, E.P. Chapter 7 passim, 1, 6–9, 16–17, 22, 98, 172
 adult education 121–3
 communism/CP 119, 123–8
 historian 121–3
 New Left 32, 124–32, 186, 188–91, 193–4, 201
 peace 32, 123–4, 128–30, 132–5
 socialist humanism 119–20, 128–32
Thompson, F. 120–1
Thompson, T. (née Jessop) 120–1
Tombs, R. 8, 16
Tribune 81, 146, 150, 152–5
Trotsky. L./Trotskyism 81, 107, 240–1
Turton (Sir) Robin 181

Union of Democratic Control (UDC) 25, 28, 44
Universities and Left Review 130, 188–91

Vallance, E. 2, 9–10, 15, 23

Walter, N. Chapter 12 passim, 3, 106, 256
 anarchism 230–42
 atheism 239–40
 Committee of 100 233–9
Ward, C. 242
Wilkinson, E. Chapter 5 passim
 communism/Communist Party 77–9
 feminism, suffrage 80–3
 Parliament 83–92
 trade unions 79–80
Williams, R. 2, 193, 196
Williams, S. 142, 156, 159
Wilson, H. 32, 151, 155, 208, 214–15, 217–18, 238
Woman's Dreadnought, The/Workers' Dreadnought, The 62–3, 66–7
Women's International League/Women's International League for Peace and Freedom (WILPF) 29, 68, 75
Women's Social and Political Union (WSPU) 23–5, 59–65, 71
Workers' Educational Association (WEA) 90, 121, 166, 172, 174
Workers' Suffrage Union/Workers' Socialist Federation (WSF) 64–5

EU authorised representative for GPSR:
Easy Access System Europe, Mustamäe tee 50,
10621 Tallinn, Estonia
gpsr.requests@easproject.com

www.ingramcontent.com/pod-product-compliance
Ingram Content Group UK Ltd.
Pitfield, Milton Keynes, MK11 3LW, UK
UKHW021847140426
5217IPUK00022B/1644